OXFORD EARLY CHRISTIAN TEXTS

General Editor

HENRY CHADWICK

LEONTIUS OF JERUSALEM

OXFORD EARLY CHRISTIAN TEXTS

The series provides reliable working texts of important early Christian writers in both Greek and Latin. Each volume contains an introduction, text, and select critical apparatus, with English translations *en face*, and brief explanatory references.

General Editor: Henry Chadwick

Leontius of Jerusalem

Against the Monophysites: Testimonies of the Saints and Aporiae

EDITED AND TRANSLATED BY

PATRICK T. R. GRAY

OXFORD
UNIVERSITY PRESS

OXFORD
UNIVERSITY PRESS

Great Clarendon Street, Oxford OX2 6DP

Oxford University Press is a department of the University of Oxford.
It furthers the University's objective of excellence in research, scholarship,
and education by publishing worldwide in

Oxford New York

Auckland Cape Town Dar es Salaam Hong Kong Karachi
Kuala Lumpur Madrid Melbourne Mexico City Nairobi
New Delhi Shanghai Taipei Toronto

With offices in

Argentina Austria Brazil Chile Czech Republic France Greece
Guatemala Hungary Italy Japan Poland Portugal Singapore
South Korea Switzerland Thailand Turkey Ukraine Vietnam

Oxford is a registered trade mark of Oxford University Press
in the UK and in certain other countries

Published in the United States
by Oxford University Press Inc., New York

British Library Cataloguing in Publication Data
Data available

Library of Congress Cataloging in Publication Data
Data available

Typeset by RefineCatch Limited, Bungay, Suffolk
Printed in Great Britain
on acid-free paper by
Biddles Ltd., King's Lynn

ISBN 0-19-926644-1   978-0-19-926644-9

PREFACE

Ever since the idea was first suggested to me by David Evans, at the opening reception of the 1975 Oxford Patristics Conference, I have wanted to publish an edition and translation of the long-neglected but fascinating sixth-century theologian, Leontius of Jerusalem. Over the decades since then, Leontius and I have become better acquainted, as my Greek improved and my knowledge of the world in which he lived and played his part deepened. We reached an understanding about my distaste for his *Against the Nestorians* as my affection for *Testimonies of the Saints* grew ever greater.

I feel fortunate that during the long gestation of this work there has been a flowering of interest in the sixth century, that amazing age of transition out of Late Antiquity into the Byzantine Period in the East, and into the Middle Ages in the West. In very recent times, the growth in interest in the church of Syria, and its vigorous anti-Chalcedonians, has been particularly noticeable. I trust the same interest will extend to the writings of the pro-Chalcedonian Leontius, whose engagement in the works published here, one essentially negative, but the other remarkably positive, is with anti-Chalcedonian followers of the great Severus in Syria.

Besides the friends and colleagues to whom this book is dedicated, I owe and gratefully offer thanks to the many people and institutions that have supported, encouraged, tolerated, and endured its long gestation. My interest in patristic christology, and particularly of the later fifth and the sixth century, was sparked in the library of Yale University, and by Jaroslav Pelikan, who taught me there; it grew into a passion at Trinity College, Toronto, encouraged by my thesis supervisor, the late Eugene Fairweather. Having discovered Leontius of Jerusalem (at first under the guise of Leontius of Byzantium) in that research, I began the present work with the support of the Killam Program, then of the Canada Council, by means of a Post-doctoral Scholarship which I

held at the Pontifical Institute of Medieval Studies in Toronto. There I was introduced by the late Walter Hayes to the mysteries of Greek manuscripts and their edition. I owe much to him. The Institute has, over decades, been unfailingly generous in allowing me access to its collections, as has also the library of St Paul's University in Ottawa. Valuable suggestions and encouragement came from many colleagues, including (besides those to whom this book is dedicated) notably the late Aloys Grillmeier, Luise Abramowski, Istvan Perczel, and Timothy Barnes. I was accompanied in the sometimes baffling task of translating Leontius by the spirit of François Combéfis who, through his hand-written Latin translation, often pointed the way to what a passage meant, and often comforted me, when I was faced by a difficult passage, by revealing through crossed-out attempts that he, too, had had a hard time of it! Marcel Richard was another giant from the past who came to my aid: Maurits Geerard, his literary executor, made available to me his unpublished work on the florilegia of Leontius of Jerusalem, without which identifying the ancient authors Leontius cites would have been an endless task. Assistance with the preparation of the text was ably provided by George Bevan, and by others. I am particularly in debt to those who have helped me with complex problems with Leontius' Greek, but who prefer to remain anonymous. I am grateful to Henry Chadwick, who, as general editor of this series, encouraged me to submit this edition and translation for publication, and to my editor, Lucy Qureshi, who has been a delight to work with. Among those who have had to live under the shadow of Leontius, perhaps with some bewilderment, and have done so with a good grace, I must thank my sons Trevor, Ben, Tim, and Geoff, and my dear wife, Cathy.

CONTENTS

ABBREVIATIONS

ACO	*Acta Conciliorum Oecumenicorum*, ed. E. Schwartz (Berlin and Leipzig, 1914–40).
BA	*Byzantina Australiensia* (Brisbane, 1981–)
BF	*Byzantinische Forschungen* (Amsterdam, 1966–)
BZ	*Byzantinische Zeitschrift* (Leipzig–Munich, 1892–)
CCSG	*Corpus Christianorum Series Graeca* (Turnhout, 1977–)
CCSL	*Corpus Christianorum Series Latina* (Turnhout, 1953–)
CSCO	*Corpus Scriptorum Christianorum Orientalium* (Louvain, 1903–)
CSEL	*Corpus Scriptorum Ecclesiasticorum Latinorum* (Vienna, 1866–)
DOS	*Dumbarton Oaks Studies* (Cambridge, Mass., 1950–)
DSp	*Dictionnaire de spiritualité, ascétique et mystique* (Paris, 1903–72)
DTC	*Dictionnaire de théologie catholique* (Paris, 1903–72)
EphThLov	*Ephemerides Theologicae Lovanienses* (Louvain, 1924–)
FC	*The Fathers of the Church* (New York, 1947–)
FCLDG	*Forschungen zur Christlichen Literatur- und Dogmengeschichte* (Paderborn, 1900–38)
GCS	*Die griechischen christlichen Schriftsteller der ersten drei Jahrhunderte* (Leipzig, 1897–)
HistJb	*Historisches Jahrbuch* (Munich–Freiburg, 1880–)
JEH	*Journal of Ecclesiastical History* (London, 1950–)
JTS	*The Journal of Theological Studies* (London, 1899–)
MSR	*Mélanges de science religieuse* (Lille, 1944–)
OCA	*Orientalia Christiana Analecta* (Rome, 1935–)
OCP	*Orientalia Christiana Periodica* (Rome, 1935–)
OECT	Oxford Early Christian Texts (Oxford, 1982–)
OLA	*Orientalia Lovaniensia Analecta* (Louvain, 1975–)
PG	*Patrologia Graeca*, ed. J. P. Migne (Paris, 1857–86)
PL	*Patrologia Latina*, ed. J. P. Migne (Paris, 1844–64)
PO	*Patrologia Orientalis* (Paris, 1903–)
RHE	*Revue d'histoire ecclésiastique* (Louvain, 1900–)

RSR	*Recherches de science religieuse* (Paris, 1910–)
SC	*Sources Chrétiennes* (Paris, 1941–)
SHCT	Studies in the History of Christian Thought (Leiden, 1966–)
StudPat	*Studia Patristica* (Berlin, 1957–)
SVTQ	*St. Vladimir's Theological Quarterly* (Crestwood, NY, 1952–)
Trad	*Traditio. Studies in Ancient and Medieval History, Thought and Religion* (New York, 1943–)
TRE	*Theologische Realenyclopädie* (Berlin, 1974–)
TU	*Texte und Untersuchungen zur Geschichte der altchristlichen Literatur* (Leipzig–Berlin, 1882–)

This book is dedicated to three friends and colleagues: David Evans, Michael Herren, and the late Maurits Geerard. Without their stimulation, support, and encouragement, it would not have been started, pursued, or finished.

INTRODUCTION

I. LITTLE-KNOWN WORKS OF A LITTLE-KNOWN WRITER

Two little-known and little-studied short works by the sixth-century theologian Leontius of Jerusalem[1]—*Testimonies of the Saints*, and *Aporiae*[2]—are presented here in the first complete edition ever made from the oldest and only textually significant manuscript, and the first accompanied by a modern-language translation.[3]

It is no surprise that these two works have remained in obscurity until now. For one thing, the 'age of the church fathers', involving the articulation of catholic Christianity in church and creed, has frequently and persistently been seen as simply ending in 451 with the Council of Chalcedon. For another, the emerging Byzantine East has not had the intrinsic interest for western scholars of western Europe's parallel emergence; fellow representatives of the sixth century in the West, such as Boethius and the Venerable Bede, are popular enough to appear routinely on reading-lists for university courses, and in paperback translations, but not so any contemporary representative of the East, least of all Leontius. Part of such a way of looking at things is the suspicion that the quarrels that consumed the eastern church after Chalcedon for

---

[1] *Fl.* 536–8. See sect. XI below.

[2] The individuality of these works was hidden by the blanket title, *Against the Monophysites*, which disguises what the text's previous editor, A. Mai, knew perfectly well but did not clearly indicate, that we actually have two works here: the manuscript's descriptions of each work are separated by the equivalent of a semicolon, and a space of eight lines is left between the two works, perhaps meant to be filled by a title which a rubricator forgot to supply. The complete corpus of extant works of Leontius, appearing, however, under the name of his contemporary, Leontius of Byzantium, is usually found in J.-P. Migne (ed.), *Patrologiae graecae cursus completus*, lxxxvi[1] (Paris, 1865), 1400A–1768[i]B (*Against the Nestorians*) and lxxxvi[2] (Paris, 1865), 1769–1901A (*Against the Monophysites = Aporiae*, 1769–1804C, and *Testimonies of the Saints*, 1804D–1901A).

[3] On previous editions, see sect. X below.

some eighty years before Leontius involved himself in them were
the product of the over-subtle Greek mind, relating to issues of no
real consequence to anyone other than the theologians concerned,
and certainly not deserving serious historical or theological analysis—presuming that anyone could make sense of this impene-
trable tangle of arguments. Another part of it is western suspicion
of the attempt, styled neo-Chalcedonianism, of which Leontius
was a part along with the Emperor Justinian, to find an accommodation with the anti-Chalcedonian schismatics traditionally,
but misleadingly, dismissed as 'Monophysite' heretics; to many
western scholars, that accommodation meant compromising the
authority and the orthodox teaching of Chalcedon and of Pope
Leo 'the Great', whose *Tome* was taken to have informed Chalcedon's statement of faith. To make matters worse, these two
works by Leontius belong to genres (the first is a sort of 'commented florilegium' or, more accurately, series of florilegia, and
the second a collection of aporiae) that are not likely to be familiar
to anyone but specialists, and which seem at first sight to justify the
charge of over-subtlety. Florilegia—literally 'bouquets of texts'—
tend to be dismissed by moderns as at best tedious catalogues of
dry proof-texts, and at worst, when full of misquotations and
forgeries—as Leontius' florilegia tend to be—sad examples of an
author's poor scholarship. Aporiae—logical arguments designed to
show the unacceptable implications, or 'impasses', into which an
opponent's position leads him if strictly analysed—tend to be
dismissed as no more than logic-chopping rhetorical display with
little real relevance. It was no help that the way in which the
Leontine corpus was transmitted from ancient times doomed
them to obscurity of a different kind for several centuries.[4] Finally,
while the one other extant work of Leontius—*Against the Nestorians*—recently engaged the passionate interest of the pre-eminent
specialist on the history of christology of our times, Aloys Grillmeier, in his monumental history of christology, Grillmeier left
Testimonies of the Saints and *Aporiae* entirely to one side; his interest
in the development of christological concepts and language quite
rightly found no original contribution of that sort in them.[5]

Testimonies of the Saints is, admittedly, not a particularly original
work in terms of concepts and terminology, but there is no

---

[4] On the years in obscurity, see sect. X below.
[5] On Grillmeier see sect. IX below.

intrinsic reason why only such works should be of historical interest. As it happens, *Testimonies of the Saints* represents, instead, a different kind of initiative of very considerable historical interest, an initiative designed to engage a specific group of anti-Chalcedonian churchmen, not high-level theologians, and to convince them, at their own level, that the arguments they give for dividing themselves from the official Church are groundless.[6] *Aporiae* makes no positive contribution to terminology, either, being concerned only with exposing the inadequacy of its opponents' terminology, but that in itself is a matter of historical interest. What is also significant about both works of Leontius here—perhaps particularly significant precisely because of their lack of originality in conceptual terms—is what they show us about how theological argument itself was being transformed in this period.

The fact that *Testimonies of the Saints* is addressed to a popular rather than an advanced audience gives us a remarkable opportunity to understand how the controversy over Chalcedon divided the Church, and how the issues were being understood in the 530s on both sides, for Leontius cites and addresses a whole series of anti-Chalcedonian concerns in a conversational, give-and-take style.[7] It is clear that Leontius, a monk of Palestine, was addressing, not the Church at large, but anti-Chalcedonian churchmen in neighbouring Syria who considered Severus of Antioch their teacher. *Testimonies of the Saints* therefore allows us to see just how the case for restoring the schismatics' union with the official Church that Justinian was so anxious to achieve, and towards which he was working so vigorously at the imperial level, was being made contemporaneously at a very specific and local level by Leontius. Because the florilegium material is built into the conversationally presented argument, and commented on at length, the text also allows us to see how the heritage of the fathers weighed on Leontius and his contemporaries, and at the same time was being deployed and, in the modern sense, 'massaged', by him to serve his purposes as a lively and potent instrument for controversy.[8] Seen in this light, *Testimonies of the Saints* is as attractive and revealing a resource for historical understanding as any other. That the sixth century is not as familiar as, say, the fourth

[6] On the specific situation, see sect. XI below.
[7] On the causes, development, and nature of the schism between Chalcedonians and anti-Chalcedonians, see sect. II below.
[8] See sect. VII below on this issue.

(the 'golden age' of patristics, according to traditional scholarship), means that it is all the more important to have texts like this available in accessible form for both scholars and general readers.

Leontius' *Aporiae* are considerably narrower in range, their whole focus being on terminology and christological formulae. Nonetheless, there is some interest to be found in how Leontius exposes inconsistencies in anti-Chalcedonian vocabulary, and in one case some intellectual fun to be had from a series of double meanings he employs to good rhetorical effect. Moreover, rival formulae really were, as we have said, at the heart of the controversy between Chalcedonians and anti-Chalcedonians. *Testimonies of the Saints* meets the *Aporiae*, then, when it proposes a way of resolving the seeming contradictions of anti-Chalcedonian formulae (the very contradictions the *Aporiae* point out) by representing the underlying christology they used those formula to express in new, non-contradictory terms, and goes on to argue that these are nothing other than the terms intended by Chalcedon and Chalcedonians. That meant, Leontius argued, that the two factions actually agreed.

Both *Testimonies of the Saints'* concentration on resolving the many and seemingly disparate testimonies of what it calls 'the select fathers' into a single, consistent christological orthodoxy, and the *Aporiae*'s concern to move anti-Chalcedonians away from attempting to express orthodoxy in inadequate and contradictory terms, are aspects of a fundamental transformation in theological method that was going on, a movement away from arguments based on the Bible and on reason, and towards scholasticism.

In the present volume, *Testimonies of the Saints* and the *Aporiae* emerge as quite distinct works, with the former given pride of place as being of inherently greater interest from many points of view. Though in the manuscript it is preceded by the *Aporiae*, there is no compelling reason to follow that practice or to see the two works as closely related in time or situation, though both are apparently addressed to the same audience, anti-Chalcedonians of Syria under the influence of Severus of Antioch.[9]

---

[9] On the close connection between *Testimonies of the Saints* and Severus and his followers, see sects VI and XI below. On the identity of the addressees of the *Aporiae*, see sect. VIII below.

II. DIVIDED OVER HISTORY: THE BACKGROUND

Leontius responded in the 530s to a highly problematic and quite real ecumenical situation that had, for over eighty years, divided the church within the eastern part of the Empire. Since 451 virtually all of the church in Egypt, and much of it in Palestine and Syria, had refused to accept the Council of Chalcedon's teaching or to be in communion with those who did accept it. The church of Rome, much of the church in the patriarchate of Constantinople, and parts of the church elsewhere in the East, did claim loyalty to Chalcedon. By the 530s the ecumenical situation was reaching crisis proportions, for the possibility was becoming stronger that anti-Chalcedonians would abandon their sense of being part of the one Church of the one Empire with a responsibility for restoring the rest of the church to orthodoxy as they understood it. The danger was that they would come to see themselves as the 'real' church contrasted with the 'heretical' imperial church. In the end, of course, that is precisely what happened, but in Leontius' time that outcome did not seem at all inevitable, just dangerously possible—if the situation was not amended. Understandably, the Emperor Justinian actively lent his potent support to various initiatives to avert the impending schism, recognizing in it a danger to the unity of the Empire itself.

The parties' quite different positions resulted from rival interpretations of a tumultuous period that began with the outbreak of the Nestorian Controversy in 428, and ended with the Council of Chalcedon in 451. This was the disputed history.

The first phase of the disputed history began with Nestorius, the recently elected patriarch of Constantinople, lending his support to attacks on the use of the title 'God-Bearer' (*theotokos*) for the Virgin Mary.[10] As someone trained in the school of Antioch, he shared the school's long-standing concern that a title like that dangerously obscured the human reality of the Word incarnate, and concealed the earlier heresy of Apollinarius. To those following in the tradition of Alexandria, however, the Antiochenes' penchant for distinguishing the human Jesus from the divine Word flew in the face of the teaching of the church fathers and of the

---

[10] The key texts from the controversy, with a useful introduction, are to be found in the sister volume from this series, L. R. Wickham (tr. and ed.), *Cyril of Alexandria: Select Letters*, OECT (Oxford: Oxford University Press, 1983).

Council of Nicaea; Cyril, patriarch of Alexandria 412–4, became
the champion of this view. The creed of Nicaea, the Alexandrians
said, spoke of 'one Lord Jesus Christ, who . . . was made man . . .',
echoing John's Gospel, which said 'the Word became flesh . . .'.
That kind of language meant that there was only one subject of
all of the Word incarnate's actions, both in His divinity before the
incarnation, and in His flesh; you could not legitimately talk about
the human Jesus as if He were a distinct subject performing His
own actions, as Nestorius was doing. The quarrel quickly escal-
ated, and in 431 Cyril presided over a council at Ephesus which
condemned Nestorius for dividing the one Christ, but without the
participation of John, patriarch of Antioch, and his bishops. John
and his bishops held a counter-council condemning Cyril, and a
period of uncertainty followed. The first phase ended in 433 when
the combatants were reluctantly brought by intense pressure from
the imperial court to an agreement of sorts. This agreement
involved the subscription by both sides to a statement of faith—
often called the Union of 433—which included the assertions that
Mary was 'God-Bearer', that the Word Himself was born 'according to his humanity' of the Virgin Mary, and that there was a
'union', rather than a 'conjunction', of His two natures.[11] All of
this was very agreeable to Cyril, and looked like a victory for his
position. On the other hand, he did have to agree that 'theologians divide [some] of the sayings [of the incarnate Word] as
pertaining to two natures . . .'.

Cyril's capitulation on that last point proved enormously problematic for the vast network of churchmen who had read his
letters, agreed with his objections to 'Nestorianism', and saw him
as the reliable voice of orthodoxy. In the episode of the disputed
history that followed, the champions of the Antiochene position
lost no time in claiming that, by agreeing that one could legitimately divide the two natures of Christ, Cyril had capitulated to
their position. Language about natures, heretofore uncontentious,
thus took on new significance. Sometime after 433, Cyril in
new letters[12] attempted to address his partisans' disquiet by clarifying what he meant by natures: Christ was indeed 'out of two

[11] Cyril, *Letter 39* (to John of Antioch, known as *Laetentur coeli*, 'Let the heavens
rejoice', from the biblical quotation with which it opens), tr. J. I. McEnerney, *FC* lxxvi[1]
(Washington, DC: Catholic University of America Press, 1987), 147–52.
[12] See esp. *Letter 45* (the first letter to Succensus), tr. Wickham, 70–83; and *Letter 46*
(the second letter to Succensus), 84–93.

natures' before the Incarnation, in that one could with the mind distinguish the human and the divine which were united in Him; concretely, in the Incarnation, there was—as he assumed Athanasius had said—only 'one incarnate nature'. The analogy used to explain how that could be the case was the time-honoured analogy of the union of body and soul in a human being: the mind could recognize somatic and psychic natures all right as the components of a human being, but in the concrete person they were united in one human nature. There was, in that sense, a 'natural union' in Christ. Since one way of talking about the dangers of Nestorianism was to say that Nestorius talked of the human and divine as separate 'hypostases' (*hupostasis* being a word often enough used to point to the concrete individual existence of an entity, as in trinitarian language about the three 'persons' or 'hypostases' of the Trinity), Cyril sometimes made the same point about the concrete oneness of Christ by saying there was a 'union by hypostasis' or 'hypostatic union'. While Cyril was clarifying his position, the Antiochenes continued to claim victory for their position, and to try to diminish the influence of Cyril. The struggle continued.

It was the elderly and influential monk of Constantinople, Eutyches, who proved the lightning-rod for hostilities in the next episode of the disputed history. The facts are clear enough: at a Home Synod of 448 presided over by Flavian, patriarch of Constantinople, Eutyches was charged and condemned for his supposed heretical belief that the human and divine were confused or mingled in one nature in the Incarnation.[13] This heresy, if really his, would make him the first genuine monophysite (*monos* meaning 'single', and *phusis* meaning 'nature'). Whatever he really thought—the issue demands more attention than it has been afforded to date—Eutyches fled to Cyril's successor as patriarch of Alexandria, Dioscorus, who certainly accepted him as an orthodox Cyrillian. In 449 Dioscorus presided over a second council at Ephesus.[14] It exonerated Eutyches, condemned the one who condemned him, Flavian, and silenced Cyril's Antiochene

---

[13] The record of the trial of Eutyches is embedded in the acts of session one of Chalcedon, ed. E. Schwartz, *ACO* ii, 1, 1 (Berlin and Leipzig: Walter de Gruyter, 1933), 55–147. The charges against him: 124 and 144.

[14] Known as the Second Council of Ephesus or, pejoratively, the Latrocinium ('Brigandage of Ephesus' or 'Robber Synod'—Pope Leo's epithet). Its records are, like those of the Home Synod that tried Eutyches, embedded in the acts of session one of Chalcedon, *ACO* ii, 1, 1, 55–147.

critics such as Theodoret of Cyrrhus. Flavian died as a result of
injuries sustained at or in connection with the council; Dioscorus,
rightly or wrongly, was widely blamed for the violence. The pap-
acy, which had been brought into the controversy by an appeal
from Flavian and others, was offended that Pope Leo's letter (the
famous *Tome*) laying out the Roman position was never read at
Ephesus. It took a sarcastic and deeply unsympathetic view of
Eutyches. Thus, while Cyril's partisans were triumphant, and saw
the council of 449 as an ecumenical council confirming Cyril's
council of 431, there was profound resistance to it in the West,
and in spheres of Antiochene influence in the East.

When a new emperor, Marcian, suddenly came to the throne,
he chose to attempt to resolve the tensions plaguing the Church by
calling yet another council, the one which eventually met at Chalcedon. He meant this council to satisfy the concerns of Rome. In
yet another dramatic reversal, Chalcedon condemned Eutyches,
and deposed Dioscorus. It approved Leo's *Tome* as expressing the
teaching of Cyril, though perhaps not paying too much attention
to the fact that it spoke in typical Western language of two
natures, each having distinct operations of its own. At Marcian's
insistence, the council went on (reluctantly) to draw up a statement of faith meant to become the agreed statement of faith unit-
ing—such was the hope!—the Church and the Empire. The first
version, though enthusiastically received by the majority of
bishops, was withdrawn and its contents suppressed. We know
only that it contained the phrase 'out of two natures', but that fact
is a clear indication that it adopted the christological language of
Cyril's post-433 letters as the touchstone of orthodoxy. That
approach would satisfy neither Rome nor the emperor. Urged to
approve something that would rule out Eutychianism—Eutyches
proving to be a useful bogeyman to spook a reluctant council
into compliance with the imperial agenda—the bishops finally
subscribed to a second and final version which radically reversed
the approach of the first. In it the language of the Antiochenes
and of the West was triumphant: Christ was 'known in two
natures'. The added phrase, 'and in one person and hypostasis',
was undoubtedly meant to deny a fully Nestorian understanding
of the distinction of natures as Cyril had construed it, i.e. that to
say there were two natures meant there were two persons and
hypostases. It was inevitable, however, that this qualification would
pass unnoticed by Cyril's partisans, for whom the combination of

the statement of faith and Leo's *Tome* gave the very clear message that it was really Nestorianism that was being affirmed.

Anti-Chalcedonians took the decisive positive moment in the disputed history to be Cyril of Alexandria's clarification of his teaching in the wake of the Union of 433 and of Antiochene attempts to hijack his authority. For them, the faith of the fathers was expressed clearly and authoritatively in the letters Cyril wrote during those years to clarify his position. Christ was 'out of two natures', and there was 'one incarnate nature of God the Word' in the actual Incarnation. The emphasis was all on what Cyril had fought for throughout his career, the oneness of the Word incarnate, the one subject who acted through both His divinity and his flesh. Chalcedon, in their view, betrayed that orthodox Cyrillian christology when it said Christ was 'in two natures'. This was exactly the heresy Nestorius had tried to perpetrate in 428. The Union of 433 used by Nestorius' friends and sympathizers to associate Cyril with Nestorian ideas was not so much an expression of what Cyril really believed as it was a generous gesture to his enemies in an attempt to bring them, eventually, to what he really believed himself. To say baldly that Christ was in two natures simply did not have Cyril's authority behind it. The episode of Eutyches was troubling for later anti-Chalcedonians, though, for they seem not to have had a clear sense of what he actually believed. What was clear to them was that Dioscorus upheld Cyril in 449 and rescued him from being totally misrepresented, and that made him in their books a hero of the faith. That Chalcedon deposed and condemned Dioscorus under suspicious circumstances two years later revealed, so they thought, its opposition to Cyril's faith. It pretended to condemn Nestorius, and to be against Eutyches, but its loyalty to Nestorius' ideas was clear in the language it espoused in its statement of faith—Christ recognized 'in two natures'—, and in its exoneration of Nestorian sympathizers like Theodoret of Cyrrhus and Ibas of Edessa. Cyrillians had shown, even before Chalcedon ended, that they were willing to go to the ramparts to defend the faith of the fathers and of Cyril against this betrayal of all they stood for, and eighty years later, in Leontius' time, anti-Chalcedonians still saw themselves in exactly that light.

By contrast, the position of the official, Chalcedonian church was by this time that the decision against Nestorianism had been made once and for all in 431. Chalcedon, in the view of

Chalcedonians, really was not about that issue, though it confirmed Ephesus and the condemnation of Nestorius. It was needed, rather, to defend the dual realities of divinity and humanity in Christ against a virulent new threat, the heresy of Eutyches. Only a clear statement about the two natures of Christ could exclude that heresy. Dioscorus had at the very least discredited himself by accepting the heretic at the illegitimate council of 449. For Chalcedonians, Cyril's decisive teaching was contained in his *Second Letter to Nestorius*, in which he said that the unity of Christ did not imply 'that the difference between the natures was abolished through their union'[15] (a text to be contrasted with the post-433 Cyril who said that Christ was 'out of two natures *before* the union'), and of course in the Symbol of Union. Those texts had special authority, in fact, because they had received synodical approval. Chalcedonians claimed that this Cyril, interpreted through the 'synodical' texts, was perfectly in agreement with Chalcedon on Christ's two natures.

At issue, then, were contrasting views of a disputed history, and especially contrasting views of what Cyril of Alexandria stood for. Cyril was defined for the disputants by two very different selections from his works. One selection privileged 'one incarnate nature' of Christ; the other privileged 'two natures'. Given the centrality of Cyril for the anti-Chalcedonians, any attempt to reconcile them to Chalcedon and to Chalcedonians had the formidable task of convincing them of something that seemed to them patently not the case. That is, anti-Chalcedonians had to be convinced, not just that Cyril spoke of 'two natures' as had Chalcedon—anti-Chalcedonians could argue with considerable plausibility that what he really meant by such talk was authoritatively explained by 'out of two natures'—but that Chalcedon actually agreed with what to them was his central article of faith, the 'one incarnate nature of God the Word'. Leontius of Jerusalem is particularly interesting for the developed way in which he attempts to make precisely that case. For better or for worse, though, by the time he made it his audience was beyond hearing it.

---

[15] Cyril, *Letter 4*, tr. Wickham, p. 7.

III. THE LESSONS OF HISTORY

That Leontius came at the end of some eighty-five years of debate and conversation between the parties goes a long way towards explaining how he addressed the issues as he did: he had learned what might succeed, and what was doomed to fail. That long history had certainly demonstrated how difficult the whole situation was. Every attempt by the state during those eighty-five years to force the anti-Chalcedonians to give up their opposition and be reunited with the official Church failed.[16] Likewise, efforts to reduce the place of Cyril and his christology in their eyes were, if anything, counter-productive. For instance, the Emperor Marcian published evidence *c.* 455 that Cyril's 'one incarnate nature of God the Word' was derived from a heretical source, not from Athanasius as Cyril had thought.[17] That revelation perhaps seemed to Marcian and his advisers to be the appropriate bombshell needed to convince anti-Chalcedonians once and for all to abandon the post-433 Cyril. There is no evidence, though, that there was any effect whatsoever on the anti-Chalcedonian resistance. The tactic, tried again in 532 during conversations between anti-Chalcedonians and Chalcedonians, again deepened the divide. The anti-Chalcedonians simply would not listen to any argument that meant compromising, as they saw it, the authority of Cyril on the central statements of doctrine they held dear, and Chalcedonians would challenge it at their peril.[18] The most positive initiative of the period immediately after Chalcedon, taken not by the state but by some anonymous scholar, was the *Cyrillian Florilegium*, an assembly of texts from Cyril showing him asserting two natures, or at least some kind of persisting duality in

---

[16] My short account of imperial policy in this period remains useful: P. T. R. Gray, *The Defense of Chalcedon in the East (451–553)*, SHCT 20 (Leiden: Brill, 1979), 17–61.

[17] *ACO* ii, 5, ed. E. Schwartz (Berlin and Leipzig: Walter de Gruyter, 1936), 4.

[18] The case for the formula's inauthenticity, made by Hypatius of Ephesus, the Chalcedonian advocate at the Conversations, was recorded by one of the Chalcedonian participants: Innocentius of Maronea, *Letter to Thomas the Priest*, ed. E. Schwartz, *ACO* iv, 2 (Berlin and Leipzig: Sumptibus Caroli J. Trübner, Librarii argentoratensis, 1914), 172–3. The absolute refusal of the equivalent anti-Chalcedonian report by John Bar Aphtonia even to mention this issue indicates how firm was the anti-Chalcedonians' denial of the forgeries: see the Syriac fragment of John's account, with translation, in S. Brock, 'The conversations with the Syrian Orthodox under Justinian (532)', *OCP* 47 (1981), 92–113.

Christ.[19] It thus moved the case for Chalcedon's compatibility with Cyril beyond the two 'synodical' letters. It did not, however, even cite the texts central to the anti-Chalcedonians, much less attempt to show that Chalcedon was true to them. Leontius evidently was familiar with Severus of Antioch's devastating critique of the *Cyrillian Florilegium* in his *Friend of Truth*, composed some fifty years after its publication.[20] Perhaps he recognized the futility of arguing that Chalcedon and Cyril agreed simply because both used 'two natures', however well the case could be documented. A more convincing resolution of the substantive issues was required if Severus and like-minded anti-Chalcedonians were to be satisfied.

The Emperor Zeno found an alternative to resolving the crisis over Chalcedon in simply putting brackets around it: he instituted the policy of the *Henoticon*, a decree which ruled that the parties should stand down from insisting on either the acceptance or rejection of Chalcedon. He thereby achieved uneasy peace for his empire (the *Henoticon* was in effect 482–518), but at the price of removing much of the impetus for any real attempt to address substantive issues.[21] We have no idea what Leontius thought about the *Henoticon*. As a Palestinian, though, he would almost certainly have been aware of the efforts of a few Palestinian residents of the previous generation to reopen the discussion with the anti-Chalcedonians. Nephalius of Alexandria, operating in Palestine *c.* 508, and John 'the Grammarian' of Caesarea (*fl.* 515), earned the wrath of Severus of Antioch by publishing defences of Chalcedon in which they took the case for Chalcedon much farther than had the *Cyrillian Florilegium*. Both took seriously—for the first time in Chalcedonian circles—the 'one incarnate nature' formula. They proposed different ways of bringing out its compatibility with,

[19] The text is preserved in Syriac within the refutation composed by Severus of Antioch called *The Friend of Truth* (*Philalethes*), ed. and tr. R. Hespel, *Le Philalèthe*, *CSCO* ccciii and ccciv = Scriptores Syri lxviii and lxix (Louvain: Imprimerie orientaliste L. Durbecq, 1952 and 1954).

[20] Ibid. Leontius seems pretty clearly to be referring—sarcastically—to Severus' title, *The Friend of Truth*, in *Testimonies of the Saints* at 1812D, when he speaks of 'friendship for the truth'. An anti-Chalcedonian, Severus was the controversial patriarch of Antioch 512–18. Dethroned in 518, he lived out his life in exile in Egypt, which remained virtually entirely, and certainly obdurately, anti-Chalcedonian. From exile he continued, through his letters and books, to be the most influential and theologically articulate voice of the anti-Chalcedonian party.

[21] The text of the *Henoticon*: Evagrius Scholasticus, *Ecclesiastical History*, iii. 14, ed. J. Bidez and L. Parmentier (Amsterdam: Hakkert, 1964), 111–14.

or in John's case complementarity to, Chalcedon.[22] Severus' responses showed that they had been successful in convincing at least some anti-Chalcedonians to return to the official Church, if not Severus himself.[23] Severus in fact became only more deeply convinced of the rightness of the anti-Chalcedonian resistance, and in his *Friend of Truth* he clarified and systematized that stance: everything that Cyril had written could and should be interpreted through and by the key formula 'one incarnate nature of God the Word'. What neither Nephalius, nor John 'the Grammarian', nor indeed anyone on the Chalcedonian side had succeeded in doing was to demonstrate convincingly how Chalcedon was fully true to that part of Cyril. It could never be sufficient to argue that it was merely compatible with, or complementary to it.

Leontius must have known, too, of the conversations Justinian sponsored in 532 between representatives of the Chalcedonians and representatives of Syrian anti-Chalcedonians who maintained connections with their exiled patriarch, Severus.[24] Those same Syrian anti-Chalcedonians were, after all, to be the intended audience of his own *Testimonies of the Saints* a few years later. He may even have been the 'Leontius, representative of the monks in [Jerusalem]', who was listed among those present.[25] The conversations had the express purpose of uncovering possible grounds for reconciliation. Though they failed after just two of the projected three days, and no official minutes were kept, we do have accounts from participants on both sides that give us a fascinating look at how the issues were formulated, where the sticking-points were, and what strategies were unproductive. Leontius seems to have

---

[22] Nephalius argued that what Chalcedon really meant was 'two united natures', and suggested that the word 'incarnate' in 'one incarnate nature' pointed to the second nature that Chalcedon asserted in a different way: Severus of Antioch, *Orations against Nephalius*, ed. and tr. J. Lebon, *Severi Antiocheni Orationes ad Nephalium: eiusdem ac Sergii Grammatici epistulae mutuae*, *CSCO* cxxx = Scriptores Syri lxv (Louvain: Apud L. Durbecq, 1949), 15; idem, *Against the Grammarian*, ed. and tr. J. Lebon, *Liber contra impium grammaticum*, *CSCO*, Scriptores Syri, series 4, vi, 48. John 'the Grammarian' made a subtle historical argument for the view that the Union of 433 showed both parties to have accepted both 'two natures' and 'one incarnate nature'. Each was necessary against one of the antithetical errors of Eutyches and Nestorius. Chalcedon affirmed one, and Cyril the other. On this argument see A. Grillmeier (with T. Hainthaler), *Christ in Christian Tradition*, ii[2], tr. P. Allen and J. Cawte (London and Oxford: Mowbray, 1995), 67–9.

[23] As is confirmed also by Severus' biographer: John Bar Aphtonia, *Life of Severus*, ed. and tr. M. A. Kugener, *PO* 2 (Paris: Firmin-Didot, 1904), 248–50.

[24] See n. 18 above on the accounts of the Conversations.

[25] Innocentius, p. 170.

been aware of precisely this information, since, as we shall see, he attempted in every case to formulate things in such a way as to go beyond the problems that led to the conversations' failure. Among the unproductive strategies, as has been mentioned, was discrediting key anti-Chalcedonian and Cyrillian articles of faith as based on forgeries. Another was any attempt to privilege as authoritative or 'synodical' only two letters of Cyril that spoke clearly in favour of 'two natures'. No anti-Chalcedonian could be convinced to leave aside the crucial post-433 letters in which their favoured formulae were found, and the attempt to get them to do so could lead only to a deepening of their suspicion that Cyril was being betrayed, not honoured. In fact, the conversations showed again that the anti-Chalcedonians could never be satisfied by anything less than convincing proof that Chalcedon meant exactly what Cyril and they meant by 'one incarnate nature'. Moreover, the conversations showed that the anti-Chalcedonians, though unwilling to say that Eutyches was orthodox, and though troubled by the fact that Dioscorus had received him, still viewed the latter as a hero of orthodoxy. They were convinced that there was something underhanded about his condemnation by Chalcedon. They likewise remained convinced that Chalcedon was made deeply suspect by its acceptance of Theodoret and Ibas, the friends of Nestorius and enemies of Cyril; their account showed that they got some pleasure out of embarrassing the Chalcedonians on that very point. The conversations showed one more thing, something that was to be central to Leontius of Jerusalem's own approach: they showed that, at least in the not-unperceptive opinion of Justinian, it was possible to conceive of winning over anti-Chalcedonians of Syria without the participation or approval of their leader-in-exile, Severus.

Shortly after the Conversations, in 533, Justinian promulgated an edict identifying 'union by hypostasis' as central to the orthodox faith.[26] Cyril, as has been observed, and his followers through the generations, had seen behind Nestorius' 'two natures' the assertion that there were two hypostases (i.e. independent subjects) in Christ, and had countered with what amounted to contrary slogans: there was 'one hypostasis' in Christ; there was a 'union by hypostasis'. The edict was aimed at allaying anti-Chalcedonian fears, as Chalcedon's addition of 'one person and hypostasis' had

---

[26] *Codex Justinianus* I, 1, 7.

been, by denying that there were two hypostases or a mere conjunction of persons, rather than at developing a christology of hypostatic union. Leontius of Jerusalem would not make a major contribution to the conceptual development of union by hypostasis in either of the works published here, but he would propose that the formula be seen as the basis on which the divided churches could discover their unsuspected unity.

IV. *TESTIMONIES OF THE SAINTS*: THE ARGUMENT FOR RECONCILIATION

Testimonies of the Saints was published at a time of great urgency about resolving the schism in the Church before it became irreversible. It was also published in the context of considerable momentum towards bringing about union on the part of the state, in that Justinian—having learned much from his earlier attempts, including the failed Conversations—was fully engaged in orchestrating, with a more and more confident hand, the great drive towards reunion that was to culminate in the Fifth Ecumenical Council of 553.

As has been remarked, *Testimonies of the Saints* seems to be not so much a theological statement debating theologians of the other side as it is a work addressed to anti-Chalcedonian churchmen at an almost popular level. It takes the form of a conversation, a long and rambling and rather informal literary conversation,[27] between Leontius as representing the Chalcedonians on one side, and various representations of anti-Chalcedonian voices on the other.[28] The latter are represented sometimes directly as 'you' (plural) or 'you' (singular), sometimes indirectly as 'they' or 'he'.[29] More than

---

[27] A certain informality has been noticed by some scholars. It is hoped that the informality is suitably reflected in the translation.

[28] A sense of the conversation as a whole can be gained from the summary provided in the Appendix.

[29] In the translation, the pronouns standing for anti-Chalcedonians in the plural are usually rendered as 'they', or 'these people' if they are being spoken about, and 'you', 'you people', or 'my friends', if they are being addressed. Leontius has the habit of slipping into the third person singular—'he says', without an antecedent—and here 'he' is rendered by 'my friend'. The intention is to capture some of the irony implied by debaters when they call opponents 'my friends', as also the ambiguous sense, implied by the language, that the opponent is being invited to listen and be won over to a better point of view, i.e. to become in fact a friend. This second sense is especially suited to this work, which overtly invites its opponents to become friends.

is the case with most of Leontius' contemporaries, the anti-Chalcedonian voices are treated with a certain respect. The agenda is quite clear: We Chalcedonians, Leontius says, 'do our winning over by charm', and we intend to 'bring your anger against us to an end by winning you over';[30] what he intends to win them over to is the 'recognition' that what they stand for in terms of genuinely Cyrillian christology is what Chalcedonians stand for too, and that therefore they have sadly misjudged Chalcedon and Chalcedonians. They really have no excuse for remaining in schism with them.

Leontius' anti-Chalcedonian voices identify two serious issues and several minor ones; the work addresses them in turn: Chalcedon's novelty, and its dishonesty, are the serious issues, and they take up almost the entire work. The first charge is the absolutely fundamental one, and the one to which *Testimonies of the Saints* devotes by far the most space, naturally enough: Chalcedonians use 'a strange [expression] we [anti-Chalcedonians] don't find being used explicitly by the fathers anywhere, i.e. "two natures, albeit undivided, of Christ"', whereas we anti-Chalcedonians use 'the fathers' teaching about Christ . . . in their own words, i.e. "one incarnate nature of God the Word", as in holy Athanasius and Cyril'.[31] What Leontius describes as 'the charge of dishonesty against the church' comes down to the suspicion, amounting to an unshakeable conviction, that the fathers of Chalcedon had 'as their pretext for convening the condemnation of Eutyches, but were really an act of zeal for Nestorius'.[32] Among the less serious charges is the claim by certain anti-Chalcedonians that the soundness of their own doctrine was confirmed by God's gift to them of superior and more abundant miracle-working power.[33]

On the first charge, Leontius tips his hand right away. He suggests that the anti-Chalcedonians' claim that Chalcedonians betrayed the teaching of the fathers when they used the novel formula of 'two natures' resulted from their refusal to investigate 'whether to speak of one incarnate nature of God the Word really is the same in meaning as speaking of a duality of natures of Christ united in one hypostasis'. They based their refusal, he says, on the fact that they didn't find the latter expression explicitly affirmed by the fathers.[34] The investigation he speaks of

---

[30] 1817A   [31] 1804D–1805A.   [32] 1876D–1877A.
[33] 1896B–C.   [34] 1805B.

is precisely what Leontius now challenges his anti-Chalcedonians to take up. For instance, he says, 'one incarnate nature' was enunciated to protect against Nestorianism, and 'a duality of natures of Christ united in one hypostasis' was enunciated later to protect against Eutychianism. Analysis shows they were not opposed formulae at all, just different ways of affirming the same thing to emphasize what needed to be emphasized against heresy. 'One incarnate nature' affirms one fundamental aspect of Christ in terms of 'unity', whereas 'a duality of natures of Christ united in one hypostasis' affirms it in terms of 'union'. The former affirms the other fundamental aspect of Christ by distinguishing implicitly between what is 'incarnated' and what 'incarnates', whereas the latter affirms it by frankly speaking of 'two'.[35] There is then, Leontius invites them to see, an underlying unity beneath the disparity in language; they and the Chalcedonians actually believe exactly the same thing.

The key to discovering this unity in meaning is getting below the surface differences in language, and the key to doing that, says Leontius, is realizing that 'to thoughtless people "nature" is a word with more than one meaning, and is often used in place of "substance" and "hypostasis"'.[36] For him, 'nature' (*phusis*) is properly identified with 'substance' (*ousia*, the essential character of a thing) rather than with 'hypostasis' (an individual entity or person).[37] When Cyril spoke of 'one incarnate nature', however, he was using 'nature' in the sense of 'hypostasis', which meant he was talking about a hypostatic union in Christ—a union in one particular entity or person—not a natural union, despite the use of the word 'nature'. (In a natural union properly speaking, things are joined by virtue of being subsumed to the same nature or substance.[38]) Similarly, when Chalcedon spoke, with the synodical Cyril, about 'two natures', it was speaking about two substances, not about two hypostases or persons.

At the centre of Leontius' proposed neutral way of talking about the allegedly shared christology beneath their rival formu-

---

[35] 1809A–B.

[36] 1808D–1809A.

[37] Throughout the translation *phusis* and *ousia* are always represented by 'nature' and 'substance' respectively. *Hupostasis* is always transliterated, or anglicized, as hypostasis, since no single English word or phrase accurately captures its meaning.

[38] At 1816A–B the example is provided of mixed gum and wax, a mixture that results in a new nature with new properties.

lae is 'union by hypostasis'. He offers not so much a conceptual explanation of what a union by hypostasis is, as some examples:

When papyrus or a sponge is dipped in water, and has drawn all the water into its whole self, it doesn't end up being one nature with the water, but one hypostasis. In the same way, iron and fire result in a hypostasis of red-hot metal. Stones and wood, too, result in a new hypostasis, that of a house, but they keep the same natures, though they're united to each other and come together in a house's structure and in the reality that underlies a single entity, i.e. the house's hypostasis.[39]

His point is that there do exist single entities in which distinct natures are united without being destroyed. A key feature of such unions is the capacity of a single hypostasis to become more composite, without losing its unity, by the addition of a second nature. Thus, in Christ, the one hypostasis of the Word, eternally possessed of a divine nature, can be understood to have become more composite by the addition of a human nature, without ceasing to be one hypostasis.

With these terminological clarifications, Leontius can approach the many texts of the fathers he adduces in the florilegia that follow, systematically interpreting all texts that refer to one nature as really meaning one hypostasis, and all texts that refer to a duality of any kind as really meaning a duality of natures understood in the sense of substance.[40] In this way, Leontius attempts to move the Chalcedonian agenda beyond the failed strategy of granting authority only to certain texts of Cyril that spoke of 'two natures': on his view even the most anti-Chalcedonian sounding texts of the post-433 Cyril speak to the one truth of a union by hypostasis, and he devotes a special section to showing that this is so: '[E]ven the sayings of the fathers that in your view agree with your doctrines rather recommend ours when they're examined, as they ought to be, in terms of their meaning . . .'.[41] The implication of accepting Leontius' argument is clearly that, if such substantive agreement is recognized, none of the issues that seem to divide anti-Chalcedonians from Chalcedonians need stand in the way of unity:

So as to demonstrate, as may be, before God and men that your secession from the Church isn't reasonable, look, we set aside every argument

---

[39] 1813D–1816A.
[40] 1817C–1841A.
[41] 1849C–D; the section devoted to this demonstration: 1849C–1852C.

we might make against your allegations, and make you the following offer: if you'll join with us in confessing the tried and true doctrines, saying both 'one incarnate nature of God the Word' and that there are two natures of Christ united in His one hypostasis, and if you also don't repudiate the council and Leo and ourselves, then we, for our part, anathematize even *an angel from heaven* sooner than we do you, if he doesn't think and speak and write likewise; we praise and accept Severus, Dioscorus, Timothy, and you, and anyone at all who shares such views; we add nothing to this . . .[42]

Leontius also brings a new approach to a related issue identified by the Conversations of 532 as a real sticking-point for the anti-Chalcedonians. Attempts to undermine the anti-Chalcedonian position by demonstrating the Apollinarian roots of its cherished 'one incarnate nature' had, as has been observed, served only to deepen the schism. The issue was inescapable in the context of Leontius' literary conversation with anti-Chalcedonians, since it was central to the latter's case to emphasize the ancient patristic pedigree of their formula over against what they described as Chalcedon's novel (and Nestorian) language.[43] Leontius is convinced that Cyril's famous one-nature formula depended on Apollinarian forgeries—he probably knew personally one man who had explored the evidence, John, Bishop of Scythopolis—and is willing to present the case in some detail here.[44] He does so, however, in the light of an extended discussion of the orthodox meaning Cyril, on his interpretation, intended by that formula, and immediately following his insistence that Cyril was not inconsistent, i.e. that what he meant by 'one incarnate nature' cohered with what he meant when he spoke of 'two natures'.[45] (It is clear that he saw, in the real or imputed tendency of such leaders as Severus to dismiss the Cyril of the Symbol of Union as inconsistent with his real position, a useful bit of rhetoric for attempting to detach Severus' followers from him.[46]) Leontius is thus at some pains to emphasize the positive nature of his presentation of Cyril. He tries to show, in fact, that Cyril used the key heretical forgery ascribed to Athanasius (and, as Leontius has already said,

---

[42] 1881A–B.
[43] The discussion is found at 1864A–1876C.
[44] Leontius mentions John of Scythopolis in this connection at 1865B–C.
[45] 1861C–1864A.
[46] Hence the odd citation from 'Timothy Aelurus' at 1849A–C that presents Severus as curing 'with his holy writings whatever of Cyril's was unsound and contradictory'. On alienating Severus and his follows, see sect. VI below.

used it in a perfectly orthodox sense) without being aware of its
origins: 'If our teacher Cyril introduces it as being Athanasius'
statement . . . it's not impossible that he was drawn to it, either
construed in terms of our meaning, or—under the influence
of certain people's forgery—mistaken for patristic rather than
heretical evidence.'[47] Moreover, even when it is the famous
pseudo-Athanasian text that he is about to show convincingly
comes from Apollinarius, Leontius makes sure first to offer a
positive interpretation of it, compatible with his own position, for
anti-Chalcedonians who could never accept its inauthenticity.[48]

V. *TESTIMONIES OF THE SAINTS*: MEETING THE CHARGE OF DISHONESTY

The second charge Leontius puts in the mouth of his anti-
Chalcedonians is the charge of dishonesty. Various anti-
Chalcedonian voices identify the suspicious circumstances:
Dioscorus was condemned, but not on the charge for which he
was cited;[49] Chalcedon accepted Theodoret and Ibas, both friends
of Nestorius, proponents of his ideas, and critics of Cyril;[50]
Chalcedon dropped the first creed it produced, and replaced it
with another;[51] votes were bought.[52] In Leontius' response to
this charge he makes careful attempts to disarm the anti-
Chalcedonians on these points.

Leontius sticks pretty well to the pro-Chalcedonian argument
used at the Conversations of 532 on the issue of Dioscorus' treatment. Dioscorus was called on suspicion of Eutychianism, and it
would not do to say his reception of Eutyches was based on the
latter's abandonment of his earlier beliefs, since Dioscorus
deposed Flavian for deposing Eutyches before he could have
abandoned them. He was therefore either shown to be a Eutychian for his defence of Eutyches against Flavian, or else he was
unjust in deposing Flavian for deposing a heretic he, Dioscorus,
did not agree with![53] That argument for the justice of Dioscorus'
deposition does not change. Unlike the participants in the

---

[47] 1865A.
[48] 1864A–B. He likewise offers an orthodox interpretation of a text from 'Gregory
Thaumaturgus' just in case, though he clearly suspects it is a forgery: 1873C–1876A.
[49] 1884C.   [50] 1877B.   [51] 1881C–D and 1884A.
[52] 1889B.   [53] 1884C–1885D.

conversations, though, Leontius sees that there are dark anti-Chalcedonian suspicions on this matter, and seeks to lay them to rest. On the one hand, Leontius uses these suspicions as one opportunity among many to attempt to detach Severus' followers from their leader. Conspiracy theories of that kind, Leontius says, are the inventions of anti-Chalcedonian leaders like Severus trying to suborn 'those not well-equipped to judge'.[54] On the other hand, he argues that the treatment of Dioscorus by Chalcedon really was a model of proper and transparent legal process. He was summoned on the charges of receiving Eutyches (i.e. on suspicion of heresy) and of unjustly deposing Flavian; he made excuses for not appearing, which were eventually found to be fraudulent; he was re-summoned, refused to appear, and was then condemned for the refusal. In legal terms, the serious charges initially brought against him were prevented from being brought to trial, not because of any conspiracy to misrepresent the case, but simply because he refused to appear and be tried.[55] In this way, Leontius attempts to present Chalcedon as scrupulously fair in its treatment of Dioscorus, and avoids associating himself with any claim that Dioscorus—a hero to the people with whom he seeks reconciliation—was in fact a heretic. The most he claims—he can hardly do otherwise—is that Chalcedon had legitimate and entirely public reasons for the deposition.

On the issue of Chalcedon's damning acceptance of Theodoret and Ibas—damning because it suggested so strongly to anti-Chalcedonians that Chalcedon was bent on restoring the Nestorianism with which these men were associated—Leontius' response represents, again, an effort to bridge the ecumenical gap. He does not deny the possibility that Theodoret and Ibas secretly persisted in Nestorian beliefs. He admits, indeed, that the charge may very well be true, though he pleads with the anti-Chalcedonians to recognize the possibility of a genuine change of heart on the part of such Antiochenes.[56] His appeal, though, is for recognition that Chalcedon as a whole should not be condemned just because two or three participants were closet Nestorians, any more than Nicaea should be condemned because a few heretics were known to be participants in it, or than Ephesus should be condemned because some of its members also participated in Chalcedon (if Chalcedon really was so heretical).[57] While not

[54] 1884c. See sect. VI below.   [55] 1884d–1885b.
[56] 1877b–1880b.   [57] 1880b–1880d.

going nearly so far as Justinian was prepared to go in the proposal he presented to the anti-Chalcedonians at the end of the Conversations of 532—a proposal that would eventually be developed into the full-fledged campaign to condemn the Three Chapters—Leontius shows himself once again to be willing to recognize some validity in anti-Chalcedonian claims. At the same time, he tries to show that remaining loyal to Chalcedon was not incompatible with those claims if the historical and theological realities were properly understood.[58]

The same may be said of Leontius' responses to three minor charges: that Chalcedon's remaking of its creed was highly suspicious; that votes were bought at Chalcedon; and that the frequent manifestations of miracle-working powers among anti-Chalcedonians was God's way of demonstrating the truth of their position. The first charge was difficult. As has been noted, Chalcedon's first statement of faith was suppressed, and the second and final statement of faith was adopted only under great pressure from the court. The patent reversal, moving from a Cyrillian statement of faith to a Nestorian-sounding one, lent instant plausibility to the anti-Chalcedonian case that there was something decidedly fishy about that second statement.[59] Leontius goes so far with his anti-Chalcedonian readers as to accept the facts, embarrassing as they are, but he does try to limit the inferences drawn from them: Chalcedon did indeed remake its definition, but to impute sinister motives to it because it did so is nothing but 'courtroom rhetoric' he will not dignify with a response.[60] He suggests instead a positive evaluation: Chalcedon simply recognized imperfections in its first definition, and tried again.[61] On the charge of bribery, Leontius again goes part way with his readers: perhaps a few people were bribed, but not the vast majority. Should not the sinners be forgiven?[62] On the issue of miracles, though Leontius does dispute the claim of superior numbers for anti-Chalcedonian miracles ('one swallow doth not a summer

---

[58] The Three Chapters were the person and work of Theodore of Mopsuestia, the writings of Theodoret of Cyrus against Cyril of Alexandria, and Ibas of Edessa's *Letter to Mari the Persian*. All were condemned, not many years after Leontius wrote, first by an imperial edict of 544, then by Constantinople II in 553.

[59] It was not Marcian's heavy hand in the affair which drew the anti-Chalcedonians' suspicion—the Church accepted without question a prominent role for the emperor in councils—but the radical reversal of position on the part of the bishops.

[60] 1884A.   [61] 1884A–B.   [62] 1889B–1892A.

make', he cannot help saying), he does not place any weight on that point.[63] As in the case of Apollinarian forgeries, he grants the possibility that the anti-Chalcedonians may even be right, but he attempts to challenge the implication drawn by some anti-Chalcedonians: there are, he says, many plausible reasons why God might grant miracle-working power other than dogmatic correctness, such as miracles' usefulness in winning over non-Christians.[64]

VI. *TESTIMONIES OF THE SAINTS*: SEVERING SEVERIANS FROM SEVERUS

While the fundamental thrust of *Testimonies of the Saints* is clearly to win over Syrian anti-Chalcedonians under the leadership-from-exile of Severus, and Leontius is well aware of the profound influence Severus continues to exercise over anti-Chalcedonians in Syria, he shares completely Justinian's apparent belief, at the time of the Conversations of 532, that Severus' said followers can be alienated from him, and reconciled independently of him. He goes out of his way to drive a wedge between them.

The dismissal of Severus as a 'nature-mixer' ('mixophysite') is a taunting way of identifying him with the standard phantom Eutychianism, but it is no more than a rhetorical flourish. From the outset, though, Leontius makes a serious, sustained attempt to make a more telling case to Severus' followers against him. His plan is to show Severus as genuinely inconsistent in his thinking, and wilful in his resistance to Chalcedon. On the point of inconsistency, Leontius says Severus claims to stand against 'two natures', yet is on record as saying that 'most of the holy fathers used the expression . . . in a blameless way', and as validating over and over again two-natures language despite himself.[65] He turns Severus' critique of Chalcedon for not saying 'out of two natures', i.e. for not talking about duality in a legitimately Cyrillian way, into an admission that Chalcedon was not incorrect in speaking of two natures. That, he argues, is inconsistent with his condemnation of Chalcedon,[66] and, having argued to his own satisfaction

---

[63] 1896c.   [64] 1896c–1900a.
[65] 1805a. The charge is repeated at some length at 1841b–d.
[66] 1841b–1844b.

that Chalcedon and Chalcedonians of his own time accept everything Severus claims they should ('out of two', 'union by hypostasis', 'combination', 'an entire nature'),[67] he tips his hand
unmistakably: 'Since [this is so,] what possible reason can these
people have for refusing to agree with us on these, using both "out
of two" and "in two", and electing to anathematize Severus,
Dioscorus, and those with them, if they don't think the same?'[68]

Leontius goes on, in a long section devoted to anti-
Chalcedonian texts that appear to support Chalcedon, to discredit
Severus again for risible inconsistency, and for the manner of his
deposition from the patriarchal throne of Antioch, ending with a
curious citation, allegedly but impossibly from Timothy Aelurus,
describing Severus as the one who 'cured' Cyril's 'inconsistency'
on two-natures language. The choice of that text can only have
been intended to leave Severus looking guilty, in the eyes of his
followers, of criticizing Cyril himself for using both one-nature
and two-natures formulae![69] That this implication is fully intended
by Leontius becomes clear from a later reference to Severus as
'patricidal'.[70] Severus later is dismissed as the anti-Chalcedonians'
'self-styled teacher',[71] and derided for individually anathematizing
a council completely outside his jurisdiction.[72] All of this suggests
that the descriptions of Severus at the very beginning of *Testimonies of the Saints* as the anti-Chalcedonians' 'authoritative guide',
and near the end, without actually naming him, as a man obsessed
with his 'status as a teacher', carry a clear message: the anti-
Chalcedonians are spinelessly letting themselves be manipulated
by an inconsistent egomaniac who sets himself against the whole
duly constituted Church, yet, as a deposed patriarch, he is a man
who has no legitimate claim over them. Moreover, in the name of
Cyril they are accepting Severus' outright doctoring of Cyril's
teaching to exclude the manifold texts in which Cyril does speak
of two natures or the equivalent.[73]

We do not need to be convinced that the strategy both Justinian
and Leontius adopted of trying to sever Severians from Severus

---

[67] 1844A–B.   [68] 1844B.

[69] 1845A–1849C. Timothy Aelurus ('the Weasel') was an anti-Chalcedonian, and
Patriarch of Alexandria at various times between 457 and his death in 477. He was
one of the first to write against Chalcedon. It is possible that Leontius intends to
attribute the text rather to Timothy III of Alexandria.

[70] 1864C.   [71] 1876D.   [72] 1888C.

[73] 'Authoritative guide': 1805A; 'status as a teacher': 1893A.

had any real chance of success. Only one anti-Chalcedonian at the Conversations changed sides, and Justinian's more developed strategy for reconciling anti-Chalcedonians at the Council of 553 certainly did not succeed, facts which suggest that Justinian and Leontius were unrealistic in their hopes. That should not prevent us from recognizing that, in the 530s, they could not know the outcome, and could and apparently did believe their strategy might succeed.

VII. *TESTIMONIES OF THE SAINTS*: THE WEIGHT OF THE FATHERS

Central to Leontius' strategy was the use of the patristic witness to what he believed he could show was the fathers' single underlying christological faith, since the sides agreed on this at least, that the faith of the fathers was what defined orthodoxy. In making the appeal to the fathers the heart of his theological argument, he exemplifies a late stage in a remarkable transformation that took place in theological argument during the fifth and sixth centuries.[74] Though the roots of the patristic argument can be traced further back, Cyril of Alexandria effectively marked its move to the centre of the stage, when he discovered it was more effective to charge Nestorius with betraying the faith of the fathers, and to demonstrate the fact with a florilegium, than to tackle him on his understanding of Scriptures (the Antiochenes had a formidable and sophisticated approach to the latter). As the focus moved to the fathers, the fathers themselves came to acquire greater authority in the minds of those who argued over what they taught, and from what they taught. Grillmeier puts it cautiously—'It was only that the proof from Scripture acquired younger siblings who

---

[74] I have explored this transformation in a number of articles: P. T. R. Gray, 'Covering the Nakedness of Noah: Reconstruction and Denial in the Age of Justinian', in L. Garland (ed.), *Conformity and Non-Conformity in Byzantium*, = BF 24 (1997), 193-206; 'Forgery as an Instrument of Progress: Reconstructing the Theological Tradition in the Sixth Century', *BZ* 81 (1988), 284-9; 'Neo-Chalcedonianism and the Tradition: From Patristic to Byzantine Theology', *BF* 8 (1982), 61-70; '"The Select Fathers": Canonizing the Patristic Past', *Papers presented to the Tenth International Conference on Patristic Studies held in Oxford 1987*, StudPat 23 (Leuven: Peeters Press, 1989), 21-36; 'Through the Tunnel with Leontius of Jerusalem: The Sixth Century Transformation of Theology', in P. Allen and E. Jeffreys (eds.), *The Sixth Century: End or Beginning?*, BA 10 (Brisbane: Australian Association for Byzantine Studies, 1996), 187-96.

wanted to sit at the same theological table and seemed for a while to demand the larger portion, which, however, must never be claimed from the "first-born" '[75]—but the truth is that, by the sixth century, the *argumentum patristicum* did not just demand a bigger place in theological argument, it exercised virtual hegemony. That fact is illustrated by the complete reliance of the Fifth Ecumenical Council on a single way of demonstrating the heresy of the Three Chapters: their works were compared minutely with patristic texts of an assumed canon of fathers who represented infallible ortho-doxy. There was not the merest hint of a demonstration from Scriptures. Scholasticism had been born, and *Testimonies of the Saints*, as its title suggests, exemplifies how scholastic theological argument functioned.

Very soon after Chalcedon, and from then on, champions of both parties had indeed turned to the fathers, collecting key texts into florilegia, or using florilegia previously collected by others. Leontius evidently had at hand various florilegia, from which he and others—his contemporary, Leontius of Byzantium, for one, and in the next century John Maron, for another—drew in com-mon. He even had one or more florilegia of anti-Chalcedonian texts. Yet unlike Leontius of Byzantium, as a comparative study shows, Leontius of Jerusalem was a careless user of sources. The one scholar ever to make a serious study of the florilegia of the period, Marcel Richard, has no kind words for our Leontius on this score: 'The little collection of definitions of Christ with which [the first florilegium] opens would have made Severus jump for joy . . . Not only does he not indicate from which works he's bor-rowed his texts, but he also altered almost all of them in his own way.'[76] He goes on to add that Leontius cut most of them so short as to leave their meaning in doubt, copied them inaccurately, and generally left them in great disorder. Whether Severus, if he ever came upon *Testimonies of the Saints*, did jump for joy or not— Richard incorrectly assumed that he was dead by the time Leon-tius wrote, as will be seen—we shall never know. Certainly

---

[75] A. Grillmeier, *Christ in Christian Tradition* II[1], tr. P. Allen and J. Cawte (London and Oxford: Mowbray, 1987), 20.

[76] M. Richard, 'Les Florilèges diphysites du Ve et du VIe siècle', *Opera Minora*, i (Turnhout: Brepols, 1976), no. 3, 741. Richard prepared a massive work with sections on the florilegia of many writers, including both Leontii, but it was never published. The section on Leontius of Jerusalem was kindly made available by M. Geerard, Richard's literary executor. Recent enquiries reveal that, sadly, at Geerard's death, Richard's papers were not preserved.

Severus' followers, if they had the means and the will to test how accurate were his citations of the fathers, will have been less impressed by Leontius' argument than they might have been.

To fault Leontius for bad historical scholarship is fair, but his bad scholarship is not the end of the story. Severus' much better historical scholarship is not the end of the story either. We know, after all, that a fierce critic of the scholarship of his opponents like Severus was well aware of a very good piece of scholarship indeed on the Chalcedonian side, scholarship which proved pretty well beyond a doubt that the anti-Chalcedonians' favourite 'authoritative' texts rested, in part, on Apollinarian forgeries. Yet he did not stop using the suspect texts. Leontius himself is able to make a decent enough scholarly case when he wants to, as he does in our text when he attacks Apollinarian forgeries, yet he is not at all scholarly—he is downright sloppy, in fact—when it comes to the texts that he himself wishes to cite. Something more, then, is at work here than scholarly capabilities.

Theologians of Leontius' era were compelled to prove the orthodoxy of what they taught by appealing to the texts of the fathers. Appealing to the fathers involved a major assumption, however: that all of the genuine fathers taught, consistently, one orthodox faith. That assumption is revealingly expressed by Leontius in *Testimonies of the Saints*: 'Surely none of the select fathers is at variance with himself or with his peers with respect to the intended sense of the faith'.[77] He can confidently assume that his anti-Chalcedonian audience agrees, and can proceed on that basis to make his argument about an underlying common faith. Yet the strains that universal assumption placed on theologians were enormous. For one thing, the tensions between, for example, an early Cyril happily affirming the continuance of two natures into the Incarnation in the *Second Letter to Nestorius*, and a late Cyril sternly insisting on only 'one incarnate nature' after the union— easily explicable, for moderns, in terms of the man's historical development—could be explained in only three ways: the reduction of the earlier statement to the later; the reduction of the later statement to the earlier; or the reduction of both (as is urged by Leontius) to a third way of talking about christology, which is what he 'really' meant. In short, the rich variety of the real historical debate had to be reduced in some way to a monolithic uniformity.

---

[77] 1849D.

That reduction could perhaps be achieved at one level by Leontius' stratagem of proposing a meta-language, but it inevitably involved also, at other levels, the reconstruction of the patristic record in the monolithic image a theologian like Leontius imposed on it. No wonder, then, that troublesome documents were misquoted, quoted out of context, cut short, or dismissed as forgeries, while helpful and consistent documents were forged to meet the need.

VIII. THE *APORIAE*

Testimonies of the Saints is not without its own examples of aporetic argument.[78] Clearly, though, whole works were devoted to aporiae systematically developed to undermine the different doctrines of an opposing group. Leontius tells us that he has responded to one such collection of aporiae (in a work now lost to us), and in the present work we find him going on to propose counter-aporiae against the very people who propounded that collection of aporiae against him and/or his party.[79] We can only guess at the length of the missing response, but *Against the Nestorians* gives us an idea of how long such a response could be.[80] The attractions of aporetic argument to all parties—Chalcedonians, Severian anti-Chalcedonians, Nestorians—were obviously great, especially as the controversies between them involved imprecise and often contradictory-sounding formulae that invited adversaries gleefully to spell out their contradictions in aporetic form. For their own positions they would always, of course, try to claim consistency and clarity.

In the present case we find Leontius—a man with a reputation for being 'all-wise' which must have signalled an aptitude for the kind of technical and logical prowess aporetic argument invited—delighting in exploring and exposing the inconsistencies of his Severian opponents' christological language. The Severians' language was based on Cyril's post-433 letters, but that language had always been difficult to explain and defend—Cyril was taunted for it, and Eutyches seems likely to have been condemned as a heretic

---

[78] e.g. at 1861B–C and at 1872C.

[79] 1769A.

[80] *Against the Nestorians* occupies 368 columns in Migne, compared with 132 columns for *Testimonies of the Saints* and the *Aporiae* combined.

because of it—fundamentally because it was inconsistent in its use of the one word 'nature' for both the christological unity ('one incarnate nature') and the christological duality ('out of two natures'). It was entirely predictable that a Chalcedonian like Leontius would, in controversy with Severians, use aporiae to hammer home the logical inconsistency inherent in saying that one incarnate nature came out of two natures before the union, and in continuing to assert that human and divine were unconfused and different in Christ while asserting that in Him they were united in one nature. He also used aporiae to undermine the paradigm used by Cyril and the Severians to explain and defend the notion of one nature out of two, the union of body and soul to produce a human nature, as well as to attack the language which that paradigm brought with it about the whole and the part.

Of the sixty-three aporiae of Leontius found in our text, sixty-one address such weak points in the Severian position, and it may be useful to categorize them roughly in terms of the point in the Severian position on which they focus their attack:

1. There is *one nature* in Christ.[81]
2. Christ's one nature came to be *out of two* natures.[82]
3. The human and divine natures became one nature just as *body and soul become one human nature*.[83]
4. A duality of natures in Christ may be recognized *only in thought*.[84]
5. There is one nature *after the union*.[85]
6. *Difference* can be affirmed at the same time as one nature is affirmed.[86]
7. There is one *incarnate nature* of God the Word, not one nature of the Word incarnate.[87]
8. Christ, though one nature, may be said to have improved or suffered.[88]
9. There is one nature *and hypostasis* in Christ.[89]

The positive case constantly implied by these arguments is that

[81] Aporiae 1–3, 5, 7, 19, 32–4, 36–8, 40–1, 53, 63.
[82] Aporiae 2, 3, 8, 20, 23–4, 29, 58, 61.
[83] Aporiae 4, 6, 15, 19, 22, 35, 45, 48, 54–5.   [84] Aporia 10.
[85] Aporia 9, 11–12, 52.
[86] Aporiae 13–14, 16–18, 25–8, 30, 39, 56–7.
[87] Aporiae 42–3, 59–60.
[88] Aporiae 44, 46–7, 49–50.   [89] Aporia 51.

for the superiority of Chalcedonian language, which has one set of terms to express Christ's unity ('person', or 'hypostasis'), and another to express His duality ('nature', or 'substance').

There is one intriguing aporia, the thirty-first, which does not resemble the others. Instead, it quite intentionally indulges in a bit of quasi-logical sleight of hand which, as Leontius certainly recognizes, depends entirely on double meanings. The point seems to have been to have some fun at the expense of the Severians. The sixty-second aporia departs from the pattern in a quite different way, and is really not an aporia except formally: Severians accuse Chalcedon of introducing new terms unknown to the fathers, but Leontius and his party find that the fathers characteristically speak of two natures; Severians therefore must find fathers who speak of one nature, or yield the point.

IX. THE THEOLOGICAL CONTRIBUTION

It is unfortunate that, from the moment of his rediscovery by Richard in the 1940s, Leontius of Jerusalem was interpreted almost exclusively in terms of conceptual and theoretical issues having little to do with his own concerns, and a great deal to do with the twentieth century. For one thing, the twentieth-century struggle between conservative champions of an asymmetrical christology (in which the human Christ is overwhelmed by His divinity), and liberal champions of a more fully human Christ, meant that liberal scholars—who were in the majority—tended to sympathize with the Antiochene school in christology because of its emphasis on the independent human reality in Christ, and to feel a commensurate antipathy towards Cyril of Alexandria and his asymmetrical christology. The Council of Chalcedon, in that it adopted the Antiochene 'two natures' over Cyril's 'one incarnate nature', came in for sympathetic treatment. Its statement of faith was seen as a balanced, statesmanlike achievement, nicely laying to rest the antithetical errors of Nestorius and Eutyches, and resolving all problems. When such scholars began to investigate the theologians like Leontius of Jerusalem who interpreted Chalcedon in a Cyrillian way, they adopted a highly suspicious attitude towards them, gave them the hostile epithet 'neo-Chalcedonian', and tended to conclude that they were, in fact, not theologians in good faith, but the instruments of an overreaching plan on the

part of the Emperor Justinian to impose on the Church his private (but not at all representative) Cyrillian-revivalist christology in place of the authentic teaching of Chalcedon.[90] (The term has since, however, lost its pejorative connotation and become merely descriptive of a certain theological tendency, which is how it is used here.) In so far as Leontius was taken to be implicated in the real or supposed ecclesiastical–political agenda of Justinian, particularly as it concerned Constantinople II and that council's relationship with Pope Vigilius, he became implicated, too, in modern concerns about the papal magisterium and how it relates to conciliar authority, about the independence of the Church from political authority, and thus about the evils of 'caesaro-papism'.

For at least myself, that interpretation of the era raised more historical questions than it answered. Could the Church really have experienced a sudden conversion from the powerfully Cyrillian faith it espoused in 431 and 449 to the remarkably Antiochene-sounding language of Chalcedon? In what way did it make sense, if at all, to speak of a person as a Chalcedonian without specifying what tradition informed that person's interpretation of the bare words of the council, a statement of faith foisted on the majority? What happened to the Cyrillians? Was it even possible for an emperor to impose his personal theology on the Church, as Justinian was often said to have done? Were the so-called neo-Chalcedonians really so unrepresentative of the mainstream? The answers to many of those questions turned out to be entirely negative, and an attempt was made to articulate a more accurate view of the post-Chalcedonian developments on purely historical grounds, which happened also to be a more positive view.[91] Orthodox scholars, for whom Cyrillian christology was, and continues to be, the authoritative expression of a living, viable faith, began to argue for a more positive evaluation too.[92] A more

---

[90] The high-water mark of this way of thinking is represented by C. Moeller, 'Le Chalcédonisme et le néo-chalcédonisme en Orient de 451 à la fin du VIe siècle', in A. Grillmeier and H. Bacht (eds.), *Das Konzil von Chalkedon* i (Würzburg: Echter-Verlag, 1951), 638–720. On 'neo-Chalcedonianism' as a historical description of certain theologians, see Gray, *Defense*, 169–72.

[91] Gray, *Defense*.

[92] e.g. J. Meyendorff, *Christ in Eastern Christian Thought* (Crestwood, NY: St. Vladimir's, 1975); K. P. Wesche, 'The Defense of Chalcedon in the 6th Century: The Doctrine of "Hypostasis" and Deification in the Christology of Leontius of Jerusalem' (Thesis, Fordham, 1986); idem, 'The Christology of Leontius of Jerusalem: Monophysite or Chalcedonian?', *SVTQ* 31 (1987), 65–95.

sympathetic treatment of Leontius and his fellow neo-Chalcedonians thus began to emerge in the later twentieth century.

The weighty contribution of Grillmeier needs to be assessed on its own. Over many decades Grillmeier undertook a complex re-evaluation of the whole development of christology that became noticeably more radical, more positive towards the neo-Chalcedonians in general, and Leontius of Jerusalem in particular, as volume II of *Christ in Christian Tradition* took shape.[93] Grillmeier's subtle assessment seems to be influenced by a number of things, including a deepening understanding (born of decades of participation in ecumenical dialogue) of the non-Chalcedonian churches of our time. That understanding surely helped him to the remarkable conclusion that Severus of Antioch actually represented, in his sternly Cyrillian christology, not a heretical 'monophysitism', but an alternative articulation of orthodoxy to that expressed in the particular conceptual vocabulary of Chalcedon.[94] That train of thought paralleled another, earlier train of thought, a reconsideration of Chalcedon and what its statement of faith represents in the light of its only partial 'reception' by the Church as an ecumenical council.[95] That train of thought led to the admission that, though Chalcedon had a certain status as ecumenical council, and one could talk about its having a positive theology, it had not spoken the final word on christology, and aspects of its implicit christology were left to be developed. In the light of those reflections, it is understandable that Grillmeier came to a positive evaluation of Leontius of Jerusalem since, whatever else Leontius was about, he was involved in arguing for a christology of hypostatic union, though not, in Grillmeier's terms, in a fully adequate way.

Grillmeier's analysis of the entire history of christology is sharply focused on the conceptual and terminological issues, however; sometimes so much so that the rarefied discussion of those issues seems to be envisaged as taking place in the stratosphere. It often seems, indeed, to take place well away from the everyday life of the Church and the very human tensions over personalities and

---

[93] Grillmeier, *Christ* II², pp. 271–312.

[94] Ibid., 152–73.

[95] The initial statement of this perspective: A. Grillmeier, *Christ in Christian Tradition* i, tr. J. Bowden (Atlanta, GA: John Knox Press, 1975), 555–7. The theme developed: idem, *Christ* II¹, 115–235.

cherished traditions and old wounds that often keep churches in schism with each other much more effectively than theological disagreements little understood by anyone other than the theologians themselves. It is no surprise, then, that Grillmeier's treatment of Leontius of Jerusalem has, literally, nothing to say about *Testimonies of the Saints*—which addresses tensions of just that sort—and devotes itself entirely to the conceptual and terminological issues addressed in the very different *Against the Nestorians*.

Setting aside the *Aporiae*'s minor, and negative, contribution to clarifying christological language, the Leontius met in this volume is not interested in conceptual issues for their own sake, nor is he original in the concepts he does use. If *Testimonies of the Saints* was written between 536 and 538, as is argued here, it followed the imperial edict on union by hypostasis by several years.[96] That means the emperor and his advisers had already recognized the potential of that expression, used by Cyril, in the campaign to reconcile the anti-Chalcedonians; we cannot credit Leontius with discovering the formula's potential. *Testimonies of the Saints* shows that what he was interested in was putting to practical use the theological language that was available. An apparently frustrating reluctance to define precisely in philosophical terms what a word like 'hypostasis' or an expression like 'union by hypostasis' meant was perhaps actually a tactical acceptance of an agreed common-sense understanding of such terms. On the basis of such an agreed sense, Leontius could and did use these words and expressions in the service of an agenda no less historically interesting, when understood on its own terms, than the intellectually more challenging achievements of Leontius of Byzantium.

X. MANUSCRIPTS, EDITIONS, AND TRANSLATIONS

For reasons we shall never know, Leontius of Jerusalem's *Aporiae*, *Testimonies of the Saints*, and *Against the Nestorians*—in that order— were copied along with works by other authors in a thirteenth-century manuscript made in Byzantium.[97] The fact that this manuscript included important works by and about Gregory of Nyssa was to prove fortuitous. No other works by Leontius, and no

[96] The argument on dating is made in sect. XI below.
[97] Codex Marcianus gr. 69.

independent copy of the works we now have, has ever been found, so that the survival of Leontius into modern times depended entirely on that single manuscript's fate. By a stroke of good luck, Gregory of Nyssa happened to be a favourite theologian of the fifteenth-century Metropolitan of Nicea, Bessarion, which explains why the manuscript was included in the extensive library of Greek fathers Bessarion took with him to Italy. It still bears his personal marking and catalogue number. Typically, in the scholion noting the contents of the volume, Bessarion writes: 'Gregory of Nyssa's *Against Eunomius*, and certain other works by different authors'; Leontius of Jerusalem was not worthy of specific mention.[98] Eventually, the MS was part of Bessarion's donation to the library of St Mark's in Venice, and there this oldest (and only textually significant) copy of Leontius' extant works has remained to this day, apart from the entire library's brief removal to Paris by Napoleon.[99]

The likelihood that Leontius' work would survive and become known improved in the sixteenth century, when two copies of the Venice manuscript were made independently by different copyists for the library amassed by the wealthy Bavarian book-collectors, the Fuggers. One copy remained in Bavaria, ending up in the Staatsbibliothek of Munich. There it attracted no scholarly attention until modern times.[100] The Fugger library in large part, however, passed to Maximilian, Elector of Bavaria, and the second copy, dated 1552, was part of Maximilian's magnificent donation to Pope Gregory XV of what came to be known as the Vatican Library's Palatine Collection.[101] Leontius thus survived in a third library, but again without, it seems, being read. (A copy of the Vatican manuscript was made in the nineteenth century either for, or destined to be retained by, the philologist Jean-Antoine Letronne (1787-1848), who may have enjoyed playing with some of Leontius' odd Greek, but who seems not to have studied him seriously or written about him.[102])

Leontius was at last read seriously, in the seventeenth century,

[98] In the upper right-hand margin of fo. 2.

[99] It bears the stamp of the Bibliothèque Nationale.

[100] Codex Monacensis gr. 67. It bears the Fugger library number (46) in the hand of Hieronymus Wolf, librarian to Johann Jakob Fugger.

[101] Codex Vaticanus Pal. gr. 342. The copyist identifies himself at the end as 'Cornelius Mourmouris of Nauplia', and says he made the copy in 1552 in Venice.

[102] Acquired, eventually, by the Bibliothèque Nationale in Paris, and held as Par. Suppl. Gr. 1288.

by the eminent French patrologist, François Combéfis, who even made rough copies of both works in his own hand, plus an equally rough Latin translation of *Aporiae* and *Testimonies of the Saints*. But Combéfis published nothing by or about Leontius, and whatever he thought about him or his significance died with him, his copies and the translation lying uncatalogued among his papers in the National Archives of France.[103]

Leontius' fortunes began to change dramatically only in the middle of the eighteenth century, when a scholar from Verona, Antonio Bongiovanni, formed the plan of editing and translating portions of the Venice manuscript. In the end, in order to please Mansi, he contributed only the closing section of *Testimonies of the Saints* and selections from the florilegium, along with his Latin translation of both, as an appendix to Mansi's 1752 *Supplement* to Cossart and Labbé's collection of conciliar documents.[104] In the process he departed from the order of the manuscript in the attempt, as Richard observed, to extract a commentary on Chalcedon from a text that has a rather different purpose.[105] Bongiovanni himself recognized that this Leontius should not be confused with Leontius of Byzantium.[106] Ominously, Mansi did not agree: he remarked, rather cavalierly, 'it is not . . . easy to see why we ought to distinguish one Leontius from the other.'[107]

Leontius was fortunate, however, to have Angelo Mai, the Vatican librarian, as the editor of the first full transcription of his two surviving works, even though Mai transcribed the Vatican manuscript that was ready to hand, rather than the Venice MS of which it is a copy.[108] His transcription was at least careful and intelligent,

---

[103] VIII, 834, no. 6: Greek of *Aporiae* and *Testimonies of the Saints*; II, M787, no. 3: Latin tr. of the same; IX, M836, no. 1: Greek of *Against the Nestorians*.

[104] J.-D. Mansi (ed.), *Supplementum* to P. Labbé and G. Cossart, *Sacrorum conciliorum et decretorum collectio nova*, vi (Luca, 1752), 467-546, and repeated in subsequent editions of Mansi's *Sacrorum conciliorum nova et amplissima collectio* (Florence: 1748-1752) as an appendix to vii, 799–208, as well as in A. Galland, *Bibliotheca veterum patrum*, xii (Venice, 1778), 719–50, and subsequent editions.

[105] M. Richard, 'Léonce de Jérusalem et Léonce de Byzance', *Opera Minora*, iii (Turnhout: Brepols, 1976), no. 59, p. 41 n. 25.

[106] Mansi, *Supplementum*, 719 n. 1: 'Our Leontius is not to be confused with the Nestorian [!] Leontius of Byzantium'. Galland agrees, *Bibliotheca*, xii, p. xxx.

[107] Mansi, *Collectio*, 798.

[108] A. Mai (ed.), *Scriptorum veterum nova collectio e vaticanis codicibus edita*, vii. 110–35 [*Against the Monophysites*] and ix. 410–610 [*Against the Nestorians*] (Rome: 1833 and 1837). In the meantime, Bessarion's MS copy remained in obscurity in Venice. F. Diekamp was the only 19th-c. scholar to register there as a reader of it, but the great

and he attributed the works, properly, to Leontius of Jerusalem. Later in the nineteenth century, though, Migne essentially republished Mai's edition of *Against the Monophysites* and *Against the Nestorians*, but included them among the collected works, both genuine and spurious, of that other theological Leontius of the same period, Leontius of Byzantium.[109] The separate identity of Leontius of Jerusalem, and the individuality of his approach, were at a stroke condemned to remain thus obscured until they were rediscovered in the mid-twentieth century. Not only that: Migne's anonymous editor was careless with the text, changed Mai's careful punctuation, and provided only a mediocre Latin translation of his own, cobbled together where possible with Bongiovanni's (awkwardly, since the latter was made from a different MS). Little help was offered to anyone who wished to approach Leontius of Jerusalem through the pages of the *Patrologia*.

XI. IDENTITY, DATE, AND CIRCUMSTANCES

The one nineteenth-century scholar besides Mai to pay any serious attention to Leontius of Jerusalem's works, Friedrich Loofs, made matters worse rather than better, for he dismissed his works as revisions of originals by Leontius of Byzantium—the work, then, of a seventh-century hack. To Loofs, Leontius of Jerusalem's works were, to use Richard's words, no more than 'a shadow of Leontius of Byzantium'; they were hardly likely to be worth studying.[110]

The credit for the modern rediscovery of Leontius of Jerusalem belongs to Marcel Richard, whose 1944 article laid out the classic case, now universally accepted, for distinguishing Leontius of Jerusalem from Leontius of Byzantium, and for letting him emerge as indeed a contemporary of the latter and of other Leontii of the period, but a contemporary with a quite different vocabulary, a quite different approach to theology, and a quite different agenda.[111] Richard's case is too long and detailed to

patrologist noted, disappointingly, not that he had studied Leontius, but that he had copied the *Life of Gregory of Nyssa*.

[109] *PG* lxxxvi[1], 1400A–1768[1]B (*Against the Nestorians*) and lxxxvi[2], 1769–1901A (*Against the Monophysites*).

[110] Loofs, *Leontius von Byzanz*, 1–2; Richard, 'Léonce', 271 n. 3.

[111] Richard, 'Léonce', 35–88.

repeat here. Suffice it to say that he shows convincingly that there are fundamental differences between the two Leontii on the philosophical terminology to be used to describe the human soul and its relationship to the body; on the use of scientific examples (for which our Leontius has a characteristic fondness quite absent from Leontius of Byzantium); and on the application of neo-Chalcedonian formulae (Leontius of Jerusalem uses them; Leontius of Byzantium does not).[112] Leontius of Jerusalem thus could stand out, at last, as an author in his own right. And scholars did at last begin to write about him. Unfortunately, as has been noted, the resonances attached to being a neo-Chalcedonian by scholars like Richard and his successors stood in the way of a full appreciation.

It would be helpful if we could identify Leontius as one of the Leontii about whom historical information is available. A plausible case can be made for only one candidate: Leontius, the 'representative of the monks in the Holy City [Jerusalem]', present at the Conversations of 532.[113] That this Palestinian monk was theologically sophisticated and knowledgeable about the issues between pro- and anti-Chalcedonians seems certain, as there would have been no other reason for his presence. We know of two Leontii who fit that description: Leontius of Jerusalem, and Leontius of Byzantium. Both are, suitably, associated with Palestine, our Leontius by the manuscript's description of him as a monk of Jerusalem, Leontius of Byzantium by Cyril of Scythopolis' information about an Origenist monk by that name active in the Judaean Desert monasteries.[114] Richard favoured the former, but knew the case could not be proven conclusively.[115] The weight of scholarly opinion at the moment favours the latter.[116] The case cannot be proven either way, and no firm conclusions can be drawn on this basis about either Leontius.

There is, however, internal evidence that helps with establishing a firm date and situation. Richard dated Leontius' activity to the period 538–44. He took Leontius to be talking of Severus as if he

---

[112] The argument on these points: 52–62.

[113] See n. 25 above.

[114] Cyril of Scythopolis, *Life of Sabas*, in E. Schwartz (ed.), *Kyrillos von Skythopolis, TU* 49² (Leipzig: J. C. Hinrichs, 1939), 176, 179.

[115] Richard, 'Léonce', 81–8.

[116] Grillmeier, *Christ* II², 183, 186; D. B. Evans, *Leontius of Byzantium: An Origenist Christology, DOS* 13 (1970), 156–83.

had died, in that he listed him with the long-deceased Dioscorus and Timothy Aelurus, and did not address him directly.[117] If Severus had died, *Testimonies of the Saints* must have been written after 538.[118] Richard noted, too, that Leontius talked of John of Scythopolis as though he was a contemporary; since he can have been Bishop of Scythopolis no earlier than 536, and no later than 550, Leontius was writing within that period.[119] In his view, Leontius' near silence about issues connected with the Three Chapters showed, too, that he wrote before 544, when the Three Chapters Controversy began to rage. Richard's dating of Leontius' *floruit* as 536–44 has generally been accepted, mostly *faute de mieux*. As will be seen, there are good reasons to modify his conclusions slightly. First, however, the few serious alternatives to Richard's dating that have been proposed should be dealt with.

Michel Breydy argued that the abbreviated citations from the fathers in *Testimonies of the Saints* compared with those in the *Doctrina patrum de incarnatione Verbi* and in John Maron's works meant that he had succeeded them, and therefore wrote in the mid-seventh century, but his argument has not found support.[120] It seems more plausible to ascribe such variations simply to different versions of an original florilegium used differently by the Leontii and others, the proliferation of florilegia in the period being extraordinary, and the difficulty of establishing clear connections between them being notorious. It is better to date Leontius of Jerusalem on the basis of more straightforward evidence.

More recently, Dirk Krausmüller has made a determined and intelligent effort to rehabilitate Loofs's late dating for Leontius' activity, though not his theory about the nature of the texts.[121] Krausmüller's case rests on odd allusions in both texts. A central instance is the reference to 'Jacobites' in the tale with which *Testimonies of the Saints* in its present form ends, since that was a way of describing Syrian anti-Chalcedonians not current until the

---

[117] Richard, 'Léonce', 44. The text is at 1881B.

[118] Richard, 'Léonce', 44–5.

[119] Richard, 'Léonce', 43–4. The text is at 1865B–C.

[120] M. Breydy, 'Les Attestations patristiques parallèles et leurs nuances chez les ps-Léonce et Jean Maron', in P. O. Scholz and R. Stempel (eds.), *Nubia et Oriens Christianus: Festschrift für C. Detlef G. Müller zum 60. Geburtstag* (Cologne: Dinter, 1987), 3–16; Breydy, *Jean Maron, Exposé de la foi et autres opuscules*, CSCO, Scriptores Syri 210 (Louvain: E. Peeters, 1988), 497–8.

[121] D. Krausmüller, 'Leontius of Jerusalem, a Theologian of the Seventh Century', *JTS*, NS 522 (2001), 637–57.

seventh century.[122] On stylistic grounds alone, though, the story is unmistakeably the work of a later writer (there is not a trace of Leontius' characteristic style in it), evidently the first copyist. The copyist's memory of this story, well known, as he says, in 'our own times and places' (implying a distinction from Leontius' times and places), was apparently triggered by Leontius' reference to miracles worked by unexpected persons. A reference to Lombards in the text is likewise said by Krausmüller to be anachronistic, but pre-seventh-century references to them are in fact to be found elsewhere.[123] A curious reference in *Against the Nestorians* to an emperor's son being crowned in early childhood or even *in utero* is said to imply familiarity on the part of Leontius' readers with a just possible, but not attested, *in utero* coronation early in the reign of Heraclius (i.e. *c.* 612). That year was marked at the very least by an intense concern about establishing a legitimate successor.[124] The reference occurs, as Krausmüller recognizes, in one of many citations from a work by a fully fledged and articulate Nestorian, otherwise unknown to us, to which Leontius is responding.[125] We cannot assume, though, that this Nestorian knew who Leontius' audience was, or what historical information they possessed, or even that he had Leontius in mind when he wrote. Moreover, given the universal condemnation of Nestorians in Byzantium, the writer may well have lived in Persia, and be referring to concerns about and practices in imperial succession there. In any case, we should be wary of mistaking what seems to be a perfectly typical display of arcane knowledge by Leontius' learned adversary for a contemporary reference. Finally, the reference to an aphorism, 'How many souls have been slaughtered during the conquest of Jerusalem!', does not necessarily imply the Persian conquest of 614.[126] It may as easily refer to either the Babylonian destruction of 587 BCE, or the Roman of 70 CE, both well known

---

[122] The passage: 1900A–1901A. The reference to Jacobites occurs at 1900C. Krausmüller, 642–7.

[123] The reference: *PG* lxxxvi¹, 1896C. Krausmüller himself has graciously conceded in correspondence the existence, after all, of early references, citing as an example Pseudo-Caesarius. See R. Riedinger (ed.), *Pseudo-Kaisarios, Die Erotapocriseis*, *GCS* (Berlin: Akademie-Verlag, 1989), 87.

[124] The reference: *PG* lxxxvi¹ 1629A; Krausmüller, 654–6.

[125] The existence of these citations from the anonymous Nestorian was first noted in print by L. Abramowski, 'Ein nestorianischer Traktat bei Leontius von Jerusalem', *III° Symposium Syriacum 1980*, *OCA* 221 (Rome: Pont. Institutum Studiorum Orientalium, 1983), 43–55.

[126] The reference: *PG* lxxxvi¹, 1768ᵇC; Krausmüller, 649–54.

in literature. Attempts at establishing a post-sixth-century date for Leontius have not, therefore, proven convincing.

It is taken, here, that Richard was close to correct about the dating, but not absolutely correct. The point at issue is the status of Severus. Some of the references to Severus, caricaturing him to anti-Chalcedonians as 'your own authoritative guide', and especially as 'your patriarch',[127] seem much more likely to be references to a living person than to a dead one. The fact that Leontius does not directly address Severus, too, has a much more natural explanation: Leontius' evident strategy of driving a wedge between Severus' followers in Syria and their exiled patriarch, bringing them to the point of returning to unity with Chalcedonians despite his opposition and without his participation. In that light the absence of direct address to Severus is very much consonant with his being alive, and quite intentional. Assuming that Severus was in fact alive at the time of writing, then, *Testimonies of the Saints* was written before 538. If John became Bishop of Scythopolis no earlier than 536, we have a fairly firm way to date at least *Testimonies of the Saints*: it was written sometime between 536 and 538.

That conclusion fits the circumstantial case perfectly. It cannot be demonstrated for a certainty that Leontius was at the Conversations of 532, though he may well have been, but it can be said that the agenda for the Conversations, including the severing of Severians from Severus, is precisely the agenda of *Testimonies of the Saints*. Moreover, Leontius is clearly familiar not only with the issues that were discussed at the conversations, but also with the strategies that had been tried but had proven counter-productive, since he takes particular care to see that his own way of addressing issues such as the Apollinarian forgeries and the deposition of Dioscorus is much more diplomatic. As was observed above, if he was not present at the conversations, he seems to have had detailed information about what happened at them. *Testimonies of the Saints* belongs to the 530s.

As for the *Aporiae*, the lack of internal clues makes their dating a good deal more problematic. Since their dating is connected with the question of other, now-missing works of Leontius (about whose existence we know something only because of Leontius' own references to them) it makes sense to turn to that question.

---

[127] 1805A and 1881A.

XII. THE CORPUS

There once existed a larger corpus by Leontius of Jerusalem, connected with works by anti-Chalcedonian and Nestorian authors now no longer extant either. On the Nestorian side, we note that *Against the Nestorians* presupposes a collection of aporiae by an unknown Nestorian to which Leontius responds, often at very great length, citing it (often at great length too) at the opening of each chapter. The sheer length and the detailed nature of these citations tells against the easy dismissal of them as inventions of Leontius' own imagination—though he is capable of putting words in his opponents' mouths in *Testimonies of the Saints*—and no less an authority on late Nestorianism than Luise Abramowski has judged them authentic.[128] In the preface to *Against the Nestorians*, Leontius lists eight themes he plans to address by way of response, one per book, but the work as we have it ends, limpingly, with the seventh book; either he did not write the eighth book after all, or else it once existed but now, like the response to the anti-Chalcedonians' aporiae, it is lost.[129]

On the anti-Chalcedonian side, we note that, at the beginning of the *Aporiae*, Leontius says: 'Seeing that we've confronted these people's aporiae, we'd now like to counter-propose aporiae ourselves on a few points out of many'.[130] At least two works in an ongoing exchange between Leontius and Severian anti-Chalcedonians preceded his *Aporiae*, then: a set of aporiae from the anti-Chalcedonian side, and a response to those aporiae by Leontius. We have neither. Richard supposes that the lost response to the anti-Chalcedonians was at least as large a work as *Against the Nestorians*, which is likewise a response to aporiae. He suggests further that Leontius' *Aporiae* and *Testimonies of the Saints* were essentially appendices to that work. In his view, the response would have taken up a complete codex, with these appendices beginning a second codex, the rest of which was taken up by *Against the Nestorians*. This would explain how we end up with the works that we have: the second codex was copied in the thirteenth century, along with works by other authors, but the first was not. Richard sees the anti-Chalcedonians' opening protestation in

---

[128] See n. 125 above.   [129] The preface: *PG* lxxxvi[1], 1400A–1401A.
[130] 1769A.

Testimonies of the Saints, '[b]ut why . . . do you push us towards your teaching, pressing us on every side?', as an imagined response to the mauling they have received in the *Aporiae*. In this reconstruction, these two extant works are thus closely tied together.[131]

Richard's case for the existence of an earlier response to anti-Chalcedonian aporiae by Leontius is convincing, but his speculation as to its size and original form of publication remains no more than speculation. The opening of the *Aporiae* shows that this work is closely connected with the missing response to anti-Chalcedonian aporiae, as he supposes, but a close connection with either is not so convincing for *Testimonies of the Saints*. For one thing, it is a fact that, though both our texts are plainly addressed to the same anti-Chalcedonian audience profoundly under the influence of Severus of Antioch, the aporiae adopt a combative, dismissive, and negative tone towards that audience suggesting a situation of conflict, while the discussion of the patristic evidence in *Testimonies of the Saints* is notably more eirenic, bespeaking a quite different situation. That conclusion stands even when account is taken of the genre involved in aporiae, a genre that requires the antagonistic demonstration of the illogicality of the opponent's position. Moreover, whereas Leontius accurately cites a text from Cyril of Alexandria in the twenty-first aporia, evidently having the text ready to hand, in *Testimonies of the Saints* he has no such text available, misquotes it rather badly from memory, and is reduced to ending with the lame assertion that this is what Cyril says, 'or something of the sort', even though an accurate citation would have been useful to him.[132] It may make sense to date the *Aporiae* to a period when imperial policy hardened against the anti-Chalcedonians, perhaps the period of the edict *On Heretics* of 527. *Testimonies of the Saints*, as has been argued, belongs to the period 536–8.

XIII. THE TEXT

The text is based on our single textually interesting manuscript, Codex Marcianus gr. 69, the source, directly or indirectly, of the

---

[131] Richard, 'Léonce', 38–9. The text: 1804D.
[132] The texts are to be found at 1781D and 1857A.

few other known copies.[133] Emendations and conjectures have been kept to a minimum, though punctuation has been modernized sparingly, and the opening words of sentences have been capitalized. The manuscript contains some variant spellings, and its approach to accenting is not always in accord with modern practice. These have been preserved, as being correct for the period; they will represent no barrier to the reader's comprehension. In order to assist the reader, column numbers and letters from the Migne edition are given in the margins of both the Greek and the English. Within the Greek text, folio numbers of the Venice manuscript are given in square brackets.

Note: The value of presenting text and translation in parallel lies in the ease and accuracy with which a reader can move from the translation to the text on which it is based. It is therefore essential that the two be aligned closely, as they are here. However, it has often been necessary to use more English than Greek words to produce a readable version in modern English of what Leontius says. On the other hand, where Leontius has cited the fathers extensively, the footnotes required to identift the citations often mean that the Greek sometimes takes up more room than the English. In these cases it has been necessary to sacrifice aesthetics to utility, and to have some pages look as though they contain less text than they should.

---

[133] The manuscript is accurately described in Mioni's catalogue: E. Mioni, *Bibliothecae divi Marci Venetiarum Codices Graeci Manuscripti I—Thesaurus Antiquus codices 1–299 = Indici e cataloghi*, NS vi (Rome: Istituto poligrafico e zecca dello stato. Libreria dello stato, 1981), 94–6.

TEXTS AND TRANSLATIONS

Τοῦ πανσόφου μοναχοῦ κύρ Λεοντίου τοῦ Ἱεροσολυμίτου μαρτυρίαι τῶν ἁγίων, καὶ ἀνάλυσις τοῦ δόγματος αὐτῶν

1804D [275ᵛ] "'Αλλὰ τί ἡμᾶς" φασὶ "πανταχόθεν περιτρέχοντες, εἰς τὴν ὑμετέραν δόξαν συνελαύνετε; Ἡμεῖς γὰρ ἦν αὐτολεξεὶ διδασκαλίαν πατρικὴν ἴσμεν περὶ Χριστοῦ, εἴτουν μίαν φύσιν τοῦ Θεοῦ Λόγου

1805A σεσαρκωμένην κατὰ τὸν ἅγιον 'Αθανάσιον καὶ Κύριλλον· ὑμεῖς δὲ ἣν φατὲ ξενοφωνίαν οὐδαμοῦ τοῖς πατράσι ῥητῶς κειμένην εὑρίσκομεν, ἤγουν δύο φύσεις εἰ καὶ ἀδιαιρέτους, Χριστοῦ."

Καίτοι γε, ὦ οὗτοι, ὁ ὑμέτερος καθηγητὴς Σεβῆρος βοᾷ, ὡς πλεῖστοι τῶν ἁγίων πατέρων ἀδιαβλήτως ἐχρήσαντο τῇ τῶν δύο φύσεων φωνῇ—πῶς οὖν τἀναντία ὑμεῖς λέγετε;—ἀλλ' ὄντως κατὰ τὸ εἰρημένον τῇ σοφίᾳ, _προφασίζεται ἀνὴρ θέλων χωρίζεσθαι φίλου._¹ Ἐπεὶ ὅτι οὐδὲν ἰσχυρὸν ἢ λόγου ἄξιον ἢ ἀκριβὲς ἔχει ὑμῖν ἡ ἀφορμὴ τῆς πρὸς ἡμᾶς διενέξεως αὕτη, ἑτοίμως καὶ πολυτρόπως σὺν Θεῷ παραστήσομεν. Πρῶτα μὲν γὰρ εἰ τὴν ἐν δυάδι φύσεων ἀδιαιρέτῳ ὁμολογίαν ἐπὶ τοῦ Κυρίου σέβοντες, περὶ τὴν ἑτέραν

1805B διεφωνοῦμεν ὑμῖν ἐξαγγελίαν τοῦ δόγματος, ἤγουν τὴν λέγουσαν μίαν φύσιν τοῦ Θεοῦ Λόγου σεσαρκωμένην, καὶ μὴ μᾶλλον ὑμῶν καὶ τήνδε ἀσμενιζόμεθα, ὄντως ἂν καλῶς διεστέλλεσθε παρ' ἡμῶν. Εἰ δὲ καὶ ταύτην ὡς τὴν αὐτήν δὲ πάντη οὖσαν τῇ ἑτέρᾳ συναποδεχόμεθα, πῶς ἀφέντες τὸ ἀνακρίνειν αὐτὸ τοῦτο, εἰ ἀληθῶς ταυτόν ἐστι τῇ δυνάμει τὸ λέγειν μίαν φύσιν τοῦ Θεοῦ Λόγου σεσαρκωμένην, καὶ δυάδα φύσεων Χριστοῦ καθ' ὑπόστασιν μίαν ἡνωμένην, τῷ μὴ ἐπὶ τῶν αὐτῶν λέξεων εὑρεῖν τοῖς πατράσι κειμένην τήνδε τὴν ἔννοιαν παραιτεῖσθαι φατὲ τὴν τοιαύτην ὁμολογίαν; Εἴπερ γὰρ μὴ ἔστι καὶ ἐκ παραλλήλου τί τὸ αὐτὸ λέγειν ἐν τῷ, _ἀκούσατε ταῦτα πάντα τὰ ἔθνη, ἐνωτίσασθε πάντες οἱ_

1805C _κατοικοῦντες τὴν οἰκουμένην,_² λεγέτωσαν ἡμῖν τί τὸ _ἀκούειν_ παρὰ τὸ _ἐνωτίζεσθαι,_ καὶ ποῖα _τὰ ἔθνη,_ ποῖοι δὲ _οἱ κατοικοῦντες τὴν οἰκουμένην;_ Εἰ δὲ καὶ τοῦ αὐτοῦ ὄντος σημαινομένου, τῷ μὴ

---

¹ Prov. 18: 1   ² Ps. 48: 2

OF THE ALL-WISE MONK LORD LEONTIUS OF JERUSALEM: TESTIMONIES OF THE SAINTS, AND AN ANALYSIS[i] OF THEIR TEACHING

'But why', they say, 'do you push us towards your teaching, press- 1804D
ing us on every side? We're the ones, after all, who know what the
fathers' teaching about Christ is in their own words, i.e. "one
incarnate nature of God the Word", as in holy Athanasius and
Cyril. The expression you use, though, is a strange one we don't 1805A
find being used explicitly by the fathers anywhere, i.e. "two
natures, albeit undivided, of Christ".'

Yet, my friends, your own authoritative guide Severus protests
that most of the holy fathers used the expression 'two natures' in a
blameless way.[ii] How does it happen that you say the opposite?
Really, it's as wisdom says: *a man finds a pretext if he wants to be divided
from a friend*. Seeing these grounds for your disagreeing with us
have no force, rational value, or accuracy to them, we'll make our
case easily with God's help, and we'll make it on several counts
too.

In the first place, if, when we honoured the confession of an
undivided duality of natures in the Lord, we disagreed with you
over the other way of expressing doctrine—the one that speaks of 1805B
the 'one incarnate nature of God the Word'—and weren't hap-
pier than you are with the latter confession too, then you were
right to separate from us. If, on the other hand, we accept the
latter as being entirely the same as the former, how does it happen
that you—abandoning any investigation as to whether to speak of
one incarnate nature of God the Word really is the same in meaning as speaking of a duality of natures of Christ united in one
hypostasis—say this kind of confession is to be avoided just
because you don't find this idea expressed by the fathers in exactly
these words? If *hear this, all you peoples; hearken, all those who dwell in the
world* isn't a case of saying the same thing through parallelism,
they should tell us what 'hearing' is, as opposed to 'hearkening', 1805C
and who 'peoples' are, as opposed to 'those who dwell in the
world'! But if they go on rejecting the confession that expresses

αὐτολεξεὶ διὰ τῶν πατέρων εἰρῆσθαι, τὴν διὰ τῆς δυάδος ὁμολογίαν
παραι[276ʳ]τοῦνται—εἴπερ ὄντως σκῶλον ἀξιόλογον, καὶ
σκανδάλου αἴτιόν ἐστι τὸ λέγειν εὐσεβῆ ἔννοιαν χωρὶς τῆς ἐπὶ
λέξεως αὐτῆς τινῶν προεγνωσμένων πατέρων εὐσεβῶν
συμφωνίας—· πρῶτον μὲν οὐδεὶς Περσῶν ἢ Ῥωμαίων ἢ Φράγγων
ἢ Ἰνδῶν οὔτε Μωσέα, οὔτε προφήτην, οὐδὲ τὸν Κύριον αὐτὸν
ἀποδέξεται τὰ εὐσεβῆ δόγματα διαλεγόμενον, ἐπεὶ οὐ γνωσταὶ
αὐτοῖς προϋπάρχουσιν αἱ λέξεις αἱ παρ' αὐτῶν ἰδικῶς λεγόμεναι, ἐὰν
μὴ δι' ἑτέρων αὐτοῖς ἑρμηνευθῶσι λέξεων ἀλλοίων τε φωνῶν καὶ
ποικίλων περιφράσεων· ἄλλως δὲ οὐδὲ Ἑβραῖοι πεισθήσονται, ὅτι
1805D   ὄντως εἰκὼν τοῦ θεοῦ³ καὶ χαρακτὴρ⁴ καὶ ἀπαύγασμα⁵ ὁ Λόγος
αὐτοῦ ἐστίν, ἐπεὶ μὴ ἔστι τοῦτο αὐτολεξεί που ἐν τῇ Παλαιᾷ· οὔτε
Σαμαρεῖται περὶ κρίσεώς τι καταδέξονται μελλούσης, ἐπεὶ οὐκ
ἐλέχθη ῥητῶς τὰ περὶ αὐτῆς Μωϋσῇ πη· ἀλλ' οὐδὲ Ἄρειοι καὶ
Εὐνόμιοι καὶ οἱ λοιποὶ τὴν τοῦ ὁμοουσίου ἢ συναϊδίου φωνὴν ἐπὶ
τοῦ Πατρὸς καὶ τοῦ Υἱοῦ καὶ τοῦ ἁγίου Πνεύματος ἀνέξονται, ἐπεὶ
μήτε τῇ ἁγίᾳ Γραφῇ πη εἴρηται αὐτολεξεὶ τάδε, μὴ δὲ τοῖς πρὸ
αὐτῶν χριστιανικοῖς συγγράμμασι. Ἀλλ' οὐδὲ αὐτὴν τὴν ὑπὸ τοῦ
πατρὸς ἡμῶν Ἀθανασίου φωνὴν ἐπὶ τοῦ Κυρίου λέγουσαν μίαν
1808A   φύσιν τοῦ Θεοῦ Λόγου σεσαρκωμένην καταδεξόμεθα· οὐ γάρ ἐστι
καὶ τοῖς πρὸ αὐτοῦ τυχὸν εἰρημένη, εἰ καὶ τῆς ἐννοίας αὐτῆς ἦν ἡ
δύναμις πάλαι ὡμολογημένη. Ὁ λόγος γὰρ σὰρξ ἐγένετο,⁶
ἠκούσαμεν ἐκ τοῦ θεολόγου·⁷ τὸ μέντοι μίαν φύσιν τοῦ Θεοῦ Λόγου
σεσαρκωμένην εἶναι, οὐκ ἠκούσαμεν σὺν αὐτῷ, ἀλλ' ἐνοήσαμεν
ἐξ αὐτοῦ τοῦδε τοῦ ὁ λόγος σὰρξ ἐγένετο·⁸ Ἁπλῶς δὲ εἰ μὴ
ταῖς ἐννοίαις ταῖς εὐσεβέσιν μᾶλλον πειθόμεθα ὁπωσοῦν
ἐξαγγελλομέναις, ἀλλὰ ταῖς λέξεσιν ἑπόμεθα, πᾶσα διδασκαλία
πρώτως λεγομένη, κἂν ὀρθῶς πάντη ἔχοι, καινοφωνεῖν κριθήσεται,
καὶ σκανδαλίσει τοὺς ἀκροατάς· διὰ καινοτέρας γὰρ συνθέσεως
λέξεων πάντως εἴρηται τὰ πρόσφατα διδάγματα, ὅπου γε πολλάκις
καὶ αὐτὰς τῆς ἁγίας Γραφῆς τὰς ῥητῶς ἐγκειμένας χρήσεις, διὰ
1808B   περινοίας γινώσκομεν ἀληθεῖς εἶναι, καὶ κατὰ ἀλληγορίας ἔσθ' ὅτε,
ἐπεί τοι γε ὡς ψευδεῖς θεωροῦμεν. Τὸ γὰρ εἰσάξω ὑμᾶς εἰς γῆν
ῥέουσαν γάλα καὶ μέλι,⁹ περὶ τῆς ἀπὸ Ἰορδάνου μέχρις Εὐφράτου
χώρας εἰρημένον, ψευδὲς ἂν εἴη, εἰ μὴ διὰ περινοίας γνῶμεν ὅτι

---

³ 2 Cor. 4: 4; Col. 1: 15   ⁴ Heb. 1: 3   ⁵ Ibid.   ⁶ John 1: 14
⁷ τῶν θεολόγων MS   ⁸ John 1: 14.   ⁹ Exod. 33: 3

itself in terms of duality, even though the identical reality is signified, because it wasn't used by the fathers in so many words—
supposing it really is a stumbling-block worth talking about, and a
cause for scandal, to express a pious idea without the literal
agreement of certain pious, pre-selected fathers—what then? In
the first place, not one of the Persians, Romans, Franks, or Indians
is going to be receptive to Moses, to a prophet, or to the Lord
Himself when whoever it is talks about pious doctrines, since the
particular expressions used by the biblical authorities aren't previously known to these people, unless they're interpreted for them
by means of different expressions, phrases, and circumlocutions.
Otherwise, Jews won't be persuaded that God's Word is really His   1805D
image, and *effulgence*, and *seal*, since this isn't stated in so many
words anywhere in the Old Testament. Nor will Samaritans admit
to anything concerning a judgement to come, since the facts about
it weren't expressly stated by Moses anywhere. Nor, for that matter, will Arians, Eunomians, and the rest embrace the assertion
about the consubstantiality or co-eternity of the Father, Son, and
Holy Spirit, since these doctrines aren't expressly stated in any
way by Holy Scripture or by Christian writings from before their
time. But then we won't accept the very expression our father
Athanasius used of the Lord when he said 'one incarnate nature
of God the Word' for, as it happens, it too wasn't used by anyone   1808A
before him, though the idea of it was confessed before that. *The
Word became flesh*; that's something we heard from the Theologian.[iii]
We certainly didn't hear along with it the assertion that there's
one incarnate nature of God the Word; rather, that's something
we came to understand from this same text, *the Word became flesh*.
It's simply the case that, if we aren't better persuaded by pious
ideas, whatever way they're proclaimed, but insist on the words in
which they're expressed, every teaching enunciated for the first
time, even though it's completely correct, will be condemned for
introducing new terms, and will scandalize its hearers. Fresh
teachings are enunciated by means of a quite new combination of
words even where, as often happens, we recognize intellectually
that the express usages of Holy Scripture themselves are true as
well. There are even times when we interpret these allegorically,   1808B
since we recognize that they are false.[iv] The statement *I shall lead
you into a land flowing with milk and honey* (referring to the land stretch-
ing from the Jordan to the Euphrates) would be false, if we didn't
know with our intelligence that the soil there is very productive

πολύφυτος καὶ βοτανώδης ἡ γῆ, οὗ δὲ πολλαὶ βοσκαί, πολλὰ κτήνη καὶ θρέμματα καὶ ποίμναι, οὗ δὲ τὰ ζῷα τάδε, καὶ γάλακτος ἀφθονία· ὁμοίως τε ὅπου πολλαὶ βοτάναι, πλεῖσταί εἰσιν αἱ ἀνθολόγοι [276ᵛ] μέλιτται, οὗ δὲ πλείους αὗται, καὶ τὸ ἐκ τῶνδε μέλι πολύ. Καὶ ὅτε οὖν λέγει ἐὰν ὁ ὀφθαλμός σου σκανδαλίζῃ σε ἔκβαλε αὐτὸν ἀπὸ σοῦ,¹⁰ τῷ ῥητῷ ἢ τῇ διανοίᾳ προσεκτέον πρώτως, εἴπερ τὸ γράμμα ἀποκτέννει, τὸ δὲ πνεῦμα ζωοποιεῖ,¹¹ ὦ οὗτοι, ἀποκρίνασθε ἡμῖν.

1808c ’Αλλ’ ἴσως πρὸς τάδε εἴποιτε· "Τί οὖν ὅλως τὴν εὐσεβῆ σημασίαν ἐχούσης τῆς πρώτης φωνῆς, δευτέραν ὑμεῖς καινουργεῖτε, εἰ μή τι σκαιωρεῖτε κατὰ τῆς ἐννοίας; ἐξὸν γὰρ εἰπεῖν καὶ πρὸς ὑμᾶς εὐκαίρως, ὅτι ὧν ἡ χρῆσις ἡ αὐτή, τούτων ἡ πολυτέλεια περιττή." ’Αλλὰ σκεπτέον ὡς τὰ αὐτὰ καὶ τοῖς τὴν ἑτέραν φωνὴν ἀρχῆθεν προβαλλομένοις, καὶ πᾶσαν τοιάνδε εὐσεβῆ ὁμολογίαν, ἀπορηθήσεται· τί γὰρ ἄν, εἰ ταυτόν ἐστι τῷ ὁ λόγος σὰρξ ἐγένετο,¹² τὸ λέγειν μίαν φύσιν τοῦ Θεοῦ Λόγου σεσαρκωμένην, αὕτη ἡμῖν ἐπεισηνέχθη; τί δὲ εἰ ταυτόν ἐστι τῷ ἐγὼ καὶ ὁ πατὴρ ἕν ἐσμεν,¹³ προσεφράσθη καὶ τὸ ὁμοούσιον τοῦ Πατρὸς πρὸς τὸν Υἱόν; Εἰ δὲ ὄντως διά τινας δύο φύσεις λέγοντας Χριστοῦ, ἰδίως ἔχουσαν

1808D ἑκατέραν οὐ μόνον κατὰ λόγον φυσικὸν, ἀλλὰ καὶ κατὰ τὴν ὕπαρξιν αὐτὴν τῆς ὑποστάσεως, ἤγουν τόν τε Λόγον καὶ τὴν σάρκα τοῦ Κυρίου, καὶ οὐκ αὐτὸν τὸν Λόγον σεσαρκῶσθαι δογματίζοντας ἐν μιᾷ τῇ καθ’ ὑπόστασιν ἑνώσει, ἀναγκαίως ἐδέησε λέγειν μίαν φύσιν τοῦ Θεοῦ Λόγου σεσαρκωμένην, ἵνα καὶ σημαίνηται τὸ διττὸν τῶν φύσεων διὰ τοῦ ὡς πρός τι λέγεσθαι τὴν σεσαρκωμένην φύσιν— πρὸς γὰρ τὴν σαρκώσασαν εἴρηται—καὶ δῆλόν ἐστιν, ὡς οὐκ ἐν μονάδι τὰ πρός τί ἐστι χώρα τὲ τοῖς δυσσεβοῦσι μὴ δοθῇ διὰ τοῦ λήμματος τῆς τῶν δύο φύσεων φωνῆς διχάζειν αὐτῶν τὴν μίαν ὑπόστασιν, ἐν τοῖς ἀπερισκέπτοις ὁμωνυμούσης τῆς φύσεως, καὶ πολλάκις ἀντὶ οὐσίας καὶ ἀντὶ, προσωπικῆς δὲ, ὑποστάσεως

1809A λεγομένης, δέον ἄρα, καὶ διὰ τὸ καινοτέρως πάλιν καὶ ἀντιθέτως ἀσεβήσαντάς τινας μίαν φύσιν κατὰ τροπὴν ἢ σύγχυσιν γενομένην τοῦ Λόγου τὴν ἐνανθρώπησιν δογματίζειν, καινουργῆσαι καὶ ἡμᾶς

---

¹⁰ Mark 9: 47   ¹¹ 2 Cor. 3: 6
¹² John 1: 14   ¹³ John 10: 30

and rich in vegetation, that where fodder abounds there are many cattle, goats, and sheep, and that where these animals are there's an abundance of milk. Likewise, wherever there are lots of plants, there are bound to be lots of bees out gathering, and where there are lots of them, there will be plenty of honey from them. Likewise, when Scripture says *if your eye offends you, pluck it out*, should you pay attention primarily to the statement, or to what it means—if *the letter kills, but the spirit gives life*? Give us an answer to that, my friends!

Your response to these points may run something like this: 1808c 'Why do you people introduce a second, novel formula, when the first captures the pious meaning completely, unless you're plotting some mischief against its meaning? We might, appropriately enough, have added the further charge against you that, when the meaning's the same, the multiplication of formulae goes beyond what's necessary.' What you have to realize, though, is that the same charge can be made against those who initially proposed the first formula too, and then there won't be any kind of pious confession at all! If saying 'one incarnate nature of God the Word' is, after all, the same thing as saying *the Word became flesh*, what did adding the former do for us? If the consubstantiality of the Father with the Son is identical to *I and the Father are one*, why was it added? Certain people say there are two natures of Christ, each (i.e. the Word, and the Lord's flesh) existing individually, not just in terms of what it means to be a nature, but in terms of the very subsist- 1808d ence of the hypostasis; they don't assert that the Word Himself became flesh in a single union by hypostasis. Suppose it really was necessary to say 'one incarnate nature of God the Word', so that the duality of the natures might also be expressed by virtue of the nature's being called 'incarnated' in relation [to something] (for 'incarnated' is predicated of the nature that became incarnate). If so, it's also clear that, as entities in relation aren't in an undifferentiated unity, so also no opportunity is offered here for godless people to divide these two natures' one hypostasis just because one accepts the expression 'two natures'. Since to thoughtless people 'nature' is a word with more than one meaning, and is often used in place of 'substance' and 'hypostasis' (when this word refers to 1809a person), we need to introduce some such new expression as well, since certain people who profane one nature in a spirit of novelty and contradiction declare that the Incarnation of the Word took place through change or commingling. The point of our expres-

τοιάνδε φωνήν, ἥτις τόν τε πρὸς τοὺς εἰρημένους αἱρετικοὺς ἐναντίως ἔχοντα σκοπόν, ὥσπερ οὖν καὶ ἡ μία φύσις τοῦ Θεοῦ Λόγου σεσαρκωμένη, φυλάττει, καὶ ἀπὸ τῶν ὕστερον ἀναφυέντων κακοδόξων διαστέλλεται, ὅπερ οὐκ εἶχεν ἡ πρώτη σαφῶς, καὶ δύο φύσεις τοῦ ἑνὸς Χριστοῦ ἡνωμένας κατὰ τὴν μίαν αὐτοῦ ὑπόστασιν διασαφεῖν. Ὁ γὰρ ἡ πρώτη φωνὴ διὰ τοῦ εἰσάγειν σεσαρκωμένον τί καὶ [277ʳ] σαρκοῦν ἔλεγε, τοῦτο καὶ αὐτὴ μόνον διὰ τῆς δυάδος λέγει· ὃ δὲ ἐν εἶναι ἐκείνη διὰ τῆς μονάδος παριστᾶν βούλεται, 1809B τοῦτο αὐτὴ διὰ τῆς τοῦ ἑνὸς Χριστοῦ καθ᾽ ὑπόστασιν ἐνώσεως ὁμολογεῖ· ἐκείνη μὲν γὰρ παρεσιώπησε τὴν ἕνωσιν καὶ τὴν ὁλότητα τῶν ἡνωμένων, ἤγουν Χριστὸν, ἀρκεσθεῖσα τῇ τῆς μονάδος καὶ συμπλοκῆς ἐννοίᾳ, ὡς ἐχούσῃ δεῖξιν τοῦ τε διπλοῦ τῶν συμπλακέντων καὶ ἑνιαίου τοῦ συμπλέγματος· αὕτη δὲ εἶναι μὲν δύο τὰ συγκείμενα φησὶ, οὔτε δὲ ἰδίως ὀνομάζειν τὰ μέρη τῆσδε τῆς ὁλότητος σύνοιδεν ἐν τῷ τῆς ἑνώσεως λόγῳ, οὔτε σιγᾶν τὴν μίαν ὑπόστασιν πείθεται, οὔτε παρατρέχειν τὴν ἕνωσιν συγχωρεῖ, οὔτε μὴ γνωρίζειν ἅπασι βούλεται, τίνος προσώπου γινώσκειν οὖσαν τῆσδε τῆς φυσικῆς δυάδος τὴν ἕνωσιν, καὶ τὴν ὑποστατικὴν μονάδα, ἐν κατ᾽ ἀμφοῖν θεῖσα τὸ ὄνομα.

Ἄρα[14] οὖν ἐπεὶ καὶ Ἄρειος μίαν φύσιν τοῦ Θεοῦ καὶ Λόγου
1809C σεσαρκωμένην φησὶ, βουλόμενος δεῖξαι ὡς οὐ πάντῃ τῆς τοῦ Πατρὸς φυσικῆς ἀτρεψίας ἐστὶ καὶ ὁ Υἱός, καὶ Ἀπολινάριος τὴν αὐτὴν λέγει ἀπαραλλάκτως φωνὴν ἀντὶ νοῦ ψυχικοῦ βουλόμενος εἶναι ἐν τῷ κυριακῷ ἀνθρώπῳ τὸν Λόγον, ἤγουν τῇ ψυχωθείσῃ σαρκὶ αὐτοῦ, ἀλόγου φύσεώς τινος ἑτεροφυοῦς ἡμῖν παριστάνων εἶναι τὴν ἐκ τῆς οἰκονομίας εὐεργεσίαν, Εὐτυχὴς δὲ τὸ αὐτὸ ἀπαρατρώτῳ φωνῇ, ἀλλ᾽ οὐχὶ ἐννοίᾳ φησί—ὡς γὰρ τοῦ Λόγου αὐτοῦ εἰς σάρκα μετουσιωθέντος, καὶ οὐδὲν ἔχοντος ἡμῖν ὁμοούσιον τοῦ Κυρίου λέγει, τὸ μίαν φύσιν τοῦ Θεοῦ Λόγου σεσαρκωμένην· καὶ καθὼς Γρηγόριος[15] ὁ θεολόγος ἐν τῷ πρὸς Κληδόνιόν φησι περὶ τούτων αὐτῶν· ὅτι "Τὰς μὲν εὐσεβεῖς λέξεις ὁμολογοῦσι περὶ ἃς τὸν νοῦν κακουργοῦσι".[16] Καὶ μετὰ βραχέα πάλιν· "Ἐπειδὴ αἱ αὐταὶ
1809D λέξεις καλῶς μὲν ἐξηγηθεῖσαι τὸ εὐσεβὲς ἔχουσι, κακῶς δὲ νοούμεναι, τὸ δυσσεβὲς ἔχουσιν"[17]—οἱ ἀπὸ Νεστορίου δὲ καὶ οἱ ἀφ᾽ ὧν Νεστόριος, δύο φύσεις Χριστοῦ ἡνωμένας ἀδιαιρέτως λέγουσι, καθὰ μαρτυρεῖ ἐν τῇ πρὸς Σούκενσον δευτέρᾳ ἐπιστολῇ

---

[14] ἄρα MS   [15] In marg. νύσσης
[16] Gregory of Nazianzus, *Letter* 102, ed. and tr. P. Gallay, *Lettres théologiques*, SC 208 (Paris: Éditions du Cerf, 1974), 74.
[17] Ibid. 78

sion is to oppose the heretics just mentioned, in much the way 'the one incarnate nature of God the Word' provides protection [against a different heresy]. It's set apart from the people of evil repute who've sprung up lately—something the first expression clearly was incapable of—and it's able to make a clear statement about the one Christ's two natures united in His one hypostasis. What the first expression asserted by introducing something incarnated and something that incarnates, this the second asserts through duality. The first wants to represent His being one in terms of an undifferentiated unity, while the second confesses this in terms of the union by hypostasis of the one Christ. The first 1809B passed in silence over the union and the wholeness of the things united, i.e. Christ, being content with the idea of the unity and of an intertwining as demonstrating both the duality of the things that intertwine and the singleness of the intertwining. The second says that the things put together are two, though it neither allows for any naming of the parts of this totality on their own in its definition of the union, nor does it acquiesce in any keeping secret of the one hypostasis, agree to any neglect of the union, or have any intention other than to make known to everyone which person the existing union of this natural duality and hypostatic unity belong to, applying the one name to both.

Arius is another person who says 'one incarnate nature of God and Word', wanting to show that the Son doesn't entirely share in 1809C the Father's natural immutability. Apollinarius, too, uses this same expression without any change, intending the Word to take the place of a psychic mind in the man belonging to the Lord, i.e. in His animated flesh, suggesting that the benefit from the Incarnation belongs to some irrational nature different in kind from us. Eutyches says the same thing in that he uses the expression without any change, though the meaning doesn't stay the same, for he uses 'one incarnate nature of God the Word' as meaning that the nature of the Word Himself changed into flesh, and that the Lord possesses nothing consubstantial with us. It's just as Gregory the Theologian says of these same people in the *Letter to Cledonius*: 'They confess pious expressions, but slander their meaning.' A little later he adds in the same vein: 'Whenever these same expres- 1809D sions are well expounded, they are pious, but whenever they are badly expounded, they fall into impiety.' Those of Nestorius' party, on the other hand, and those to whose party Nestorius belonged, speak of 'two natures of Christ indivisibly united', as

Κύριλλος ὁ διδάσκαλος, λέγουσι δὲ τὸ ἀδιαίρετον καὶ τὴν ἕνωσιν καὶ οὗτοι ὑπούλως—οὐ καθ᾽ ὑπόστασιν γὰρ οὐ κατὰ τὴν τῶν φύσεων αὐτῶν συμπλοκήν, ἀλλὰ τῇ ἰσοτιμίᾳ, τῇ ταυτοβουλίᾳ, τῇ αὐθεντίᾳ, ἑνώσασθαι ἀδιαιρέτως μέν, σχετικῶς δὲ ὁμολογοῦντες τὸν λόγον τῇ σαρκί, εἰ καὶ τὰς φύσεις αὐτὰς εἶναι, τῶν προσώπων, τὰς ἡνωμένας κατὰ γνώμην φασίν—ἀναγκαῖον δέδεικται εἶναι, ὡς οἶμαι, μὴ ταῖς φωναῖς ἁπλῶς προσέχειν, ἀλλὰ τοῖς νοήμασι· καὶ εἴ
1812A τις μὲν καινοτέρα φωνή ἐστι, τῇ ἀνέκαθεν δὲ καὶ ἐξ ἀρχῆς ὁμολογουμένῃ ὀρθοδοξίᾳ συμφωνεῖ κατὰ τὸ σημαινόμενον, ταύτην ποτνιᾶσθαι καὶ ὡς οἰκείαν ἀσμενίζεσθαι· εἴ τις δὲ τετριμμένη τέ τῇ ἁγίᾳ [277ʳ] Γραφῇ πάσῃ καὶ τοῖς πατράσιν ὅλοις ἔστι φωνή, κατά τινα δὲ δυσσεβῆ καινοτομίαν νοήματος ὑπό τινος προφέρεται εἰς διαφθορὰν ὀρθῆς ἐννοίας, ταύτην ἀποδοκιμάζειν καὶ βδελύττεσθαι ὡς καλοὺς τραπεζίτας δέον ἡμᾶς, μὴ τῷ ἐπιπολαίῳ χαρακτῆρι τῶν νομισμάτων καὶ τοῖς χαράγμασι προσέχοντας μόνον, ἀλλὰ καὶ αὐτὸ τὸ ἀργύριον ἐντέχνως παρακονοῦντας καὶ κατεξετάζοντας εἰ ὄντως δόκιμόν ἐστι· τὰ γὰρ λόγια κυρίου, ἀργύριον πεπυρωμένον[18] δοκίμιον εἴρηται· ὅσοι γὰρ[19] κατὰ πρώτην ἀκοὴν τῶν λέξεων κρίνουσι τὴν δύναμιν, ἐπεὶ καὶ τὰ γράμματα λέξεών εἰσιν
1812B ἀπογραφαί, μανθανέτωσαν ὅτι οὕτως πολλάκις τὸ γράμμα ἀποκτέννει, τὸ δὲ πνεῦμα ζωοποιεῖ,[20] εἴτουν ὁ νοῦς.

Τί δὴ ἄρα μοι δεήσει λόγων μακρῶν περὶ τοῦδε; Πᾶσι γὰρ γνωστὸν ὡς Μανιχαῖοι Χριστιανοί,[21] καὶ Σαμαρεῖται, καὶ Ἑβραῖοι, καὶ Ἀρειανοί, καὶ Σαβελλιανοί, καὶ Οὐαλεντιανοί, καὶ Μαρκιωνισταί, καὶ Νεστοριανοί, καὶ Ἀπολιναριασταί, καὶ πᾶσα ἁπλῶς ὁμολογουμένη κακοδοξία, ἔκ τε τῆς ἁγίας Γραφῆς Παλαιᾶς τε καὶ Νέας, καὶ τῶν προλαβόντων πατέρων τινὰς χρήσεις παρέσπασαν[22] πρὸς μαρτυρίαν τοῦ οἰκείου φρονήματος, ὡς τὰ αὐτὰ βουλομένους αὐτοῖς· ἆρα[23] οὖν οὐχὶ τὴν ἔννοιαν εἰ ὀρθῶς αὐτοῖς ἔχοι κρίνοιμεν, καὶ οὐ τὰς φωνὰς ἁπλῶς; ἀλλὰ παράγοντος Σαβελλίου
1812C τό ἐγὼ καὶ ὁ Πατὴρ ἕν ἐσμεν,[24] καὶ ἀναιροῦντος τὴν τριαδικὴν ὑπόστασιν· καὶ Εὐνομίου προβαλλομένου τό, ὁ ἀποστείλας με Πατήρ, μείζων μού ἐστι,[25] καὶ ἀνατρέποντος τὴν μονάδα καὶ τὴν ἰσοφυῖαν τῆς θεότητος, οὑτωσὶ ἀνοήτως συμπεριφερόμεθα μὲν τοῖς ἀσεβέσι, μᾶλλον δὲ καὶ ἀντιπεριφερόμεθα παντὶ ἀνέμῳ τῆς διδασκαλίας[26] πρὸς τὴν μωρίαν τῆς πλάνης[27] κλυδωνιζόμενοι, οὕτω τε ἑαυτῇ ἀσύμφωνον ὅσον ἀπὸ τῶν φωνῶν τὴν ἁγίαν Γραφὴν λογισόμεθα, καὶ τὸ κήρυγμα τοῦ εὐαγγελίου εἶναί τε καὶ οὐκ εἶναι[28]

---

[18] Ps. 17: 31   [19] τῇ (sic MS) delevi   [20] 2 Cor. 3: 6

[21] Μανιχαῖοι] Μανιχαιοⁱ sic MS

[22] παρέσπασαν] conieci, παρασπασθη σ sic MS

[23] ἀρα MS   [24] John 10: 30   [25] John 14: 28

[26] Cf. Eph. 4: 14   [27] Cf. Gen. 4: 16   [28] Cf. 2 Cor. 1: 18

Cyril the teacher witnesses in his *Second Letter to Succensus*, but these people are talking of what's indivisible, and talk of union in a deceitful way: they confess that the Word was united with the flesh, not by hypostasis, nor by the intertwining of the natures themselves, but by identity of honour, identity of will, identity of authority, indivisibly, yet only relationally—though they also say that the natures themselves, united in will, are of persons. All of these instances have shown the necessity, in my view, of paying attention, not just to expressions, but to what's understood by them. If some expression's new, but is nonetheless in harmony in what it signifies with orthodoxy as confessed from the very first, 1812A this expression needs to be trumpeted abroad and greeted as one that belongs. If some expression's everywhere in Holy Scripture and the fathers, however, but is trotted out by someone for the purpose of destroying a correct way of understanding through some impious innovation in interpretation, we must reject and loathe this expression, like good money-changers who don't pay attention just to the superficial impress and inscriptions on coins, but skilfully pare^v the silver itself, and test whether it really is valuable, for *the words of the Lord* are said to be *tested*, valuable silver. The kind of people who judge the meaning of expressions on the first hearing need to learn that that's often the way *the letter kills, but* 1812B *the spirit* (i.e. the sense) *gives life*—letters being just written versions of expressions.

Why should I go on and on about this issue? Everyone knows that Manichaean Christians, Samaritans, Jews, Arians, Sabellians, Valentinians, Marcionites, Nestorians, Apollinarians, and, in short, every heresy ever confessed, twisted certain expressions from both the Old and the New Testaments, as from the fathers who went before us, into evidence for their own understanding, as if these authorities intended the same things by them as they did. Are we not to judge, not just expressions, but whether these expressions carry the correct idea for them? When Sabellius twists the meaning of *I and the Father are one*, and destroys the triple 1812C hypostasis, and when Eunomius proposes the text *the Father who sent me is greater than I* as overthrowing the divinity's oneness and iden- tity by nature, are we thus foolishly turned aside with the ungodly—rather, are we turned right around, *tossed about by every wind of doctrine* into the foolishness of wandering—so that, on the basis of expressions, we'll consider Holy Scriptures totally self- contradictory, and admit that the proclamation of the gospel is

καταδεξόμεθα; οὐχ᾽ οὕτως οἱ εὐσεβεῖς, οὐχ᾽ οὕτως. ἀλλ᾽ ὄντως
δοκιμάζοντες τὰ διαφέροντα οἱ διὰ τῶν γεγυμνασμένων
αἰσθητηρίων τὰς συγκρίσεις τῶν καλῶν τε καὶ κακῶν ποιούμενοι,
πάντα δοκιμάζοντες, τὸ καλὸν κατέχοιμεν.²⁹

1812D   Οὐκοῦν φιλαλήθως πάντας τοὺς κατά τινα σκοπὸν τῶν αἱρετικῶν
λέγοντας τὸ, μίαν φύσιν τοῦ Θεοῦ Λόγου σεσαρκωμένην,
ἀποσκορακιστέον· ἀλλὰ καὶ ὅσοι κατά τινα ἔννοιαν δυσσεβῆ φασὶ
δυάδα φύσεων τῶν Χριστοῦ ἡνωμένων ἀδιαιρέτως, καταπτυστέον·
ἀποδεκτέον δὲ πάλιν πάντας τούς τε μίαν φύσιν λέγοντας τοῦ Θεοῦ
Λόγου σεσαρκωμένην ὡς ἑτέρᾳ φύσει, ἤγουν τῇ τῆς σαρκός,
ἡνωμένην τὴν φύσιν τοῦ Λόγου καθ᾽ ὑπόστασιν, καὶ πάντας δὲ τοὺς
ὁμολογοῦντας δυάδα φύσεων Χριστοῦ ἡνωμένων ἀδιαιρέτως, [278ʳ]
οὐ κατά τι τῶν περὶ τὴν οὐσίαν θεωρουμένων, ἀλλὰ κατὰ τὴν
ὑπόστασιν αὐτὴν τῶν φύσεων τουτέστιν, εἰς ἑνὸς προσώπου δεῖξιν
τοῦ ἐξ ἀμφοῖν, ὡς τὴν αὐτὴν οὖσαν ἑκατέραν ὁμολογίαν
ποτνιωμένους.

1813A   Ὅτι γὰρ καὶ Κύριλλος ὁ πατὴρ τὴν αὐτὴν οἶδεν ἔννοιαν εἶναι³⁰
τῆς μιᾶς φύσεως τοῦ Θεοῦ Λόγου σεσαρκωμένης, κατὰ τὴν αὐτοῦ
ἔννοιαν λεγομένης καὶ τῶν ὀρθῶς νοούντων δύο φύσεις Χριστοῦ
καθ᾽ ὑπόστασιν μίαν ἡνωμένας, κατὰ τὴν Λέοντός τε τοῦ
σοφωτάτου καὶ τῶν ἁγίων πατέρων τῶν ἐν τῇ συνόδῳ
Χαλκηδόνος ὁμολογίαν, ἀκουστέον αὐτοῦ ἐν τῇ πρὸς Εὐλόγιον
πρεσβύτερον ἐπιστολῇ τάδε λέγοντος· "Κἀκεῖνο δὲ μὴ
ἀγνοείτωσαν· ὅπου γὰρ ἕνωσις ὀνομάζεται, οὐχ᾽ ἑνὸς πράγματος
σημαίνεται σύνοδος, ἀλλ᾽ ἢ δύο ἢ καὶ πλειόνων καὶ διαφόρων
ἀλλήλοις κατὰ τὴν φύσιν. Εἰ τοίνυν λέγομεν τὴν ἕνωσιν,
ὁμολογοῦμεν ὅτι σαρκὸς ἐψυχωμένης νοερῶς καὶ Λόγου, καὶ οἱ
δύο δὲ λέγοντες φύσεις οὕτως νοοῦσι· πλὴν τῆς ἑνώσεως
1813B   ὁμολογουμένης, οὐκέτι διῒστανται ἀλλήλων τὰ ἑνωθέντα, ἀλλ᾽ εἷς
λοιπὸν Υἱός, μία φύσις αὐτοῦ ὡς σαρκωθέντος τοῦ Λόγου· ταῦτα
ὡμολόγησαν οἱ τῆς Ἀνατολῆς."³¹

Ἔτι μὴν καὶ ἐν τῇ δευτέρᾳ πρὸς Σούκενσον ἐπιστολῇ οὕτως
φησί, ἀποσκευαζόμενος τοὺς, κατ᾽ ἔννοιαν μειώσεως ἢ φύρσεως τῶν
συνελθόντων, διαβάλλοντας αὐτὸν λέγειν τὴν μίαν φύσιν· "Εἰ μὲν
γὰρ εἰπόντες φύσιν τοῦ Λόγου σεσιγήκαμεν, οὐκ ἐπενέγκαντες, τὸ
σεσαρκωμένην, ἀλλ᾽ οἷον ἔξωθεν τιθέντες τὴν οἰκονομίαν, ἦν αὐτοῖς
τάχα που καὶ οὐκ ἀπίθανος ὁ λόγος, προσποιουμένοις ἐρωτᾶν ποῦ
τὸ τέλειον ἐν ἀνθρωπότητι, πῶς ὑφέστηκεν ἡ καθ᾽ ἡμᾶς οὐσία·

---

²⁹ 1 Thess. 5: 21
³⁰ ἔννοιαν οἶδεν εἶναι a. corr.
³¹ Cyril of Alexandria, *Letter* 44, *ACO* i, 1, 4, 36.

both 'yes' and 'no'? This isn't the way pious people behave! Not at all! Rather, *testing all things, may we hold fast what's good*, really weighing the different things, being people who make comparisons between good and bad by means of trained facilities.

The upshot is that, out of friendship for the truth,[vi] one has to reject utterly all who say 'one incarnate nature of God the Word' in any sense intended by heretics, but one also has to spit on as many as speak of a duality of natures of Christ indivisibly united in some impious sense. Again, one has to accept all who speak of 'one incarnate nature of the Word of God' as being the Word's nature united by hypostasis to another nature, i.e. that of flesh, as also all who confess a duality of natures of Christ indivisibly united, not with any reference to what's understood about substance, but rather in terms of the hypostasis itself of the natures, that is, so as to show the one person out of both of them. Both groups we have to accept as being people who openly affirm that both confessions are the same. 1812D

You'd realize that the father Cyril knew the meaning of 'one incarnate nature of God the Word', used in his sense, to be the same as that of those who correctly think of two natures of Christ united in one hypostasis—in accordance with the proclamation of the most-wise Leo and the holy fathers at the Council of Chalcedon—if you'd just listen to what he says in the letter to the priest Eulogius: 'They mustn't ignore the former. Wherever the name "union" is used, what's indicated is a coming together, not of one entity, but of two or more things that differ by nature from each other. If, accordingly, we speak of union, we're confessing a union of flesh endowed with a rational soul, and of the Word, and those who speak of two natures also think in this way, except that, when the union's confessed, the things united no longer stand apart from each other, but rather there's one Son from then on, His one nature being of the Word thus incarnated. This is what the Anatolians confessed.' 1813A

1813B

Moreover, this is how he talks in the *Second Letter to Successus*, when he refutes those who misrepresent him as speaking of the one nature as meaning a diminution or commingling of the things that come together: 'If we had spoken of the one nature of the Word without making the overt addition "incarnate", to the exclusion, evidently, of the divine plan, there might have been some plausibility to their pretended question about the complete humanity or the possibility of our substance's continued existence.

ἐπειδὴ δὲ καὶ ⟨ἡ⟩ ἐν ἀνθρωπότητι τελειότης, καὶ τῆς καθ᾽ ἡμᾶς
οὐσίας ἡ δήλωσις εἰσκεκόμισται διὰ τοῦ λέγειν σεσαρκωμένην,
1813c παυσάσθωσαν".³² καὶ τὰ ἑξῆς. Τί οὖν, πρὸς τῇ μιᾷ φύσει τοῦ
Λόγου καὶ ἀνθρωπίνην τελείαν οὐσίαν εἰσκομίζων διὰ τοῦ
"σεσαρκωμένην", οὐ δύο εἶναι λογίσεται τὰς φύσεις, ἀκούων "μίαν
φύσιν τοῦ Θεοῦ Λόγου σεσαρκωμένην"; φησὶ γὰρ καὶ μετὰ βραχέα·
"Τί γάρ ἐστιν ἀνθρωπότητος φύσις, πλὴν ὅτι σὰρξ ἐψυχωμένη
νοερῶς;"³³

Τοῦ πατρὸς οὖν σαφῶς ἡμῖν μαρτυροῦντος τὴν πρὸς αὐτὸν καὶ
τὴν ἀλήθειαν συμφωνίαν, τῶν νοημάτων ἄρα μὴ εὐσεβῶς ἔχειν
δηλουμένων, ταῖς φωναῖς ἡμεῖς οὐ προσκείμεθα, οὐδ᾽ αὖ πάλιν
εὐσεβῶς ἐχόντων τὰς φωνὰς ἀποστεφόμεθα· οὔτε γὰρ ἕνωσις ἢ
μονὰς, ἁπλῶς ὁπωσοῦν συμφραζομένη τισί, τὰς φύσεις αὐτῶν
ἀναιρεῖ, εἰ μὴ εἰς φύσεως αὐτῆς μονάδα ἥκει, νοοῦσα³⁴ τὰ ἴδια τῆς
1813D κατὰ σύγχυσιν ἑνώσεως—ἑτέρα γὰρ ἕνωσις τοῦτο οὐ ποιεῖ—οὐδὲ
ἡ δυὰς πάντως κατηγορηθεῖσα τινός, καὶ εἰς πρόσωπα διαιρεῖ
τοῦτο, εἰ μὴ εἰς προσωπικὴν δίπλωσιν εἴη ληφθεῖσα. Τίς γὰρ ἂν
εἴποι [278ᵛ] διότι ἕνωσίς τις λέγεται καὶ μονὰς ἡ τοῦ ὅλου
Ῥωμαϊκοῦ τυχὸν στρατοῦ, καὶ ἓν ἐπὶ πάντων τῶν ἐν ταύτῃ
περιλαμβανομένων κεῖται ὄνομα τῶν ἀνθρώπων καὶ ἡμιόνων καὶ
καμήλων τῶν ἐν αὐτῷ, διὰ τόδε, καὶ μία φύσις ἐστὶν ὁ πᾶς στρατός;
Ἀλλ᾽ αὕτη, φησίν, οὐκ ἔστι καθ᾽ ὑπόστασιν φύσεων ἕνωσις.

Σκεπτέον οὖν, ὃ ἔφην, ὡς οὐκ ἔστιν ἕνωσιν ἁπλῶς ποιεῖν μίαν
φύσιν· ἀλλ᾽ οὐδὲ εἰ καθ᾽ ὑπόστασιν ἕνωσις εἴη μόνον λεγομένη,
μονάδα ποιήσει φύσεως, ἀλλ᾽ ἢ μόνης ὑποστάσεως· οὔτε γὰρ βύβλος
ἢ σπόγγος ὕδατι ἐμβαφεὶς καὶ ἀνιμησάμενος ἐν ὅλῳ ἑαυτῷ ὅλον
1816A τόδε, εἰς φύσιν ἦκε μίαν σὺν τῷ ὕδατι, ἀλλ᾽ εἰς ὑπόστασιν μίαν,
ὥσπερ οὖν καὶ σίδηρος καὶ πῦρ εἰς μύδρου ὑπόστασιν. Καὶ λίθοι
γὰρ καὶ ξύλα εἰς οἴκου μὲν ὑπόστασιν ἑτέραν ἦκαν, φύσεις δὲ τὰς
αὐτὰς ἀλλ᾽ ἡνωμένας ἀλλήλαις τὰς συνελθούσας εἰς τὴν τοῦδε
σύστασιν καὶ τὴν ὑφ᾽ ἓν στάσιν, εἴτουν ὑπόστασιν τοῦ οἴκου,
ἔχουσιν. Εἰ μέντοι καὶ εἰς φύσιν μίαν ὥσπερ οὖν καὶ ὑπόστασιν
γένοιτο ἕνωσις, οἷον γίνεται ἐπὶ τῆς κλαύρας Χίας καὶ τοῦ
μαλθακτοῦ κηροῦ, εἰς μαστιχήματος σύστασιν ἑνουμένων, ὄντως
καὶ φύσιν μίαν ἀνάγκη λέγειν ἐπὶ τῇ ἑνώσει· σκεπτέον δὲ ὡς οὔτε ἡ
μαστίχη οὔτε ὁ κηρὸς ἐν ταῖς οἰκείαις φυσικαῖς ἰδιότησι τότε καὶ

---

³² Cyril of Alexandria, *Letter* 46, *ACO* i, 1, 6, 160.
³³ Cyril of Alexandria, *Letter* 46, *ACO* i, 1, 6, 162.
³⁴ ἥκει, νοοῦσα] ἥκειν νοοῦν MS

In view, though, of the fact that the introduction of the word "incarnate" expresses completeness in manhood and our nature, they should cease . . .', and so on.[vii] What reason is there, then, for concluding that he doesn't consider the natures to be two, if he's adding a complete human substance to the one nature of the Word by means of the word 'incarnate', when he hears 'one incarnate nature of God the Word'? He does, after all, add after a bit: 'What is human nature, other than flesh endowed with a rational soul?' ⟨margin: 1813C⟩

Since the father so clearly demonstrates to us his harmony with himself and with the truth, we for our part don't cling to expressions when their meanings are shown not to be pious, nor, on the other hand, do we reject the expressions of those who are pious. A union or unity doesn't destroy things' natures just by being somehow connected with them, not unless it goes so far as to produce a unity of nature itself, which implies the properties of union by confusion—for no other kind of union does this. Neither does duality, positively predicated of something, also divide that thing into persons, unless it's assumed to be a case of the compounding of persons. Who would ever say that, just because, as it happens, there's said to be a kind of union and unity belonging to the whole Roman army, and one name is given for all—men, mules, camels—contained in it, the whole army is therefore one nature too? But this, my friend says, is not a union of natures by hypostasis. ⟨margin: 1813D⟩

One therefore needs to reflect on the fact, as I said, that it's not possible for a union to produce one nature just like that, nor, if it's a union by hypostasis alone that's spoken of, will that union produce a unity of nature, just a unity of a single hypostasis. When papyrus or a sponge is dipped in water, and has drawn all the water into its whole self, it doesn't end up being one nature with the water, but one hypostasis. In the same way, iron and fire result in a hypostasis of red-hot metal. Stones and wood, too, result in a new hypostasis, that of a house, but they keep the same natures, though they're united to each other and come together in a house's structure and in the reality that underlies a single entity, i.e. the house's hypostasis. Should there be a union in one nature, as in one hypostasis—the kind of thing that happens in the case of Syrian gum and soft wax when they're united in combination as plaster—in that case it really is necessary to speak of one nature in the union. Observe that, in that union, neither mastic nor wax ⟨margin: 1816A⟩

1816B συστάσεσι καὶ χροιαῖς καὶ λοιπαῖς ποιότησι πάντη μένουσι λοιπὸν κατὰ τήνδε τὴν ἕνωσιν, οὔτε ἔστι θατέρῳ τῶν ἰδίων μερῶν ὁμοιότης ἐν τῷ μαστιχήματι σωζομένη πρὸς τὰ ὁμοειδῆ· οὔτε γὰρ Χίας, οὐδὲ κηροῦ τί ὅμοιον πάντη ἔχει τὸ σύνθετον μαστίχημα, οὐδὲ ὁ ἤλεκτρος πάντη χρυσοῦ εἶδος καὶ ἀργύρου σώζει.

Καὶ εἰ οὕτως λέγειν ἐπὶ Χριστοῦ εὔλογον τὴν ἕνωσιν, ὑμῖν ἐγκαταλειπτέον κρῖναι, ὡς μήτε ὄντως Θεὸν μήτε ἄνθρωπον εἶναι. Εἰ δὲ αὐτὸν μὲν οὐ φατὲ τόδε, τινὰ δὲ τῶν ἐκκρίτων πατέρων ταύτην τὴν εἰς φύσιν ἕνωσιν δείξοιτε λέγοντα, παυσόμεθα τῆς πρὸς ὑμᾶς ἀμφισβητήσεως. Εἰ δὲ τόδε τὸ τῆς εἰς φύσιν ἑνώσεως δόγμα διαξαινόμενον καὶ διασαφούμενον κατὰ τὴν ἔννοιαν, οἷον τί ἐστι,
1816C μήτε ὑμῖν δεκτέον, μήτε τινὶ τῶν θεοφόρων λεκτὸν, πῶς ὅσιον οὕτως διὰ τὴν ἕνωσιν ἁπλῶς ἢ καὶ τὴν ὑπόστασιν, τὴν μίαν φύσιν ὑμᾶς προφασίζεσθαι, μὴ ὀρρωδοῦντας εὐσεβῶς, ὥσπερ τὴν διαίρεσιν τῶν συνελθόντων, οὕτως καὶ τὴν τροπὴν αὐτῶν καὶ σύγχυσιν, διὰ τῆς ἀπερισκέπτου φωνῆς ὑπογράφειν;

Καὶ γὰρ κἀκεῖνο μὴ ἀγνοείτω ὑμᾶς, ὡς τοῖς περὶ φυσικὰ γεγυμνασμένοις ὤφθη πολλάκις, καὶ διακεκριμένων τῶν ὑποστάσεων, γενομένη τισὶ φυσικὴ ἕνωσις· [279ʳ] τῷ γὰρ ὄξει ὑποκειμένῳ, ἐξ ὀλίγου διαστήματος ὑπερκείμενος χαλκός, αὐτὸς μὲν ὀξύνεταί τε τὴν γεῦσιν ἰούμενος, καὶ ὀπτίζεταί πως τὴν σύστασιν ἐκδιαινόμενος καὶ ἀναχεόμενος, τὸ δὲ ὄξος συστρέφεταί
1816D τε εἰς παχύτητα γλοιούμενον τὴν σύστασιν, πικραίνεταί τε τὴν γεῦσιν καὶ ἐρυθαίνει πως τὸ χρῶμα, καὶ ἁπλῶς ἀντικίρνανται τὰς φυσικὰς ποιότητας, καὶ διεστῶτά τε καὶ διωρισμένα τὰς ὑποστάσεις. Οὐκ ἄρα οὖν ἡ εἰς φύσιν ἕνωσις, τοῦ ἀδιαιρέτου τῶν ἑνωθέντων πίστωσις, ἀλλὰ μόνον τῆς κατ᾽ οὐσίαν ἀλλοιώσεως αὐτῶν εἰς δεῖξιν λαμβάνεται καὶ νοεῖται σαφῶς· τοῦτο γὰρ ἰδίως ἕπεται τῇδε.

Ἀλλ᾽ οὕτως μὲν τάδε· ἵνα ἐκ περιουσίας ὑμᾶς δείξωμεν, ὡς οὐδὲ τήνδε τὴν ἄλογον ἀφορμὴν τῆς ταυτολεξίας ἔχετε,³⁵ εἰς τὴν διένεξιν τὴν πρὸς ἡμᾶς, μόνον δὲ διά τινα προσπάθειαν καὶ ἀλόγιστον συνήθειαν καὶ ἀβασάνιστον πρόληψιν περὶ τοῦ ἀρχῆθεν τῆς ἀληθοῦς εὐσεβείας ἀποδεδρακότες, καὶ αἱρεσιαρχήσαντες ὑμεῖς ἀφορίζεσθε

---

³⁵ ἔχετε] ἔχῃ a. corr. MS

retains from that moment on its common natural characteristics, combinations, appearances, or other qualities. Nor is any likeness 1816b preserved in the plaster to things of the same form as either of its parts, for the plaster compounded from them has absolutely nothing in common with Syrian gum or wax. Neither does electrum preserve anything at all of the form of gold and silver.

If it makes sense to speak of the union in Christ like that, it's left to you to draw the conclusion that He's really neither God nor man. If you don't say that's what He is, but instead put on display specific texts of the select Fathers that speak of this as a union in a nature, we'll abandon our dispute with you! If, however, this doctrine of union into a nature—a doctrine torn to pieces and exposed by intelligent analysis—is the kind of thing that's unacceptable to you, and couldn't possibly have been uttered by 1816c any of the God-bearing fathers, how then can it be permissible for you to make a sham case for the one nature on the basis of union alone, or on the basis of hypostasis as well? How can you do this, refusing to shudder at the changing and confusing of the entities that come together in the same pious way as you shudder at their division, just because of your subscription to an expression you haven't thought through?

Don't let the following escape your notice either: something often observed by people trained in physics is the occurrence of a natural union between certain things even though their hypostases remain separate. When copper is placed at a little distance above vinegar, it's made sharp and acrid in taste, and is observed somehow turning liquid in structure, and becoming fluid. The vinegar, on the other hand, is compressed into a sticky sediment in struc- 1816d ture, and turns bitter in taste, and sort of red in colour. They simply mingle their natural qualities, while keeping separate and distinct in their hypostases. Therefore union in a nature isn't any confirmation of the undividedness of the things so united; on the contrary, it's taken as, and clearly understood to be, an indication only of their alteration in substance, for this is what properly follows from this kind of union.

The effect of all this is that we have, out of an abundance [of arguments that could be made] on our side, the following to lay against you: you no longer have the irrational pretext of words' identity in meaning for differing from us. It was on account just of a certain prejudice, irrational habit, and unexamined preconception about the origin of true piety that you were the ones who,

1817A ἡμῶν. Ἢ τὴν Βίβλον ἤ τοὺς γραφέας χορηγοῦντες ὑμεῖς μὴ
ἀποκάμητε, καὶ οὐκ ἐκλείψωμεν ὑμῖν διὰ βίου παντὸς πατρικὰς
χρήσεις κατεπάδοντες, ἵνα τοῦ πρὸς ἡμᾶς ἀγριαίνεσθαι
ὑποθωπεύσαντες καταπαύσωμεν.

Εἰ δὲ καὶ τοῦτο ὑμῖν φορτικόν, ὅσον ἐκ προχείρου ἀρκεῖν καὶ εἰς
σύμμετρον ἔλεγχον ἀποχρώντως ἔχει, τέως παραθήσομεν ὑμῖν, οὐ
μόνον ταῖς τῶν ἐκκρίτων ἡμῶν πατέρων μαρτυρίαις δυσωποῦντες
εἰδέναι φύσεις ἐπὶ τοῦ Κυρίου σωζομένας μετὰ τὴν ἔνωσιν, ἀλλὰ
καὶ τῶν ὑμετέρων καθηγεμόνων ὁμολογίας περὶ τούτου
προάγοντες. Εἰ δέ, ὡς ἔθος ὑμῖν πολλάκις, γελωτοποιεῖτε καὶ πρὸς
ταῦτα ἐφευρίσκοντες λέγειν, ὡς, ἀληθῶς φύσεις μὲν εἴρηνται,
ἀλλ' οὐ δύο αἱ μετὰ τὴν ἔνωσιν ἐπὶ τοῦ Κυρίου, ὑμῖν ἐγκαταλείψομεν
1817B τὸ λοιπὸν διδάσκειν ἡμᾶς, ὅσας δέον τάσδε νοεῖν. Εἴπερ ἄρα τὴν
φύσιν ταυτὸν ἴστε εἶναι καὶ τὰς φύσεις, κατά γε τὸ ποσὸν
νοούμενα—οὐδὲ γὰρ τοσῆσδε ἀμαθίας κατάγνωσιν φέρετε, μὴ
διακρίνοντες τὸ ἑνικὸν ἀπὸ τοῦ πληθυντικοῦ—, ἐξ ἀνάγκης ἤ
πλείους ἤ δύο τό γε ἐλάχιστον δώσετε εἶναι τάσδε τῷ ποσῷ τὰς
ἐνούσας Χριστῷ, καὶ οὔσας Χριστόν, καὶ ἐν αἷς ἐστι Χριστός· ἐκ
δύο γὰρ καὶ μόνων ἀτρέπτων καὶ ἀμειώτων καὶ ἡ ἔνωσις Χριστοῦ
ὡμολόγητο, καὶ ὑμῖν καὶ ἡμῖν. Πλὴν καὶ δύο ῥητῶς λέγοντας
δείξωμεν· οὐ μόνον δὲ τοῦτο, ἀλλὰ καὶ τὴν ἀντιλεγομένην ἡμῖν μίαν
φύσιν, ἥν φασιν οἶδε, προδήλως ἀποδοκιμάζοντας, ἵνα μηδὲν ἡμῖν
εἰς παντελοῦς ἀνατροπῆς χρείαν ὑπολείπηται πρὸς αὐτούς. Πρῶτον
μὲν οὖν τοὺς οἰονεὶ ὑπογραφικοὺς ὁρισμοὺς Χριστοῦ ὑπὸ τῶν
1817C πατέρων εἰρημένους ἀκουστέον· φασι γὰρ οὕτως·

Τί ἐστι Χριστὸς ὁ προσκυνητὸς ἡμῖν

Ἀθανασίου· [279ᵛ] "Θεὸς καὶ ἄνθρωπος ὁ αὐτός, εἷς ὢν
καθ' ὕπαρξιν, ἀνελλιπῆ τὰ ἑκάτερα."³⁶ Τί δέ ἐστι τάδε "τὰ
ἑκάτερα", καὶ τί "Θεός καὶ ἄνθρωπος"; Εἴπατε εἰ φύσεις ἤ οὐχί.

Βασιλείου, τί ἐστι Χριστός· "Θεότης ἐμψύχῳ σαρκὶ
κεχρημένη."³⁷

Γρηγορίου, τί ἐστι Χριστός· "Καινὴ μίξις, Θεὸς καὶ ἄνθρωπος,
ἓν ἐξ ἀμφοῖν, καὶ δι' ἑνὸς ἀμφότερα."³⁸

---

³⁶ Ps.-Athanasius, *On the Incarnation (against Apollinarius)* i, 16, *PG* xxvi, 1124A.
³⁷ Basil, *Letter* 236, Y. Courtonne (ed. and tr.), *Lettres*, iii (Paris: Les Belles Lettres, 1966), 49.
³⁸ Gregory of Nazianzus, *Oration* 2, ed. and tr. J. Bernardi, *Discours*, *SC* 247 (Paris: Éditions du Cerf, 1978), 120.

turning away and separating from us, became the founders of a heresy. Don't get tired of producing texts from the Bible or the writings, and we—who do our winning over by charm—won't abandon the texts of the fathers to you for a lifetime, our point being to bring your anger against us to an end by winning you over.

1817A

If that task's too much for you, we'll take a turn at serving up to you just so much from what we have at hand as will best serve the purpose of disproving your position in the appropriate way. In doing so, we'll not just be eager to observe—in citations taken from our select Fathers—the Lord's natures being preserved after the union; we'll also produce confessions on this point by your very own guides!^{viii} If, as is so often your custom, you make a joke of it, and come up with the idea of saying, by way of rebuttal, 'It's true that natures are mentioned, but there aren't two natures in the Lord *after* the union', we'll leave to you the further task of teaching us what quantity one ought to consider these natures as having. Now if you know the nature to be the same thing as the natures, when they're considered in terms of quantity—for don't you invite condemnation for great ignorance in failing to distinguish the single from the multiple?— you have no choice but to grant that these natures that are in Christ, that are Christ, and in which Christ exists, are multiple (two at the very least!); or Christ's union out of only two unchangeable and indivisible natures is proclaimed both by you and by us. We're going to point out, furthermore, people who speak quite clearly of two. Not only this, but we'll also show them openly rejecting as unworthy the one nature adduced in opposition to us that our opponents speak of, our purpose being that nothing should be left out on our part that's useful for their complete overthrow. The first order of business, then, is to hearken to the definitions of Christ, as it were, enunciated by the fathers. This is how they talk:

1817B

1817C

What is Christ, whom we are to adore?
Athanasius: 'The same God and man, being one in existence, both being complete.' What are these 'both', and what are 'God' and 'man'? Tell us whether they're natures or not.

Basil on what Christ is: 'Divinity making use of animated flesh.'

Gregory on what Christ is: 'A new mixture, God and man, one out of both, and both through one.'

1817D Τοῦ αὐτοῦ· "Κρᾶσις Θεοῦ καὶ σαρκός, διὰ μέσης ψυχῆς νοερᾶς, μεσιτευούσης θεότητι καὶ σαρκὸς παχύτητι".³⁹—" Ὁ Υἱὸς Θεοῦ ὤν, καὶ υἱὸς ἀνθρώπου γενόμενος, ἄμφω εἰς Υἱὸς καὶ Θεός, τοῦ κρείττονος ἐκνικήσαντος· ἔστιν ἄρα τὸ νικηθὲν καὶ τὸ νικῆσαν."⁴⁰— "Ἀνθρωπότης χρισθεῖσα θεότητι, καὶ γενομένη ὅπερ τὸ χρίσαν, καὶ οἷον εἰπεῖν ὁμόθεος."⁴¹

Κυρίλλου, τί ἐστι Χριστός· "Εἷς Υἱός, Θεὸς καὶ ἄνθρωπος, ὁ αὐτὸς τοῦτο κἀκεῖνο ὑπάρχων τὲ καὶ νοούμενος."⁴²—" Ὁ τοῦ Θεοῦ Λόγος καὶ Υἱὸς ἐνανθρωπήσας καὶ σεσαρκωμένος."⁴³—"Θεὸς ἐν προσλήψει σαρκὸς νοερῶς ἐψυχωμένης, εὐδοκήσας γενέσθαι καὶ ἄνθρωπος."⁴⁴—"Μία φύσις τοῦ Θεοῦ Λόγου σεσαρκωμένη."⁴⁵

1820A Ἆρα οὖν εἴ γε καὶ ἑαυτοῖς καὶ ἀλλήλοις συμφωνοῦσι τοῖς νοήμασιν οἱ ὁρίσαντες τάδε, πῶς οὐχὶ ἀμφότερα τὰ συνελθόντα ἐν Χριστῷ οἴδασι σώζεσθαι, καὶ μίαν φύσιν τοῦ Θεοῦ Λόγου σεσαρκωμένην ὅτε λέγοιεν; Εἰ δὲ τὸ "ἀμφότερα", τὰ δύο πράγματα σημαίνει κυρίως, καὶ οὔτε τρία, οὔτε ἕν, τὰ δὲ πράγματα τάδε οὐ συμβεβηκότα τινὰ ἢ φαντασίαι ψιλαί, ἀλλ' οὐσίαι τινές εἰσι, τί ἄλλο συνάγεται διὰ τῶνδε τῶν φωνῶν νοεῖν, ἢ ὅτι δύο φύσεις τοῦ Χριστοῦ ἡνωμέναι εἰσὶ κατὰ μίαν τὴν ὑπόστασιν αὐτοῦ; Ἀλλ' ἐπιδράμωμεν καὶ ταῖς σαφῶς τῶν φύσεων Χριστοῦ μνημονευούσαις μαρτυρίαις πατρικαῖς, καὶ μάλιστα ὧν μὴ ὁπωσοῦν τολμῶσι ποιεῖσθαι παραγραφὴν οἱ ἀντιλέγοντες

1820B Γρηγορίου τοῦ Θεολόγου· "Φύσεις μὲν γὰρ δύο, Θεὸς καὶ. ἄνθρωπος, ἐπεὶ καὶ ψυχὴ καὶ σῶμα, υἱοὶ δὲ οὐ δύο, οὐδὲ ἄνθρωποι."⁴⁶

Γρηγορίου· "Ἄμφω δὲ οὖν ἐν ταυτῷ εἷς, Θεός τε ὁμοῦ καὶ ἄνθρωπος, ὁ Ἐμμανουήλ."⁴⁷

Ποίαν φασὶ τὴν ἐπὶ Χριστοῦ ἕνωσιν οἱ πατέρες

Γρηγορίου τοῦ Θεολόγου· "Εἴ τις ὡς ἐν προφήτῃ λέγει κατὰ χάριν ἐνηργηκέναι, ἀλλὰ μὴ κατ' οὐσίαν συνῆφθαί τε καὶ συναναπεπλάσθαι, εἴη κενὸς τῆς κρείττονος ἐνεργείας."⁴⁸

1820C Κυρίλλου ἐκ τῆς ἑρμηνείας τῶν ἰδίων κεφαλαίων· "Ἀναγκαίως ἡμεῖς τοῖς Νεστορίου μαχόμενοι λόγοις, τὴν καθ' ὑπόστασιν ἕνωσιν γενέσθαι φαμέν."⁴⁹

Τοῦ αὐτοῦ ἐκ τῆς πρὸς Σούκενσον· "Οὐκοῦν καὶ εἰ λέγοιτο

---

³⁹ Gregory of Nazianzus, *Oration* 38, ed. and tr. P. Gallay, *Discours 38–41, SC* 358 (Paris: Éditions du Cerf, 1990), 134.

⁴⁰ Gregory of Nazianzus, *Oration* 29, ed. and tr. P. Gallay, *Discours 27-31 (Discours théologiques), SC* 250 (Paris: Éditions du Cerf, 1978), 218.

⁴¹ Gregory of Nazianzus, *Oration* 45, 13, *PG* xxxvi, 641A.

⁴² Cyril of Alexandria, *Letter* 45, *ACO* i, 1, 6, 153.   ⁴³ Ibid. 152 and 154.

⁴⁴ Cyril, *Letter* 46, *ACO* i, 1, 6, 159.   ⁴⁵ Cyril, *Letter* 45, *ACO* i, 1, 6, 153.

⁴⁶ Gregory of Nazianzus, *Letter* 101, *SC* 208, 44.

⁴⁷ Actually Cyril of Alexandria, *Against Nestorius* III, 2, *ACO* i, 1, 6, 61.

⁴⁸ Gregory of Nazianzus, *Letter* 101, *SC 208*, 46.

⁴⁹ Cyril of Alexandria, *Defence of the Twelve Anathemas, ACO* i, 1, 6, 115.

The same: 'A commixture of God and flesh, through a median 1817D
intellectual soul that mediates between divinity and the grossness
of flesh'; 'being the Son of God, and having become Son of
Man, one Son and God is both, since the superior of these is the
one that conquered. He therefore is both what was conquered
and what conquered'; 'humanity anointed by divinity, and
become like that which did the anointing and, so to speak, one
with God'.

Cyril's view of what Christ is: 'One Son, God and man, the
same being and understood to be both the former and the latter';
'the Word and Son of God become man and made flesh'; 'God,
pleased in the addition of rationally animated flesh to become
man as well'; 'one incarnate nature of God the Word'.

Well then: if the fathers who made these definitions agree in 1820A
their thinking both with themselves and with one another, how
could they not know that both the things that came together in
Christ are preserved, even though there are times when they speak
of one incarnate nature of God the Word? If the word 'both'
properly signifies the two realities (and not three, or one), yet these
realities are not just any entities that come together, nor mere
products of the imagination, but specific substances, what else are
we supposed to think follows from these expressions than that
there are two natures of Christ united in His one hypostasis? But
let's also run over those patristic citations that clearly call to mind
Christ's natures, and above all those to which our opponents don't
dare to take exception.

Gregory the Theologian: 'There are two natures, God and 1820B
man, seeing that there are both soul and body, but not two sons,
not two men.'

Gregory: 'Both, then, are one in the same thing, at once God
and man, the Emmanuel.'

What kind of union do the fathers say the union in Christ is?

Gregory the Theologian: 'If anyone says He acted by grace, as in
the case of a prophet, but was not conjoined and put together in
substance, let him be empty of the power from above.'

Cyril, from the *Explanation of his own Chapters*: 'Necessarily, we 1820C
who fight against Nestorius' arguments say that it is a union by
hypostasis that has taken place.'

The same, from the *Letter to Succensus*: 'Therefore, even if a

ἀνθρωπότητος καὶ θεότητος φύσις ἐπὶ τοῦ Ἐμμανουήλ, ἀλλ' ἡ
ἀνθρωπότης, ἰδία γέγονε τοῦ Λόγου· καὶ ὁ εἷς Υἱὸς νοεῖται σὺν
αὐτῇ."⁵⁰ Ἆρα οὖν φύσεις τὸ ἰδιοποιησάμενον καὶ τὸ ἰδιοποιηθὲν εἰς
τὴν τοῦ οἰκειωσαμένου ὑπόστασιν, ἢ οὔ;

　　　Τοῦ αὐτοῦ· " Ἡμέτερον γὰρ τὸ λέγειν ἤτοι ὀνομάζειν δύο φύσεις
1820D μέχρι τοῦ γινώσκειν τὴν διαφορὰν τοῦ Λόγου καὶ τῆς σαρκός."⁵¹
Δῆλον οὖν ὡς ὁ μὴ λέγων δύο φύσεις ἤρνηται τὴν διαφορὰν καὶ οὐ
γινώσκει αὐτὴν ἐν Χριστῷ.

　　　Τοῦ αὐτοῦ ἐκ τῶν Γλαφυρῶν· "Δύο μὲν γὰρ" φησὶ [280] "ὀρνίθια
κελεύει ληφθῆναι ζῶντα καὶ καθαρά, ἵνα νοήσῃς διὰ πετεινῶν τὸν
οὐράνιον ἄνθρωπον, ἄνθρωπόν τε ὁμοῦ καὶ Θεόν, εἰς δύο φύσεις,
ὅσον ἧκεν εἰς τὸν ἑκάστῃ πρέποντα λόγον, διαιρούμενον· Λόγος γάρ
ἦν ὁ ἐκ Θεοῦ Πατρὸς ἀναλάμψας, ἐν σαρκὶ τῇ ἐκ γυναικός."⁵²

　　　Γρηγορίου τοῦ θεολόγου· "Θεὸς δὲ λέγοιτο ἄν, οὐ τοῦ Λόγου,
τοῦ ὁρωμένου δέ—πῶς γὰρ ἂν εἴη τοῦ κυρίως Θεοῦ, Θεός;—
ὥσπερ καὶ Πατήρ, οὐ τοῦ ὁρωμένου, τοῦ Λόγου δέ· ἡνίκα γὰρ αἱ
1821A φύσεις διΐστανται ταῖς ἐπινοίαις, συνδιαιρεῖται καὶ τὰ ὀνόματα."⁵³
Ἐπισκεπτέον δὲ ὅτι οὐ τῇ ἐπινοίᾳ εἶναι τὰς φύσεις, ἀλλὰ διΐστασθαι
ταῖς ἐπινοίαις τὰς φύσεις φησίν.

　　　Τοῦ αὐτοῦ· "Κιρναμένων ὥσπερ τῶν φύσεων, οὕτω δὴ καὶ τῶν
κλήσεων, καὶ περιχωρουσῶν εἰς ἀλλήλας τῷ λόγῳ τῆς συμφυΐας."⁵⁴

　　　Βασιλείου, ἐκ τοῦ πρώτου τοῦ πρὸς Εὐνόμιον· "Οὐ δύο λέγομεν
Θεὸν ἰδίᾳ καὶ ἄνθρωπον—εἷς γὰρ ἦν—ἀλλὰ κατ' ἐπίνοιαν τὴν
ἑκάστου φύσιν λογιζόμενοι· οὐδὲ γὰρ ὁ Πέτρος δύο ἐνόησεν εἰπών,
Χριστοῦ οὖν <u>παθόντος</u> ὑπὲρ ἡμῶν <u>σαρκί</u>.⁵⁵,⁵⁶ Ὁ αὐτὸς δὲ μέγας
Βασίλειος φησὶ πρὸς Εὐνόμιον εἶναι τινὰ μὲν ἐπίνοιαν, τὴν ἀληθῆ
1821B νοητὴν θεωρίαν, καὶ εἶναι ἑτέραν, τὴν κατὰ ἀνάπλασμα ψεύδους,
οἷα τῶν μυθοποιῶν καὶ ζωγράφων. Εἰ μὲν οὖν πρὸς τὸν Θεὸν καὶ
ἄνθρωπον, τὴν ἀληθῆ, εἰ δὲ πρὸς τὸ ἰδίᾳ τὴν ἐπίνοιαν ἀκούωμεν, τὴν
ἀναπλαστικὴν λογιστέον· μόνον γὰρ διὰ τὸ διαρθρῶσαι ἑαυτοῖς τὸ
διάφορον τῶν ἡνωμένων, ταῖς φαντασίαις ἰδίᾳ ἕκαστον ἀφορίζομεν,
ἕως ἴδωμεν τί μὲν ἰδίως τοῦδε, τί δὲ τοῦ ἑτέρου.

　　　Τοῦ αὐτοῦ· "Ἐκ τούτου δεῖ συνορᾶν ὅπως ἐν τῷ ἑνὶ καὶ τῷ αὐτῷ

---

⁵⁰ Cyril of Alexandria, *Letter* 46, *ACO* i, 1, 6, 162.
⁵¹ Actually Severus of Antioch, *Against the Grammarian* iii, 9, ed. and tr. J. Lebon,
CSCO xciv = Scriptores Syri xlvi = Scriptores Syri, series 4, v, 124 (tr.). Cited in part
also at 1845D.
⁵² Cyril of Alexandria, *Glaphyra on the Pentateuch* 4, *PG* lxix, 576B.
⁵³ Gregory of Nazianzus, *Oration* 30, *SC* 250, 240 and 242. Cited in part at 1861A.
⁵⁴ Gregory of Nazianzus, *Letter* 101, *SC* 208, 48.
⁵⁵ 1 Pet. 4: 1
⁵⁶ [Ps.-] Basil, *Against Eunomius* iv, *PG* xxix, 704C.

nature of humanity and a nature of divinity are spoken of in the Emmanuel, still the humanity has become the Word's own humanity, and the one Son is understood along with it.' Well then: are what makes something its own, and what is made that thing's own in the hypostasis of what appropriates it, natures—or are they not?

The same: 'It is our position to speak of, indeed to name, two natures, to the point of recognizing the difference between the Word and the flesh.' It's clear, then, that the man who doesn't   1820D
speak of two natures has denied the difference, and doesn't recognize it in Christ.

The same, from the *Glaphyra*: 'He orders two small, living, clean birds to be taken', he says, 'so that you might understand from winged creatures the *man from heaven*, at once man and God, in two natures, inasmuch as he came to be in the separate definition that belongs to each. He who shone forth from God the Father was Word, in flesh from a woman.'

Gregory the Theologian: 'He's said to be God, not of the Word, but of the visible realm—how could He be God of the one who is God in His own right?—just as He's also called Father, not of the visible realm, but of the Word, for whenever natures differ in thought, their names are distinguished too.' Notice that he says,   1821A
not that the natures exist in thought, but that they differ in the ideas one has of them.

The same: 'When appellations are mixed in the same way as natures are, and interpenetrate each other by reason of their coming together'.

Basil, from *Against Eunomius* I: 'We do not say God and man are separately two—for He was one—though we do infer the nature of each in thought, for Peter wasn't thinking of two when he spoke of *Christ* therefore *suffering* for us *in the flesh*.' The same great Basil says, against Eunomius, that there's one sort of thought that's the true intellectual apprehension, and another sort that   1821B
works by false invention, such as are the thoughts of myth-makers and painters. If, then, we take the thought that refers to 'God and man', it's the true one, but if we take the thought that refers to 'separately', it's the invented kind. It's only by articulating united things' difference from each other that we distinguish each individually from illusions, until we get to know what properly belongs to one, and what to the other.

The same: 'What you need to realize from this is how the truth

ἑκατέρας φύσεως ἀποδειχθῇ ἡ ἀλήθεια."⁵⁷

Γρηγορίου τοῦ θεολόγου· "'Απεστάλη μέν, ἀλλ' ὡς ἄνθρωπος· διπλοῦς γὰρ ἦν."⁵⁸

1821C Κυρίλλου ἐκ τοῦ πρὸς Θεοδόσιον τὸν βασιλέα· "Τὰς γὰρ εὐαγγελικὰς περὶ τοῦ Κυρίου φωνὰς ἴσμεν τοὺς θεολόγους ἄνδρας, τὰς μὲν κοινοποιοῦντας ὡς ἐφ' ἑνὸς προσώπου, τὰς δὲ διαιροῦντας ὡς ἐπὶ δύο φύσεων, καὶ τὰς μὲν θεοπρεπεῖς, κατὰ τὴν θεότητα αὐτοῦ, τὰς δὲ ἀνθρωποπρεπεῖς κατὰ τὴν ἀνθρωπότητα αὐτοῦ διδόντας."⁵⁹

Τοῦ Θεολόγου ἐκ τοῦ περὶ Υἱοῦ δευτέρου λόγου· "Τὸ γὰρ συναμφότερον, ἕν· ἀλλ' οὐ τῇ φύσει, τῇ δὲ συνόδῳ."⁶⁰

Κυρίλλου· "Μετὰ μέντοι τὴν ἕνωσιν οὐ διαιροῦμεν τὰς φύσεις ἀπ' ἀλλήλων, οὐδὲ εἰς δύο υἱοὺς τέμνομεν τὸν ἕνα καὶ ἀμέριστον."⁶¹

1821D Δῆλον ἄρα, ὡς εἰ καὶ ἀδιαιρέτους, ἀλλ' οὖν φύσεις οἶδε τὰς μετὰ τὴν ἕνωσιν, καὶ οὐ φύσιν μίαν.

Γρηγορίου Νύσσης ἐκ τῶν κατὰ Εὐνομίου· "Οὔτε ζωοποιεῖ τὸν Λάζαρον ἡ ἀνθρωπίνη φύσις, οὔτε δακρύει τὸν κείμενον ἡ ἀπαθὴς ἐξουσία."⁶² Καὶ πάλιν· "Τὸν μεσίτην Θεοῦ καὶ ἀνθρώπων,⁶³ καθὼς καὶ ὠνόμασεν ὁ θεῖος 'Απόστολος, οὐδὲν οὕτως ὡς τὸ τοῦ Υἱοῦ δείκνυσιν ὄνομα, ἑκατέρᾳ φύσει τῇ θείᾳ καὶ ἀνθρωπίνῃ κατὰ τὸ ἴσον ἐφαρμοζόμενον."⁶⁴

Τοῦ Χρυσοστόμου, ἐκ τοῦ κατὰ 'Απολιναριαστῶν· "Οὕτω κἀνταῦθα τῆς θείας ἐνιδρυσάσης τῷ σώματι φύσεως, ἕνα Υἱόν, ἓν 1824A πρόσωπον τὸ συναμφότερον ἀπετέλεσε, γνωρι[280ᵛ]ζόμενον μέντοι ἀσυγχύτῳ καὶ ἀδιαιρέτῳ λόγῳ, οὐκ ἐν μιᾷ μόνῃ φύσει, ἀλλ' ἐν δυσὶ τελείαις· ἐπὶ γὰρ μιᾶς, πῶς τὸ ἀσύγχυτον, πῶς τὸ ἀδιαίρετον, πῶς ἡ ἕνωσις λεχθείη ποτέ; Ἡ γὰρ μία ἑαυτῇ ἑνοῦσθαι, ἢ συγχεῖσθαι, ἢ ἐξ ἑαυτῆς διαιρεῖσθαι, οὐ δύναται."⁶⁵ Καὶ μετὰ βραχέα· "Πάλιν ἐπ' ἄλλο μεταπηδῶντες, φασὶ μετὰ τὴν ἕνωσιν μὴ χρῆναι λέγειν δύο φύσεις. Πρόσεχε τῇ σημασίᾳ τοῦ ῥητοῦ· ἕνωσιν εἶπας, ἕνωσιν δὲ μιᾶς οὐκ ἂν εὕροις γινομένην."⁶⁶ Καὶ μετὰ βραχέα· "Εἰώθασι δὲ καὶ τοῦτο προτείνειν· "Ἀρα οὐ τὸ σῶμα καὶ τὸ αἷμα τοῦ Θεοῦ λαμβάνομεν πιστῶς καὶ εὐσεβῶς;' Ναὶ, λεκτέον, οὐχ' ὅτι σῶμα καὶ αἷμα, τὸ θεῖον πρὸ τῆς ἐνανθρωπήσεως ἐκέκτητο φύσει, ἀλλ' ἐπειδὴ

---

⁵⁷ Actually Origen, *On First Principles* ii, 6, 2. Latin: P. Koetschau (ed.), *Origenes Werke* v, *GCS* (Leipzig: J. C. Hinrich'sche Buchhandlung, 1913), 141.

⁵⁸ Gregory of Nazianzus, *Oration* 38, *SC* 358, 138. Cited also at 1861A.

⁵⁹ Actually Cyril of Alexandria, *Letter* 39 (to John of Antioch), *ACO* i, 1, 1, 17. Cited also at 1829A and 1852B–C.

⁶⁰ Gregory of Nazianzus, *Oration* 30, *SC* 250, 242.

⁶¹ Cyril of Alexandria, *Letter* 45, *ACO* i, 1, 6, 153.

⁶² Gregory of Nyssa, *Against Eunomius* v, 3, 65, in W. Jaeger (ed.), *Gregorii Nysseni Opera*, ii (Leiden: E. J. Brill, 1960), 130.

⁶³ 1 Tim. 2: 5   ⁶⁴ Gregory of Nyssa, *Against Eunomius* iii, 1, 92, Jaeger 35.

⁶⁵ Ps.-Chrysostom, *Letter to Caesarius*, *PG* lii, 758–9.

⁶⁶ Ibid. 759.

of each nature may be demonstrated in one and the same [Christ].'

Gregory the Theologian: 'He was sent, but as a man, for he was twofold.'

Cyril, from *To Theodosius the Emperor*: 'We recognize that theologians hold some evangelical and apostolic texts about the Lord to be common, as concerning one person, but distinguish others of them as concerning two natures; they agree the God-befitting statements apply to His divinity, but the man-befitting ones to His humanity.' 1821C

[Gregory of Nazianzus] the Theologian, from the second work *Concerning the Son*: 'The combination is one; however, it is not one by nature, but by union.'

Cyril: 'After the union we of course do not separate the natures from each other, nor do we sever the one and undivided [Christ] into two sons.' It's clear, then, that he does recognize natures— though they're undivided natures—after the union, and not one nature. 1821D

Gregory of Nyssa, from *Against Eunomius*: 'The human nature does not bring Lazarus to life, nor does the impassable power weep over him who lies dead.' And further on: 'The *mediator between God and man*, as the divine Apostle styles Him, is nothing like what the name of Son signifies, for it is adapted to each nature, the divine and the human, as is appropriate.'

Chrysostom, from *Against Apollinarians*: 'The moment the divine nature thus dwelt in the body, the combination completed one Son, one person, known in an unconfused and undivided way, not in just one nature, but in two complete natures. In one nature, after all, how could there be unconfusedness? How could there be undividedness? How could union ever be talked about? That is because the one nature cannot be united with itself, or confused with itself, or divided from itself.' A little later: 'Shifting their ground to yet another position, they say one must not speak of two natures after the union. Stick to the sense of what is said: you spoke of a union, but you will never find a union of one nature happening.' And a little later: 'They have been in the habit of putting this objection forward as well: "Do we not receive the body and the blood of God faithfully and piously?" Yes, this has to be admitted, but the divine is said to have these things, not because it had acquired body and blood by nature before His incarnation, but rather because it appropriated to itself what 1824A

τὰ τῆς σαρκὸς ἰδιοποιεῖται, ἔχειν λέγεται ταῦτα. Ὦ τοῦ
1824Β ἀτοπήματος, Ὦ τῆς ἀσεβοῦς διανοίας· κινδυνεύει γὰρ παρ' αὐτοῖς
τῆς θεότητος τὸ ἀξίωμα, καὶ πάλιν τὸ κυριακὸν σῶμα ὡς ἀληθινὸν
σῶμα ὁμολογεῖν οὐκ ἀνέχονται· δι' ἐπινοίας γὰρ λέξεων τετράφθαι
τοῦτο εἰς θεότητα φαντάζονται, μίαν ἐντεῦθεν κατασκευάζοντες
φύσιν, καὶ αὐτὴν τίνος εἶναι μὴ εὑρίσκοντες λέγειν."[67] Καὶ
μετ' ὀλίγα· "Φύγωμεν τοὺς διαιροῦντας· εἰ γὰρ καὶ διττὴ ἡ φύσις,
ἀλλ' οὖν ἀδιαίρετος καὶ ἀδιάσπαστος ἡ ἕνωσις, ἐν ἑνὶ τῆς υἱότητος
ὁμολογουμένῃ προσώπῳ, καὶ μιᾷ ὑποστάσει. Φύγωμεν τοὺς μίαν
φύσιν μετὰ τὴν ἕνωσιν τερατευομένους· τῇ γὰρ τῆς μιᾶς ἐπινοίᾳ τῷ
ἀπαθεῖ Θεῷ πάθος προσάπτειν ἐπείγονται."[68]

1824C Κυρίλλου ἐκ τῶν κατὰ Νεστορίου ἐν τῷ δευτέρῳ λόγῳ·
"Ὁμολόγησόν ἕνα, μὴ διαιρῶν τὰς φύσεις, μετὰ τοῦ εἰδέναι ὅτι
σαρκὸς μὲν ἕτερος λόγος, θεότητος δὲ ὁ αὐτῇ καὶ μόνῃ πρέπων."[69]
Ἰδοὺ οὖν σαφῶς οὐκ ἀναιρεῖν τὴν δυάδα, ἀλλὰ μὴ διαιρεῖν παραινεῖ
τήνδε τὴν κατὰ τὰς φύσεις, γινώσκειν τὲ πρὸς τῷ ποσῷ καὶ τὴν
διαφορὰν τοῦ λόγου θατέρας πρὸς ἑτέραν βούλεται, φύσεις τὲ εἰπὼν
καὶ ἑτέρους λόγους.

Τοῦ αὐτοῦ ἐκ τῆς ἑρμηνείας τῆς πρὸς Ἑβραίους δευτέρου τόμου·
"Συνέβησαν δὲ ἀλλήλαις ἀπορρήτως τὲ καὶ ὑπὲρ νοῦν θεότης καὶ
1824D ἀνθρωπότης· καὶ διάφοροι μὲν αἱ φύσεις ὁμολογουμένως, πλὴν εἷς
τε καὶ μόνος ἐξ ἀμφοῖν Υἱός."[70] Ὅτι τὲ οὖν διάφοροι, καὶ ὅτι καὶ
φύσεις εἰσὶ οἶδεν· εἰ οὖν μὴ φύσεις μετὰ τὴν σύμβασιν λέγει, οὔτε
διαφόρους θεότητα καὶ ἀνθρωπότητα.

Τοῦ αὐτοῦ ἐκ τῆς αὐτῆς τόμου ϛ'· "Εἰ γὰρ καὶ νοοῦνται διάφοροι,
καὶ ἀλλήλαις ἄνισοι τῶν εἰς ἑνότητα συνδεδραμηκότων αἱ φύσεις
σαρκὸς δὴ λέγω καὶ Θεοῦ, ἀλλ' οὖν εἷς τὲ καὶ μόνος ὁ ἐξ ἀμφοῖν Υἱὸς
ἀληθῶς."[71] Δῆλον ἄρα ὅτι ὅτε εἷς ὁ ἐξ ἀμφοῖν, τότε [281ʳ] καὶ
νοοῦνται καὶ φύσεις, καὶ ἀλλήλαις ἄνισοι ἐπὶ Χριστοῦ μετὰ τὴν
ἕνωσιν.

Τοῦ αὐτοῦ ἐκ τοῦ ιά κεφαλαίου τῶν Σχολίων· "Ὅτι δὲ
1825Α ἀσύγχυτοι μεμενήκασιν αἱ φύσεις, εἴτ' οὖν ὑποστάσεις."[72] Ἰδοὺ οὖν,
ὅτι οἶδε τὰς φύσεις μενούσας με⟨τὰ⟩ τὴν ἕνωσιν ἐν Χριστῷ,
διωνύμως ὁμολογεῖ εἰπὼν "εἴτ' οὖν ὑποστάσεις"· λέγεται γὰρ καὶ
ὑπόστασις παρὰ τὸ ὑφεστηκέναι ἡ φύσις. Εἰ δέ, ὥσπερ εἰώθασι
γελωτοποιῶς ἀποκρίνεσθαι, "Οὐκοῦν καὶ πρόσωπα δύο μένουσιν·
ἔφη γὰρ καὶ 'ὑποστάσεις'", πρῶτον μὲν σαφῶς ἑαυτοὺς

---

[67] Ibid. 759–60.　　　[68] Ibid. 760. Cited also at 1825c below.

[69] Cyril of Alexandria, *Against Nestorius* ii, *ACO* i, 1, 6, 46.

[70] Cyril of Alexandria, *On Hebrews*, *PG* lxxiv, 1005B.　　　[71] Ibid. 1005C.

[72] Cyril of Alexandria, *Scholia*. Attested in John 'the Grammarian' of Caesarea:
ACO i, 5, 227.

belongs to the flesh. What an absurdity! What an impious idea! 1824B
The dignity of the divinity is put at risk with them, and again they
do not stand firm in confessing the dominical body as a true body.
From their understanding of passages, they imagine this body to
have been turned into divinity, building the case for one nature
from that premise. Whose nature it is, they are at a loss to say.' A
little later: 'Let us flee those who divide. Even if the nature is
twofold, the union is nonetheless undivided and inseparable,
being confessed in one person of sonship, and in one hypostasis.
Let us flee those who devise one nature after the union, for by
means of the notion of the one nature they are eager to attribute
suffering to the impassable God.'

Cyril, from *Against Nestorius* ii: 'Confess one, not dividing the 1824C
natures, with the knowledge that there is another definition of
flesh, but the definition of divinity fits only itself.' Observe: he
clearly exhorts him not to abolish the duality, but not to divide this
duality of natures either, and wants him to recognize also the
numerical difference in definition of the one over against the
other, for he speaks of natures, and of different definitions.

The same from the *Commentary on Hebrews* ii: 'Divinity and
humanity came together with each other ineffably and incompre-
hensibly. The natures are different, as all admit, yet there is one 1824D
single Son out of both.' He recognizes, then, that they're different,
and that they're natures as well. If, then, he's not talking about
natures after the coming together, he isn't talking about a divinity
and a humanity that differ either.

The same, from the same commentary, book vi: 'Even if the
natures of the things come together into a unity are thought to be
different, and unequal to each other—I am talking about the
natures of flesh and of God—still the Son who is from them both
is truly one and single.' It's clear, then, that when there's one [Son]
from them both, that's when natures are understood too, and
natures unequal to each other in Christ after the union.

The same, from the *Scholia*, chapter 11: 'because the natures,
that is, hypostases, have remained unconfused'. Observe: he con- 1825A
fesses by his use of the two names that he recognizes that the
natures remain after the union in Christ when he says 'that is,
hypostases'. Nature is also called hypostasis on account of having
subsisted. If, as they're in the foolish habit of responding, 'then
there remain two persons, for he spoke of "hypostases"', what
follows, in the first place, is that they've unmistakably revealed

ἀπεκάλυψαν ἰδίῳ πάθει δουλεύοντας, καὶ τοὺς πατέρας βάλλειν, καὶ
πατραλοῖαι γίνεσθαι μὴ ὑφορώμενοι, μόνον δὲ τῆς πλάνης ἑαυτῶν
προεστηκότες. Τοῦ γὰρ πατρὸς τάδε λέγοντος, εἰ οὕτως νοοῦσι καὶ
νῦν πρόσωπον τὴν ὑπόστασιν, ἀνάγκη τοὺς τοῖς εἰρημένοις
προσέχοντας, καὶ μηδὲν προσεπινοοῦντας ἢ ὑφαιροῦντας νόημα—
οὐ γὰρ θέμις τῷ ὀρθῶς κρίνοντι—τὸν πολεμιώτατον τῇ δυσσεβείᾳ
1825Β   Νεστορίου, συνομολογοῦντα αὐτῷ νῦν τὰ αὐτὰ καθορᾶν, μαχόμενον
δὲ αὐτῷ μυριάκις κράζοντι ἐν τῇ πρὸς Ἑβραίους ἐξηγήσει καὶ ἐν
ἑτέροις, οὐ δύο εἶναι προσώπων ἕνωσιν—ἔφη γὰρ περὶ τοῦ
ματαιόφρονος—"Τὴν τῶν προσώπων ἕνωσιν οὐκ οἶδα πόθεν
ἐξευρηκώς",[73] τὰ δὲ ἑνωθέντα, ταῦτά φησι, καὶ μεῖναι ἀσύγχυτα
νῦν. Εἰ οὖν ὡς πρόσωπα λέγει τὰς ὑποστάσεις ἀσυγχύτους, γέγονεν
ὑπόσπονδος τῷ ἀσεβεῖ ὁ πολέμιος· ἀλλ' οἱ τῶν ἰδίων ἀμνήμονες, πῶς
νῦν οὐκ ἀποφαίνονται, ὅτι " Ἐπὶ τοῦ τῆς οἰκονομίας λόγου, φύσιν
τέ καὶ ὑπόστασιν ταὐτὸν οἶδεν ὅ τε διδάσκαλος Κύριλλος καὶ
ἡμεῖς"; Ἔκ τε οὖν τούτων, τὸ ἐκεῖ ψευδές, καὶ ἐκ τῶν ἐκεῖ, ἡ
ἐνθάδε εὑρεσιλογία αὐτῶν κατάδηλος.

    Ἰωάννου τοῦ Χρυσοστόμου ἐκ τῆς πρὸς Καισάριον ἐπιστολῆς·
1825C   "Γνωριζόμενον μὲν τῷ ἀσυγχύτῳ καὶ ἀδιαιρέτῳ λόγῳ, οὐκ ἐν μιᾷ
φύσει, ἀλλ' ἐν δυσὶ τελείαις".[74] Καὶ μετ' ὀλίγα· "Ποῖος οὖν Ἅδης
ἐξηρεύξατο μίαν ἐπὶ τοῦ Χριστοῦ λέγειν φύσιν;"[75] Καὶ μετὰ
βραχέα· "Εἰ γὰρ καὶ διττὴ ἡ φύσις, ἀλλ' οὖν ἀδιαίρετος καὶ
ἀδιάσπαστος ἡ ἕνωσις, ἐν ἑνὶ τῆς υἱότητος ὁμολογουμένῃ
προσώπῳ."[76]

    Τοῦ ἁγίου Ἰουστίνου καὶ μάρτυρος ἐκ τοῦ τρίτου βιβλίου τοῦ
περὶ τῆς ἁγίας Τριάδος κεφαλαίου ιζ'· " Ὅταν οὖν ἀκούσῃς τοῦ ἑνὸς
Υἱοῦ τὰς ἐναντίας φωνάς, καταλλήλως μέριζε ταῖς φύσεσι τὰ
λεγόμενα."[77] Καὶ μετὰ βραχύ· "Ἑκάστης ἃ πέφυκε δεχομένης
φύσεως."[78] Καὶ μετ' ὀλίγα· " Ὅσπερ εἷς μέν ἐστιν ἄνθρωπος, ἔχει δὲ
1825D   δύο φύσεις διαφόρους, καὶ κατ' ἄλλο μὲν λογίζεται, κατ' ἄλλο δὲ τὸ
λογισθὲν ἐνεργεῖ".[79] Εἶτα ἐπάγει· "Οὕτως ὁ Υἱὸς εἷς ὢν καὶ δύο
φύσεις, κατ' ἄλλην μὲν τὰς θεοσημίας ἐργάζεται, κατ' ἄλλην δὲ τὰ
ταπεινὰ παρεδέξατο."[80] Καὶ μεθ' ἕτερα· "Εἷς ἥλιος, φύσεις δὲ δύο,
ἡ μὲν φωτός, ἡ δὲ σώματος ἡλιακοῦ· οὕτως κἀνταῦθα [281ᵛ] εἷς μὲν
Υἱὸς καὶ Κύριος καὶ Χριστὸς καὶ Μονογενής, φύσεις δὲ δύο, ἡ μὲν
ὑπὲρ ἡμᾶς, ἡ δὲ ἡμετέρα."[81]

[73] Cyril, *On Hebrews*, PG lxxiv, 1004B.
[74] Ps.-Chrysostom, *Letter to Caesarius*, PG lii, 758.   [75] Ibid. 759.
[76] Ibid. 760. Cited at 1824B above.
[77] Actually Theodoret, *Exposition of the Correct Faith*, PG vi, 1225A.
[78] Ibid.   [79] Ibid. 1225B–C.   [80] Ibid. 1225C.   [81] Ibid. 1232A.

themselves to be slaves to their own sad situation, since they haven't a clue that they're casting aside the fathers and becoming parricides, and that they're standing up for nothing but their own error! Cyril does say this. If these people who pay attention to what's said, and don't read anything in or subvert its meaning— not the way of a man of sound judgement!—thus think, even now, that the hypostasis is a person, they must agree that the very man who was most hostile to Nestorius' impiety now takes the same 1825B view of things as he did! This means he's in conflict with what he himself cries out a thousand times in his commentary on Hebrews and elsewhere, that there's no union of two persons. He was talking about that fool—'I have no idea where he came upon the union of persons'—but says that whatever realities were united now remain unconfused. If, then, he's saying the hypostases are unconfused as being persons, the man who was hostile to the impious Nestorius has become his ally! How can these people, being so careless about their own affairs, escape the implication that they're declaring that 'Cyril the teacher recognizes nature and hypostasis to be the same thing in the Word's Incarnation, as do we'? It was from these conclusions that the old error arose, and it's from the old controversies that these people's present sophistical ingenuity is exposed.

John Chrysostom, from the *Letter to Caesarius*: 'made known in 1825C an unconfused and undivided sense, not in one nature, but in two complete natures'. And after a bit: 'What hell belched forth the idea of saying one nature in Christ?' And after a bit: 'Even if the nature is twofold, the union is nonetheless undivided and inseparable, being confessed in one person of sonship.'

Justin, saint and martyr, from *On the Trinity* iii, 17: 'Whenever you hear contradictory sayings of the one Son, then, distribute what is said between the natures as is appropriate.' And after a little: 'each nature receiving what was natural to it'. After a few more things: 'who is one man, yet has two different natures, and makes decisions in one reality, but does what He has decided in 1825D the other'. Next he adds: 'Thus the Son, being one and also being two natures, works the miracles in one of them, but took upon Himself humble things in the other.' And after other things: 'There is one sun, but two natures: one is the nature of light, the other the nature of a solar body. In this case, similarly, there is one Son and Lord and Christ and Only Begotten, but two natures, one that is beyond us, one that is our own.'

Τοῦ ἁγίου Ἀμβροσίου ἐπισκόπου Μεδιολάνων ἐκ τῆς ἑρμηνείας τοῦ ἁγίου συμβόλου· "Τοὺς δὲ λέγοντας" μετὰ τὰ ἐν μέσῳ τινὰ "τὰς φύσεις τοῦ Χριστοῦ κατὰ ἀνάκρασιν συγχυθείσας μίαν γενέσθαι φύσιν, καὶ μὴ ὁμολογοῦντας τὸν Κύριον ἡμῶν Ἰησοῦν 1828A Χριστόν, δύο εἶναι φύσεις ἀσυγχύτους, ἐν δὲ πρόσωπον, καθὸ καὶ εἷς ὁ Χριστὸς καὶ εἷς Κύριος, τούτους ἀναθεματίζει ἡ καθολικὴ καὶ ἀποστολικὴ Ἐκκλησία."[82] Ἀναγκαζόμεθα δὲ περιτέμνειν τὰς χρήσεις διὰ τὸ μὴ εἰς πλῆθος καὶ ὄγκον ἄγειν τὸ σύγγραμμα.

Τοῦ αὐτοῦ, ἐκ τοῦ περὶ τῆς θείας ἐνανθρωπήσεως· "Ἀνεφύησάν τινες τὴν σάρκα τοῦ Κυρίου καὶ τὴν θεότητα μιᾶς εἶναι φύσεως λέγοντες. Ποῖος Ἅδης τὴν τοιαύτην βλασφημίαν ἐξήμεσεν;"[83] Ἰουλίου ἐπισκόπου Ῥώμης, ἣν καὶ Κύριλλος παρήγαγε χρῆσιν ἐν τῇ κατ᾽ αὐτὴν συνόδῳ· "Ὁ δὲ καὶ τὰ ἴδια γινώσκων, καὶ τὴν ἕνωσιν φυλάττων, οὔτε τὰς φύσεις ψεύσεται, οὔτε τὴν ἕνωσιν ἀγνοήσει."[84]

1828B Γρηγορίου Νύσσης πρὸς Φίλιππον μονάζοντα περὶ τῆς τῶν Ἀρειανῶν ἀντιθέσεως, ἧς ἡ ἀρχή· "Ἡ κακία γέννημά ἐστι ψυχῇ·" "Κἂν γὰρ ἀρρήτῳ καὶ ἀφράστῳ ἑνώσει τὰ συναμφότερα ἕν, ἀλλ᾽ οὐ τῇ φύσει, διὰ τὸ ἀσύγχυτον φημί".[85] ἕτερον γὰρ τὸ θεῖον παρὰ τὸ σῶμα, ἐπείσακτον γάρ. Ὁ τοίνυν Χριστὸς δύο ὑπάρχων φύσεις, καὶ ἐν αὐταῖς ἀληθῶς γνωριζόμενος, μοναδικὸν πρόσωπον, ἀσύγχυτον ὅμως.

Τοῦ αὐτοῦ ἐκ τῶν πρὸς αὐτούς· "Εἰ γὰρ καὶ ἐν δύο φύσεσι νοεῖται καὶ ἔστιν ὁ Χριστός, ἀλλ᾽ ἕνα ἴσμεν Υἱόν."[86]

Ἰωάννου τοῦ Χρυσοστόμου ἐκ τοῦ εἰς τὸν Λάζαρον· "Ὁ 1828C κασσίτερος μολίβδου καὶ ἀργύρου μετέχει, ἀργύρου τὴν ὄψιν, μολίβδου τὴν φύσιν. Τὸν αὐτὸν τρόπον καὶ ὁ Χριστὸς θεότητος καὶ ἀνθρωπότητος τελείως τὰς φύσεις ἐν ἑαυτῷ ἀποσώζει· ὥσπερ οὖν ἐν ἑαυτῷ ἔχει τὰς φύσεις, οὕτω καὶ αὐτὸς ἐν αὐταῖς ἐστιν, οὐχ᾽ ὑπάρχων ἕτερος παρ᾽ αὐτάς."[87]

---

[82] Ambrose, *Explanation of the Creed*. Greek attested in Theodoret, *Eranistes*, Florilegium 2, ed. G. H. Ettlinger, *Eranistes* (Oxford: Clarendon Press, 1975), 163.

[83] Ambrose, *On the Incarnation*, ed. O. Faller, *Sancti Ambrosii opera pars nova*, CSEL lxxix (1964), 248 (Latin).

[84] Ps.-Julius of Rome, *On the Union* = H. Lietzmann, *Apollinaris von Laodicea und seine Schule: Texte und Untersuchungen* (Tübingen: J. C. B. Mohr, 1904), 193. Cited at 1841B as a comment by Severus.

[85] Gregory of Nyssa, *Letter to Philip the Monk*. Attested in John of Damascus, *PG* xlvi, 1112C; Latin attestation in G. Mercati, *Codici latini Pico Grimani Pio e di altra biblioteca ignota del secolo XVI esistenti nell'Ottoboniana e i codici greci Pio di Moderna*, ST 75 (Vatican City: Biblioteca apostolica vaticana, 1938), 195.

[86] Not otherwise attested.   [87] Not otherwise attested.

Saint Ambrose, Bishop of Milan, from his *Interpretation of the Holy Symbol*: 'The Catholic and Apostolic Church anathematizes those who say,' after some things in the middle, 'that Christ's natures became one nature as a result of being confused by mixture, and who do not confess our Lord Jesus Christ to be two unconfused natures but one person, just as there is one Christ and one Lord.'[ix] We're compelled, though, to cut short our citations so as not to make our book too long and heavy.

The same, from *On the Divine Incarnation*: 'Certain people sprang up who said the Lord's flesh and His divinity were of one nature. What hell vomited up so great a blasphemy?'

Julius, Bishop of Rome, the text that Cyril brought forward in the council about [union]: 'He who recognizes the properties, and preserves the union, will not speak falsely about the natures, nor will he fail to recognize the union.'

Gregory of Nyssa to Philip the monk on the opposition of the Arians, a text of which the opening words are 'Wickedness is what is begotten by a soul': 'What I am saying when I use the word "unconfused" is that, even though the things combined are one in an inexpressible and ineffable union, they are not one by nature'—for the divine is different from the body, being alien to it. This means that the Christ who exists as two natures, and is truly recognized in them, is a single person, and at the same time unconfused.

The same, from his works against [the Arians]: 'Even though Christ is understood and exists in two natures, we still observe one Son.'

John Chrysostom, from the [sermon] on Lazarus: 'Tin partakes of lead and of silver: it partakes of silver's appearance, and of lead's nature. In the same way Christ preserves in Himself perfectly the natures of divinity and humanity. Just as He has their natures in Himself, so also He is in them, since He does not subsist as someone different from them.'

1828A

1828B

1828c

Ἐφραὶμ τοῦ Σύρου, ἐκ τοῦ εἰς τὸν μαργαρίτην· " Ἐπίβλεψον τῷ
μαργαρίτῃ, καὶ βλέπεις τὰς δύο φύσεις συνέχοντα· φαιδρότατός
ἐστι διὰ τὴν θεότητα, λευκὸς διὰ τὴν πρόσληψιν."[88]

Ἰσιδώρου τοῦ Πιλουσιώτου πρὸς τὸν πάπαν Κύριλλον τὸν
Ἀλεξανδρείας· "Ὅτι δὲ ὁ ἀληθινὸς καὶ ἐπὶ πάντων Θεὸς[89]
ἄνθρωπος γέγονε, οὔτε ὃ ἦν τραπείς, καὶ ὃ οὐκ ἦν προσλαβών, ἐν
δύο φύσεσιν εἷς ὑπάρχων Υἱός, ἄτρεπτος καὶ ἀναλλοίωτος,
1828D πρόσφατος καὶ ἀΐδιος, οὐδ' ἂν αὐτὸς ἀρνηθείης, πλείστας ἔχων τοῦ
ἁγίου πατρὸς ἡμῶν τοῦ μεγάλου Ἀθανασίου περὶ τούτων
συναινέσεις".[90]

Παύλου ἐπισκόπου Ἐμέσης ἐκ τοῦ ῥηθέντος ἐν τῇ Ἀλεξανδρέων
ἐκκλησίᾳ λόγου ὑπ' αὐτοῦ παρουσίᾳ Κυρίλλου πατριάρχου, ὃν
εὐφήμησε καὶ ἀπεδέξατο καὶ ἐνεκωμίασεν εὐθὺς ἐπειπὼν καὶ αὐτὸς
λόγον ἐν ᾧ φησί· "Ἠντλήσαμεν ἡμῖν ὕδωρ"· "Ὅρα καὶ τὸν
Ἰωάννην δύο φύσεις κηρύττοντα καὶ ἕνα Υἱόν· ἕτερον σκηνὴ, καὶ
ἕτερον τὸ σκηνοῦν· ἕτερον ναός, καὶ ἕτερον ὁ ἐνοικῶν Θεός.
Πρόσεχε τῷ λεγομένῳ· οὐκ εἶπον 'ἕτερος καὶ ἕτερος' ὡς ἐπὶ δύο
προσώπων, ἢ χριστῶν ἢ δύο υἱῶν, ἀλλ' 'ἕτερον καὶ ἕτερον' ὡς ἐπὶ
δύο φύσεων".[91]

1829A Κυρίλλου ἐκ τῆς ἐπιστολῆς τῆς πρὸς Ἰωάννην Ἀντιοχείας καὶ
τὴν ὑπ' αὐτοῦ ἁγίαν σύνοδον, ἐν ᾗ φησιν ἀποδέξασθαι αὐτοῦ τὰ
γράμματα, ὀρθῶς ἔχοντα τάδε· [282ʳ] "Τὰς δὲ εὐαγγελικὰς καὶ
ἀποστολικὰς περὶ τοῦ Κυρίου φωνὰς ἴσμεν τοὺς θεηγόρους ἄνδρας,
τὰς μὲν κοινοποιοῦντας ὡς ἐφ' ἑνὸς προσώπου, τὰς δὲ διαιροῦντας
ὡς ἐπὶ δύο φύσεων."[92] Ἰδοὺ γοῦν οὗτος καὶ διαίρεσιν τῶν κατὰ τὰς
φύσεις σημαινομένων ὁμολογῶν, οὐ τὴν ἕνωσιν διαλύειν ἐνεβλήθη.
Περὶ δὲ αὐτοῦ καὶ τῆς συνόδου αὐτοῦ, τάδε γράφει πρὸς
Οὐαλεριανὸν ἐπίσκοπον Ἰκονίου· "Οἱ γάρ τοι κατὰ τὴν Ἑῴαν
ἄπαντες θεοσεβέστατοι ἐπίσκοποι ἅμα τῷ θεοσεβεστάτῳ
ἐπισκόπῳ τῆς Ἀντιοχέων Ἰωάννῃ καὶ δι' ἐγγράφου καὶ σαφοῦς
ὁμολογίας φανερὸν ἅπασι κατέστησαν, ὅτι τὰς μὲν βεβήλους
1829B Νεστορίου κενοφωνίας κατακρίνουσί τε καὶ ἀναθεματίζουσι
μεθ' ἡμῶν, καὶ οὐδενὸς αὐτὰς ἠξίωσαν πῶ ποτε λόγου, ἀλλὰ τοῖς
ἀποστολικοῖς ἕπονται δόγμασι, καὶ τὴν τῶν πατέρων ὁμολογίαν
κατ' οὐδένα λυποῦσι τρόπον."[93] Εἶτα εἰπὼν ἃ φασίν, ἐπάγει· "Ἂν

---

[88] Ps.-Ephrem, *Homily on the Pearl*. Not otherwise attested.
[89] Rom. 9: 5
[90] Isidore of Pelusium, *Letters* i, 323, *PG* lxxviii, 369B.
[91] Paul of Emesa, *Sermon on the Nativity*, *ACO* i, 1, 4, 13.
[92] Cyril of Alexandria, *Letter* 39, *ACO* i, 1, 4, 17. Cited also at 1821C and 1852B–C.
[93] Cyril of Alexandria, *Letter* 50, *ACO* i, 1, 3, 100.

Ephrem of Syria, from the homily on the pearl: 'Look closely at the pearl, and you see it encompassing two natures: it is brilliant on account of the divinity, and it is white on account of the assumption.'

Isidore of Pelusium, to Pope Cyril of Alexandria: 'You yourself would not deny that the true *God over all* became a man, not changing what He was, yet taking on what He was not, one existing Son in two natures, immutable and unchangeable, both new and eternal, since you have an exceedingly large number of proofs concerning these issues from our holy father, the great Athanasius'. 1828D

Paul, Bishop of Emesa, from the statement made by him in the Alexandrian church in the presence of the patriarch Cyril, whom he honoured and approved and praised, then instantly added a statement of his own in which he says 'We drew water to us': 'Consider John when he proclaims two natures and one Son, one a tent, and the other the one who dwells in that tent, one a temple, and the other the indwelling God. Pay attention to what is said: he did not say "one [person] and another", as of two persons or Christs, or as of two sons, but "one [thing] and another", as of two natures.'

Of Cyril, from the letter to John of Antioch and the holy synod held under him, in which he says the latter's writings are received, since they're correct: 'We recognize that theologians hold some evangelical and apostolic texts about the Lord to be common, as concerning one person, but distinguish others of them as concerning two natures.' Notice: this man, though he also confesses a difference of things signified in terms of natures, wasn't driven to dissolve the union. Here's what he writes to Valerian, Bishop of Iconium, about John and his synod: 'All the most pious bishops of the Orient, along with John the most pious bishop of Antioch, made it evident to everyone in writing and by a clear confession that they condemn and anathematize along with us the profane babblings of Nestorius, never thought them worthy of any kind of rational regard, follow instead the apostolic doctrines, and do not compromise the fathers' confession in any way.' Then, using their words, he adds: 'Though certain deluded men may say [the bishops of the Orient] think something different from this, they are not to be trusted, but must be dismissed as cheats and liars like their father the Devil, lest they throw into confusion people who want to walk in the right way.' Since Cyril bears witness to these 1829A 1829B

τοίνυν ψευδόμενοί τινες λέγωσιν ἕτερά τινα παρ' αὐτὰ φρονεῖν αὐτούς, μὴ πιστευέσθωσαν, ἀλλ' ὡς ἀπατεῶνες καὶ ψεῦσται κατὰ τὸν αὐτῶν πατέρα διάβολον[94] ἀποπεμπέσθωσαν, ἵνα μὴ θορυβῶσι τοὺς ἐθέλοντας ὀρθοποδεῖν."[95] Ταῦτα Κυρίλλου μαρτυροῦντος ἡμῖν, τί ὥσπερ ἀπ' αὐτοῦ πολεμεῖν τῇ τῶν δύο φύσεων Χριστοῦ ὁμολογίᾳ προσποιοῦνται οἱ συκοφάνται;

Κυρίλλου παραγωγὴ χρήσεως Ἀμβροσίου· "Φυλάξωμεν τὴν
1829C διαφορὰν τῆς θεότητος καὶ τῆς σαρκός· ἐν ἑκατέρᾳ λαλεῖ ὁ τοῦ Θεοῦ Υἱός· ἑκατέρα γὰρ φύσις ἐν αὐτῷ ἐστι."[96]

Κυρίλλου, ἐκ τῆς περὶ τῆς ἐνανθρωπήσεως ἐπιστολῆς· "Οὐ διαιρετέον οὖν ἄρα τὸν ἕνα Κύριον καὶ Υἱὸν καὶ Χριστὸν εἰς ἄνθρωπον ἰδικῶς καὶ εἰς Θεὸν ἰδικῶς, ἀλλ' ἕνα καὶ τὸν αὐτὸν Χριστὸν καὶ Υἱὸν εἶναι φαμέν, τὴν τῶν φύσεων εἰδότες διαφοράν, καὶ ἀσυγχύτους ἀλλήλαις τηροῦντες αὐτάς."[97]

Τοῦ αὐτοῦ· "Νοεῖται δὲ πάντως ἕτερον ἐν ἑτέρῳ, τουτέστιν ἡ θεία φύσις ἐν ἀνθρωπότητι."[98]

Τοῦ αὐτοῦ ἐκ τῆς ἑρμηνείας τῆς πρὸς Ἑβραίους ἐπιστολῆς·
1829D "Νοουμένης δὲ μᾶλλον καὶ ὑπαρχούσης ἑκατέρας ἐν τῷ τῆς ἰδίας φύσεως ὅρῳ πεπρᾶχθαι τὴν ἕνωσιν".[99] Καὶ πάλιν· "Οὐκ ἀνάχυσίν τινα τὴν εἰς ἄλληλα τῶν φύσεων πεπρᾶχθαι φαμέν, μενούσης δὲ μᾶλλον ἑκατέρας τοῦτο ὅπέρ ἐστιν, ἡνῶσθαι σαρκὶ νοοῦμεν τὸν Λόγον."[100]

Τοῦ αὐτοῦ ἐκ τοῦ τρίτου τόμου πρὸς Νεστόριον· "Οὐκοῦν ὅσον μὲν ἧκεν εἰς ἔννοιαν, καὶ εἰς μόνον τὸ ὁρᾶν τοῖς τῆς ψυχῆς ὄμμασι τίνα τρόπον ἐνηνθρώπησεν ὁ Μονογενής, δύο τὰς φύσεις εἶναι φαμέν, ἕνα δὲ Χριστὸν καὶ Υἱὸν καὶ Κύριον τὸν τοῦ Θεοῦ Λόγον ἐνανθρωπήσαντα καὶ σεσαρκωμένον."[101] Ἀλλ' οἱ σαρκοβλέπται
1832A ὄντες, καὶ μόνον εἰ μὴ τοῖς σαρκὸς ὄμμασι θεωρεῖταί τι, οὐκ ὄντως εἶναι τόδε οἴονται. Ἄρα οὖν οὐδὲ ἄγγελος, οὐδὲ Θεὸς ἔσται, οὐδέ τι τῶν νοητῶν ἁπλῶς.

---

[94] Cf. John 8: 44
[95] Cyril of Alexandria, *Letter* 50, *ACO* i, 1, 3, 101.
[96] Ambrose, *On the Faith (to Gratian)* ii, ed. O. Faller, *Sancti Ambrosii opera pars* viii, *CSEL* lxxviii (1962), 84 (Latin).
[97] Cyril of Alexandria, *Scholia, ACO* i, 5, 222.
[98] Ibid. *ACO* i, 5, 228.
[99] Cyril of Alexandria, *On Hebrews, PG* lxxiv, 1004A.   [100] Ibid.
[101] Actually Cyril of Alexandria, *Letter* 45, *ACO* i, 1, 6, 153–4. Cited in part at 1857C.

facts for us, why do the slanderers pretend it's on his behalf that they attack the confession of Christ's two natures?

A text of Ambrose introduced by Cyril: 'Let us preserve the difference between divinity and flesh. The Son of God speaks in each of them, for each nature is in Him.'   1829C

Cyril, from the letter on the Incarnation: 'One must not divide the one Lord and Son and Christ independently into a man and a God. What we say, rather, is that there is one and the same Christ and Son, while recognizing the difference of natures, and while keeping them from being confused with each other.'

The same: 'What is perfectly understood is that one thing is in another, i.e. the divine nature is in humanity.'

The same, from the interpretation of the Epistle to the Hebrews: 'each rather being understood and existing in the defin-   1829D
ition of its own nature, that the union has been effected'. And again: 'We do not say that any confusion of the natures with each other has been effected, but rather, since each instead remains precisely what it is, we understand that the Word has been united with flesh.'

The same, from the third book against Nestorius: 'Therefore, it is inasmuch as the Only Begotten has become present to our understanding, and became man in some way perceptible only to the eyes of the soul, that we say there are two natures, but one Christ and Son and Lord, the Word of God become man and incarnate.' Those who are materialists, however, don't recognize something as really existing unless it's beheld with eyes of flesh. In   1832A
that case there will exist neither angel, nor God, nor—to put it simply—any of the realities apprehended by the intellect.

Τοῦ αὐτοῦ, ἐκ τῆς πρὸς Ἰοῦστον τὸν ἐπίσκοπον Ῥώμης ἐπιστολῆς· "Ἐγὼ γὰρ οὔτε ἐλέγχομαι πεφρονηκὼς ἕτερόν τι πῶ ποτε παρὰ τὸ δοκοῦν τῇ ἀληθείᾳ, οὔτε παθητὴν εὕρηκα ποτὲ τὴν θείαν τοῦ Λόγου [282ᵛ] φύσιν."¹⁰² Καὶ μετὰ βραχύ· "Οἶδα δὲ καὶ ἀπαθῆ τὴν τοῦ Θεοῦ φύσιν καὶ ἄτρεπτον καὶ ἀναλλοίωτον κἂν τῇ τῆς ἀνθρωπότητος φύσει, καὶ ἕνα ἐν ἀμφοῖν καὶ ἐξ ἀμφοῖν τὸν Χριστόν."¹⁰³

Ἀθανασίου ἐν τῇ ἐξηγήσει τοῦ <u>Ἀμὴν ἀμὴν λέγω ὑμῖν πρὶν Ἀβραὰμ γενέσθαι ἐγώ εἰμι</u>·¹⁰⁴ "'Αναισχυντία σαφῶς τὸ μὴ διχῶς νοεῖν τὸν Χριστόν θεϊκῶς τε καὶ ἀνθρωπίνως."¹⁰⁵ Ἐν δὲ τῷ κατὰ Ἀρειανῶν τρίτῳ λόγῳ φησί· "Πάντα τὰ κατὰ τὸν καιρὸν τῆς ἐνανθρωπήσεως τῷ Σωτῆρι Χριστῷ πεπραγμένα, ἤγουν λελεγμένα πράγματά τε καὶ ῥήματα, τὸ μονοειδὲς οὐκ ἔχει, διάφορα δέ ἐστι."¹⁰⁶

Τοῦ ἁγίου Κυρίλλου ἐκ τοῦ πρὸς Ἀλεξανδρεῖς προσφωνητικοῦ λόγου· "Ἡ δὲ ἄρρητος ἕνωσις, παρὰ τῶν ὀρθῶς φρονούντων ὁμολογουμένη, ἀμφοτέρας σώζει ἀσυγχύτους τὰς φύσεις, καὶ ἕνα ἀποτελεῖ καὶ ἐξ ἀμφοῖν τὸν ὀφθέντα Χριστόν, Θεὸν τὲ ὁμοῦ καὶ ἄνθρωπον γενόμενον τὸν αὐτόν, καὶ οὐ δύο Χριστοὺς, ἕνα δὲ μόνον ἑνωθέντα καὶ οὐ κεκραμμένον· εἰ γὰρ κέκρανται αἱ δύο φύσεις εἰς μίξιν μίαν, ἑτεροούσιοι τυγχάνουσαι, οὐδὲ ὁποτέρα σώζεται, ἀλλ' ἀμφότεραι συγχυθεῖσαι ἠφανίσθησαν. Καὶ οὔτε χωρισμὸν ἀπ' ἀλλήλων ἢ διαίρεσιν ἐπιδέχονται κεκραμμέναι, διῃρέθησαν δὲ τῷ καιρῷ τοῦ θανάτου καὶ ἐχωρίσθησαν, καὶ ψυχὴ ἀπὸ σώματος εἰς Ἅδου μετὰ τῆς θεότητος κατελθοῦσα, καὶ σῶμα ἀπὸ ψυχῆς ἐν μνήματι καινῷ ἀποτεθὲν κατὰ τὰς ἀψευδεῖς τοῦ Χριστοῦ φωνὰς τὰς λεγούσας <u>Λύσατε τὸν ναὸν τοῦτον, καὶ ἐν τρισὶν ἡμέραις ἐγερῶ αὐτόν</u>.¹⁰⁷ Καὶ λύεται μὲν ὁ ναὸς ἐν τῷ καιρῷ τῆς τριημέρου ταφῆς, βουλομένου αὐτοῦ, καὶ πάλιν ἀνέστησεν αὐτόν, καὶ ἡνώθη αὐτῷ ἀρρήτῳ καὶ ἀφράστῳ λόγῳ, οὐ κεκραμμένος ἐν αὐτῷ ἢ ἀποσεσαρκωμένος, ἀλλ' ἀποσώζων ἐν ἑαυτῷ τῶν φύσεων τῶν ἑτεροουσίων ἀσυγχύτους τὰς ἰδιότητας· οὐ γὰρ δήπου ἐκράθησαν αἱ φύσεις."¹⁰⁸ Εἶτα ἐπάγεται μαρτυρίαν τοῦ ἐν ἁγίοις Ἀθανασίου αὐτὸς τήνδε· "Δύο φύσεων τῶν ἑτεροουσίων ἐν ἑνὶ Χριστῷ καὶ Υἱῷ τοῦ Θεοῦ σωζομένων, καὶ μήτε συγχεομένων μήτε ἀπολλυμένων ἢ διαιρεθεισῶν."¹⁰⁹

---

¹⁰² Cyril of Alexandria, *Letter 53, to Xystus, Bishop of Rome*. Not otherwise attested.
¹⁰³ Ibid.   ¹⁰⁴ John 8: 58
¹⁰⁵ Athanasius, *On the text 'Amen, amen, I say unto you'*. Attested by John 'the Grammarian' of Caesarea, cited by Severus, *Against the Grammarian* iii, 32, ed. J. Lebon, *CSCO*, Scriptores Syri, series 4, vi (1933), 97.
¹⁰⁶ Actually Severus, *Against the Grammarian* iii, 33, 98.   ¹⁰⁷ John 2: 19
¹⁰⁸ Cyril of Alexandria, *Sermon on the Faith Addressed to the Alexandrians*, PG lxxvii, 1112C–1113A and n. 1.
¹⁰⁹ Ibid. 1113A. The citation from 'Athanasius' cannot be authentic.

The same, from the letter to Justus, Bishop of Rome: 'I have never yet been put to shame for thinking anything except what is consonant with the truth, nor have I ever called the Word's divine nature passible.' And after a little: 'I know that God's nature is impassible, immutable, and unchangeable even in the humanity's nature, and that Christ is one in both of them, and out of both of them.'

Athanasius, in his exegesis of *Amen, amen, I say to you, before Abraham was I am*: 'It is clearly a shameless thing not to understand Christ in two ways, a divine way, and a human way.' In *Against the Arians* iii he says: 'All the various things done by Christ our Saviour at the time of the Incarnation—stories, actions, sayings—do not fit into one category; they are different.'   1832B

Holy Cyril, from the work addressed to the Alexandrians: 'The ineffable union, as confessed among right-minded people, keeps both natures unconfused, and completes the one visible Christ out of both of them, the same being at once God and man, not two Christs, but a single Christ, united, not mixed. That is so because, if two natures that happen to be different in substance are mixed in a single mixture, neither is preserved; actually, both are destroyed when they are confused. They admit of no separation or distinction from each other when they are mixed, yet they were distinguished and divided at the time of death: a soul divided from a body descended into Hell with the divinity, and a body divided from a soul was laid in a new tomb, in accordance with what Christ accurately said, *Destroy this temple, and in three days I shall raise it up*. The temple was destroyed at the time of His three-day entombment, as He willed, and He raised it again, and was united with it in an ineffable and unutterable way. He was not mingled in it, nor was He turned into flesh. Rather, He kept unconfused in Himself the properties of natures that differed in substance, for the natures were never mingled.' He himself then introduces the following testimony of Athanasius, who is among the saints: 'there being two natures, different in essence, preserved in one Christ and one Son of God, neither confused, nor destroyed or divided'.   1832C   1832D

Τοῦ αὐτοῦ, ἐκ τῆς βίβλου τῶν χρήσεων· "Καὶ οἱ μὲν μίαν φύσιν
πρὸς ἀναίρεσιν τῆς προσληφθείσης ἐξ ἡμῶν ὑπὸ τοῦ Θεοῦ Λόγου
τελείας ἀνθρωπότητος ἐπὶ σωτηρίᾳ τῶν ὅλων ἐκδιδάσκουσιν, οἱ
δὲ δύο ὑποστάσεις, ἤγουν φύσεις, κατὰ διαίρεσιν καὶ χωρισμὸν
ἐκπαιδεύουσιν, ἀλλ' οὐ καθ' ἕνωσιν τὴν κατ' οὐσίαν ὡς τοῖς ἁγίοις
δοκεῖ πατράσιν, ὡς ἑκατέρους αὐτοὺς τῆς ἀληθείας
διαμαρτάνειν."[110] Τί τούτων σαφέστερον; μόνον γὰρ τῷ κατὰ
1833A   διαίρεσιν καὶ χωρισμὸν τὸν ἀπ' ἀλλήλων εἰδέναι τὰς δύο φύσεις
τούτους ἐμέμψατο, ὡς καὶ ὑπόστασιν ἰδίᾳ ἑκάστῃ συνεισάγεσθαι,
καὶ μὴ τῇ κατ' οὐσίαν πρὸς οὐσίαν ἑνώσει, ἐν πρόσωπον [283ʳ]
τὰς δύο ὑφιστάνειν· τὴν μέντοι μίαν φύσιν καὶ παντοίως
ἀπεστράφη.

Κυρίλλου ἐκ τοῦ περὶ πίστεως λόγου· "'Ἀλλὰ γὰρ ναὸν ἑαυτῷ
ἔμψυχον καὶ τέλειον κατεσκεύασεν ἐν τῇ ἁγίᾳ παρθενικῇ μήτρᾳ, καὶ
ἐνδυσάμενος αὐτὸν καὶ ἑνωθεὶς αὐτῷ ἀρρήτῳ λόγῳ, σωζομένων δὲ
ἀμφοτέρων τῶν φύσεων καὶ οὐ κεκραμένων, προῆλθε φαινόμενος
μὲν ἄνθρωπος, νοούμενος δὲ Θεὸς Ἰησοῦς Χριστός."[111]
1833B   Τοῦ αὐτοῦ ἐκ τῆς πρὸς Σούκενσον ἐπιστολῆς· "Δύο τὰς φύσεις
εἶναι φαμέν, ἕνα δὲ Χριστὸν καὶ Υἱὸν τὸν τοῦ Θεοῦ Λόγον
ἐνανθρωπήσαντα καὶ σεσαρκωμένον."[112]
Τοῦ αὐτοῦ· "Οὐχ' ὡς τῆς τῶν φύσεων διαφορᾶς ἀναιρεθησομένης
διὰ τὴν ἕνωσιν."[113]

Τοῦ αὐτοῦ ἐκ τῆς πρὸς Σούκενσον δευτέρας ἐπιστολῆς,
δηλοῦντος ὡς οὐ τῷ λέγειν σεσαρκῶσθαι τὸν Υἱόν, καὶ φύρειν τὰς
φύσεις βούλεται. "Εἰ γὰρ καὶ λέγοιτο πρὸς ἡμῶν ὁ μονογενὴς Υἱὸς
τοῦ Θεοῦ σεσαρκωμένος καὶ ἐνανθρωπήσας, οὐ πέφυρται διατοῦτο
κατὰ τὸ ἐκείνοις δοκοῦν, οὔτε μὴν εἰς τὴν τῆς σαρκὸς φύσιν
μεταπεφοίτηκεν ἡ τοῦ Λόγου, ἀλλ' οὔτε ἡ τῆς σαρκὸς εἰς τὴν αὐτοῦ,
1833C   ἀλλ' ἐν ἰδιότητι τῇ κατὰ φύσιν ἑκατέρου μένοντος κατά γε τὸν
ἀρτίως ἡμῖν ἀποδοθέντα λόγον."[114] Εἰ δὲ μήτε κατὰ φύρσιν μήτε
κατὰ τροπήν, πῶς ἔσται μία φύσις, λεγέτω τις. Τί δέ ἐστι καὶ τὸ
μένον ἑκάτερον, καὶ ἐν ἰδιότητι φυσικῇ ὄν;

---

[110] Not otherwise attested.
[111] Cyril of Alexandria, *On the Faith*. Not otherwise attested.
[112] Cyril of Alexandria, *Letter* 45, *ACO* i, 1, 6, 154.
[113] Cyril of Alexandria, *Letter* 4, *ACO* i, 1, 1, 27.
[114] Cyril of Alexandria, *Letter* 46, *ACO* i, 1, 6, 159–60.

The same, from the *Book of Citations*: 'The former teach one nature, with the effect of destroying the complete humanity from us added by God the Word for the salvation of complete human beings. The latter teach two hypostases, i.e. natures, in the sense of division and separation, but not in the sense of the union by substance favoured by the holy fathers. Thus both of them fall short of the truth.' What could be clearer than that? The only thing he found fault with was the way they saw these two natures   1833A
in terms of division and separation from each other, so that an hypostasis was introduced for each of them individually, rather than envisaging one person subsisting under the two natures in a union by substance in [one] substance. In all kinds of ways, then, he rejected one nature.

Cyril, from *On Faith*: 'Rather, He made a temple for Himself in the Virgin's holy womb, a temple animated by a soul and complete. When He had put it on and been united with it in an ineffable way, though both the natures were preserved and not mingled, there came forth Jesus Christ, seen as a man, understood as God.'

The same, from the *Letter to Succensus*: 'We say there are two   1833B
natures, but one Christ and Son, the Word of God become man, and incarnate.'

The same: 'the difference of the natures thus not being destroyed by the union'.

Of the same from the *Second Letter to Succensus*, showing that he doesn't intend, by saying that the Son has been incarnated, to mix the natures: 'If the only-begotten Son of God is said on our part to be incarnated and made man, that does not mean He is mixed, as seems to our opponents to be the case, nor has the Word's nature turned into the flesh's nature, but neither has the flesh's nature turned into the Word's nature. On the contrary, each   1833C
remains in the property that belongs to it by nature, as we just explained.' Someone needs to tell us how there exists one nature, if it's not by mixing or change. What is it that each remains, and that exists in its natural property?

Τοῦ αὐτοῦ ἐκ τῆς πρὸς Εὐλόγιον ἐπιστολῆς, καὶ ὅτι οὐ τὸ δύο
λέγειν, ἀλλὰ τὸ μὴ ἡνωμένας καθ᾽ ὑπόστασιν, ἀποβάλλεται· "Οὕτω
καὶ ἐπὶ Νεστορίου, κἂν λέγῃ δύο φύσεις, τὴν διαφορὰν σημαίνων
τῆς σαρκὸς καὶ τοῦ Θεοῦ Λόγου—ἑτέρα γὰρ ἡ τοῦ Θεοῦ Λόγου
φύσις καὶ ἑτέρα ἡ τῆς σαρκὸς—, ἀλλ᾽ οὐκέτι τὴν ἕνωσιν ὁμολογεῖ
1833D   μεθ᾽ ἡμῶν."¹¹⁵ Ὥστε οὖν τὸ δύο εἶναι φύσεις, μεθ᾽ ἡμῶν καὶ αὐτὸς
ὁμολογεῖ, φησί.

Τοῦ αὐτοῦ, ἐκ τῆς πρὸς Ἰωάννην ἐπιστολῆς· "Εἷς γὰρ Κύριος
Ἰησοῦς Χριστός, κἂν ἡ τῶν φύσεων μὴ ἀγνοῆται διαφορά."¹¹⁶ Τῶν
ἄρα οὐσῶν, ἢ τῶν μὴ οὐσῶν, ἔστιν ἡ διαφορά;

Γρηγορίου Νύσσης, ἐκ τοῦ κατὰ Ἀπολιναρίου· "Εἰ οὖν ἐν τοῖς
ἐναντίοις ἰδιώμασιν ἡ ἑκατέρου τούτων θεωρεῖται φύσις, τῆς
σαρκὸς λέγω καὶ τῆς θεότητος, πῶς μία αἱ δύο φύσεις εἰσίν;"¹¹⁷

Κυρίλλου, ἐκ τοῦ πρώτου βιβλίου τῶν Θησαυρῶν, ὅτι οὐσῶν
τῶν οὐσιῶν, ἀνάγκη εἶναι τὰς οὐσιώδεις διαφοράς· "Οὐκοῦν
προϋποκειμένης τῆς οὐσίας, αἱ διαφοραὶ προσεπινοοῦνται."¹¹⁸

1836A   Ἰσιδώρου τοῦ Πιλουσιώτου, ἐκ τῆς πρὸς Τιμόθεον ἀναγνώστην
ἐπιστολῆς· "Πάσῃ τοίνυν φυλακῇ τήρει σὴν καρδίαν, μήπου μίαν
φύσιν Χριστοῦ μετὰ τὴν σάρκωσιν δέξῃ."¹¹⁹

Θεοδότου ἐπισκόπου Ἀντιοχείας, ἐκ τοῦ κατὰ Συνουσιαστῶν·
"Εὖ ἴστωσαν ὅτι ἡμεῖς τὸν Χριστὸν δύο φύσεις ὁμολογοῦντες,
ἑκατέρᾳ μὲν φύσει τὰ πρόσφορα νέμομεν, ἀλλὰ πάντα καθ᾽ ἑνὸς
προσώπου τοῦ Υἱοῦ κατηγοροῦντες."¹²⁰

Κυρίλλου Ἱεροσολύμων, ἐκ τοῦ εἰς τὸ Ἐγὼ πορεύομαι πρὸς τὸν
Πατέρα μου·¹²¹ "Φαίνεσθαι δὲ τὴν διάγνωσιν τῶν φύσεων ἐκ τῆς
[283ᵛ] διαφορᾶς τῶν λεγομένων".¹²²

1836B   Πέτρου μάρτυρος πάπα Ἀλεξανδρείας, ἐκ τοῦ περὶ τῆς
ἐπιδημίας τοῦ Χριστοῦ· "Τὸ συναμφότερον τοίνυν δείκνυται, ὅτι
Θεὸς ἦν φύσει, καὶ γέγονεν ἄνθρωπος φύσει."¹²³

Σεβηριανοῦ Γαβάλων· "Οὕτω Θεόν τε καὶ ἄνθρωπον ὁμολογεῖ
τὸν Χριστὸν τὸν Υἱὸν τοῦ Θεοῦ, δύο φύσεων, παθητῆς καὶ
ἀπαθοῦς."¹²⁴

---

¹¹⁵ Cyril of Alexandria, *Letter* 44, *ACO* i, 1, 4, 35.
¹¹⁶ Cyril of Alexandria, *Letter* 39, *ACO* i, 1, 4, 18–19.
¹¹⁷ Gregory of Nyssa, *Against Apollinarius*, ed. F. Mueller, *Gregorii Nysenni Opera Dogmatica Minora* 1 = W. Jaeger (ed.), *Gregorii Nysseni Opera* iii, 1 (Leiden: E. J. Brill, 1958), 196.
¹¹⁸ Cyril of Alexandria, *Thesaurus* 2, *PG* lxxv, 28D.
¹¹⁹ Isidore of Pelusium, *Letters* i, 102, *PG* lxxviii, 252C.
¹²⁰ Not otherwise attested.   ¹²¹ John 14: 12
¹²² Not otherwise attested.
¹²³ Peter of Alexandria, *On the Lord's Advent*. Attested in Leontius of Byzantium, *Against the Nestorians and Monophysites*, *PG* lxxxvi, 1312B, and in Justinian, *Against the Monophysites*, E. Schwartz (ed.), *Drei dogmatische Schriften Iustinians* = M. Amelotti *et al.* (eds.), *Legum Iustiniani imperatoris vocabularium*, Subsidia ii (Milan: A Giuffrae, 1973), 50.
¹²⁴ Not otherwise attested.

The same, from the *Letter to Eulogius*, saying that what he rejects is not the use of the word 'two', but the refusal to speak of two [natures] united by hypostasis: 'It is the same in the case of Nestorius: even if he speaks of two natures, signifying the difference between the flesh and God the Word—for God the Word's nature is one, and the flesh's nature is another—all the same he does not confess the union along with us.' He's saying, in effect, that Nestorius does confess along with us that there are two natures. 1833D

The same, from the *Letter to John*: 'There is one Lord Jesus Christ, though the difference between the natures is not to be ignored.' Is this difference, then, between existent things, or non-existent?

Gregory of Nyssa, from *Against Apollinarius*: 'If, then, the nature of each of these is to be observed in their opposite properties—I am referring to the properties of flesh and of divinity—how can the two natures be one?'

Cyril, from the *Treasuries* i, saying that, since substances exist, there must exist differences in substance: 'Therefore, since the substance is already in existence, the differences are brought to mind.'

Isidore of Pelusium, from the *Letter to Timothy the Reader*: 'Guard 1836A your heart with all care, therefore, lest you accept at any time one nature of Christ after the Incarnation.'

Theodotus, Bishop of Antioch, from *Against the Synousiasts*: 'Let them realize full well that we who confess Christ as two natures distribute to each nature what is appropriate, but ascribe all things to one person of the Son'.

Cyril of Jerusalem from [his commentary] on *I go to my Father*: 'that the distinction between natures is disclosed on the basis of the difference between things said'.

Peter, Pope and martyr of Alexandria, from *On the Coming of* 1836B *Christ*: 'The combination therefore shows He was God by nature, and has become man by nature.'

Severian of Gabala: 'Thus he confesses Christ the Son of God to be both God and man, of two natures, a passible nature and an impassible one.'

Πρόκλου Κωνσταντινουπόλεως εἰς τὸ Παιδίον ἐγεννήθη ἡμῖν·[125]
"Καὶ ἔστιν εἷς Υἱός, οὐ τῶν φύσεων εἰς δύο ὑποστάσεις διῃρημένων,
ἀλλὰ τῆς φρικτῆς οἰκονομίας τὰς δύο φύσεις εἰς μίαν ὑπόστασιν
ἐνωσάσης."[126]

1836c   Σιλβέστρου ἐπισκόπου Ῥώμης, ἐκ τῶν πρὸς Ἰουδαίους· "Δύο
κατὰ ταὐτὸν ἡνωμένων φύσεων, ἡ μὲν μία περιπίπτει τῇ ὕβρει, ἡ δὲ
ἑτέρα κρείττων πάθους παντὸς ἀπεδείχθη."[127]

Πρόκλου εἰς τὴν γέννησιν τοῦ Κυρίου· "Ἐκεῖνος ἀφθάρτως
ἐγεννήθη, οὗ τὴν συζυγίαν τῶν φύσεων θεωρῶν ὁ Θωμᾶς κέκραγε
λέγων· Ὁ Κύριός μου καὶ ὁ Θεός μου.[128][129]

Τοῦ ἁγίου Ἱππολύτου, ἐκ τῶν εὐλογιῶν τοῦ Βαλαάμ· "Ἵνα
δειχθῇ τὸ συναμφότερον ἔχων ἐν ἑαυτῷ· τήν τε τοῦ Θεοῦ οὐσίαν καὶ
τὴν ἐξ ἀνθρώπων."[130]

Τοῦ ἁγίου Ἱλαρίου τοῦ Πικταβῶν, ἑνὸς ὄντος τῶν ἐν Νικαίᾳ, ἐκ
1836d τοῦ περὶ πίστεως ζ΄ λόγου· "Ταῦτα δὲ τούτου χάριν διὰ βραχέων
ὑπέδειξα, ἵνα ἑκατέραν φύσιν ἐν τῷ Κυρίῳ ἡμῶν Ἰησοῦ Χριστῷ
νοεῖσθαι μνημονεύωμεν."[131]

Σχόλιον· Ἐπειδὴ ἑκάτερα ταῖς οἰκείαις γεγένηνται[132] φύσεσιν,
ἕνα μὲν Κύριον Ἰησοῦν Χριστὸν ἐκεῖνον μνημόνευε τὸν ὄντα
ἀμφότερα.

Τοῦ αὐτοῦ Ἱλαρίου τοῦ ὁμολογητοῦ ἐν τῷ αὐτῷ λόγῳ· " Ἕν καὶ
ταὐτὸν δι᾽ ἑκατέρας φύσεως, πλὴν οὕτως, ὡς ἑκατέρῳ μηδετέρου
χηρεύειν."[133]

1837a   Τοῦ ἁγίου Ἀμβροσίου, ἐκ τοῦ τρίτου λόγου· "Διάστιξον οὖν καὶ
ἐνταῦθα τὰς φύσεις· βοηθὸν γὰρ εἶχεν ἡ σάρξ, οὐκ εἶχε δὲ ἡ
θεότης."[134]

---

[125] Isa. 9: 5 LXX
[126] Proclus of Constantinople, *Sermon on the Doctrine of the Incarnation*, PG lxv, 841–4.
Attestation elsewhere: C. Martin, 'Un florilège grec d'homélies christologiques des
IVᵉ et Vᵉ siècles sur la nativité (Paris Gr. 1491)', *Le Muséon*, 54 (1941), 46.
[127] Sylvester of Rome, *Against the Jews*. Attested also in John Maron, *Exposé de la foi et
autres opuscules, CSCO*, Scriptores Syri, ccx, (1988), 23–4.
[128] John 20: 28
[129] Proclus of Constantinople, *Sermon in Praise of Holy Mary, ACO* i, 1, 1, 104.
[130] Ps.-Hippolytus, *From the Praises of Balaam*. Other attestations: H. Achelis (ed.),
Hippolytus kleinere exegetische und homiletische Schriften, Hippolytus Werke, GCS 1 (1897), 82.
[131] Hilary of Poitiers, *On the Trinity* ix, ed. and tr. G-M. de Durand *et al.*, *La Trinité, SC*
462 (2001), 40.
[132] γεγένηνται] (γεγένη)ν(ται) supra lin. MS
[133] Hilary of Poitiers, *On the Trinity* ix, SC 462, 18.
[134] Ambrose, *On the Faith (to Gratian)* iii, *CSEL* lxxviii, 118 (Latin).

Proclus of Constantinople, on *Unto us a child is born*: 'There is also one Son, since the natures have not been divided into two hypostases, but rather the awe-inspiring Incarnation united the two natures into one hypostasis.'

Sylvester, Bishop of Rome, from *Against the Jews*: 'Of the two 1836c natures united in Him, one succumbs to injury, but the other is shown to be greater than any suffering.'

Proclus, *On the Nativity of the Lord*: 'He was born in a way untouched by corruption; when Thomas saw His combination of natures, he cried out saying *My Lord and my God.*'

Saint Hippolytus, from *Eulogies of Balaam*: 'so that He might be shown to have the combination in himself, both the substance of God, and the substance from men'.

Saint Hilary of Poitiers, one of those present at Nicaea, from *On Faith* vii: 'He indicated these things in few words for this pur- 1836d pose: that we might remember that each nature is understood in our Lord Jesus Christ.'

Scholion: Since both have been engendered by their proper natures, he calls to mind that one Lord Jesus Christ who is both.

The same Hilary, the Confessor, in the same work: 'One and the same through each nature, but in such a way that, for either, there should be no deprivation of the other.'

Saint Ambrose, from the third volume: 'Mark the difference 1837a between the natures here too: the flesh had an assistant, but the divinity did not.'

Τοῦ αὐτοῦ, ἐκ τῆς πρὸς τοὺς ὄχλους διαλέξεως· "Ὁ μίαν ἐκ δύο κατασκευάζων φύσιν, κρᾶσιν καὶ σύγχυσιν πάντως εἰσάγει."[135] Καὶ μετὰ βραχέα· "Δύο ἐπὶ τοῦ Χριστοῦ ὁμολογοῦμεν φύσεις ἡνωμένας ἀρρήτῳ ἑνώσει, καὶ μηδαμῶς ἀλλήλων χωριζομένας ἢ συγχεομένας, δηλονότι τοῦ ἑκάστῃ πρέποντος ἰδιώματος νοουμένου τε καὶ σωζομένου, εἰ καὶ ἕνα οἴδαμεν Χριστὸν Υἱὸν μονογενῆ· τὰ γὰρ συναμφότερα ἕνα ἀπετέλεσαν ἡμῖν Χριστόν, καὶ οὐ μίαν φύσιν."[136]

1837B　Τοῦ αὐτοῦ, ἐκ τῆς ἑρμηνείας τοῦ ἁγίου συμβόλου· "Λύεται γὰρ Χριστός, κατὰ τὴν ἐμὴν οὐσίαν ἣν ἀνέλαβε, καὶ λελυμένον ἐγείρει τὸν ναὸν αὐτοῦ κατὰ τὴν θείαν οὐσίαν.[137],[138]

Τοῦ αὐτοῦ, ἐκ τῆς πρὸς τοὺς φιλοπόνους· "Κἂν δύο ἐπιστάμεθα ἐν τῷ Χριστῷ φύσεις, οἴδαμεν μή δύο εἶναι υἱοὺς, ἀλλ' ἕνα, ὅμοιον τῷ Πατρὶ κατὰ τὸ ἀόρατον, ὅμοιον τῇ μητρὶ κατὰ τὸ ὁρατόν."[139]

Τοῦ αὐτοῦ, ἐκ τοῦ κατὰ Ἀπολιναρίου θ' λόγου· " Ὅτι ὁ Χριστὸς Υἱὸς ἐστὶ τοῦ Θεοῦ καὶ ἀΐδιος ἐκ Πατρὸς, καὶ τεχθεὶς ἐκ παρθένου· ὃν ὡς γίγαντα[140] ὁ ἅγιος Δαβὶδ ὁ προφήτης ἐξέφρασεν, ὅτι μόνος δίμορφος καὶ διττῆς εἴη φύσεως, κοι⟨νω⟩νῶν θεότητος καὶ
1837C　ἀνθρωπότητος".[141]

Τοῦ αὐτοῦ, ἐκ τοῦ ⟨πρὸς⟩ Ἀντωνῖνον ἐπίσκοπον λόγου· "Ἵνα τέλειος ἐν ἑκατέρᾳ φύσει τυγχάνῃ".[142]

Τοῦ αὐτοῦ ἐκ τοῦ πρὸς Γρατιανὸν β' λόγου· "Εἷς γὰρ Θεοῦ Υἱὸς ἐν ἑκατέρᾳ [284ʳ] λαλεῖ, ἐπειδήπερ ἑκατέρα φύσις ἐστὶν ἐν αὐτῷ."[143]

Ἀμφιλοχίου ἐπισκόπου Ἰκονίου πρὸς Ἀρειανούς· "Διάκρινον τὰς φύσεις, τήν τε τοῦ θεοῦ καὶ τοῦ ἀνθρώπου."[144]

Τοῦ αὐτοῦ, ἐκ τῆς πρὸς Σέλευκον ἐπιστολῆς· " Ἕνα Υἱὸν δύο
1837D　φύσεων, παθητῆς τε καὶ ἀπαθοῦς".[145] Καὶ μετὰ βραχέα· "Ὁ Χριστὸς ὁ Υἱὸς τοῦ Θεοῦ, ὁ δύο τελείων φύσεων εἷς Υἱός".[146] Καὶ μετ' ὀλίγα· "Ἕνα μὲν τὸν Υἱὸν τοῦ Θεοῦ δύο φύσεων φημί".[147] Καὶ μετ' ὀλίγα· "Οἰκειοῦται οὖν αὐτὸς ὁ Θεὸς Λόγος, πάσχων οὐδέν, τὰ τοῦ ναοῦ, ἐπειδὴ εἰς ἓν πρόσωπον συντελοῦσιν αἱ δύο φύσεις."[148]

---

[135] Ambrose, *To the Crowds*. Not otherwise attested.　　[136] Ibid.

[137] Cf. John 2: 19　　[138] See n. 82 above.

[139] Ambrose, *To the Diligent*. Not otherwise attested.

[140] Ps. 19: 5 LXX

[141] Actually Ambrose, *On the Incarnation* v, CSEL lxxix, 240 (Latin).

[142] Ambrose, *Letter* 46, PL xvi, 1196D.　　[143] See n. 96 above.

[144] Amphilochius of Iconium, *Oration on 'the Father is greater than I'*. Attested in Theodoret, *Eranistes* Florilegium II, Ettlinger, *Eranistes*, 107.

[145] Amphilochius of Iconium, *To Seleucus* = fragment 11 B2 in F. Cavallera, 'Fragments de Saint Amphiloque dans l'Hodegos et le Tome Dogmatique d'Anastase le Sinaïte', RHE 8 (1907), 489.

[146] Ibid. fr. 11 D2.　　[147] Ibid. fr. 11 E1, 490.　　[148] Ibid. fr. 11 E7–8.

The same, from his *Address to the Crowds*: 'Whoever makes one nature out of two introduces complete mixture and confusion.' And after a bit: 'We confess two natures in Christ united by an ineffable union, and in no way separated from or confused with each other, since clearly the property appropriate to each is recognized and preserved, though we know one Christ, the only-begotten Son, for the two together made one Christ for our sake, and not one nature.'

The same, from his *Interpretation of the Holy Symbol*: 'For Christ is destroyed in my substance, which He assumed, and in the divine substance raises up His destroyed temple.' 1837B

The same, from *To the Diligent*: 'Though we are aware of two natures in Christ, we know there are not two sons, but one, who is like His Father in terms of what is invisible, and like His mother in terms of what is visible.'

The same, from *Against Apollinarius* ix: 'because Christ is the Son of God and eternally from the Father, and is also born from a virgin, whom holy David the prophet described as being *like a giant*, because He alone is in two forms, and is double in nature, because He shares in divinity and humanity'. 1837C

The same, from the work *Against Antoninus the Bishop*: 'so that He might achieve completeness in each nature'.

The same, from *Against Gratian* ii: 'One Son of God speaks in each nature, seeing that each nature is in Him.'

Amphilochius, Bishop of Iconium, *Against Arians*: 'Distinguish the natures, the nature of God, and the nature of man.'

The same, from the *Letter to Seleucus*: 'one Son belonging to two natures, one passible, the other impassible'. And after a bit: 'Christ the Son of God, the one Son belonging to two complete natures'. And after a few things: 'I speak of one Son of God belonging to two natures.' And after a few things: 'God the Word Himself makes the things that pertain to the temple His own, without suffering at all, since the two natures belong to one person.' 1837D

Αὐγουστίνου ἐπισκόπου Ῥηγιτῶν πρὸς Βολοσιανὸν ἐπιστολή· "Νῦν δὲ οὕτως μεταξὺ Θεοῦ καὶ ἀνθρώπων ἀνεφάνη μεσίτης,[149] ὥστε αὐτὸν ἐν τῇ τοῦ προσώπου ἑνότητι συνάπτειν ἑκατέραν φύσιν".[150] Καὶ μετὰ βραχέα· "Ἐπίγνωθι τὴν διττὴν φύσιν τοῦ Χριστοῦ, τὴν θείαν δὴ λέγω, τὴν ἴσην ὑπάρχουσαν τῷ Πατρὶ, καὶ τὴν ἀνθρωπείαν, ἧς μείζων ἐστὶν ὁ Πατήρ.[151],[152]

1840A   Φλαβιανοῦ ἐπισκόπου Ἀντιοχεί⟨ας⟩, ἐκ τοῦ κατὰ Ἰωάννην εἰς τὸ Ὁ μὴ τιμῶν τὸν Υἱόν, οὐ τιμᾷ τὸν Πατέρα·[153] "Ἵνα ἀμφοτέρας αὐτοῦ διδαχθῶμεν τὰς φύσεις."[154]

Τοῦ αὐτοῦ εἰς τὴν ἀνάληψιν τοῦ Κυρίου· "Ἀνθρωπίνῃ φύσει θεότης συνάπτεται, μενούσης ἐφ᾽ ἑαυτῆς ἑκατέρας φύσεως."[155]

Τοῦ αὐτοῦ εἰς τὸ κατὰ Ἰωάννην· "Ἵνα ἀμφοτέρας αὐτοῦ διδαχθῶμεν τὰς φύσεις, καὶ τὸν ὁρώμενον ἄνθρωπον, καὶ τὴν διὰ τοῦ σώματος ἐνεργοῦσαν θεότητα."[156]

Ἰσιδώρου ἀσκητοῦ τοῦ Πιλουσιώτου, ἐκ τῆς πρὸς Θεοδόσιον διάκονον ἐπιστολῆς· "Οὐ ψιλὸς ἄνθρωπος ὁ Χριστὸς ἐνανθρωπήσας μᾶλλον δὲ Θεός· ἐν ἑκατέραις ταῖς φύσεσιν εἰς ὑπάρχει Υἱός."[157]

1840B   Τοῦ ἁγίου Κυρίλλου, ἐκ τοῦ κατὰ διάλογον συντάγματος "Ὅτι εἷς ὁ Χριστός"· "Ἆρα οὖν συγκέχυνται καὶ μία γεγόνασιν ἄμφω αἱ φύσεις; Εἶτα τίς οὕτως ἐμβρόντητός τε καὶ ἀμαθὴς εἴη;"[158]

Τοῦ αὐτοῦ, ἐκ τοῦ ⟨περὶ τῆς⟩ ἐν πνεύματι λατρείας λόγου ἐννάτου· "Λαμπρὸς γὰρ ἐν γῇ καὶ διαφανὴς ὁ Χριστός, κατά γε τὸ Θεὸς Κύριος καὶ ἐπέφανεν ἡμῖν,[159] καὶ οἱονεὶ διφυᾶ τὴν γνῶσιν ἔχων· νοεῖται γὰρ ἐν ταυτῷ Θεὸς καὶ ἄνθρωπος."[160]

Τοῦ αὐτοῦ, ἐκ τῶν κατὰ Ἰουλιανοῦ λόγου η´· "Μία γὰρ φύσις πῶς ἂν εἰσδέξηται τὸ διάφορον ἐφ᾽ ἑαυτῆς;"[161]

---

[149] 1 Tim. 2: 5

[150] Augustine, Letter 137, PL xxx, 519 (Latin).   [151] John 14: 28

[152] Cf. Augustine, Tractate on John 99, 1, in In Iohannis evangelium tractatus cxxiv, CCSL xxxvi (1954), 582 (Latin).

[153] John 5: 23

[154] Flavian of Antioch. Attested in John Maron, Exposition of the Faith, 24.

[155] Not otherwise attested.

[156] Flavian of Antioch, On John. Attested by Leontius of Byzantium, PG lxxxvi¹, 1313D.

[157] Isidore of Pelusium, Letters 1, 405, PG lxxviii, 409A.

[158] Cyril of Alexandria, That Christ is One, ed. and tr. G.-M de Durand, Deux dialogues christologiques, SC 97 (1964), 372.

[159] Ps. 117: 27 LXX

[160] Cyril of Alexandria, On Worship in Spirit and in Truth iv, PG lxviii, 637A.

[161] Cyril of Alexandria, Against Julian viii, PG lxxvi, 916C.

Augustine, Bishop of Regium, a letter to Volusianus: 'Thus there appeared at this time a *mediator* between *God and men*, so that He might bind together each nature in the unity of person.' And after a bit: 'Recognize the twofold nature of Christ—I am referring to the divine nature, that is the equal of the Father, and to the human nature, than which *the Father is greater*.'

Flavian, Bishop of Antioch, from the *Commentary on John* concerning the text *He who does not honour the Son, does not honour the Father*: 'so that we may teach both of His natures'. 1840A

The same, *On the Ascension of the Lord*: 'Divinity is united with a human nature, though each nature remains by itself.'

The same, the *Commentary on John*: 'so that we may teach both of His natures, the man who's seen, and the divinity that works through the body'.

Isidore, the monk of Pelusium, from his *Letter to Theodosius the Deacon*: 'Christ become man is not a mere man, but God; one Son exists in both of the natures.'

Saint Cyril, from the work in dialogue form, *That Christ is One*: 'Have the two natures then been commingled and become one nature? Who would be so stupid and ignorant as that?' 1840B

The same, from *On Worship in Spirit* ix: 'Christ is radiant and luminous on earth, in accordance with the text *the Lord God appeared to us*, and gives rise as it were to a double kind of knowledge, for He is understood to be God and man in the same [person].'

The same, from *Against Julian* viii: 'How is one nature to take on difference all by itself?'

Εὐσταθίου Ἀντιοχείας, ἐκ τῆς ἑρμηνείας τοῦ ιε΄ ψαλμοῦ·
1840c "Ἐξαπέστειλεν ὁ Θεὸς τὸν Υἱὸν αὐτοῦ γενόμενον ἐκ γυναικός·[162] οὐ
'γενομένους', ἀλλὰ 'γενόμενον'· μοναδικὸν γὰρ τὸ πρόσωπον. Οὐκ
εἶπον μοναδικὴν τὴν φύσιν—ἄπαγε, μὴ γένοιτο—οὐδὲ τὴν αὐτὴν
οὐσίαν σαρκὸς καὶ θεότητος, ἀλλ' εἶπον ἕνα Κύριον Ἰησοῦν Χριστόν,
δι' οὗ τὰ πάντα, ἐν τῷ διαφόρῳ τῶν φύσεων γνωριζόμενον κατὰ
πάντα."[163]

Ἰωάννου τοῦ Χρυσοστόμου, ἐκ τῆς πρὸς Καισάριον ἐπιστολῆς·
"Μίξιν θεσπεσίαν θεότητος καὶ σαρκός, μίαν δὲ ἐντεῦθεν
τελεσθῆναι φύσιν, τοῦτο τοῦ παράφρονος Ἀπολιναρίου τὸ
ἀτόπημα, αὕτη τῶν εἰσαγόντων κρᾶσιν καὶ συναλοιφὴν ἡ
δυσσεβεστάτη αἵρεσις."[164] Καὶ πρὸς τῷ τέλει· "Φύγωμεν τοὺς μίαν
1840d φύσιν μετὰ τὴν ἕνωσιν τερατευομένους· τῇ γὰρ τῆς μιᾶς ἐπινοίᾳ, τῷ
ἀπαθεῖ Θεῷ πάθος προσάπτειν ἐπείγονται."[165]

Ἀμφιλοχίου Ἰκονίου, ἐκ τῆς πρὸς Σέλευκον δευτέρας ἐπιστολῆς·
"Ἐὰν εἴπωσιν ὡς μιᾶς οὐσίας ἐστί,[284ᵛ] ἐρωτήσατε αὐτούς· 'Πῶς
οὖν, κατὰ μὲν τὴν θεότητα ἀπαθῆ, κατὰ δὲ τὴν σάρκα παθητόν; τὸ
γὰρ μιᾶς ὑπάρχον οὐσίας, ὅλον ὅμοιον. Ἢ γὰρ ἀπαθὲς ὅλον, ἢ
παθητόν.'"[166] Καὶ μετὰ βραχέα· "Ἕνα οὖν Υἱὸν τὸν Χριστὸν δύο
φύσεων φημί, οὐκ ἀρνούμενος τὴν θείαν, οὐδὲ τὴν ἀνθρωπείαν.
Πάσχει τοίνυν, οὐ θεότητι, ἀλλ' ἀνθρωπότητι, τουτέστι Χριστὸς
1841a ἔπαθε σαρκί, ἀλλ' οὐχ' ἡ θεότης ἔπαθεν—ἄπαγε τὸ δυσμενὲς τοῦτο
καὶ βλάσφημον, ὦ δείλαιε—, ἡ ληφθεῖσα πάσχει φύσις, ἡ δὲ
λαβοῦσα, ἀπαθὴς μένει."[167]

Γρηγορίου Νύσσης, ἐκ τοῦ εἰς παρθενίαν ἐπαίνου· "Ἦλθε Θεὸς
θνητός τε, φύσεις δύο εἰς ἓν διείρας, τὴν μὲν κευθομένην, τὴν
δ' ἀμφαδίην μερόπεσι."[168]

[169]Ἀλλ' αὗται μὲν τῶν ἡμετέρων· αὐτῶν δὲ τῶν καθ' ἡμῶν
λυττώντων, εἰ ἑκούσιοι κατὰ θείαν συνέλασιν ἢ ἀκούσιοι οὐκ οἶδα,
τοιαίδε δὲ ὅμως φωναὶ φέρονται.

1841b Ἀμφιλοχίου τοῦ Σίδης, ὃν φασὶ μόνον ἀπροσπαθῶς καὶ ἀδεῶς
ἔχειν τὴν ⟨μίαν φύσιν⟩ ἐν τῇ συνόδῳ, ἐκ τῆς κατ' αὐτῆς γραφείσης
αὐτῷ ἐπιστολῆς πρὸς Λέοντα τὸν βασιλέα· "Καταφεύξονται γὰρ εἰς
τινας διδασκάλους δύο φύσεις εἰρηκότας."[170]

[162] Gal. 4: 4
[163] Ps.-Eustathius of Antioch, *Commentary on Psalm 15*. Not otherwise attested.
[164] Ps.-Chrysostom, *Letter to Caesarius*. Not otherwise attested.
[165] Ibid. Latin attested *PG* lii, 760.
[166] Amphilochius of Iconium, *To Seleucus* = fr. 11A, Cavallera, 488.
[167] Ibid. = fr. 11 E 1-6, Cavallera, 490.
[168] Actually Gregory of Nazianzus, *Poems* I, 2, 1, *PG* xxxvii, 533D (Latin).
[169] in marg. σχ°(λιον) MS
[170] Amphilochius of Side, *Letter to the Emperor Leo*, cf. *PG* lxxvii, 1515. For other attestations see M. Geerard, *Clavis patrum graecorum*, iii (Turnhout: Brepols, 1979), 5965 n.

Eustathius of Antioch, from his *Exposition of the Fifteenth Psalm*: '*God sent His son, born of a woman*—not the plural of "born", but the 1840C singular, for the person is a single entity. I did not say the nature is a single entity—Perish the thought! God forbid!—nor did I say the same substance belongs to flesh and divinity, but I did say there is one Lord Jesus Christ, through whom all things exist, made known in the difference of natures in all respects.'

John Chrysostom, from the *Letter to Caesarius*: 'To think that one nature was completed from that moment, an ineffable mixture of divinity and flesh, is the absurd notion of the deranged Apollinarius. This is the exceedingly impious heresy of those who introduce mixing and coalescence.' And towards the end: 'Let us flee those who make up the fairy-tale of one nature after the union. Through the idea of the one nature they hasten to attribute 1840D suffering to the impassible God.'

Amphilochius of Iconium, from the *Second Letter to Seleucus*: 'If they say He is of one substance, ask them "How is He impassible in His divinity, then, but passible in His flesh? Whatever is of one essence is the same through and through; either it is all impassible, or it is all passible."' And after a little: 'I say there is one Christ, the Son, belonging to two natures, denying neither the divine nature nor the human. He suffers, therefore, not in His divinity, but in His humanity. That is, Christ suffered in flesh, but the divinity did not suffer—give up that hostile and blasphemous 1841A business, you wretch! The nature that was assumed suffers, but the nature which did the assuming remains impassible.'

Gregory of Nyssa, from his *Praise of Virginity*: 'God came as a mortal, drawing two natures—one hidden, the other open to all articulate beings—together into one.'

But these texts belong to our people. Phrases of the very same sort are produced, nonetheless, that belong to people who rave against us. Whether [in these phrases] they're speaking of their own free will, at God's prompting, or involuntarily, I have no idea.

Amphilochius of Side, whom these people describe as the only 1841B one to maintain one nature in the synod dispassionately and voluntarily, from the letter written by him to the Emperor Leo against the council: 'They will have recourse to certain teachers who have spoken of two natures.'

Σεβήρου τοῦ αἱρετικοῦ τοῦ μιξοφυσίτου, ταῖς Ἰουλίου καὶ Ἀμβροσίου χρήσεσιν οὕτως ἐπιλέγοντος· "Ὁ δὲ καὶ τὰ ἴδια γινώσκων, καὶ τὴν ἕνωσιν φυλάττων, οὔτε τὰς φύσεις ψεύδεται, οὔτε τὴν ἕνωσιν ἀγνοήσει."[171]

Τοῦ αὐτοῦ ἐκ τῶν κατὰ τοῦ Γραμματικοῦ· "Δύο τὰς φύσεις ἐν τῷ Χριστῷ νοοῦμεν, τὴν μὲν κτιστήν, τὴν δὲ ἄκτιστον."[172]

"Ἀλλ᾽ οὐδεὶς ἐγράψατο τὴν ἐν Χαλκηδόνι σύνοδον, τὴν ἄλογον
1841C ταύτην γραφήν· 'Τί δήποτε δύο φύσεις ὠνόμασαν περὶ τῆς τοῦ Ἐμμανουὴλ ἐνώσεως διαλαμβάνοντες;' Οὐδεὶς ταύτην ἐστήσατο τὴν κατηγορίαν, ἀλλ᾽ ἐκείνην μάλα δικαίως· 'Τί δήποτε μὴ ἀκολουθήσαντες τῷ ἁγίῳ Κυρίλλῳ ἐκ δύο φύσεων ἔφασαν εἶναι τὸν Χριστόν;'"[173] "Οὐ παυσόμεθα λέγοντες τοίνυν, ὡς 'Δειξάτω τίς τὴν ἐν Χαλκηδόνι σύνοδον, ἢ τὸν τόμον Λέοντος, τὴν "καθ᾽ ὑπόστασιν ἕνωσιν" ὁμολογήσαντας, ἢ "σύνοδον φυσικὴν", ἢ "ἐξ ἀμφοῖν ἕνα Χριστόν", ἢ "μίαν φύσιν τοῦ Θεοῦ Λόγου σεσαρκωμένην", καὶ τότε γνωσόμεθα, ὡς κατὰ τὸν σοφώτατον Κύριλλον θεωρίᾳ μόνῃ ἀνακρίνοντες τὴν οὐσιώδη διαφορὰν τῶν συνενεχθέντων ἀπορρήτως εἰς ἕν, ἴσασι. Καὶ ὡς ἑτέρα ἡ τοῦ Λόγου φύσις, καὶ ἑτέρα ἡ τῆς σαρκός, καὶ ὡς δύο τὰ ἀλλήλοις
1841D συνενηνεγμένα καθορῶσι τῷ νῷ, διϊστῶσι δὲ οὐδαμῶς.'"[174]

Καίτοι γε ὁ ταῦτα λέγων, ἐν τῇ ἐκθέσει τῆς πίστεως αὐτοῦ πρὸς Νηφάλιον ὁ αὐτὸς φησί· "Τὸ λέγειν δύο φύσεις ἐπὶ Χριστοῦ, πάσης κατηγορίας ἐπίμεστον, εἰ καὶ ὑπὸ πλειόνων ἁγίων πατέρων εἴρηται."[175] Καὶ μεθ᾽ ἕτερα· "Καὶ μὴ εἴπῃς ὡς τῇ λέξει τῶν 'δύο φύσεων' τινὲς τῶν πατέρων ἐχρήσαντο· ἐχρήσαντο γὰρ
1844A ἀδιαβλήτως ὥσπερ εἴπομεν, κατὰ δὲ τὸν χρόνον τοῦ ἁγίου Κυρίλλου, τῆς νόσου τῶν Νεστορίου καινοφωνιῶν τὰς ἐκκλησίας ἐπινεμομένης, ἐπὶ πλέον ἡ λέξις ἀπεδοκιμάσθη."[176]

---

[171] Actually Ps.-Julius, *On the Union* = Lietzmann, *Apollinaris*, p. 193. Cited as a text of Julius at 1828A above.
[172] Severus, *Against the Grammarian* iii, 17, CSCO xciv, 196. Cited also at 1845C below.
[173] Ibid. iii, 9, 120.　　　[174] Ibid. 29.
[175] Original not extant. Cited in *Against the Grammarian* iii, 22, ed. J. Lebon, CSCO, Scriptores Syri, series 4, vi (1933), 1.
[176] Ibid. 3.

Severus the heretic, the nature-mixer, who adds this comment to citations from Julius and Ambrose: 'Yet the man who both recognizes the properties and protects the union does not speak falsely about the natures, nor is he ignorant of the union.'

The same, from *Against the Grammarian*: 'We understand there are two natures in Christ, one created, the other uncreated.' 'But no one indicted the Council of Chalcedon on this irrational charge: "Why ever did they specify two natures, introducing division into the Emmanuel's union?" No one laid that charge. 1841C Rather, and quite justly, people laid the following charge: "Why did they not, following holy Cyril, say that Christ is out of two natures?"' 'That is why we will not stop saying "Someone needs to demonstrate that the Council of Chalcedon, or the *Tome* of Leo, confesses 'union by hypostasis', or 'a natural combination', or 'one Christ out of both', or 'one incarnate nature of God the Word'. Then we shall know that, like the supremely wise Cyril, it is in thought only that they recognize the substantial difference between things brought together ineffably into one. It is by the mind that they need to observe that the Word's nature is one thing, the flesh's another, and that two things have been brought together with each other; they must not separate them in any 1841D way."'

Indeed, the same person who makes that assertion says the following in his exposition of the faith *Against Nephalius*: 'To speak of two natures in Christ is completely blameworthy, even though the expression is used by the majority of the holy fathers.' After other things: 'You must not say that some of the fathers made use of the two-natures formula, for they made use of it in a blameless way, as we said. In holy Cyril's time, though, when the sickness of 1844A Nestorius' new formulations spread through the churches, that expression was rejected all the more as unworthy.'

Ὥστε οὖν, ὦ οὗτος, καὶ πάλαι ἀδόκιμα, καὶ ἐπὶ πλέον μετὰ
Νεστόριον. Πῶς οὖν "ἀδιαβλήτως [285ʳ] ἐχρήσαντο" αὐτῇ; Εἶτα
δέ, εἰ διαβέβληται καὶ ἀπεδοκιμάσθη κατὰ Νεστόριον, πῶς οὐ κατὰ
τόδε γράφεταί τις ἢ κατηγορεῖ τῆς ἐν Χαλκηδόνι συνόδου μετὰ
Νεστόριον οὔσης, ἀλλὰ διότι μὴ καὶ "ἐκ δύο" λέγει καὶ "τὴν καθ'
ὑπόστασιν ἔνωσιν" Χριστοῦ; Ὅτι δὲ λέγει τάδε, τίς ἀμφιβάλλει;
Εἰ γὰρ ἡ σύνοδος ψηφιζομένη φησὶν οὕτως· "Τὰς τοῦ μακαρίου
Κυρίλλου τοῦ τῆς Ἀλεξανδρέων ἐκκλησίας γενομένου ποιμένος
συνοδικὰς ἐπιστολὰς πρὸς Νεστόριον, καὶ πρὸς τοὺς τῆς Ἀνατολῆς
1844ʙ δεχόμεθα ἁρμοδίας οὔσας εἰς ἔλεγχον τῆς Νεστορίου
φρενοβλαβείας", ἐν αἷς ἐπιστολαῖς καὶ τὴν φυσικὴν καὶ τὴν
καθ' ὑπόστασιν ἔνωσιν ἔφη ὁ πατήρ, πῶς οὐχὶ τὰ αὐτὰ ὁμολογεῖ ᾧ
συμφωνεῖ, καὶ ὃν ἀποδέχεται ἐν τοῖσδε;

Ἡμῶν δὲ προλεγόντων τέ καὶ συλλεγόντων τὸ "ἐκ δύο φύσεων"
εἶναι τὸν Κύριον, μετὰ τοῦ καὶ "ἐν δύο φύσεσιν" εἶναι, καὶ λεγόντων,
καὶ τὴν σύνοδον καὶ πᾶσαν φύσιν καὶ ἄγγελον ἐξ οὐρανοῦ,[177] εἰ μὴ
οὕτως ἐφρόνουν, ἀναθεματιζόντων, διὰ τί μὴ καταδέχονται αὐτοὶ
τάδε συνομολογεῖν, λέγοντες καὶ τὸ "ἐκ δύο" μετὰ τοῦ "ἐν δύο" σὺν
ἡμῖν, καὶ Σεβῆρον καὶ Διόσκορον καὶ τοὺς μετ' αὐτῶν, εἰ μὴ οὕτως
ἐφρόνουν, ἀναθεματίζειν αἱρούμενοι; Φλαβιανοῦ τε τοῦ μακαρίτου
1844ᴄ τῆς ἐκθέσεως ἐχούσης· "Καὶ μίαν δὲ φύσιν τοῦ Θεοῦ Λόγου,
σεσαρκωμένην μέντοι καὶ ἐνανθρωπήσασαν, λέγειν οὐ
παραιτούμεθα διὰ τὸν ἐξ ἀμφοῖν ἕνα Κύριον ἡμῶν Ἰησοῦν
Χριστόν",[178] καὶ τοῦτο τῆς συνόδου ποτνιωμένης, πῶς οὐχὶ κατὰ
πάντα τάδε τούτοις συμφθέγγεται ἡ σύνοδος;

Λέων δὲ ὁ θαυμάσιος, μιᾷ κυρώσει καὶ συνόψει, πάντα τάδε τὰ
κατὰ Νεστορίου εἰρημένα ἐν τῇ ἐν Ἐφέσῳ συνόδῳ ὑπὸ τοῦ
μακαρίου Κυρίλλου, ἐπισφραγίζεται καὶ κυροῖ, λέγων· "Τὰ
μέντοι γε τῆς πρότερον ἐν Ἐφέσῳ συνόδου, ἧστινος ὁ τῆς ὁσίας
μνήμης Κύριλλος τότε προήδρευεν κατὰ Νεστορίου ἰδικῶς
πραχθέντα διαμενέτωσαν· μήπως ἡ τότε καταδικασθεῖσα
1844ᴅ δυσσέβεια δι' αὐτὸ τοῦτο καθ' ὁτιοῦν ἑαυτὴν ἀπατήσῃ, ὅτιπερ
Εὐτυχὴς δικαίως ἀναθεματισθεὶς καταβέβληται· ἡ καθαρότης γὰρ
τῆς πίστεως καὶ διδασκαλίας, ἣν τῷ αὐτῷ πνεύματι κηρύττομεν,
ὥσπερ οἱ ἅγιοι πατέρες ἡμῶν, καὶ τὴν Νεστορίου, καὶ τὴν
Εὐτυχοῦς μετὰ τῶν ἡγουμένων αὐτῶν, ἐπίσης καταδικάζει καὶ
διώκει κακοδοξίαν."[179]

---

[177] Gal. 1: 8
[178] Flavian of Constantinople, *Letter to Theodosius*, *ACO* ii, 1, 1, 35.
[179] Leo the Great, *Letter* 52, *ACO* ii, 1, 2 (1933), 32.

Well then, my good man: this saying was both rejected some time ago, and rejected all the more after Nestorius, was it? How is it, then, that 'they made use of it in a blameless way'? How is it that, if it was calumniated and rejected on account of Nestorius, no one indicts or condemns the Council of Chalcedon—which took place after Nestorius—for this, but rather because it doesn't say 'out of two', or speak of Christ's 'union by hypostasis'? But who doubts that it does say these things? If the synod, when it votes, says 'We accept the synodical letters to Nestorius and to the Anatolians of blessed Cyril, pastor of the Alexandrian church, as being suitable for the refutation of Nestorius' folly'—in which 1844B letters the father speaks both of 'natural union', and of 'union by hypostasis'—in what way is the synod not confessing exactly what the one with whom it agrees confesses, and whom it accepts in these letters?

Since we publicly assert and maintain the statement that the Lord is 'out of two natures' along with the statement that He is 'in two natures', since we speak of a combination, and of an entire nature, and since we anathematize even an *angel from heaven* if he doesn't think likewise, what possible reason can these people have for refusing to agree with us on these, using both 'out of two' and 'in two', and electing to anathematize Severus, Dioscorus, and those with them, if they don't think the same? Since blessed Flavian's explanation says 'We are not looking for an excuse not 1844C to speak of one nature of the Word of God—made flesh, of course, and become man—because our one Lord Jesus Christ is out of both', and since the synod loudly proclaims this, in what way, in the light of all this, does the synod not agree with these assertions?

The admirable Leo confirms and ratifies in one comprehensive ratifying statement everything said against Nestorius at the Council of Ephesus under blessed Cyril, when he says: 'They must certainly stand stoutly by the actions, particularly against Nestorius, of the first Council of Ephesus that Cyril of blessed memory presided over at the time, lest the impiety condemned at that time should on this very account deceive itself over any issue at all, 1844D seeing that Eutyches, being rightly anathematized, was deposed. The purity of the faith and of the teaching, which we proclaim by the same spirit as did our holy fathers, condemns and banishes Nestorius' and Eutyches' infamy equally, along with their predecessors.'

Ἀκουστέον δὲ ἔτι τοῦ λέγοντος, ὅτι καὶ "πλείους τῶν πατέρων ἀδιαβλήτως ἐχρήσαντο φωνῇ" τῇ "ἐν δύο" ἐπὶ Χριστοῦ, καὶ ὅτι οὐχ' ὡς λέγουσαν τὸ "ἐν δύο" γράφεται τὴν σύνοδον, ἀλλ' ὡς τὸ "ἐκ δύο" μὴ εἰποῦσαν, καὶ τὰ λοιπὰ ἃ φησίν. Οὐκ οἶδα γὰρ πῶς
1845A λαθὼν ἑαυτὸν ὥσπερ ἐν ὕπνῳ λαλῶν, ἐν τοῖς ἑαυτοῦ συγγράμμασι πάλιν φησί· "Νύκτωρ καὶ μεθ' ἡμέραν ταῖς βίβλοις τῶν πατέρων στρεφόμενος, οὔπω τινὰ μέχρι καὶ νῦν τῶν πατέρων εὑρεῖν ἐδυνήθην [285ʳ] φύσεις ἐπὶ Χριστοῦ δύο δοξάζοντα, καθάπερ οἱ ἐν Χαλκηδόνι συνελθόντες ἐδόξασαν, καὶ ἐν δυσὶν αὐτὸν ἀπεφήναντο φύσεσιν."[180]

Ταῦτά γε, εἰ μὴ τὸ τῆς ὑποθέσεως τῶν ζητουμένων σεπτὸν πρὸς εὐλάβειαν ἄγχει τὸν ἀκροατὴν, οὐκ εἰς ἄμετρον ἐγχύσει γέλωτα, οὑτωσὶ αὐτοῦ ἑαυτὸν ἀμνημόνως ἢ ἀταλαφρόνως ἢ θεηλάτως, οὐκ οἶδα πῶς λέγειν, ἀντικαταρράσσοντος; Καὶ ἡμῖν μὲν σκοπὸς οὐκ ἦν, ὡς ὁ Κύριος μάρτυς, ἀνδρὸς ὁμοφυοῦς ἄγνοιαν ὀνειδίζειν, ἢ σαθρότητα λόγων ἀλλοτρίων ἑτέροις δημοσιεύειν, ἀλλ' ἐπεὶ τὸ μὲν κατ' αὐτὸν δόγμα κεκίνηται, ὁ δὲ θερμῶς ἀντιποιησάμενος
1845B τοῦδε τοῦ δόγματος, αὐτὸς οὔπω ἔφθη πανεκκλησίῳ συνόδῳ κατακριθῆναι, ἀλλὰ ψήφοις βασιλικαῖς καὶ ἱερατικαῖς ἐκβληθῆναι τοῦ θρόνου τῆς Ἀντιοχέων, ἀναγκαῖον παραστῆσαι τὴν ποιότητα τοῦ ἀνδρός, μήπως ἐκ τῆς τινῶν περὶ αὐτοῦ φατριαστικῆς τὸ ὅλον προλήψεως ἐνδόξου, ταῖς ἐκείνου διδασκαλίαις ἀβασανίστως οἱ νηπιώτεροι κατασύροιντο. Ἔστι γὰρ τοιόσδε ὁ ἀνὴρ καὶ ἐν ἄλλοις τοῖς ὑποτεταγμένοις αὐτοῦ συγγράμμασι θεωρούμενος καὶ σύμφωνος, ὡς εἰπεῖν, τὴν ἀσυμφωνίαν ἑαυτοῦ γινωσκόμενος.

Σεβήρου ἐκ τῶν κατὰ τοῦ Γραμματικοῦ λόγου τρίτου, κεφαλαίου θ' ἢ ιγ· "Ἀλλὰ λέγεις ὡς οὐκ ἀρνεῖται ὁ δοκιμώτατος
1845C Κύριλλος δύο φύσεις ὀνομάζειν· ἑτέρα γὰρ ἡ τοῦ Λόγου, καὶ ἑτέρα ἡ τῆς ἐμψύχου καὶ ἐννου σαρκός. Σύμφημι κἀγώ."[181] "Καὶ ὡς οἱ ἐν Χαλκηδόνι συνελθόντες, ἃ μὲν συνομολογεῖ καὶ Νεστόριος ἡμῖν ἐκ τῶν Κυρίλλου φωνῶν παρατίθενται, δηλαδὴ τὸ φύσεις εἶναι δύο καὶ διαφόρους τὴν οὐσίαν, θεότητά τε καὶ ἀνθρωπότητα."[182]

Τοῦ αὐτοῦ ἐκ τῶν κατὰ τοῦ αὐτοῦ Ἰωάννου Γραμματικοῦ τοῦ Καισαρέως, λόγου γ', κεφαλαίου ιζ· "Τὴν διαφορὰν δεξάμενοι, δύο τὰς φύσεις ἐν αὐτῷ νοοῦμεν, τὴν μὲν κτιστὴν, τὴν δὲ ἄκτιστον."[183]
1845D Τοῦ αὐτοῦ, κεφαλαίου θ'· "Τὸ δύο φύσεις λέγειν, εἴτουν ὀνομάζειν, κοινὸν ἡμῖν καὶ Νεστορίῳ μέχρι τοῦ γινώσκειν τὴν διαφορὰν τοῦ Θεοῦ Λόγου καὶ τῆς σαρκός."[184]

---

[180] Not otherwise attested.
[181] Severus, *Against the Grammarian* iii, 9, *CSCO* xciv, 127.   [182] Ibid. 163.
[183] Ibid. iii, 17, 196. Cited in part at 1841B above.
[184] Ibid. iii, 9, 124. Cited also at 1820C–D above.

Listen once more to the man who says that 'the majority of the fathers . . . used the expression "in two" of Christ "in a blameless way"', and who says he indicts the Council, not for saying 'in two', but for not saying 'out of two', and so on and so forth. I have no idea how he, like someone who forgets himself when he talks in his sleep, can say again in his own writings: 'Though I am occupied 1845A night and day with the books of the fathers, never to the present day have I been able to find any of the fathers who honours two natures in Christ in the way that those assembled at Chalcedon honoured them, proclaiming Him in two natures.'

If the seriousness of the subject into which we're inquiring didn't compel an attitude of reverence in the reader, wouldn't the fact that [Severus] so completely turns the case against himself induce unrestrained laughter? (Whether he does so out of absent-mindedness, or inexperience, or God-induced madness, I couldn't say.) As the Lord is my witness, it wasn't our intention to reproach a man of like nature to ourselves with ignorance, or to publicize to others the unsoundness of other people's statements. Still, since legal proceedings against him were set in motion, but he, hotly contesting these proceedings, was not at all eager to be judged by a council of the whole church, [preferring] rather to be deposed 1845B from the throne of the Antiochene church by imperial and clerical votes, it's necessary to demonstrate what kind of man he is, lest the immature be carried away unthinkingly by his teachings as a result of certain people's remarkable and entirely factional prejudice in his favour. This is the sort of man who's on view also in his other, secondary writings, and who's consistent, so to speak, only in knowing his own inconsistency!

Severus, from *Against the Grammarian* iii, 9 or 13: 'But you say that the most-esteemed Cyril does not refuse to name two natures, one that belongs to the Word, and another belonging to flesh endowed 1845C with a soul and a mind. I agree completely.' 'Likewise those who came together at Chalcedon commend what even Nestorius confesses along with us from Cyril's sayings, that is, evidently enough, that there are two natures different in substance, divinity, and humanity.'

The same, from his work against the same John the Grammarian of Caesarea, iii, 17: 'Since we accept the difference, we understand two natures in Him, one created, the other uncreated.'

The same, from chapter 9: 'To speak of—that is, to name—two 1845D natures is something we and Nestorius have in common so far as recognizing the difference between God the Word and the flesh goes.'

Τοῦ αὐτοῦ ἐκ τῆς πρὸς Σόλωνα ἐπιστολῆς, ἧς ἡ ἀρχή· "Ἦλθεν εἰς τὴν ἐμὴν μετριότητα"· "Τὰ ἐξ ὧν ὁ Ἐμμανουήλ, ὑφέστηκε[185] καὶ μετὰ τὴν ἕνωσιν, καὶ οὐ τέτραπται· ὑφέστηκε δὲ ἐν τῇ ἑνώσει καὶ ἐν μιᾷ ὑποστάσει θεωρούμενα, καὶ οὐκ ἐν μονάδι κατ᾽ ἰδίαν ὑπόστασιν, ἕκαστον ἰδιοσυστάτως θεωρούμενον."[186]

1848A   Τοῦ αὐτοῦ ἐκ τῶν πρὸς τὸν Γραμματικὸν λόγου β΄ κεφαλαίου πρώτου· "Καὶ τῶν ἐξ ὧν ἡ ἕνωσις μενόντων ἀμειώτων καὶ ἀναλλοιώτων, ἐν συνθέσει δὲ ὑφεστώτων, καὶ οὐκ ἐν μονάσιν ἰδιοσυστάτοις".[187] Ἰδοὺ τό τε ἀμείωτον κατὰ ποσὸν καὶ ἀναλλοίωτον κατὰ ποιὸν λέγειν φυσικὸν συνωθεῖται. Καὶ μετά τινα· "Καὶ ὡς τὰ ἐξ ὧν εἷς ὁ Χριστὸς ἐν τῇ συνθέσει τελείως καὶ ἀμειώτως ὑφέστηκεν."[188]

Τοῦ αὐτοῦ Σεβήρου [286ʳ] ἐκ τῆς πρὸς Σέργιον τὸν Γραμματικὸν δευτέρας ἐπιστολῆς· "Καὶ καταπέπληγμαι λίαν πῶς
1848B   καὶ σύνθεσιν ὀνομάζεις τὴν σάρκωσιν, ἔστιν ὅπου καὶ πάλιν λέγεις ᾽μιᾶς γεγενημένης καθάπαξ οὐσίας ἢ ποιότητος᾽. Ἄρα γὰρ ἤρχθη μὲν ἡ ἕνωσις ἐκ συγχύσεως, καὶ πέπαυται δὲ ἡ σύνθεσις, καὶ εἰς μίαν οὐσίαν μετεχώρησεν, ἵνα, ὡς λέγεις, ἡ ἁγία Τριὰς φυλαχθῇ τριάς, καὶ μὴ περιττὸν πρόσωπον παραδέξηται."[189] Καὶ πάλιν· "Καὶ οἴει τοῦτο πρὸς μίαν οὐσίαν ἄγειν τὰ τῇ φυσικῇ ποιότητι διαφέροντα, θεότητα καὶ ἀνθρωπότητα, ἐξ ὧν ἀσυγχύτως καὶ ἀμειώτως ὑπάρχει Χριστός."[190]

Τοῦ αὐτοῦ αἱρετικοῦ ἐκ τῆς πρὸς τὸν αὐτὸν Σέργιον τρίτης ἐπιστολῆς· "Ἴσθι οὖν μὴ οὕτως ἔχειν τὸ ἀληθές, καὶ προσαποφήσαντός μου καὶ διὰ πλειόνων μαρτυριῶν ἀποδείξαντος, ὡς οὐ χρὴ λέγειν τὸν Ἐμμανουὴλ μιᾶς οὐσίας τε καὶ ποιότητος καὶ
1848C   ἑνὸς ἰδιώματος."[191] Καὶ πάλιν· "Οὐκ ἄν τις νοῦν ἔχων εἴποι τὴν τοῦ Θεοῦ Λόγου καὶ τὴν ἔμψυχον καὶ ἔννουν σάρκα, τὴν ἑνωθεῖσαν αὐτῷ καθ᾽ ὑπόστασιν, γεγενῆσθαι μιᾶς οὐσίας καὶ ποιότητος."[192]

---

[185] ὑφεστήκε] ὑφεστήκει MS   [186] Not otherwise attested.
[187] Not otherwise attested.   [188] Ibid.
[189] Severus, Letter 2 to Sergius the Grammarian, ed. J. Lebon, CSCO cxx = Scriptores Syri, series 4, vii (1949), 93.
[190] Ibid. 94.   [191] Letter 3 to Sergius the Grammarian, 123.
[192] Ibid. 125.

The same from the *Letter to Solon*, which begins 'He came to my moderation': 'The things out of which the Emmanuel comes existed after the union too, and did not change. They existed in the union, being observed in one hypostasis; neither is observed existing on its own in a single entity by its own hypostasis.'

The same, from *Against the Grammarian* ii, 1: 'since the things out of which the union [came] remain undiminished and unchanged, subsisting in a composition, and not in single entities that exist independently'. Notice: he's driven to use the language of nature for what's undiminished in quantity, and unchanged in quality. After other things he goes on to say: 'Thus the things out of which there exists one Christ in the composition existed in a complete and undiminished way.' 1848A

The same Severus, from the second letter to Sergius the Grammarian: 'I am utterly astonished at the way you call the Incarnation a composition, and yet there is a place where you say again "one substance or quality having been brought forth once and for all". On those grounds the union took its start from confusion, and composition came to an end, and it changed into one essence so that, as you put it, the Holy Trinity might be kept a trinity, lest an extra person be accepted.' And again: 'You also think this draws things that differ by natural quality—divinity and humanity, out of which Christ exists unconfusedly and without diminution—into one substance.' 1848B

The same heretic, from the third letter to the same Sergius: 'Know, then, that this is not the truth of the matter, since I went on to declare—and demonstrated from many testimonies—that one does not need to say the Emmanuel is of one substance, quality, and property.' And again: 'No one who has a mind would say that the nature of God the Word, and the flesh possessed of a soul and a mind that was united with Him by hypostasis, came to be of one substance and quality.' 1848C

The same, from the letter to the same person: 'Accordingly, when we anathematize those who divide the one Christ after the union by the duality of natures, we do not say this, and place them under anathema, just because they speak of "natures", "properties", or "actions", but because they speak of "two".' If even an unlearned person isn't going to say the natures are one, though, yet you anathematize those who say there are two of them, you'll be driven to confess that there are three, or four, or ten, or a hundred of them, for there's no such thing as a magnitude that has no numerical value, except for infinity.

Τοῦ αὐτοῦ ἐκ τῆς πρὸς τὸν αὐτὸν ἐπιστολῆς· "᾽Αναθεματίζοντες τοίνυν τοὺς διαιροῦντας τὸν ἕνα Χριστὸν μετὰ τὴν ἕνωσιν τῇ δυάδι τῶν φύσεων, οὐ δι' αὐτὸ τὸ λέγειν 'φύσεις' ἢ 'ἰδιότητας' ἢ 'ἐνεργείας' ὑπ' ἀνάθεμα τιθέντες τοῦτό φαμεν, ἀλλὰ διὰ τὸ λέγειν 'δύο'."[193] ⟨᾽Α⟩λλ' εἰ μίαν εἶναι τὰς φύσεις οὐδ' ἀγράμματός τις ἐρεῖ, δύο δὲ τοὺς λέγοντας αὐτὰς εἶναι ἀναθεματίζεις, ἢ τρεῖς, ἢ τέσσαρας, ἢ δέκα, ἢ ἑκατὸν εἶναι αὐτὰς ἐξ ἀνάγκης ὁμολογήσεις· πλῆθος γὰρ οὐδὲν ἀναρίθμητον, εἰ μὴ τὸ ἄπειρον.

1848D   Τοῦ αὐτοῦ ἐκ τῆς κατὰ τοῦ Γραμματικοῦ Ἰωάννου τοῦ καὶ ἐπισκόπου Καισαρείας βίβλου. Τοῦ αὐτοῦ Σεβήρου· "Εἰ καὶ τὸ λέγειν 'ἐν δύο φύσεσιν' ἀδιαιρέτοις ὑφιστάναι τὸν Χριστὸν μετὰ τὴν ἕνωσιν εἴρητο τισὶ τῶν πάλαι διδασκάλων τῆς ἐκκλησίας, ἢ καὶ αὐτῷ Κυρίλλῳ, μετὰ ταῦτα δὲ ἀπηγόρευτο, καθάπερ καὶ τὸ λέγειν 'τῇ φύσει τῆς ἀνθρωπότητος παθεῖν τὸν Χριστὸν', καλῶς ὑπὸ τῶν ὀρθοδόξων λεγόμενον, ἀπηγόρευσε λέγειν, τοῖς νοσοῦσι τὴν

1849A   διαίρεσιν ἀνθιστάμενος, οὐδὲ οὕτω τοῖς ἐν Χαλκηδόνι συνελθοῦσιν, ἀπολογίας τις ὑπελείπετο τρόπος, ὁρισαμένοις 'ἐν δύο φύσεσιν' ἀδιαιρέτοις γνωρίζεσθαι τὸν Χριστόν."[194]

Τοῦ αὐτοῦ ἐν τῷ ὅτι ἀπαθὴς ὁ Λόγος· "Καὶ τῇ διδασκαλίᾳ τῶν ἱερῶν γραμμάτων πειθόμενοι, κηρυττόντων αὐτὸν <u>πεπονθέναι σαρκί</u>,[195] καὶ σαφῶς εἰδότες ὡς τὸ πάθος οὐ πέρα τοῦ παθητοῦ διαβήσεται σώματος· προσψαύει γὰρ οὐδαμῶς τοῦ ἀπαθοῦς τῆς θεότητος."[196]

Τιμοθέου τοῦ Αἰλούρου τοῦ αἱρετικοῦ τοῦ Μονοφυσίτου, ἐκ τῆς πρὸς τὸν Ἀλεξανδρέα Καλώνυμον διαλέξεως· "Κύριλλός ἐστιν ὁ

1849B   τῆς Ἀλεξανδρέων ἐπίσκοπος. Οὗτος γὰρ διαφόρως τὸ σοφὸν τῆς ὀρθοδοξίας διαρθρώσας κήρυγμα, [286ᵛ] παλίμβολος φανείς, τἀναντία δογματίσας ἐλέγχεται, ἐπεὶ 'μίαν φύσιν τοῦ Θεοῦ Λόγου σεσαρκωμένην' χρὴ λέγειν ὑποθέμενος, ἀναλύει τὸ ὑπ' αὐτοῦ δογματισθὲν καὶ δύο φύσεις ἐπὶ Χριστοῦ πρεσβεύων ἁλίσκεται, καὶ ὅ γε σαρκὶ παθεῖν τὸν Θεὸν ἀποφηνάμενος Λόγον, τοὐναντίον φησὶν οὐδενὶ τρόπῳ τὸ ὑπὲρ ἡμῶν ἀναδέξασθαι πάθος. Ἀλλ' ἐναντίος τοῖς οἰκείοις λόγοις γενόμενος, τὴν νῦν κρατοῦσαν ἐν ταῖς ἐκκλησίαις δυσδιάλλακτον μάχην ἐνέσπειρε, καὶ ὥσπέρ τινα φλόγα λαβροτάτην ἐξάψας, τὸν τῆς ὑγιοῦς πίστεως λόγον ἐνέπρησεν, εἰ μὴ θεόθεν φανεὶς ὁ πατριάρχης Σεβῆρος, τοῖς ἱεροῖς αὐτοῦ συγγράμμασιν ἰάσατο Κυρίλλου τὸ ἄστατον καὶ παλίμβολον,

1849C   καθάπερ τις φιλοπάτωρ υἱός, λώβην τοῦ φύσαντος οἰκείοις ἐσθήμασιν ἀμφιάσας.[197],[198]

---

[193] *Letter 1 to Sergius the Grammarian*, 59.
[194] Original not extant. Cited in *Against the Grammarian* iii, 22, *CSCO*, Scriptores Syri, series 4, vi, 1.
[195] Cf. 1 Pet. 4: 1   [196] Not otherwise attested.
[197] Cf. Gen. 9: 23   [198] Not possibly by Timothy Aelurus, who died in 477.

The same (that is, the same Severus), from the work against 1848D John the Grammarian, who's also Bishop of Caesarea: 'Even if saying that Christ existed "in two natures" undivided after the union was something asserted by certain teachers of the church in times gone by, or even by Cyril himself, nonetheless he gave up doing so afterwards, just as he gave up saying "Christ suffered in the nature of humanity" (though that was said in a correct way by the orthodox), when he took a stand against those who caught the disease of dividing. Thus no kind of defence was handed to those 1849A who gathered at Chalcedon when they determined that Christ was made known "in two natures" that are undivided.'

The same, in *That the Word is Impassible*: 'Those who are persuaded by the teaching of Holy Scriptures, which proclaim that He *suffered in the flesh*, and who see clearly that suffering will not go beyond the suffering body, for it in no way touches the impassibility of divinity'.

Timothy Aelurus, the heretic, the Monophysite, from the *Argument against Calonymus of Alexandria*: 'Cyril is the bishop of the Alexandrian church. In that this man articulated the wise proclam- 1849B ation of orthodoxy in different ways, seeming to be unstable, he is accused of teaching contradictory doctrines. This is because, having laid down as fundamental the necessity of saying "one incarnate nature of God the Word", he cancels what he asserted, and is caught in the act of giving pride of place to "two natures in Christ!" The man who declared that God the Word suffered in the flesh says the opposite: that He did not take on suffering for our sake in any way. But when he became an opponent of his own statements, he gave root to the implacable battle that currently rages in the churches and, as if kindling a violent flame, set the definition of sound faith ablaze—except that the patriarch Severus, appearing with God's aid, cured with his holy writings whatever of Cyril's was unsound and contradictory, covering, like some loyal son, his progenitor's shame with fitting garments'. 1849C

Ἀλλὰ τί πρὸς ταῦτα πάντα φασὶ πάλιν ἡμῖν οἱ ὡς <u>ἀσπίδες τὰ ὦτα</u>
<u>βύοντες</u>,[199] καὶ τῆς τῶν πατέρων σοφῆς ἐπῳδῆς οὐκ εἰσακούοντες;
Τοιάδε γὰρ πάντως ἡμῖν ἀντιλέξουσι καὶ πρὸς τάδε· "Τί δῆτα
μελιττῶν δίκην πᾶσι τοῖς πατρικοῖς συγγράμμασιν ἐφιπτάμενοι, τὸ
μὲν καθ᾽ ἡδονὴν ὑμῖν ἀνθολογεῖτε τῶν χρήσεων, καὶ περιβομβεῖτε
ἡμᾶς τούτοις ἐνδελεχῶς, τὰ δὲ πολέμια τοῖς ὑμετέροις φρονήμασιν
ὑπερίπτασθε, σιγῇ τούτων ἀποπηδήσαντες;"Καὶ πρὸς τοῦτο γοῦν
ἐροῦμεν, ὡς ὄντως καὶ τὰ δοκοῦντα ὑμῖν συμφωνεῖν πατρικὰ
1849D   ῥήματα τοῖς ὑμετέροις δόγμασι, μᾶλλον τὰ ἡμέτερα συνιστάνει,
δεόντως ἐξεταζόμενα κατὰ τὴν ἔννοιαν, καθὼς ἐξ ἀρχῆς ἐλέγομεν·
οὐ γὰρ δή τις τῶν ἐκκρίτων πατέρων ἀσύμφωνος ἑαυτῷ ἐστιν ἢ τοῖς
ὁμοτίμοις αὐτῷ κατὰ τὴν ἔννοιαν τῆς πίστεως, εἰ καί, δι᾽ ἑτέρων
λέξεων καὶ λόγων φερόμενος, ἐναντίος ὑμῖν δοκεῖ εἶναι, τὰς
1852A   λέξεις καὶ οὐ τὰς δυνάμεις τῶν λόγων συμβιβάζειν ἐθέλουσιν.
Ἀλλ᾽ εἰκότως καὶ τοῦτο ὑμᾶς λανθάνει, τό γε ὅμοιον
προηγνοηκότας. Ὥσπερ γάρ ἐστι διὰ τῶν αὐτῶν φωνῶν διάφορον
ἔννοιαν σημαίνεσθαι ἐπὶ τῶν δισεμφάτων λόγων, οὕτω καὶ ἐκ
διαφόρων λόγων τὴν αὐτὴν ἔννοιαν συνάγεσθαι ἐπὶ τῶν
πολυφράδων νοημάτων. Εἰ οὖν τινὰ ἔχετε τῶν ὡμολογημένων καὶ
γνωστῶν πατέρων ὀρθοδόξων, καὶ διὰ τεύχους παλαιοῦ καὶ
ἀνοθεύτου ἐπιδεικνύναι τι τοῖς ὑμετέροις συνᾷδον εἰρηκότα,
προσαγάγετε· τὰς γὰρ κρυψωνύμους καὶ φαλσογράφους ὑμῶν
χρήσεις, ἅπαξ καὶ δὶς φωραθείσας ἐν ἀκεραίῳ ἁπλότητι, λοιπὸν οὐ
παραδεχόμεθα.

Προδιαμαρτυρόμεθα δὲ ὅμως ὅτι ἐν καταχρήσει ἐστὶ πολλάκις
1852B   μεταγενόμενα εὑρεῖν καὶ τὰ τῆς φύσεως καὶ οὐσίας καὶ ὑποστάσεως
καὶ προσώπου ὀνόματα ἐπὶ τῆς οἰκονομίας· οὐ γὰρ κυρίως ἀεὶ
κεῖται. Ἀθανάσιός τε γὰρ ὁ μέγας καὶ "προσώπων ἔνωσιν" ἐπὶ τοῦ
Χριστοῦ διϊσχυρίζεται, καὶ Πρόκλος "ὑποστάσεων", Κύριλλός τε
ὁ μακάριος, "εἴ τις [287ʳ] διαιρεῖ τὰς ὑποστάσεις",[200] ἔφησεν. Ἐὰν
οὖν ὡς κυριολεξίας ὄντα καὶ τάδε νοοῦνται, ἰδοὺ καὶ οἱ Νεστοριανοὶ
καλῶς ἡμῖν ταῦτα ἀεὶ προβάλλονται, ὑποστάσεων καὶ προσώπων
ἔνωσιν δογματίζοντες ἐν τῇ οἰκονομίᾳ. Πῶς δὲ ἂν τόδε οὕτως ἔφη,
ὁ ἐν τετάρτῳ ἀναθεματισμῷ εἰπὼν πατὴρ Κύριλλος, "Εἴ τις
προσώποις δυσὶν ἤγουν ὑποστάσεσι διανέμει φωνάς",[201] καὶ τὰ
ἑξῆς, ἐν δὲ τῇ πρὸς τὸν βασιλέα Θεοδόσιον ἐπιστολῇ ἀλλὰ καὶ πρὸς
Ἰωάννην τὸν Ἀντιοχείας φησί· "Τὰς εὐαγγελικὰς καὶ ἀποστολικὰς
1852C   περὶ τοῦ Κυρίου φωνὰς ἴσμεν τοὺς θεηγόρους ἄνδρας, τὰς μὲν
κοινοποιοῦντας ὡς ἐφ᾽ ἑνὸς προσώπου, τὰς δὲ διαιροῦντας ὡς ἐπὶ
δύο φύσεων."[202]

---

[199] Ps. 57: 5 LXX
[200] Cyril of Alexandria, *Letter* 17, *ACO* i, 1, 1, 40.   [201] Ibid. 41.
[202] Actually Cyril of Alexandria, *Letter* 39, *ACO* i, 1, 4, 17. Cited also at 1821C and
1829A.

But what do these people who *stop their ears like adders*, and don't listen to the wise incantation of the fathers, have to say against all this? Here are exactly the kinds of things they'll offer in opposition to what we've said: 'Why do you, when you buzz around patristic texts like bees, harvest honey from whatever example pleases you, and continually bombard us with your buzzing about them, but fly right over others that are hostile to your purposes, darting away from them in silence?' Our response to what you say is that, actually, even the sayings of the fathers that in your view agree with your doctrines instead recommend ours when they're examined, as they ought to be, in terms of their meaning—which is what we've been saying from the outset. Surely none of the select fathers is at variance with himself or with his peers with respect to the intended sense of the faith, even though, when he expresses himself through different words and expressions, he seems to you people who want to compare words, rather than the force of words, to be contradictory. Likely this escapes your notice, however, since you were ignorant on the same point before. The very man who's able to signify a different sense by means of the same sounds, when it's a case of expressions that have two meanings, is likewise able to infer the same sense from different expressions when eloquent speech is involved. If, then, you have any [texts] of orthodox fathers everyone agrees about and knows, and these texts from an old and genuine book are said to demonstrate something that accords with your views, bring them into court. We're not allowing your anonymous and spurious texts any more, though, not now that they've quite plainly been detected once or twice!

We likewise give testimony in advance that it's often possible to find names that change in cases of misuse—names for nature, essence, hypostasis, and person in the Incarnation—for they aren't always properly applied. The great Athanasius confidently affirms a 'union of persons' in Christ, and Proclus one of 'hypostases'. The blessed Cyril said 'if anyone divides the hypostases . . .'. If, then, our opponents suppose that these expressions are used in the literal sense, then notice what follows: the Nestorians are right when they always use these texts as a defence against us, asserting a union of hypostases and persons in the Incarnation. But how could the father Cyril have used this expression in their sense, since he says in the fourth anathema 'If anyone apportions sayings to two persons or hypostases . . .', and so on, though in the *Letter to the Emperor Theodosius*, but also to John of Antioch, he says: 'We recognize that theologians hold some evangelical and apostolic texts about the Lord to be common, as concerning one person, but distinguish others of them, as concerning two natures.'

1849D

1852A

1852B

1852C

Εἰ γὰρ πανταχῇ ἐπὶ τῆς οἰκονομίας ἀποκληρωτικῶς φύσιν καὶ ὑπόστασιν ταὐτὸν οἶδεν ὁ πατήρ, οἱ διαιροῦντες ὡς ἐπὶ δύο φύσεων τὰς φωνάς, τῷ ἀναθέματι τῷ ἐπὶ τῶν δύο ὑποστάσεσι διανεμόντων φωνὰς κειμένῳ καθυποβέβληνται πάντες οἱ θεηγόροι. Μὴ οὖν τὰ μὴ κυρίως κατὰ τῶν κυρίως εἰρημένων προφέροιτε, ἀλλ᾽ ἐκ τοῦ πρέποντος λόγου καὶ συμφώνου καὶ κοινοτέρου καὶ πᾶσιν ὡμολογημένου, τῆς ἀληθείας στοχαστέον ἡμῖν τὲ καὶ ὑμῖν κατὰ πάντα τὰ παραγόμενα.

1852D

Πρῶτον μὲν οὖν εἰπεῖν, "Νεστόριος" φασὶ "κατεχρήσατο τῇ τῶν δύο φύσεων φωνῇ ἐπὶ Χριστοῦ, ᾗ καὶ ὑμεῖς." ⟨Λ⟩έγομεν οὖν ὅτι καὶ γραφικαῖς φωναῖς πολλαῖς ἐχρήσατο· μὴ δὲ αὗται οὖν ὀνομαζέσθωσαν ἡμῖν, εἰ συνορᾶτε. Ἀλλὰ καὶ "τῇ μιᾷ φύσει τοῦ Λόγου σεσαρκωμένῃ", οἱ Ἀρειανοὶ πρῶτοι καὶ Ἀπολινάριοι καὶ ἕτεροι αἱρετικοὶ προσχρῶνται· σιγητέον οὖν καὶ τήνδε διὰ τούσδε; Οὐχί, ἀλλ᾽ ἐμφράξει πᾶσα ἀνομία τὸ στόμα αὐτῆς,[203] ἡμεῖς δὲ

1853A παρρησιασώμεθα ὡς δεῖ λαλῆσαι[204] κατὰ τὸν θεοθαρσῆ κήρυκα· ὁ γὰρ τῆς ἀληθείας λόγος[205] ἐν τῷ θριαμβεύεσθαι, οὐκ ἐν τῷ περικαλύπτεσθαι, νικᾷ τὸ ψεῦδος, καὶ δοξάζειν αὐτὸς οἶδε τοὺς λαλοῦντας αὐτόν, οὐκ ἐκ τῶν λαλούντων αὐτὸς δοξάζεται. Καὶ περὶ μὲν τοῦδε τάδε. Λοιπὸν δὲ ἴδωμεν, οἷα ἐστὶ καὶ ἃ φασιν αὐτοὶ σαφῶς μίαν φύσιν ἐπὶ τοῦ Κυρίου λέγειν, καὶ τὰς δύο ἀπαγορεύειν φύσεις παντελῶς, πατρικὰ δόγματα.

Τοῦ ἁγίου Κυρίλλου ἐκ τῆς πρὸς Σούκενσον Β΄ ἐπιστολῆς· "Τὸ λέγειν δύο φύσεις ὑφεστάναι μετὰ τὴν ἕνωσιν ἀδιαιρέτως, μάχεσθαί ἐστι τοῖς μίαν εἶναι λέγουσι τὴν τοῦ Λόγου φύσιν

1853B σεσαρκωμένην."[206] Ἀλλὰ πρὸς Νεστοριανοὺς τοῦτο λέγων, ἐπιφέρει μετὰ βραχέα, ὦ οὗτοι· "Τὸ γὰρ ἀδιαιρέτως προστεθέν, δοκεῖ μὲν παρ᾽ ἡμῖν ὀρθῆς εἶναι δόξης σημαντικόν, αὐτοὶ δὲ οὐχ᾽ οὕτως νοοῦσι. Τὸ γὰρ ἀδιαίρετον παρ᾽ αὐτοῖς κατὰ τὰς Νεστορίου κενοφωνίας, καθ᾽ ἕτερον λαμβάνεται τρόπον· φησὶ γὰρ ὅτι τῇ ἰσοτιμίᾳ, τῇ ταυτοβουλίᾳ, τῇ αὐθεντίᾳ, ἀδιαίρετός ἐστι [287ᵛ] τοῦ Λόγου ὁ ἐν ᾧ κατῴκησεν ἄνθρωπος, ὥστε οὐχ᾽ ἁπλῶς τὰς λέξεις λέγουσιν, ἀλλὰ μετά τινος κακουργίας."[207] Ἰδοὺ οὖν σκοπεῖτε εὐγνωμόνως ὅτι τὴν μὲν φωνὴν οἶδεν ὀρθῆς δόξης, τὸ δὲ κακούργως ἔχον νόημα, ἀποβάλλεται, ὅπερ ἐξ ἀρχῆς καὶ ἕως τέλους ποιεῖν καὶ ὑμᾶς καὶ ἡμεῖς δυσωποῦμεν. Ἔστιν οὖν τὴν αὐτὴν ἀσεβῶς εἰπεῖν τινα φωνήν, ἀλλὰ καὶ τὴν ἑτέραν φωνὴν τὴν

---

[203] Ps. 106: 42 LXX   [204] Eph. 6: 20, modified   [205] Eph. 1: 13
[206] Cf. Cyril of Alexandria, *Letter* 46, *ACO* i, 1, 6, 161.
[207] Ibid. 162.

If the father recognizes nature and hypostasis as being absolutely and without distinction the same thing in the Incarnation, all of the theologians who divide the sayings as of two natures have been implicated in the anathema applied to those who apportion sayings to two hypostases! That's why you mustn't adduce things said in the improper sense against things that are said in the proper sense. Rather, on the basis of the fitting and harmonious and more universal understanding confessed by all, what we and you must aim at, with all the evidence we adduce, is the truth.   1852D

This is their first objection: 'Nestorius', they say, 'used the expression "two natures in Christ", which you people also use.' Well, we say he also used many scriptural expressions, but then these aren't to be cited by us either, if you see what I mean. Moreover, Arians were the first, along with Apollinarians and other heretics, to use 'one incarnate nature of the Word'. Is a person, just because of them, to keep silent about this expression too? Certainly not! Rather, *all wickedness will stop its mouth*, but we, on the other hand, *shall speak boldly, as we ought to speak*, as God's   1853A confidence-infused herald puts it, for *the word of truth* defeats falsehood when it's shouted from the housetops, not when it's concealed, and itself knows how to glorify those who speak it; it doesn't acquire glory from those who do the speaking. But enough of that. Let's go on to see what kind of doctrines these patristic doctrines are, the ones these people say clearly speak of one nature in the Lord, and completely rule out two natures.

Saint Cyril, from the *Second Letter to Succensus*: 'To say that two natures exist indivisibly after the union is to oppose those who say there is one incarnate nature of the Word.' But when he says this against Nestorians, my friends, he adds after a bit: 'Though the   1853B added word "indivisibly" seems, in our use of it, to signify a correct opinion, that is not the way they understand it. The word "indivisible" is taken in a different sense when they use it, one that accords with the empty babblings of Nestorius. He says it is by equality of honour, sameness of will, and [equality of] authority that the man in whom the Word dwelt is undivided from Him. That means they do not use these phrases in a straightforward way, but with a kind of mischievous intent.' See? It's with good reason that you notice that, while he recognizes the expression as enunciating correct opinion, he rejects the mischievous way of understanding it—just what we've been urging both you and us to do from start to finish. It's possible to use this same particular expression in an impious way, but it's also possible, in the way of Arius, to conceive of the other expression (the one that says 'one

1853C λέγουσαν "μίαν φύσιν τοῦ Θεοῦ Λόγου σεσαρκωμένην" ἔστι κατὰ
Ἄρειον, ὡς οὐ πάντῃ ἀτρέπτου φύσεως ὄντος τοῦ Υἱοῦ, νοεῖν, καὶ
κατὰ Ἀπολινάριον, ὡς αὐτοῦ τοῦ Λόγου ἀντὶ νοῦ ψυχικοῦ
γενομένου, τῇ ἐμψυχωθείσῃ ἀλόγῳ σαρκί, λογίζεσθαι, καὶ κατὰ
Εὐτυχέα, ὡς αὐτοῦ τοῦ Λόγου εἰς σάρκα μεταποιηθέντος,
ἐκδέχεσθαι. Ἐὰν οὖν²⁰⁸ μὴ τὰ νοήματα ἀνακρίνωμεν τῶν
ὁμολογούντων, καὶ ταύτην κἀκείνην οὐκ ἄλλως προσιέμεθα τὴν
φωνήν. Τοῦτο γὰρ ὁ πατὴρ φησὶ, ὅτι, ὡς κακουργοῦντας περὶ τὴν
ἔννοιαν τῆς ἑνώσεως τῶν φύσεων, μὴ ἀποδέχεσθαι τοὺς αἱρετικοὺς
δεῖ, κἂν εὔηχοι εἶεν αἱ φωναί· οὐ γὰρ τὴν καθ᾽ ὑπόστασιν ⟨ἕνωσιν⟩
λέγουσι τῶν φύσεων, ἀλλὰ κατὰ σχέσιν ἀδιαίρετον. Ἐν πολλαῖς γὰρ
χρηστολογίαις²⁰⁹ οἶδε τὴν ἀπάτην καὶ ὁ ἀπόστολος γινομένην. Ὅτι
1853D δὲ τοῦτο οὕτως νοεῖ καὶ ἐν τῇ ἑξῆς ἣν παράγουσι χρήσει, σαφὲς
ἔσται.

Τοῦ αὐτοῦ Κυρίλλου ἐκ τῶν εἰς τὴν πρὸς Ἑβραίους δευτέρου
τόμου· "Ἀποδιϊστάντες γὰρ ἀλλήλων τὰς δύο φύσεις, καὶ ἀνὰ μέρος
ἡμῖν ἑκατέραν ἀσυναφῆ θατέραν δεικνύοντες, ἐν μόνοις προσώποις
φασὶ γενέσθαι τὴν ἕνωσιν, καὶ ὡς ἔν γε ψιλῇ συναινέσει καὶ
ταυτοβουλίᾳ καὶ θελημάτων ῥοπαῖς, κατ᾽ ἐκεῖνό που τάχα τὸ ἐν ταῖς
Πράξεσι τῶν ἁγίων ἀποστόλων γεγραμμένον, τοῦ δὲ πλήθους τῶν
1856A πιστευσάντων, ἦν ἡ καρδία καὶ ἡ ψυχὴ μία.²¹⁰ Ἑκάστου γὰρ τῶν
πεπιστευκότων κατά γε τὸν τῆς ἰδίας ὑποστάσεως λόγον
διεσχοινισμένου τῶν ἄλλων, ὅσον ἧκεν εἰς ταυτοβουλίαν καὶ τὴν
ἑνότητα τῆς πίστεως, ψυχὴ πάντων εἶναι μία λέγεται καὶ καρδία.
Ἆρα οὖν κατὰ τοῦτον καὶ αὐτοὶ τὸν τρόπον, τῶν προσώπων τὴν
ἕνωσιν ὁμολογεῖν ἐγνώκασιν."²¹¹ Ἰδοὺ διασαφεῖ ἐκδήλως τί ἐστιν ὃ
μέμφεται δόγμα τῶν δὲ καὶ ἕνωσιν ἀδιαίρετον λεγόντων ἐπὶ δύο
φύσεων. Καὶ μετὰ βραχέα· "Καὶ οὐ δήπου φαμὲν ἐν τῷ ἀνθρωπίνῳ
σώματι τὴν τοῦ Θεοῦ Λόγου περιγεγράφθαι φύσιν· ἄποσον γὰρ τὸ
θεῖον."²¹² Εἶτα ἐπάγει, ὅτι· "Ὄψεταί τις ἐν Χριστῷ τὸ ἀνθρώπινον
τελείως ἔχον, κατά γε τὸν τῆς ἰδίας φύσεως λόγον, ὁμοίως τὲ
τέλειον τὸν ἐκ Θεοῦ φύντα Λόγον, πλὴν ἕνα τὸν ἐξ ἀμφοῖν
1856B ὁμολογήσει Χριστὸν καὶ Υἱόν, οὐ προσώπων ἑνώσει μόνον
συντιθεὶς τὴν οἰκονομίαν, συλλέγων δὲ μᾶλλον εἰς ἓν τὰς φύσεις
ἀπορρήτως γε καὶ ὑπὲρ λόγον, ὡς αὐτὸς ἔγνω ὁ Θεός. Καὶ οὐ δήπου
φαμὲν ἀνάχυσιν ὥσπέρ τινα συμβῆναι περὶ τὰς φύσεις, ὡς
μεταστῆναι τὴν τοῦ Λόγου φύσιν [288ʳ] εἰς τὴν τοῦ ἀνθρώπου
τυχόν, ἀλλ᾽ οὐδὲ αὖ τὴν ἀνθρωπίνην εἰς τὴν τοῦ Λόγου, νοουμένης δὲ

---

²⁰⁸ οὖν] supra lin. MS   ²⁰⁹ Rom. 16: 18   ²¹⁰ Acts 4: 32
²¹¹ Cyril of Alexandria, *On Hebrews* ii, *PG* lxxiv, 1004A–B.   ²¹² Ibid. 1004B.

incarnate nature of God the Word') as belonging to the Son who 1853c doesn't have an altogether immutable nature, and, in the way of Apollinarius, to take it as belonging to the Word Himself who took the place of a psychic mind for the animate but irrational flesh, and, following Eutyches, to accept it as belonging to the Word Himself changed into flesh. If we're not to inquire into the intentions of the people who make confessions, we have no other basis on which to accept the former or the latter expression. What the father's saying is this: the heretics ought not to be accepted, being people who falsify what's understood by the union of natures, even if the expressions they use sound good, for they don't speak of the union of natures by hypostasis, but of a union that's undivided in terms of relationship. The apostle, too, recognizes the deceit that lurks in lots of *flattering words*. It will become clear that Cyril takes the same approach to this matter in the next 1853D text they trot out.

The same Cyril, from *On Hebrews* ii: 'When they separate the two natures from each other, and point each of them individually out to us in turn, they're saying that the union took place in persons only, and thus [has its reality] in mere agreement, identity of inclination, and harmony of wills, the kind of union found in that passage, probably somewhere in the Acts of the Holy Apostles, that goes *the heart and the soul of the company of those who believed* 1856A *were one*. Though each of those who had come to believe was separate from the others by reason of his own hypostasis, the soul and heart of all are said to be one in so far as each tends towards identity of inclination and oneness of faith. In this way, then, even these people have learned to confess the union of persons.' Notice: he makes it quite clear just what opinion on the part of those who speak of an undivided union in two natures it is that he censures. After a bit he goes on: 'We certainly are not saying the nature of the Word of God is contained in the human body, for the divine is without quantity!' Then he adds: 'Anyone will observe the human existing completely in Christ by reason of its own nature, and likewise the complete Word sprung from God. He will, moreover, confess the one Christ and Son out of both, not 1856B putting the Incarnation together just by a union of persons, but rather bringing the natures together into one in a way that is ineffable and beyond reason, as God Himself understood. We certainly do not speak of a confusion, as if the Word's nature changed into the man's nature in the same way as some things

μᾶλλον καὶ ὑπαρχούσης ἑκατέρας ἐν τῷ τῆς ἰδίας φύσεως ὅρῳ, πεπράχθαι φαμὲν τὴν ἕνωσιν."²¹³ Καὶ μετ' ὀλίγα· "Εἰ τις οὖν ἄρα λέγοι μόνων προσώπων τὴν ἕνωσιν, ἀποδιϊστὰς ὁλοτρόπως ἀλλήλων τὰς φύσεις, ἔξω τῆς εὐθείας φέρεται τρίβου."²¹⁴ Τούτων τίς ἀγνοήσει τὴν ἔννοιαν, καὶ μίαν φύσιν λέγειν οἰήσεται τὸν πατέρα
1856c ἐπὶ Χριστοῦ, οὐχὶ δὲ ἓν πρόσωπον μᾶλλον, ἡνωμένων αὐτοῦ τῶν φύσεων, οὐχ' ἁπλῶς ἀδιαιρέτως ἀλλὰ καθ' ὑπόστασιν αὐτοῦ αὐτήν;
Κυρίλλου ἐκ τῆς πρὸς Σούκενσον ἐπιστολῆς· "Ὥστε τὰ δύο μηκέτι εἶναι δύο, δι' ἀμφοῖν δὲ τὸ ἓν ἀποτελεῖσθαι ζῷον".²¹⁵ ⟨Ε⟩ἰ οὖν τοῦτό φησιν, ὅτι αἱ φύσεις οὐκ εἰσὶ λοιπὸν φύσεις, ἔδει εἰπεῖν ὥστε τάς ποτὲ δύο, ταύτας μὴ εἶναι καὶ νῦν δύο· ἢ ὥστε τὸ ἓν τὸ νῦν μηκέτι εἶναι ὡς καὶ πρῴην δύο. Εἰ δὲ ἔστι²¹⁶ καὶ νῦν δύο τὰ δύο, δι' ἀμφοῖν τὲ καὶ οὐκ ἐξ ἀμφοῖν ἁπλῶς τὸ ἓν ὁρᾶται, δῆλον ὡς κατ' ἄλλο καὶ ἄλλο· ὡς μὲν γὰρ φύσεις, δύο, ὡς δὲ σύνθετόν τε τοιόνδε ζῷον, ὅπερ καὶ ῥητῶς ἔφη, ἕν ἐστι. Προσεκτέον δὲ ὡς καὶ "δι' ἀμφοῖν ζῷον ἀποτελεῖσθαι" λέγων, ἑκατέραν φύσιν τῷ ἑνὶ
1856d τούτῳ Χριστῷ ζωὴν συνεισάγειν φησίν, ἀλλὰ τὴν μέν, τὴν φυσικὴν ἀνθρώπῳ, τὴν δέ, τὴν φυσικὴν Θεῷ ζωήν, ὡς ἓν εἶναί τι θεανδρικῶς ζῶν πρόσωπον τόδε· καὶ γάρ ἐσθίων καὶ πίνων,²¹⁷ διήρκει καὶ ηὔξανε²¹⁸ καθ' ἡμᾶς καὶ ἦν καὶ αὐτάρκης καὶ παντέλειος θεϊκῶς ὁ αὐτὸς εἷς Χριστὸς ὁ Κύριος ἡμῶν.
"'Ἀλλ' ἅπαν ἓν ζῷον καὶ μία φύσις" φασίν· "εἰ οὖν ἓν ζῷον, καὶ μία φύσις ὁ Χριστός." Ἀλλ' εἰ ἀποδεικτικῶς ἀπαντᾶν βούλεσθε, μὴ ἀγνοεῖτε τὰ κοινῶς δεδομένα πᾶσι τοῖς ἀποδεικτικοῖς καὶ διαλεκτικοῖς· τῶν γὰρ ἀντιστρόφως ἀλλήλοις κατηγορουμένων, τούτων ἀνάγκη θατέρου δοθέντος, καὶ τὸ ἕτερον συνεπάγεσθαι, τῶν δὲ οὐκ ἀντιστρεφόντων, οὐ δῆτα. Εἰ μὲν οὖν καὶ πᾶσα φύσις ζῷον,
1857a ὥσπερ οὖν καὶ πᾶν ζῷον φύσις, καλῶς ἐλέγετε, ἐπεὶ ζῷον τὸ

---

²¹³ Ibid. 1004B–1005A.
²¹⁴ Ibid. 1005A.
²¹⁵ Cyril of Alexandria, *Letter* 46, *ACO* i, 1, 6, 162.
²¹⁶ ἔστι] supra. lin. MS
²¹⁷ Matt. 11: 19; Luke 7: 34
²¹⁸ Luke 2: 40

come together in terms of their natures, but neither again do we say that the human nature changed into that of the Word. What we do say, rather, is that union was achieved even though each nature is understood, and exists, in the definition of its own nature.' And after a bit: 'If anyone speaks of the union of individual persons, therefore, separating the natures completely from each other, he is turned aside from the straight path.' Who's going to ignore the intent of these statements, and suppose that the father speaks of one nature in Christ, and not rather of one person, since His two natures are united, not only indivisibly, but by His hypostasis itself? 1856c

Of Cyril, from the *Letter to Succensus*: 'so that the two things may no longer be two, but rather the one living thing may be completed through both of them'. If what he's saying is that the natures are no longer natures, then what he should have said is that the natures that once were two aren't two anymore, or that the one thing that now exists is no longer, as it formerly was, two. If, however, the two things continue to be two, and it's simply a matter of the one entity being perceived through both of them and not out of both of them, it's clear that there are two by virtue of there being one reality over against another, for just as the natures are two, so too this kind of compound living thing is one entity—and that is exactly what Cyril was saying. You should pay attention to the fact that the man who says 'a living thing is completed through both of them', says each living nature comes together with this one Christ, but one is the nature natural to a man, the other the nature natural to God. That's why this person is one entity living theandrically, for the same one Christ, our Lord, lived and *grew* like us, *eating and drinking*, yet He was both self-sufficient and, in divine terms, complete. 1856d

'But every one living thing is also one nature', they say. 'If Christ is one living thing, then, He is also one nature.' If you want to prove your case against us with logic, though, you'd better not show your ignorance of what's universally granted by everyone trained in logic and dialectic: when things are signified in ways that are interchangeable with each other, then when one of them is granted, the other inevitably follows, but when it's a case of things that aren't interchangeable, it's quite a different story. If, then, every nature is a living thing, just as every living thing is a nature, you were right to say that, since the composite entity [that 1857a

σύνθετον, καὶ φύσιν ἀποτελεῖσθαι. Εἰ δὲ ἔστιν ὁ λίθος φύσις, οὐ μὴν διά τόδε καὶ ζῷον, οὐκ ἀναγκαῖον εἴ τι ζῷον ἕν ἐστι, διὰ τόδε ἁπλῶς καὶ φύσιν μίαν εἶναι. Καὶ ἄλλως γάρ. Εἰ διότι ἓν ζῷόν ἐστιν ὁ Χριστός, καὶ μία φύσις ἐστί, καὶ διότι ἐκ δύο φύσεών ἐστι, καὶ δύο ζῷα ἔσται, ὅ φησι Νεστόριος ἀσεβῶν μόνος. Εἰ δὲ λέγοιτε, ὅτι "Καὶ ἐκ δύο ζῴων,[219] ὡς ἀπὸ κοινῆς τῆς θεότητος καὶ τῆς ἀνθρωπότητος, τῶν διαφόρων φυσικῶν εἰδῶν, φαμεν αὐτόν", ἆρά γε καὶ ἓν ζῷον οὖν, ὡς κοινόν τι καὶ ὡς εἶδος ἕτερον, παρὰ τὴν θεότητα καὶ ἀνθρωπότητα λέγετε αὐτόν. Καὶ πῶς φησὶν οὗτός τε ὁ πατὴρ καὶ οἱ λοιποί, "τὸ Χριστὸς ὄνομα μήτε οὐσίας ὅρον, μήτε φύσεως ὄνομα εἶναι, μήτε ὅρου δύναμιν ἔχειν, μήτε εἶδος φύσεως σημαίνειν", ἢ
1857в τι [288ᵛ] τοιοῦτον;[220] Ζῷον ἄρα τὸ ὡς ὑφεστὼς πρόσωπόν ἐστιν ἕν. Ἀλλ' εἴποιτε ἴσως, ὅτι ὥσπερ ζωῆς τῆς ἀϊδίου καὶ τῆς προσκαίρου μετέχων ἓν ζῷόν ἐστιν, οὕτως καὶ φύσεως προσκαίρου καὶ τῆς ἀϊδίου μετασχών, μία φύσις ἐστίν. Ἀλλ' ἔστιν εὔδηλος ὁ παραλογισμός. Ἀντὶ γὰρ τοῦ μετέχοντος, τὸ μετεχόμενον ἔφητε τὸ δεύτερον. Εἰ μὲν γὰρ τὸ μετέχον ἑκατέρας ζωῆς, ζωὴ ἦν καὶ οὐ ζῷον, εἴτουν τὸ μετέχον τῶν ζωῶν πρόσωπον, καλῶς εἴρητο. Εἰ δὲ τὸ ἐν δύο ζωαῖς θεωρούμενον, ζῷόν ἐστί, καὶ τὸ δύο οὐσιῶν μετειληφός, οὐσιωμένον ἐστὶ τί· οὐ μὴν ἡ οὐσία, εἴτουν φύσις, ἀπρόσωπος. Τί δέ ἐστι τὸ οὐσιωμένον καὶ τὸ ζῷον, ἢ τὸ πρόσωπον κυρίως, τό τε κατὰ διαφόρους φύσεις καὶ ζωὰς ὑφεστώς; Ὥστε ζῷον μὲν ἓν ὀρθῶς φαμέν, φύσιν δὲ μίαν οὐδαμῶς, ὥσπερ οὐδὲ ζωὴν ἐπὶ τοῦ συνθέτου προσώπου Χριστοῦ.

1857с Κυρίλλου ἐκ τῆς πρὸς Ἀκάκιον ἐπιστολῆς· "Ὁρῶμεν ὅτι δύο φύσεις συνῆλθον ἀλλήλαις καθ' ἕνωσιν ἀδιασπάστως, ἀσυγχύτως, καὶ ἀτρέπτως· ἡ γὰρ σάρξ, σάρξ ἐστι καὶ οὐ θεότης, εἰ καὶ γέγονε Θεοῦ σάρξ· ὁμοίως δὲ καὶ ὁ Λόγος, Θεός ἐστι καὶ οὐ σάρξ, εἰ καὶ ἰδίαν ἐποιήσατο τὴν σάρκα οἰκονομικῶς. Ὅταν οὖν ἐννοῶμεν τοῦτο, οὐδὲν ἀδικοῦμεν τὴν εἰς ἑνότητα συνδρομήν, ἐκ δύο φύσεων γεγενῆσθαι λέγοντες· μετὰ μέντοι τὴν ἕνωσιν οὐ διαιροῦμεν τὰς φύσεις ἀπ' ἀλλήλων, οὐδὲ εἰς δύο τέμνομεν υἱοὺς τὸν ἕνα καὶ ἀμέριστον, ἀλλ' ἕνα φαμὲν Υἱόν, καὶ ὡς οἱ πατέρες εἰρήκασιν μίαν

---

[219] p. corr.
[220] Cyril of Alexandria, *Scholia*, *ACO* i, 5, 219, apparently cited (badly) from memory. The text is cited correctly in *Aporiae* at 1781D.

is Christ] is a living thing, it constitutes a nature. Yet if stone's a nature, but it's certainly not on that account a living thing, then there's no necessity that, if some living thing is one entity, it on that account alone be one nature too. There are other considerations. If Christ is one nature because He's one living thing, then He'll be two living things because He's out of two natures—and that's something only the impious Nestorius says! If, however, you say 'We say He's also out of two living things, as from the different natural forms of universal divinity and humanity', then you're saying He's also one living thing as being some different universal form from divinity and humanity! And how does it happen that Cyril, along with all the other fathers, says that 'the name "Christ" is neither the definition of a substance nor the name of a nature, nor does it have the meaning of a definition, nor does it signify the form of nature'—or something of the sort? The person subsisting in this way is, then, one living thing. You may say, by the same 1857B token, that, just as He who shares in both eternal and transitory life is one living thing, so also He who shared in a transitory and an eternal nature is one nature. The falsity of your reasoning is patent, though: you substituted the second thing, the thing shared in, for the thing that does the sharing in. If what shared in each life was life, and not a living thing, that is, the person that shares in living things, what you said was correct. If, however, what's understood in two lives, and participated in two substances, is a living thing, it's something invested with substance. Certainly there exists no substance, i.e. nature, that's without a person. What is the thing invested with substance, the living thing, except the person in the strict sense, that which subsists in respect of various natures and lives? That's why we're right when we speak of one living entity as regards the compound person of Christ, but absolutely not of one nature or life.

Cyril, from the *Letter to Acacius*: 'We observe that two natures 1857C came together in a union inseparably, indivisibly, and immutably, for flesh is flesh, and not divinity, even though it became God's flesh. Likewise, the Word is God and not flesh, even though He made the flesh His own by His Incarnation. Whenever we think in this way, we are not doing any injustice to the coming together into unity when we say it came to be out of two natures. We certainly do not divide the natures from each other after the union, nor do we cut the one and indivisible Son into two Sons! Rather, we speak of one Son and—as the fathers have put it—of

φύσιν τοῦ Λόγου σεσαρκωμένην. Οὐκοῦν ὅσον μὲν ἧκεν εἰς ἔννοιαν
καὶ εἰς μόνον τὸ ὁρᾷν τοῖς τῆς ψυχῆς ὄμμασι, τίνα τρόπον ὁ
Μονογενὴς ἐνηνθρώπησε, δύο τὰς φύσεις φαμέν."²²¹

1857D   'Αλλ' εἴπωμεν καὶ πρὸς τάδε, ὅτι ἀρκεῖ ἡμῖν αὐτὸς ἑαυτὸν
διασαφῶν· "Οὐ γὰρ διαιροῦμεν", ἔφη, καὶ οὐχ "ἑνοῦμεν", καὶ "τὰς
φύσεις", οὐ μὴν "τὴν φύσιν" ὡς οὗτοι λέγουσιν, οὐδὲ τεμνόμενον
1860A   τὸν ἕνα Υἱόν, οὐ μὴν τὴν μίαν φύσιν, ἔφη, "τοῖς δὲ τῆς ψυχῆς
ὄμμασιν", οἷς καὶ διαφέρει ἄνθρωπος κτήνους, τοῦ ἐν τοῖς τοῦ
σώματος ὄμμασι μόνον βλέποντος. Δύο ἄρα καί φησιν εἶναι ὁ πατὴρ
τὰς φύσεις τοῦ Λόγου σεσαρκωμένου, ἀληθῶς.

Τοῦ αὐτοῦ ἐκ τῆς αὐτῆς ἐπιστολῆς· "Δεξώμεθα πρὸς
παράδειγμα τὴν καθ' ἡμᾶς αὐτοὺς σύνθεσιν, καθ' ἣν ἐσμὲν ἄνθρωποι·
συντιθέμεθα γὰρ ἐκ ψυχῆς καὶ σώματος, καὶ ὁρῶμεν δύο φύσεις,
ἑτέραν μὲν τοῦ σώματος, ἑτέραν δὲ τῆς ψυχῆς, ἀλλ' ἐξ ἀμφοῖν
καθ' ἕνωσιν ἄνθρωπον. Καὶ οὐχ' ὅτι ἐκ δύο φύσεων συντέθειται ὁ
ἄνθρωπος, δύο τὸν ἕνα νομιστέον, ἀλλ' ἕνα τὸν αὐτὸν κατὰ σύνθεσιν,
ὡς ἔφην, τὴν ἐκ σώματος καὶ ψυχῆς."²²² Ἰδοὺ πάλιν σαφῶς, μὴ δύο
1860B   ἀνθρώπους τὸν ἕνα νομίζειν, λέγει· οὐχί, μὴ δύο φύσεις τὴν μίαν
φύσιν λογίζεσθαι, ἔφη, ὅπου γε τοῦ ἀνθρώπου οὐδὲ κατὰ πάντα
ἐλήφθη τὸ παράδειγμα.

"'Αλλ' ἐν τῷ δευτέρῳ πρὸς Σούκενσον ὑπομνηστικῷ ῥητῶς",
φασίν, "ὁ πατὴρ Κύριλλος εἴρηκε, τὸ τοῦ ἀνθρώπου λαβών, ἐκ
ψυχῆς καὶ σώματος ὄντος, παράδειγμα· ὥστε 'τὰ [289ʳ] δύο,
μηκέτι εἶναι δύο.'²²³" Καὶ πῶς οὐ δῆλον, ὡς καὶ τοῦτο οὕτως λέγει,
ὅτι καθὸ γέγοναν, οὐκ εἰσὶ δύο ἤγουν ἄνθρωποι; Ἰδοὺ γὰρ αὐτὸς
ἀνωτέρω φησί· "Δύο μὲν γὰρ καὶ ἐπ' αὐτοῦ νοοῦμεν τὰς φύσεις, μίαν
μὲν ψυχῆς, ἑτέραν δὲ τοῦ σώματος",²²⁴ εἰ καὶ μὴ ἀνὰ μέρος δῆλον.
1860C   Καὶ γὰρ ἐπάγει· "'Αλλ' ἑνὸς εἶναι νοοῦμεν".²²⁵ ὥστε οἶδεν αὐτὰ δύο,
ἐν τῷ εἶναι αὐτὰ ἑνός. Οὐ γὰρ ἂν ἔφη, μήποτε εἰδὼς τὴν δυάδα, τὸ
"ἀλλ' ἑνὸς" τοῦ ἀνθρώπου, ὡς ἕκαστα ἔχοντος, οὐκέτι δὲ ἔμεινε δύο,
τουτέστι μόνον καὶ ἁπλῶς ὄντα, ἀλλὰ καὶ ἕν τι ποιήσαντα τὸν
ἄνθρωπον—καὶ ἕν τι γὰρ ὁρῶνται καὶ νοοῦνται· ἐπεὶ πῶς, εἰ
πάντη οὐκ εἰσὶ δύο, ψυχὴ ἔτι ἐστὶ καὶ σῶμα σωζόμενα; Ὅμως ἐπὶ
Χριστοῦ, οὐδὲ κατὰ τὸν τῆς φύσεως λόγον, ἀλλὰ κατὰ τὸν τῆς

---

²²¹ Actually Cyril of Alexandria, *Letter* 45, *ACO* i, 1, 6, 153–4.
²²² Ibid. 154.
²²³ Cyril of Alexandria, *Letter* 46, *ACO* i, 1, 6, 162.
²²⁴ Ibid. 162.   ²²⁵ Ibid.

one incarnate nature of the Word. Therefore, it is inasmuch as the Only-Begotten has become present to our understanding, and became man in some way perceptible only to the eyes of the soul, that we say there are two natures.'

Here's what we'd like to say in rebuttal: Cyril himself is on our side, for he explains himself. 'We do not divide', he said, not 'we unite', and he spoke of 'natures', not 'nature', as our opponents do. He talked of the one Son not being cut into two, not the one nature. No indeed. He said 'with the eyes of the soul'—which is how a man differs from a beast, which sees only with the eyes of the body. What the father's saying, therefore, is that there are two natures of the incarnate Word, and that's the truth. 1857D 1860A

Of the same, from the same letter: 'Let us take as our paradigm the composition that has to do with ourselves, the composition that makes us human beings. We are composed of a soul and a body, and we discern two natures, one of the body, another of the soul, but we discern out of both, by union, a man. You should not consider that the one man is two just because he was composed out of two natures, but rather, as I said, that the same man is one by virtue of his composition out of body and soul.' Notice once again, and notice well: he's telling us not to consider the one man to be two men; he didn't say the one nature wasn't to be considered two natures, and there are cases where the paradigm of man was not applied in every respect. 1860B

'But in the second memorandum to Succensus', they say, 'the father Cyril expressly said, when he adopted the paradigm of man (who is out of soul and body), that "the two are no longer two." ' How is it anything but clear that he says this in the following sense: there aren't two, vis-à-vis the way they've come to exist, that is, there aren't two men? Notice what he himself says earlier: 'We recognize two natures in him, one of soul, another of body', though it's clear they don't exist one after the other. He also adds: 'but we understand that [they are] of one.' He therefore recognizes them to be two in their being 'of one'. He didn't, refusing to recognize the duality, use the expression 'but . . . of one' for the man who possessed both. Rather, they didn't remain two, i.e. two things existing separately and by themselves, but they made man one thing—for they are observed and understood to be one thing. How, after all, are body and soul preserved if there really aren't two realities? Similarly, in the case of Christ, the paradigm is applied to Him, not in the sense of nature, but in the sense of 1860C

ὑποστάσεως εἴληπται αὐτῷ τὸ παράδειγμα· πρὸς γὰρ Νεστόριον δύο τὰς ὑποστάσεις αὐτοῦ λέγοντα εἴρηται. Εἰ γὰρ καὶ ἐπὶ φύσεως λόγῳ εἴληπται τὸ παράδειγμα τοῦ ἀνθρώπου ἐπὶ Χριστοῦ, ἄρα καί, ἐπεὶ οὐκ ἐκ προϋπαρχουσῶν δύο φύσεων ὁ Ἀδὰμ ψυχῆς καὶ σώματος, οὐδὲ ὁ Κύριος ἐκ δύο φύσεων· ἔτι μὴν ὁ Λόγος καὶ πρὸ 1860D τῆς σαρκός, τοῦ δὲ ἀνθρώπου, οὐδὲν μέρος τοῦ ἑτέρου προϋπάρχειν εἴρηται· ἔτι ὁ ἄνθρωπος δυνάμει διαιρετὸς εἰς τὰς αὐτοῦ δύο φύσεις ἐστὶν ἀεί, ἀλλὰ καὶ ἐνεργείᾳ ποτέ. Ἆρα οὖν καὶ ἐπὶ Χριστοῦ εἴποι τίς τάδε, μὴ παραφρονῶν; Πῶς οὖν τὸ καθ᾽ ὑπόστασιν ληφθέν, καὶ ποτὲ εἰς φύσιν τὴν ὡς ὑπόστασιν καὶ αὐτὴν λεγομένην, εἰς οὐσίας παράδειγμα βιάζεσθε πάντως λαμβάνειν ἡμᾶς; Δέδειχε γοῦν καὶ ἐν τοῖς ἐπιχειρήμασιν ἐπὶ Χριστοῦ τὸ μίαν λέγειν φύσιν, εἰ καὶ ἔστιν εἰπεῖν ἐπ᾽ ἀνθρώπου μίαν, ὁ λόγος ἀδύνατον.

"Ἐν πολλοῖς" φησὶν "εὑρίσκομεν ἀπαρεσκόμενον τὸν πατέρα 1861A Κύριλλον καὶ τῇ τοῦ διπλοῦ ὀνομασίᾳ ἐπὶ τοῦ Κυρίου· πόσῳ γε μᾶλλον τῇ τῶν δύο φωνῇ·"

Ἆρα οὖν ἐναντίος Γρηγορίῳ τῷ πολλάκις κατακεχρημένῳ τῇδε, ἐστίν· "Ἀπεστάλη γάρ," φησίν, "ἀλλ᾽ ὡς ἄνθρωπος, διπλοῦς γὰρ ἦν".[226] καὶ "Πατὴρ οὐ τοῦ ὁρωμένου, τοῦ νοουμένου δέ· καὶ γὰρ ἦν διπλοῦς",[227] καὶ ἄλλοι δὲ πλεῖστοι τῶν πατέρων τὰ ὅμοιά φασιν. Ἢ δῆλον, ὅτι μὲν διπλοῦς κατὰ τὰς φύσεις ἦν, ἔφη, ὅτι δὲ οὐ διπλοῦς Χριστὸς ἢ Υἱὸς ὀρθῶς λέγεται, Κύριλλος ὁ πατὴρ φησί· τοῦτο γὰρ Νεστόριος ἐπινοεῖ. Εἰ γὰρ τὸ κατὰ φύσιν διπλοῦν οὐκ ἐγκρίνει, πῶς καὶ αὐτὸς ἔφη ἐν τῷ κατὰ Ματθαῖον, "Ὁ στατὴρ ὁ ἀληθινὸς καὶ νοητὸς καὶ ὡς ἐν τύπῳ τῷ ἐξ ὕλης νοούμενος, οὗτός ἐστιν ὁ Κύριος ἡμῶν Ἰησοῦς Χριστός, ὁ διπλοῦς χαρακτήρ"·[228]

1861B Κυρίλλου ἐκ τῶν πρὸς τὰς ἀπορίας ὑπαντήσεων· "Ἐν ἰδιότητι τῇ κατὰ φύσιν ἑκατέρου μένοντός τε καὶ νοουμένου, κατά γε τὸν ἀρτίως ἡμῖν ἀποδοθέντα λόγον, ἀρρήτως καὶ ἀφράστως ἑνωθείς, μίαν ἡμῖν ἔδειξεν Υἱοῦ φύσιν, πλὴν σεσαρκωμένην· οὐ γὰρ ἐπὶ μόνων τῶν ἁπλῶν κατὰ τὴν φύσιν τὸ ἕν ἀληθῶς λέγεται."[229] "Ἰδοὺ" φασὶ "τοῦ Υἱοῦ, ὅς ἐστι Χριστός, 'μίαν φύσιν' ἔφη." Ἀλλὰ καὶ τὸ ἐπαγόμενον συνάψαντες, διακρινέτωσαν, εἰ ὀρθῶς συλλογίζονται. Εἰ γὰρ τὸ τοῦ Υἱοῦ ὄνομα [289ʳ] καὶ πρὸ τῆς σαρκώσεως

---

[226] Gregory of Nazianzus, *Oration* 38, SC 358, 138. Cited also at 1821B–C.
[227] Gregory of Nazianzus, *Oration* 30, SC 250, 240. Cited more extensively at 1820D.
[228] Cf. Cyril of Alexandria, *On Matthew*, PG lxxii, 429B–C.
[229] Cyril of Alexandria, *Letter* 46, ACO i, 1, 6, 159–60.

hypostasis. It's used against Nestorius, who spoke of His two hypostases. If the paradigm of man was applied to Christ in the sense of nature as well, then, since Adam wasn't out of two pre-existing natures of soul and body, neither was the Lord out of two natures. The Word certainly existed also before the flesh, but nei- 1860D ther of man's parts is said to have pre-existed the other. Moreover, man is always potentially divisible into his two natures, but sometimes that happens in actuality too. Could anyone say that about Christ unless he were mad? How, then, can you press us to take unreservedly what was accepted as applying to hypostasis (and sometimes to nature, when the word's used in the sense of hypostasis) as a paradigm applying to substance? Reason has shown, then, in these demonstrations too, that to speak of one nature with reference to Christ is impossible, even though it's possible to speak of one nature in the case of a man.

'In many places', my friend says, 'we find the father Cyril showing displeasure even at the mention of two-foldedness vis-à-vis the 1861A Lord; how much more [would he show disapproval], then, at the assertion of the two [natures]?'

That means he's opposed to Gregory, who often made use of this expression. 'He was sent,' he says, 'but as a man, for He was twofold.' He also says 'Father, not of what's seen, but of what's understood, for He was twofold'. Most of the other fathers say much the same thing. It's clear, though, that he was saying Christ was of two kinds in respect of natures, but that the father Cyril says He can't correctly be called a twofold Christ or Son, for that's what Nestorius thinks. If Cyril doesn't accept the twofold reality vis-à-vis nature, how is it that he himself said, in *On Matthew*, 'The true coin known to the mind, and understood as in the type of a material coin, this is our Lord Jesus Christ, the two-fold impress'?

Cyril from *Responses to the Objections*: 'Since each thing remains 1861B and is understood in its natural property according to the definition given by us just now, He, being united in an inexpressible and unutterable way, displayed to us one nature of a Son, only it is an incarnate nature, for the word "one" is not truly used for things that are single and simple by nature.' 'Notice,' they say, 'he said "one nature" of the Son, who is Christ.' But they have to ask, now that they've assembled their evidence, whether they're drawing the correct conclusions! If the name 'Son' is fixed on and used in place of 'Christ' even before the Incarnation, then it'll be demon-

τεταγμένον ἀντὶ τοῦ Χριστοῦ εἴρηται, οὑτωσὶ φρασθήσεται, "μίαν
ἡμῖν ἔδειξε Χριστοῦ φύσιν, πλὴν σεσαρκωμένην", τοῦτο δὲ ἢ ὡς
ἀσάρκου Χριστοῦ δυναμένου ληφθῆναι, ὅπερ ἀνεπινόητον, ἢ ὡς καὶ
1861C πρὸς τῇδε τῇ μιᾷ αὐτοῦ φύσει, καὶ σάρκα ἐπενδυσαμένου Χριστοῦ.
Ἔσται οὖν ἐκ Λόγου τὲ καὶ σαρκός, καὶ ἑτέρας φύσεως σαρκὸς ὢν ὁ
Χριστός, καὶ οὐ μόνον δύο φύσεις ἁπλῶς, ἀλλ' ἐκ μιᾶς μὲν τῆς θείας
ἁπλῆς, ἐκ δύο δὲ συνθέτων ἤγουν τῶν ἀνθρωπίνων νοούμενος, ἐκ
τριῶν τὲ φύσεων λεγόμενος λοιπόν· οὐδὲν δὲ ἧττον καὶ δύο φύσεις,
ἐκ μιᾶς τῆς καθ' ὑμᾶς Χριστοῦ φύσεως, καὶ τῆς ἐπεισαχθείσης
Χριστῷ κατὰ τὴν δευτέραν σάρκωσιν αὐτοῦ σαρκὸς φύσεως.

Ἀλλὰ τί μή, τούτων ἀφέμενοι τῶν παραβλωπισμάτων, ὄμμασιν
ὀρθοῖς τὸν σκοπὸν τῶν εἰρημένων κατανοεῖτε; Ὅτι γὰρ υἱότητος
φυσικῆς νῦν φησὶ τὴν αὐτὴν μίαν φύσιν μένειν τῷ Υἱῷ, κἂν
1861D προσελάβετο ἄλλην φύσιν, ἰδοὺ αὐτὸς τρανοῖ λέγων· "Οὐ γὰρ ἐπὶ
μόνων τῶν ἁπλῶν κατὰ τὴν φύσιν", υἱῶν δηλαδὴ, "τὸ ἓν ἀληθῶς
λέγεται." Ἆρα οὖν τοῦτο ὑμᾶς μᾶλλον διδάξει, ὅτι οὐχ' ἁπλοῦς
κατὰ τὴν φύσιν ὁ περὶ οὗ τάδε φησὶν Υἱὸς εἷς, ἀλλὰ διπλοῦς· ἔστι
γὰρ κατὰ τὸν πατέρα, ὃ πολλάκις καὶ ἡμεῖς ὑμῖν ἐνηχοῦμεν, καὶ
πλειόνων οὐσῶν τῶν φύσεων, ἓν εἶναι τό τε πρόσωπον καὶ ἕνα τὸν
αὐτὸν Υἱὸν φύσει, καὶ οὐ τὴν μὲν τῶν φύσεων Υἱὸν φύσει, τὴν δὲ
Υἱὸν χάριτι εἶναι. Ὥστε σαφῶς τὰ ἡμέτερα λέγων ἢ τὰ ὑμέτερα
δείκνυται, κἂν τούτοις ὁ διδάσκαλος, ὅπου γε εἰ καὶ οὕτως εἶχεν, ὡς
βούλεσθε, πάντα ἂν τὰ ἐν ἑτέροις εἰρημένα τῷ πατρὶ ὡς περὶ δύο
1864A φύσεων Χριστοῦ, τοῖσδε τοῖς αὐτοῦ ἂν διεμάχετο· ὅπερ <u>οὐδεὶς ἐν
πνεύματι Θεοῦ λαλῶν</u>[230] παθεῖν ὑποπτεύεται.

Τοῦ μεγάλου Ἀθανασίου· " Ὁμολογοῦμεν καὶ εἶναι αὐτὸν Υἱὸν
τοῦ Θεοῦ καὶ Θεὸν κατὰ πνεῦμα, Υἱὸν ἀνθρώπου κατὰ σάρκα, οὐ
δύο φύσεις τὸν ἕνα Υἱόν, μίαν προσκυνητὴν καὶ μίαν ἀπροσκύνητον,
ἀλλὰ μίαν φύσιν τοῦ Θεοῦ Λόγου σεσαρκωμένην, καὶ
προσκυνουμένην μετὰ τῆς σαρκὸς αὐτοῦ μιᾷ προσκυνήσει."[231]
"'Ἰδοὺ" φασὶ "τὴν δυάδα σαφῶς ἀναιρεῖ τῶν φύσεων ὁ πατὴρ ἐπὶ
τοῦ ἑνὸς Υἱοῦ." Ἀλλ' οὐ τὰς δύο φύσεις, ὦ οὗτοι, ἀνεῖλεν, ἀλλὰ τὸ
μὴ θατέραν μὲν εἶναι τῶν δύο φύσεων "προσκυνητὴν" ἐν τῷ Υἱῷ,
θατέραν δὲ "ἀπροσκύνητον" ἐν αὐτῷ. Διὰ γάρ τοι τόδε καὶ
1864B ἐπήγαγεν, ὅτι ἐν μιᾷ καὶ τῇ αὐτῇ προσκυνήσει, τοῦ ἑνὸς Υἱοῦ οὐ

---

[230] 1 Cor. 12: 3
[231] Actually Apollinarius, *To Jovian* = Lietzmann, *Apollinaris*, 250–1.

strated that the assertion, 'He displayed one nature of Christ to us, only it is an incarnate nature', is to be taken as either about a Christ capable of being without flesh—which is inconceivable—or about a Christ who takes on flesh beyond this one nature of His. In that case the actual Christ will be out of Word, flesh, and a further nature of flesh. He'll be understood not only and simply to be two natures, but to be out of the one and simple divine nature, yet also out of two compound natures (i.e. the human ones), and besides that He'll be said to be out of three natures. It's no less the case that there are two natures out of that one nature of Christ you hold to, plus the nature added to Christ by the second incarnation of His flesh! 1861C

But why don't you give up these distorted views, and consider with right eyes the intention behind what's said? Notice that Cyril himself makes it clear that he's saying there continues to be the same one nature of natural sonship for the Son, even though He took on another nature, when he says 'for the word "one" isn't truly used for things'—that is, sons, clearly enough—'that are solitary and simple by nature.' He'll teach you, rather, that the one Son of whom he says these things isn't simple by nature, but twofold. What's true for the father is exactly what, for our part, we've often urged against you: that the person is one, though of several actual natures, and the same Son is one by nature, not that one of the natures is a Son by nature, and the other a Son by grace. When he's thus clearly shown to be saying what we say, rather than what you say—even though he's 'the teacher' to these people!—then, even though in some passages things are just as you would wish them to be, everything said by the father about the two natures of Christ in other passages contradicts those texts of his. He's suspected of enduring exactly what *no one who speaks in the Spirit of God* endures.[x] 1864A

The great Athanasius: 'We confess that He is both Son of God and God in spirit, but Son of Man in flesh. We don't confess that the one Son is two natures, one that's to be worshipped, and another that's not to be worshipped, but one incarnate nature of God the Word, worshipped along with His flesh in one act of worship.' 'Observe', they say, 'how the father clearly rules out the duality of natures in the one Son.' But it wasn't the two natures that he ruled out, my friends, but having one of the two natures that's 'to be worshipped' in the Son, and the other that's 'not to be worshipped' in Him. This is undoubtedly why he went on to say that [this worship] is in one and the same act of worship of the 1864B

φύσεως λέγων· ὡς γὰρ διὰ καθολικωτέρου τινὸς τοῦ ὅλου
προσώπου, ἅμα προσκυνεῖσθαι τὰ μέρη αὐτοῦ, ἤγουν τάσδε τὰς
φύσεις, συμβαίνει, ὡς ἐμπεριεχομένας τῷ προσκυνουμένῳ Υἱῷ
ὁμοίως ἄμφω. Ὑμεῖς δὲ σοφιστικῶς τελείᾳ στίζοντες, καὶ
οὐχ' ὑποστιγμῇ καθ' ἡμᾶς, "τὸν ἕνα Υἱὸν", τὰ πρῶτα μὲν τῶν
ῥησειδίων, κατὰ σκοπὸν ἑαυτοῖς ἀποτίλλαντες, διορίζετε, τὰ δὲ
ἑξῆς ἀσυνάρτητα παρέλκοντες, ἐν τῷ νοήματι τοῦ ὅλου χωρίου,
διελέγχεσθε [290ʳ]. Οὕτως μὲν οὖν νοείσθω, εἰ ὄντως Ἀθανασίῳ
εἴρηται· οὐ γὰρ ἑαυτῷ περὶ τὰ αὐτά τις θεοφόρος στασιάζει. Ὅτι δὲ
Ἀπολιναρίῳ²³² εἴρηται τάδε κατὰ τὴν ὑμετέραν ἔννοιαν, Τιμόθεός
τις τούτου μαθητὴς ἐν τῇ Ἐκκλησιαστικῇ ἱστορίᾳ λέγει καὶ
1864c Πολέμων ὁ συνουσιαστής, οὗ Κύριλλος ὁ πατὴρ καὶ Σεβῆρος ὁ
πατραλοίας μνημονεύουσι, φήσαντος οὕτως· "Θεὸν γὰρ λέγοντες
καὶ ἄνθρωπον τὸν αὐτόν, οὐκ αἰσχύνονται μίαν φύσιν τοῦ Θεοῦ
Λόγου σεσαρκωμένην, οἷόν τινα σύνθετον, ὁμολογοῦντες· εἴ γε
Θεὸς τέλειος καὶ ἄνθρωπος τέλειος ὁ αὐτός, δύο φύσεις ἄρα ὁ αὐτός,
καθάπερ ἡ τῶν Καππαδοκῶν εἰσηγεῖται καινοτομία, Διοδώρου
τὲ καὶ Ἀθανασίου ἡ οἴησις, καὶ τῶν ἐν Ἰταλίᾳ ὁ τύφος. Καὶ
σχηματίζονται μὲν οἱ δῆθεν ἡμέτεροι φρονεῖν τὰ τοῦ ἁγίου πατρὸς
ἡμῶν Ἀπολιναρίου, κηρύττουσι δὲ καθάπερ Γρηγόριοι, τὴν τῶν
φύσεων δυάδα".²³³ Καὶ μετὰ βραχέα· "Τί δὲ Ἀπολιναρίῳ τῷ θείῳ
μαθητιᾷν σχηματίζονται; Ταύτην γὰρ ἐπ' ἀναιρέσει τῆς τῶν φύσεων
1864d δυάδος, μόνος ἡμῖν ἀπεκύησε, γεγραφὼς ὧδέ πη σαφῶς· "Καὶ εἶναι
αὐτὸν Υἱὸν τοῦ Θεοῦ, καὶ Θεὸν κατὰ πνεῦμα, Υἱὸν ἀνθρώπου κατὰ
σάρκα, οὐ δύο φύσεις τὸν ἕνα Υἱόν, μίαν προσκυνητὴν καὶ μίαν
ἀπροσκύνητον, ἀλλὰ μίαν φύσιν τοῦ Θεοῦ Λόγου σεσαρκωμένην,
καὶ προσκυνουμένην μετὰ τῆς σαρκὸς αὐτοῦ μιᾷ προσκυνήσει."²³⁴
⟨Τ⟩ίς οὖν οὐ θαυμάσει, εἰ ὁ μετὰ Διοδώρου τοῦ ἀσεβοῦς
διαβαλλόμενος αὐτῷ Ἀθανάσιος τὰ ὅμοια ῥήματα πάντα ἔφη; Εἰ δὲ
1865a καὶ τάδε ἔλεξε, πῶς καὶ ἐπὶ τῆς αὐτῆς διανοίας τῷδε τάδε εἰπὼν
διεβλήθη Ἀπολιναρίῳ καὶ Τιμοθέῳ; Πῶς τὲ πρῶτος Ἀπολινάριος
τάδε ἀπεκύησεν, ὥς φασιν οἱ τοῦδε μαθηταί, εἰ τῷ διδασκάλῳ ἡμῶν
Ἀθανασίῳ προείρηται; Πῶς δὲ καὶ ὁ οὕτως ταῦτα εἰπών, ἔφη ἂν ἐν

---

²³² Ἀπολιναρίῳ] Ἀποναρίῳ a. corr. MS
²³³ Timothy, *Ecclesiastical History* = Lietzmann, *Apollinaris*, 274, q.v. for other
attestations.
²³⁴ Ibid.

one Son, not of the one nature. What happens is that His parts, i.e. these natures, are worshipped together by virtue of the whole person's becoming in some way more comprehensive, so that both natures alike are encompassed within the Son who's worshipped. You people, though—by sophistically putting a period after 'the one Son [is two natures]', and not, as we do, a comma—divide off the first part of the sentence, taking it out of context for your own purposes. However, since [by doing so] you render the next isolated phrases extraneous, you're utterly refuted by the sense of the passage as a whole. So then, one needs to think about whether this was actually said by Athanasius, for not one of the God-bearers is at odds with himself on identical issues. A certain Timothy, a disciple of Apollinarius, affirms in his *Church History* that these things were said by Apollinarius in the sense intended by you, and so does his companion Polemon, whom both the father Cyril and the patricidal Severus mention. Here's what he says: 'Those who say that the same [Christ] is both God and man aren't ashamed of confessing one incarnate nature of God the Word as being some sort of compound [Christ]. That is to say, if the same [Christ] is complete God and complete man, then He is two natures—just what the Cappadocians' innovation introduces, as do the opinion of Diodore and Athanasius and the vanity of the Italians. They pretend that they really belong to our party, and that they hold the opinions of our holy father Apollinarius, but they proclaim just what the Gregories proclaim: the duality of natures.' And after a bit: 'Why do they pretend they want to become disciples of the divine Apollinarius? All by himself he produced for us this [formula] with the aim of destroying the duality of natures, having somehow openly written as follows: "[We confess] that He is both Son of God and God in spirit, but Son of Man in flesh. We do not confess that the one Son is two natures, one that is to be worshipped, and another that is not to be worshipped, but one incarnate nature of God the Word, worshipped along with His flesh in one act of worship." '

Who wouldn't be shocked if the Athanasius who, in company with the impious Diodore, opposed Apollinarius used exactly the same words as he? If he did say these things, how can it be that, though he said them in the very same sense as Apollinarius, he was condemned by the latter and by Timothy? How can it be that Apollinarius was the first to produce these things, as the relevant experts say, if they were said before that by our teacher Athanasius? How could the man who put things in this way say, in his

1864c

1864D

1865A

τῷ Περὶ τῆς ἁγίας Τριάδος λόγῳ· "Οὐκ ἐπιμίγνυται ἡ τοῦ δημιουργοῦ φύσις καὶ τῶν δημιουργημάτων εἰς ἑνότητα φύσεως, ἀλλὰ δυσφημίας τὸ τοιοῦτον μεγίστης τὴν ὑπεροχὴν τῆς θεότητος καταγούσης εἰς ἑνότητα τῆς ἐκτισμένης οὐσίας";[235] Εἰ οὖν καὶ Κύριλλος αὐτὴν παράγει ὁ διδάσκαλος ὡς Ἀθανασίου, οὐκ ἀδύνατον ἢ κατὰ τὴν ἡμετέραν ἔννοιαν, ἢ κατὰ ῥᾳδιουργίαν τινῶν, 1865b ταύτῃ προσελχθῆναι αὐτόν, ὡς πατρικῇ καὶ οὐχ᾽ αἱρετικῇ μαρτυρίᾳ.

Ἰουλίου τοῦ Ῥώμης ὡς δοκεῖ ἐκ τῆς ⟨ ⟩· "Ὁμολογεῖται δὲ ἐν αὐτῷ, τὸ μὲν εἶναι κτιστὸν ἐν ἑνότητι τοῦ ἀκτίστου, τὸ δὲ ἄκτιστον ἐν συγκράσει τοῦ κτιστοῦ, φύσεως μιᾶς ἐξ ἑκατέρου μέρους συνισταμένης, μερικὴν ἐνέργειαν καὶ τοῦ Λόγου συντελέσαντος εἰς τὸ ὅλον, μετὰ τῆς θεϊκῆς τελειότητος· ὅπερ ἐπὶ τοῦ κοινοῦ ἀνθρώπου ἐκ δύο μερῶν ἀτελῶν γίνεται, φύσιν μίαν πληρούντων καὶ ἑνὶ ὀνόματι δηλουμένων."[236] Ταύτην πρῶτα μὲν Ῥωμαῖοι οὐ καταδέχονται εἶναι Ἰουλίου—οὐδὲ γὰρ εὕρηται ἐν ταῖς βίβλοις τῶν 1865c ἀρχαίων τί τοιόνδε τοῦ ἀνδρός—, Ἰωάννης δὲ ὁ Σκυθο[290ᵛ] πόλεως ἐπίσκοπος, φιλοπονήσας ἐν τοῖς παλαιοτάτοις Ἀπολιναρίου συγγράμμασιν, εὗρεν ἐπὶ λέξεως τὴν χρῆσιν. Ὅτι δὲ Ἀπολιναρίου ἐστί, δηλοῖ καὶ τὸ ἐπαγόμενον ἐν τῷ αὐτῷ λόγῳ μετά τινα φύλλα· ἔφη γὰρ μὴ ζωοῦσθαι καὶ ὑπὸ ψυχῆς τὸ σῶμα τοῦ Κυρίου, ὅπερ Ἰούλιος οὔ ποτε ἂν ἔφη· ἔχει δὲ οὕτως· "Οὕτω γὰρ ἔζησε τὸ σῶμα θεότητος ἁγιασμῷ, καὶ οὐκ ἀνθρωπίνης ψυχῆς κατασκευῇ."[237] Ὅτι δὲ πάλαι καὶ ἄψυχον ἐδογμάτισεν Ἀπολινάριος εἶναι τὸν Κύριον, εἶτα ὡς ἐκ μεταμέλου ἄνουν καὶ οὐκ ἄψυχον λέγειν αὐτὸν μετέμαθε, Σωκράτης ἐν τῇ Ἐκκλησιαστικῇ ἱστορίᾳ φησὶν οὕτως περὶ αὐτοῦ, καὶ τῶν ἀμφ᾽ αὐτόν· "⟨Κ⟩αὶ πρότερον μὲν ἔλεγον, μὴ ἀνειληφέναι 1865d ψυχήν, ὑπὸ τοῦ Θεοῦ Λόγου ἐν τῇ οἰκονομίᾳ τῆς ἐνανθρωπήσεως· εἶτα ὡς ἐκ μετανοίας ἐπιδιορθούμενοι προσέθηκαν ψυχὴν μὲν ἀνειληφέναι, νοῦν δὲ οὐκ ἔχειν, ἀλλ᾽ εἶναι τὸν Θεὸν Λόγον ἀντὶ νοῦ εἰς τὸν ἀναληφθέντα ἄνθρωπον."[238]

1868a Τοῦ αὐτοῦ Ἰουλίου ἐπισκόπου Ῥώμης ἐκ τῆς πρὸς Διονύσιον ἐπιστολῆς· "Μία φύσις ἐστίν, ἐπειδὴ πρόσωπον ἕν, οὐκ ἔχον εἰς δύο διαίρεσιν· ἐπεὶ μὴ ἰδία φύσις τὸ σῶμα, καὶ ἰδία φύσις ἡ θεότης κατὰ τὴν σάρκωσιν, ἀλλ᾽ ὥσπερ ἄνθρωπος μία φύσις, οὕτως καὶ ὁ ἐν

---

[235] Ps.-Athanasius, *On the Trinity*, PG xxvi, 1191–1218 (Latin).

[236] Actually Apollinarius, *On the Union* = Lietzmann, *Apollinaris*, 187. Cited with minor variations also at 1873b–c.

[237] Ibid. 190.

[238] Socrates, *Ecclesiastical History* ii, 46, ed. G. C. Hansen, *Sokrates Kirchengeschichte*, GCS, ns 1 (Berlin: Akademie-Verlag, 1995), 185–6.

work on the Holy Trinity, 'The nature of the Creator is not min-gled with that of created things into a unity of nature; rather, that sort of thing partakes of the greatest blasphemy, the blasphemy that reduces the superiority of divinity to oneness with created substance'? If our teacher Cyril introduces it as being Athanasius' statement, then, it's not impossible that he was drawn to it either as invested with our meaning, or—under the influence of certain people's forgery—mistaken for patristic rather than heretical evidence. 1865B

Julius, Bishop of Rome, or so it seems, from the < >:[xi] 'What is confessed in Him is that the created is in unity with the uncreated, but the uncreated is in mixture with the created, since one nature is completed out of each part, for the Word contributes His par-ticular activity to the whole with the divine perfection. This is exactly what happens in the case of the universal "man" who is out of two incomplete parts, parts which complete one nature and are signified by one name.' In the first place, the people of Rome don't admit that this is Julius' statement—nothing of the sort is to be found attributed to the man in books of the ancients—but John, Bishop of Scythopolis, who did painstaking work on the 1865C oldest writings of Apollinarius, did find the passage in a text. What follows a few pages later in the same volume makes it clear that it's a work of Apollinarius, for it says the Lord's body wasn't animated by a soul, surely something Julius never said. This is how the text goes: 'Thus the body came to life by the divinity's sanctifi-cation, not by the formation of a human soul.' That Apollinarius at first declared the Lord to be without a soul, then later, as it were in repentance, learned to say that He was without a mind, not without a soul, is something Socrates attests in his *Ecclesiastical History* when he says the following about Apollinarius and those around him: 'At first they would say a soul was not assumed by the Word of God in the Economy of His becoming man. Then, revis- 1865D ing their position as if out of repentance, they asserted that He assumed a soul for Himself but had no mind, and that instead of a mind God the Word took its place for the man who was assumed.'

Of the same Julius, Bishop of Rome, from the *Letter to Dionysius*:; 1868A 'There is one nature, there being one person which does not admit of division into two, since the body is not a distinct nature, and the divinity is not a distinct nature either in terms of the Incarnation, but as a man is one nature, so is the Christ *born in the likeness of men.*

ὁμοιώματι ἀνθρώπων γενόμενος[239] Χριστός. Εἰ δὲ οὐκ
ἐπιγινώσκουσι τὸ καθ᾽ ἔνωσιν ἕν, δύνανται καὶ εἰς πολλὰ
καταμερίζειν τὸν ἕνα, καὶ πολλὰς λέγειν φύσεις, ἐπειδὴ πολυειδὲς
τὸ σῶμα ἐξ ὀστέων καὶ νεύρων, καὶ φλεβῶν καὶ σαρκῶν, καὶ
δέρματος καὶ ὀνύχων, καὶ τριχῶν, καὶ αἵματος, καὶ πνεύματος,
ἅπερ πάντα διαφορὰν μὲν ἔχει πρὸς ἄλληλα, μία δὲ φύσις
ἐστίν. Ὥστε καὶ ἡ τῆς θεότητος ἀλήθεια, μετὰ τοῦ σώματος ἕν ἐστι,
1868Β καὶ εἰς δύο φύσεις οὐ μερίζεται."[240] Καὶ μετὰ βραχέα· "᾽Ανάγκη
γὰρ αὐτοὺς δύο λέγοντας φύσεις, τὴν μὲν μίαν προσκυνεῖν, τὴν δὲ
ἑτέραν μὴ προσκυνεῖν· εἰς μὲν τὴν θεϊκὴν βαπτίζεσθαι, εἰς δὲ τὴν
ἀνθρωπίνην, μὴ βαπτίζεσθαι. Εἰ δὲ εἰς τὸν θάνατον τοῦ Κυρίου
βαπτιζόμεθα,[241] μίαν ὁμολογοῦμεν φύσιν τῆς ἀπαθοῦς θεότητος καὶ
τῆς παθητῆς σαρκός, ἵνα οὕτως εἰς Θεὸν ᾖ τὸ βάπτισμα ἡμῶν, καὶ
εἰς τὸν θάνατον τοῦ Κυρίου[242] τελούμενον."[243] Καὶ μετ᾽ ὀλίγα πάλιν·
"Μὴ οὖν τοῖς διατέμνουσι πρόφασιν δότωσαν οἱ δύο λέγοντες
φύσεις· οὔτε γὰρ τὸ σῶμα καθ᾽ ἑαυτὸ φύσις, μὴ δὲ ζωοποιὸν
καθ᾽ ἑαυτό, μὴ δὲ διατέμνεσθαι δυνάμενον, ἄνευ τοῦ ζωοποιοῦ· οὔτε
ὁ Λόγος καθ᾽ ἑαυτὸν εἰς ἰδίαν μερίζεται φύσιν ἣν ἔχει κατὰ τὸ
ἄσαρκον, ἐπειδὴ ἐν σαρκὶ Κύριος, καὶ οὐκ ἄσαρκος ἐπεδήμησε τῷ
1868C κόσμῳ· οὔτε τὸ κτιστὸν σῶμα ζῇ χωρὶς τῆς ἀκτίστου θεότητος, ἵνα
χωρίζῃ τίς φύσιν κτιστήν· οὔτε μὴν ὁ ἄκτιστος Λόγος ἐπεδήμησε
χωρὶς σώματος, ἵνα μερίζῃ τίς ἀκτίστου φύσιν.[291ʳ] Εἰ δὲ ἐν
ἑκάτερόν ἐστι κατὰ τὴν ἔνωσιν καὶ τὴν σύνοδον καὶ τὴν σύνθεσιν
τὴν ἀνθρωποειδῆ, ἓν καὶ τὸ ὄνομα τῷ συνθέτῳ προσαρμόζεται· ἀπὸ
μὲν τῆς θεότητος, τὸ ἄκτιστον, ἀπὸ δὲ τοῦ σώματος, τὸ κτιστόν·
ἀπὸ μὲν τῆς θεότητος τὸ ἀπαθές· ἀπὸ δὲ τοῦ σώματος τὸ παθητόν.
Καὶ ὥσπερ ἀκούοντες τοῦ Παύλου τὸν Χριστὸν παθητόν,[244] οὔτε
μερικῶς ἠκούσαμεν, οὔτε τὴν θεότητα παθητὴν ἐνομίσαμεν, οὕτως
καὶ τὸ κτιστὸν καὶ δοῦλον, οὔτε μερικῶς λέγεται, οὔτε τὴν θεότητα
1868D ποιεῖ κτιστήν, οὔτε δούλην."[245] Ταύτην τὴν χρῆσιν, εἴ γε
προσεχόντως ἐπισκέπτοιεν οἱ ἐντυγχάνοντες, οὔτε διαβολῆς
οἰόμεθα χρῄζειν εἰς τὸ ψευδεπίγραφον, οὔτε ἀνατροπῆς εἰς τὸ
ἀνίσχυρον. Ὅτι μὲν γὰρ πρόσφατος ἡ ταύτης σκαιωρία, συνίδοι τίς
ῥᾶστα τῷ μὴ δὲ Διοσκόρῳ, μὴ δὲ Σεβήρῳ, μὴ δὲ τοῖς παλαιοτέροις
1869A τῆσδε τῆς ἀσεβείας αἱρεσιάρχαις παράγεσθαι· δῆλον γὰρ ὅτι ἢ διὰ
τὴν διαβολὴν τοῦ εἰπόντος, ἢ τὴν ὑπερβολὴν τοῦ ἀσεβήματος,
καὶ ἐκείνοις τοῖς λίαν προσκειμένοις τῷ δόγματι παρώφθη, πάντα
τὰ Ἰουλίου καὶ τῶν λοιπῶν πατέρων μυριάκις σπουδαίως
περιεργασαμένων, ἵνά τι πρὸς συνηγορίαν τοῦ οἰκείου φρονήματος

---

[239] Phil. 2: 7
[240] Actually Apollinarius, *Letter to Dionysius* = Lietzmann, *Apollinaris*, 257–8.
[241] Cf. Rom. 6: 3   [242] Ibid.
[243] Actually Apollinarius, *Letter to Dionysius* = Lietzmann, *Apollinaris*, 258–9.
[244] Acts 26: 23.
[245] Actually Apollinarius, *Letter to Dionysius* = Lietzmann, *Apollinaris*, 259–69.

If they don't acknowledge the one entity in union, they are capable also of cutting the one [Christ] into many, and of speaking of many natures, since the body is complex, being made out of bones, sinews, veins, muscles, skin, nails, hair, blood, and breath, all of which differ from each other, yet is nonetheless one nature. Likewise the reality of the divinity with the body is one, and is not divided into two natures.' And after a bit: 'It is necessary for those who speak of two natures to worship one of them, but not to worship the other, to be baptized into the divine nature, but not to be baptized into the human nature. If, however, *we are baptized into the death of the Lord*, we confess one nature of the impassible divinity and of the passible flesh, so that in this way our baptism into God, and *into the death of the Lord*, may be accomplished.' And again, after a few things: 'Those who speak of two natures must not provide a pretext for those who cut in two. The body is not a nature of itself, neither is it life-giving by itself, nor can it be severed from what gives it life. Nor is the Word divided of Himself into a distinct nature, a nature He has without flesh, since He is Lord in flesh, and did not live in the world without flesh. The created body does not live without the uncreated divinity, so that someone might separate off a created nature, nor did the uncreated Word live in the world without a body, so that someone might separate off an uncreated nature. If each thing is one by the union, the coming together, and the human composition, so is the name one that is attached to what is compounded. The uncreated is from the divinity, but the created is from the body; the impassible is from the divinity, but the passible is from the body. Though we heard Paul's *Christ must suffer*, we did not hear it as applying to a particular part, nor did we consider the divinity to be passible. In the same way terms like "creature" and "slave" are not used with reference to a particular part, nor do they make the divine a creature or a slave.'

We think this text, if its readers would only examine it closely, doesn't lack the fraudulent character that points to pseudepigraphy, nor is there any lack of the grounds for undermining it as invalid. Anyone could see, just at a glance, that this fraud is a recent phenomenon from the fact that it isn't cited by Dioscorus, or Severus, or this impiety's earlier heresiarchs. It's clear that all of Julius' works, and all the works of the rest of the fathers who so earnestly laboured time after time, were overlooked for the purposes of consolidating something useful in support of their shared understanding even by those people—people so exceedingly devoted to the doctrine—either because of the fraudulent character of the speaker, or because of the enormity of the blasphemy

1868B

1868C

1868D

1869A

ἀναλέξωνται. Ἄλλως τε τῷ γε ψιλῶς πῶς τοῖς Ἀπολιναρίου
ἐντυγχάνοντι προγενεστέροις συγγράμμασι περὶ τῆς οἰκονομίας,
οὐδ' ἀμφιβολίας εἶναι ἄξιον δόξει τὸ γνήσιον αὐτῷ τῆσδε τῆς
χρήσεως. Ἄνω τε γὰρ καὶ κάτω, τὰ δύο μέρη τῆς φύσεως Χριστοῦ,
σῶμα μόνον καὶ θεότητά φησί, καὶ σάρκα τὴν ὡς σῶμα, οὐ μὴν ὡς
ἀνθρωπότητα, λαμβανομένην καὶ Λόγον, ἀνθρωποειδῆ δὲ τὴν
Χριστοῦ ἔνωσιν καλεῖ· ὅπερ ἦν ἰδιαίτατον ἐκείνου πρώτου δόγμα,
1869B λέγοντος πάλαι μὲν ἀντὶ ψυχῆς σώματι ἀνθρωπείῳ ἐγγενέσθαι τὴν
θεότητα, καὶ μίαν φύσιν ἀπαρτίσαι ἄψυχον θείαν τὸν Χριστόν·
ὕστερον δὲ ὑφήσαντος ποσῶς τῇ ἀσεβείᾳ, ἀντὶ νοῦ ψυχικοῦ ἐνεῖναι
τὴν θεότητα ἐν Χριστῷ μετὰ τοῦ ἀλόγου τῆς ψυχῆς μέρους
δογματίζοντος. Ἀλλ' οὕτω μὲν εὐφώρατος ἡ κατὰ τοῦ πατρὸς διὰ
τῆς ἐπιγραφῆς συκοφαντία· ἡ δὲ κατὰ τοῦ Κυρίου βλασφημία, ὅση
ἐστὶν ἐν τοῖσδε τοῖς ῥησειδίοις, ἐξεταστέον λοιπόν, τὰ πλεῖστα ἐν
αὐτοῖς ἀλόγιστα καθ' ἓν βασανίζοντ⟨ε⟩ς. "Μία φύσις ἐστί," φησί,
"ἐπειδὴ πρόσωπον ἕν". Ἄρα οὖν ὅπου πλείονα πρόσωπα, πάντως
καὶ φύσεις πλείους· καὶ μὴν τρία τὰ θεῖα πρόσωπα, φύσις δὲ μία,
1869C οἷς ἔμπαλιν ἔχει ὁ τῆς οἰκονομίας λόγος, ᾗ φησιν ὁ θεολόγος
Γρηγόριος.²⁴⁶ Ἔτι μὴν ἐπεὶ καὶ τοῦ μύδρου ὑπόστασις μία εἴτουν
πρόσωπον, μία καὶ τοῦ ἐν αὐτῷ πυρὸς καὶ σιδήρου φύσις ἐστίν, ἢ
παρὰ τὰς κοινὰς ἐννοίας δοξάζομεν τάδε. Εἶτα φησί· "Οὐκ ἔχον εἰς
δύο διαίρεσιν, ἐπεὶ μὴ ἰδίᾳ φύσις ἡ θεότης κατὰ τὴν σάρκωσιν"· τὸ
οὖν "ἰδίᾳ" [291ᵛ] τούτου φησίν. Εἰ μὲν κατὰ τόπον, ὄντως οὐκ
ἔστιν ἰδίᾳ θάτερον ἀπὸ θατέρου· οὐκ ἔστι γὰρ αὐτοῖς τοπικῶς
διορισμός, ὅτι ἐν τῷ ἀνθρωπίνῳ τοῦ Χριστοῦ, κατοικεῖ πᾶν τὸ
πλήρωμα τῆς θεότητος σωματικῶς.²⁴⁷ Εἰ δὲ κατὰ λόγον, οὐκ ἔστιν
ἑκατέρα ἰδιάζουσα φύσις ἐκ θατέρας—τοῦτο γὰρ ἐσαφήνισε διὰ
τῶν μετὰ βραχέα, λέγων· "Μίαν ὁμολογοῦμεν φύσιν τῆς ἀπαθοῦς
θεότητος καὶ τῆς παθητῆς σαρκός"—καὶ οὔτε ἡ ἀπάθεια τοῦ
1869D Λόγου, οὔτε τὸ πάθος τῆς σαρκὸς ἴδιον. Δῆλον πᾶσιν, ὡς καὶ ὁ
Λόγος αὐτῆς εἰς ἴδιον λόγον ἔπαθε, καὶ ἡ σὰρξ ἰδίῳ λόγῳ οὐκ
ἔπαθεν, ἐζωοποίησέ τε οὐ μόνον ὁ Λόγος τὴν σάρκα, ἀλλὰ καὶ ἡ
σὰρξ τὸν Λόγον, εἴτουν ἡ ἀνθρωπότης, ἢ, ὡς οὗτος λέγει, τὸ σῶμα

---

²⁴⁶ Referring to Gregory of Nazianzus, *Letter* 101, SC 208, 44. The text is cited in
Aporiae at 1780D.
²⁴⁷ Col. 2: 9

involved. For the person who reads the earlier writings of Apollinarius on the Incarnation to any extent at all, though, the fact that the text is authentically his won't seem worth a moment's doubt. From beginning to end it speaks of the two parts of Christ's nature—a body alone, and divinity; flesh taken on (as body, not as humanity), and Word—but characterizes Christ's union as 'in human form', which was precisely Apollinarius' most characteristic doctrine at first, he being the one who began by saying that divinity was born in a human body in place of a soul, 1869B and that Christ completed one divine nature that had no soul, but later gave up his impiety to a certain extent and articulated the doctrine of the divinity's being in Christ in place of a psychic mind, but along with the irrational part of the soul. The false accusation against the father [Julius] is thus easy to detect by means of its false ascription. On the other hand, the blasphemy against the Lord found in these short statements is so great that we need to go on to scrutinize the extensive inanities in them, testing them one at a time.

'There is one nature,' Apollinarius says, 'there being one person'. It follows that, whenever there is more than one person, there will always be more than one nature too. The divine persons are three, but there's one nature. However, the understanding of the Incarnation is the reverse of this, as Gregory the Theologian 1869C says. Surely, though, since there's one hypostasis, i.e. person, of a red-hot mass of metal, then there's also one nature of the fire and of the iron in it—unless we hold opinions about these things that differ from the general understanding! He goes on to say 'which does not admit of division into two, since . . . the divinity is not a distinct nature . . . in terms of the Incarnation'. He uses the word 'distinct' here. If he uses the word with reference to place, one thing really isn't apart from the other by virtue of having a 'distinct' nature; there's no topical separation for these things, since in the humanity of Christ *all the fullness of the godhead dwells bodily*. On the other hand, if he uses the word with reference to definition, there isn't one nature that's essentially distinct from the other—he made this clear in what follows shortly after when he said 'We confess one nature of the impassible divinity and of the passible flesh'—and neither the impassibility of the Word nor the suffering 1869D of the flesh is distinct. It's clear to all that this one nature's Word also suffered in its own definition, and the flesh didn't suffer in its own definition, and not only did the Word make the flesh alive, but also the flesh, i.e. the humanity, made the Word alive or—as

τὴν θεότητα· ὧν τίς βλασφημίας ὑπέρτερος λόγος; Ἀλλὰ τὸν περὶ
τὰς ἀσεβεῖς διανοίας συμβαίνοντα σάλον ἐξ ἀδρανείας τοῦ ψεύδους
καὶ διὰ τῶν ἑξῆς σκοπητέον. "Οὔτε γὰρ τὸ σῶμα καθ᾽ ἑαυτὸ φύσις"
φησί, "μὴ δὲ ζωοποιὸν καθ᾽ ἑαυτό, μὴ δὲ διατέμνεσθαι δυνάμενον"
1872A 〝Ἄρα[248] γοῦν ὥσπερ οὐκ ἔχει τὸ ζωοποιὸν ἐκ τοῦ ἰδίου λόγου,.
οὕτως οὐδὲ τὸ διατέμνεσθαι ἔχει ἐκ τοῦ ἰδίου λόγου τὸ σῶμα· ἢ ἐκ
μὲν τοῦ λόγου τῆς ἰδίας φύσεως θάτερον ἔχει, ἕτερον δὲ οὔ, ἐκ δὲ
τῆς πρὸς τὸ ζωοποιὸν καὶ ἀδιάτμητον φύσει ὂν ἑνώσεως, ἀμφότερα
ἔλαβεν. Ἄλλως δέ, εἰ μὴ ἔχει τὰ ἴδια, καὶ ἐπεδείξατο ἐνεργείᾳ ἡ
φύσις τοῦ σώματος τὸ διατμητὸν αὐτῆς ἐν Χριστῷ, οὔτε τοῦ
Λόγου, οὔτε τῆς σαρκὸς οὔσης διατμητῆς, τίς περιετμήθη; τίς δὲ
ἥλοις κατεπερονήθη; τίς δὲ λόγχῃ διῃρέθη, πλὴν εἰ μὴ φαντασία τίς
καὶ σκιᾶς τύπος;

　　Τὸ δὲ ἐπαγόμενον, ὅσης γέμει τῆς ἀνοίας, προσεκτέον· φησὶ γάρ·
1872B "Οὔτε ὁ Λόγος εἰς ἰδίαν μερίζεται φύσιν, ἢν ἔχει κατὰ τὸ ἄσαρκον".
Ἔχει οὖν, ὦ σοφοί, "κατὰ τὸ ἄσαρκον" "ἰδίαν φύσιν" ὁ Λόγος, ἔτι
καὶ "ἐπιδημήσας" ἐν σαρκί. Καὶ πῶς τῶν ὑμετέρων οὐκ ἐπαΐοιτε; τί
τὲ ἡμῖν προσεπερωτῶσιν ὑμᾶς ἀποκριθήσεσθε; Ἄρα γὰρ καὶ ὁ
κυριακὸς ἄνθρωπος ἔχει ἰδίαν φύσιν κατὰ τὸ σαρκικόν, εἰ καὶ
ἐνθέως "ἐπεδήμησεν", ἢ τοῦ Λόγου μόνον σώζεται ἡ φύσις ἡ
ἄσαρκος, δόκησις δὲ ἦν ἡ φανέρωσις τῆς σαρκὸς τοῦ Κυρίου; εἰ γὰρ
ἀληθείᾳ ἦν, δύο φύσεις ἑκατέρα τῶνδε συνάγουσιν, εἰς μίαν κοινὴν
ὑπόστασιν συνηγμένας τὴν αὐτοῦ. Ἀλλ᾽ ἐπὶ τούτοις τί φησιν; Εἰ δὲ
"ἓν ἑκάτερόν ἐστι κατὰ τὴν σύνοδον", ὦ ἄνθρωπε, εἰ ἕν, πῶς
1872C ἑκάτερον; εἰ δὲ ἑκάτερον, πῶς ἓν κατὰ τὸ αὐτὸ ἔσται; Οὐκοῦν
σαφές, ὅτι ἓν μὲν κατὰ τὸ πρόσωπον, ἑκάτερον δὲ κατὰ τὰς φύσεις
ἐστίν. Οὐχὶ φησίν, ἀλλὰ "κατὰ τὴν ἀνθρωποειδῆ σύνθεσιν". Τί οὖν,
σωζομένης φύσεως ψυχῆς καὶ σώματος, ἴσμεν καὶ ἑτέραν [292ʳ]
φύσιν εἶναι τὸν ἄνθρωπον παρὰ τάσδε, ἢ οὐχί; Εἰ μὲν οὖν οὐχί, οὐδὲ
ἐπὶ τοῦ Κυρίου σωζομένης θεότητος καὶ ἀνθρωπότητος ἔτι, φύσις
ἐστὶ αὐτῷ ἡ καθολικωτέρα μία. Εἰ δὲ σωζομένων τούτων, οἰόμεθα

---

248 ἄρα] ἄρα MS

this man puts it—the body made the divinity alive. Is there any understanding that outdoes this in blasphemy?

The tossing about that accompanies impious ideas as a result of falsity's impotence is something one needs to examine also throughout what comes next. 'The body is not a nature of itself,' he says, 'neither is it life-giving by itself, nor can it be severed'. It follows that the body doesn't, on the basis of its own definition, have the ability to be severed, just as it doesn't have the power to give life on the basis of its own definition, or else it has one of these capabilities by the definition of its own nature, but not the other. It received both of these, though, from its union with what is life-giving and indivisible by nature. Otherwise, if there are no distinct realities, and the nature of the body actually revealed its indivisibility in Christ, then—since neither the Word nor the flesh is indivisible—who was it that was circumcised, who was perforated by nails, who was pierced by a spear, unless it was some kind of illusion or phantom? _{1872A}

Take note: what my friend has proposed is rife with lack of understanding, for he says: 'Nor is the Word . . . divided into a distinct nature, a nature He has without flesh'. Then, O wise ones, the Word does have a distinct nature in respect of unfleshly reality when it *dwells in* flesh. Why don't you pay attention to your own statements? What answer will you give us if we put this additional question to you: does the dominical man have a distinct nature in respect of the fleshly reality, if He *dwelt in* it in a divine way, or is only the Word's unfleshly nature preserved, whereas the manifestation of the Lord's flesh was an illusion? If it truly was a manifestation, both of these realities imply two natures, two natures united in His one common hypostasis. What answer does he give to these charges? If 'each thing is one by . . . the coming together', my good man, if there is 'one', how can there be 'each'? But if there is 'each', how is there going to be 'one', when these words have the very same referent? It's therefore clear that there is 'one' vis-à-vis person, but there is 'each' vis-à-vis natures. That's not [how he says there's one], but rather 'by the human composition'. What then? Though the nature of soul is preserved, and so is that of body, do we recognize that there is also another nature, man, beyond those natures, or don't we? If not, then there exists for Him the one more inclusive nature, neither divinity nor humanity being preserved in the Lord any longer. If, since these natures are preserved, we recognize that the more common nature of man, _{1872B} _{1872C}

ἐπιγενέσθαι καὶ τὴν κοινοτέραν τοῦ ἀνθρώπου φύσιν, παρὰ ταύτας
ἑτέραν οὖσαν, τίς ἂν εἴη καὶ ἡ ἐπὶ Χριστοῦ ἡ ἐπιγενομένη φύσις, ἡ
οὔτε θεία οὔτε ἀνθρωπίνη ἐστί; Καὶ τί τὸ φυσικὸν τοῦτο εἶδος,
1872D   τὸ ὑπέρθεον, εἴπατε· ἀλλ' οὕτως μὲν τάδε. "Ἐν" δὲ "τῷ συνθέτῳ
ὄνομα", τὸ ποῖον φατὲ "προσαρμόζεσθαι"; Εἰ μὲν τὸ ὑποστατικόν,
ἀναντίρρητος ὁ λόγος· εἰ δὲ ⟨τὸ⟩ φυσικόν, τίς αὐτῷ ἡ ὑποκειμένη
φύσις, καὶ διὰ τοῦδε προσαγορευομένη; Εἰ μὲν γὰρ ἑτέρα παρά τε
τὴν θεότητα καὶ ⟨τὴν⟩ ἀνθρωπότητα, ποία ἂν εἴη; Εἰ δὲ ἡ τῆς
θεότητος, οὐ τοῦ συνθέτου ἰδίως ἡ ὀνομασία ὡς συνθέτου· καὶ πρὸ
γὰρ τῆς συνθέσεως ἦν ἥ τε φύσις καὶ τὸ ὄνομα. Εἰ δὲ ⟨ἡ⟩ τῆς
ἀνθρωπότητος, καὶ οὕτως οὐ τοῦ συνθέτου ἡ προσηγορία· καὶ πρὸ
1873A   γὰρ τῆς ἑνώσεως τῆσδε ἦν ἥ τε φύσις καὶ ἡ κλῆσις αὕτη
ὡμολογημένως πᾶσιν. Ἀλλ' ἵνα πάντα παρίδωμεν, πῶς ἓν ὄνομα
φυσικὸν δεῖν εἰδέναι κατὰ τοῦ συνθέτου λέγοντες ὅλου, δύο τὲ καὶ
ἐναντία αὐτοῦ καταφάσκετε, κτιστόν τε καὶ ἄκτιστον αὐτὸ
λέγοντες, καὶ τό γε λίαν παραδοξότερον, ὅτι "ἀπὸ μὲν τῆς
θεότητος", μόνον "τὸ ἄκτιστον" καὶ "ἀπαθὲς" φάσκοντες εἶναι
αὐτοῦ, "ἀπὸ δὲ τοῦ σώματος τὸ κτιστὸν" καὶ "παθητόν", "οὔτε
μερικῶς ἀκούειν", "οὔτε λέγειν" τάδε ἐπὶ Χριστοῦ εἰρήκατε, ἀλλ' ἐκ
τοῦ ὅλου Χριστοῦ. Συγχωρήσαντες δὲ ὑμῖν ὡς ἂν καὶ βούλεσθε
παλιλλογεῖν, ἐπαγάγοιμεν τοῖς παρ' ὑμῶν ἀναγκαίως, ὡς εἴπερ
ὁμοτίμως περὶ ἑκατέρου τῶν ἐν Χριστῷ τὰ ἐναντία δοξάζετε, καὶ
τὸ ὅλον κατὰ φύσιν ἴστε τοιόνδε Χριστοῦ, ὃ ἂν ἐκ θατέρας τῶν ἐν
1873B   αὐτῷ φύσεων λέγεται κατὰ τῆς ὅλης ὑποστάσεως αὐτοῦ, ἆρά γε
ὥσπερ ἀληθῶς παθητὴ καὶ κτιστὴ ἡ σὰρξ αὐτοῦ, οὕτως γε καὶ ἡ
θεότης αὐτοῦ, καὶ ὥσπερ ἀπαθὴς καὶ ἄκτιστος ἡ θεότης αὐτοῦ,
οὕτως γε καὶ ἡ σάρξ· ἃ πρὸς τῷ βλασφήμῳ, ἔχει καὶ τὸ ἀδύνατον
σαφῶς· οὐ γὰρ ἔστιν ἐν ταυτῷ καὶ κατὰ τὸ αὐτὸ καὶ ὡσαύτως
πάντῃ τὰ ἐναντία πώποτέ τινος καταφάσκεσθαι.

being a different nature beyond these, has come into existence, what would the nature be that has come into existence in Christ—the nature that's neither divine nor human? Tell us, what is this natural form, this form beyond God? So much for that!

What kind of 'one name', though, are you saying 'is attached to what is compounded'? If it's the kind of name that pertains to hypostasis, the statement is unexceptionable. But if it's the kind of name that pertains to nature, what's the nature that underlies it, and on account of which it's called that kind of name? If it's a different nature than divinity and humanity, what sort of nature could it be? If it's the nature of divinity, this isn't properly the name of the composite *qua* composite, for it was [divinity's] nature and name before the composition too. If, on the other hand, it's the nature of humanity, it's likewise not the appellation for the compound, for this nature and form of address existed before this union too, as is universally confessed. So that we may take account of everything, though, how is it that you who say it's necessary to recognize one natural name for the composite whole affirm two opposite names for it, calling it both 'created' and 'uncreated'? What's even more incredible is the fact that, though you say that only 'the uncreated' and 'the impassible' about Him are 'from the divinity', but 'the created' and 'the passible' are 'from the body', you've asserted that you 'do not hear', that you 'do not say', these things about Christ as applying to a particular part, but on the basis of the whole Christ! We concede that you'd like to go over the whole thing again, but we just have to make the point to your partisans that, if you really think opposite things about each of the realities in Christ, giving them equal honour, and if you recognize the whole of Christ by nature to be of this kind—something that's surely said about His whole hypostasis on the basis of both of the natures that are in Him—then His divinity is just as truly passible and created as is His flesh, and His flesh is just as impassible and uncreated as His divinity. Such assertions aren't just rife with blasphemy; they're also clearly impossible. It's never yet been possible for opposites to be affirmed of anything in the same sense, in the same respect, and in precisely the same way.

1872D
1873A
1873B

Τοῦ αὐτοῦ ἐκ τοῦ περὶ τῆς ἐν Χριστῷ ἑνώσεως· " Ὡμολόγηται δὲ ἐν αὐτῷ τὸ μὲν εἶναι κτιστὸν ἐν ἑνότητι τοῦ ἀκτίστου, φύσεως μιᾶς ἐξ ἑκατέρου μέρους συνισταμένης, μερικὴν ἐνέργειαν καὶ τοῦ Λόγου συντελέσαντος εἰς τὸ ὅλον, μετὰ τῆς θεϊκῆς τελειότητος, ὅπερ ἐπὶ 1873c τοῦ κοινοῦ ἀνθρώπου ἐκ δύο μερῶν ἀτελῶν γίνεται, μίαν φύσιν πληρούντων, καὶ ἑνὶ ὀνόματι δηλουμένων."²⁴⁹ Σαφὲς ἄρα ὡς τῆς φύσεως τοῦ οἰκείου ὅλου, τῆς μιᾶς ἤγουν τῆς Χριστοῦ, ἡ θεϊκὴ τελειότης· μέρος οὖν φυσικὸν καὶ ἐλάττων ἐστὶ φύσις, καὶ οὐ μόνον γυμνὴ σαρκὸς κρίνοιτο τοῦ Λόγου πρὸς Χριστόν· ὅπερ εἰ ὁ Ἰούλιος ἔφη, ὄντως ὁ βουλόμενος σκοπείτω. [292ᵛ]

Γρηγορίου τοῦ Θαυματουργοῦ, ὡς φασίν, ἐν τῇ Κατὰ μέρος πίστει· "Τὸ δοξάζειν δύο φύσεις τὸν ἕνα Χριστόν, τετράδα τὴν ἁγίαν Τριάδα ποιεῖ", φασί· "ἔφη γὰρ οὕτως· Καὶ ἔστι Θεὸς ἀληθινός, ὁ ἄσαρκος ἐν σαρκὶ φανερωθείς,²⁵⁰ τέλειος τῇ ἀληθινῇ καὶ θείᾳ τελειότητι. Οὐ δύο πρόσωπα, οὐ δύο φύσεις, οὐδὲ τέσσαρας προσκυνεῖν λέγομεν, Θεὸν καὶ Υἱὸν Θεοῦ καὶ ἄνθρωπον καὶ Πνεῦμα 1873d ἅγιον."²⁵¹" Πρῶτον μὲν ἀγνοεῖται καὶ ἀμφιβάλλεται λίαν ἡ χρῆσις καὶ ἥδε· ὅμως μέντοι μὴ "δύο πρόσωπα" ἐπὶ Χριστοῦ λέγειν φησί, ἵνα μὴ ὁμολογοῦντες αὐτὸν Θεὸν, καὶ ἐν τελείᾳ θεότητι, δύο δὲ αὐτοῦ πρόσωπα, τετράδα παριστῶμεν τῶν θείων προσώπων, Θεοῦ τοῦ Πατρὸς ἕν, καὶ Υἱοῦ Θεοῦ ἕν, καὶ ἀνθρώπου ἕν, καὶ Πνεύματος ἁγίου ἕν, ἀριθμοῦντες. Ἀλλ' οὐδὲ δύο φύσεις, θείας μέντοι, εἰδέναι αὐτοῦ φησί, ἀλλ' ἐν μιᾷ φυσικῇ θείᾳ τελειότητι, τέλειον αὐτὸν θεὸν ὁμολογεῖν, καὶ οὐκ ἐν δύο· ὅτι γὰρ ἀτρέπτως ἐσαρκώθη, καὶ 1876a ἀδιπλασιάστως τὴν θεότητα ἔχει, βούλεται δεῖξαι. Ὁ γοῦν αὐτὸς πρὸ βραχέος φησί· "Καὶ τῶν περὶ σάρκα παθῶν γινομένων, τὴν ἀπάθειαν ἡ δύναμις εἶχε τὴν ἑαυτῆς. Ἀσεβὴς οὖν ὁ τὸ πάθος ἀνάγων εἰς τὴν δύναμιν· ὁ γὰρ τῆς δόξης Κύριος²⁵² ἐν ἀνθρωπίνῳ σχήματι πέφηνε, τὴν ἀνθρωπίνην οἰκονομίαν ἀναδεξάμενος."²⁵³

Γρηγορίου τοῦ ⟨θεολόγου⟩ ἐκ τοῦ κατὰ Ἀπολιναριαστῶν· "Κατηγοροῦσιν ἡμῶν ὡς δύο φύσεις εἰσαγόντων, ἀπηρτημένας ἢ 1876b μαχομένας, καὶ μεριζόντων τὴν ὑπερφυᾶ καὶ θαυμασίαν ἕνωσιν."²⁵⁴ Ἀλλ' ὦ οὗτοι σαφές, ὅτι τὴν ἀπάρτησιν καὶ μάχην λέγειν ἐπὶ τῶν φύσεων οὐ συνέθετο—τάδε γὰρ μερίζει τὴν θαυμαστὴν ἕνωσιν— ἐπεὶ ἔδει λέγειν μόνον οὕτως, ὡς "δύο φύσεις εἰσαγόντων, καὶ μεριζόντων τὴν ὑπερφυᾶ ἕνωσιν".

---

²⁴⁹ Actually Apollinarius, *On the Union* = Leitzmann, *Apollinaris*, 187. Cited with minor differences also at 1865b above.

²⁵⁰ 1 Tim. 3: 16

²⁵¹ Actually Apollinarius, *On the Faith, Point by Point* = Lietzmann, *Apollinaris*, 178–9.

²⁵² 1 Cor. 2: 8

²⁵³ Actually Apollinarius, *On the Faith, Point by Point* = Lietzmann, *Apollinaris*, 171.

²⁵⁴ Gregory of Nazianzus, *Letter* 102, SC 208, 82.

Of the same, from *On the Union in Christ*: 'It has been confessed that the created is in union with the uncreated in Him, one nature being put together out of each part, and the Word contributing part of the activity to the whole with the divine perfection. This is exactly what happens in the case of man, who comes to be out of two incomplete parts that complete one nature, and are signified 1873C by one name.' It's clear, then, that the 'divine perfection' belongs to the nature of the common whole, to the nature, i.e. of Christ. There is, therefore, a nature—the Word's—that's a natural part and inferior, and it's judged to be inferior to Christ, and not just because it's stripped of flesh. If that's what Julius said, then really anyone who likes is welcome to look into it!

Of Gregory Thaumaturgus (or so they claim) in *On the Faith, Point by Point*: 'To believe that the one Christ is two natures', they say, 'makes the Holy Trinity a quartet, for this is what [Gregory] says: "and He is true God, who being fleshless *was made manifest in flesh*, complete with the true and divine perfection. We do not speak of two persons, nor do we speak of two natures, nor do we say one should worship four—God, Son of God, man, and Holy Spirit."' A first point: this text, too, is unknown, and it's exceed- 1873D ingly limited. All the same, surely he says one shouldn't speak of two persons in Christ lest, when we confess He's God and in perfect divinity, but also confess His two persons, we set up a quartet of divine persons, counting one for God the Father, one for God the Son, one for man, and one for the Holy Spirit. He says he doesn't recognize two natures—divine natures, of course—belonging to Him, but confesses Him to be perfect God in one natural divine completeness, not in two, for he wants to demonstrate that He was incarnate in an immutable way, and has His divinity in a way that isn't double. He himself, at any rate, says 1876A shortly before this: 'though sufferings happened vis-à-vis the flesh, the divine power possessed its own impassibility. The man, there- fore, who refers suffering to the divine power is impious, for the *Lord of glory* appeared in human form, taking the human condition upon himself.'

Of Gregory the Theologian, from *Against Apollinarius*: 'They accuse us of introducing two natures that are separated or opposed, and of dividing the marvellous and wonderful union.' 1876B But, my friends, it's clear what he doesn't agree with is speaking of separation and opposition vis-à-vis the natures—these things div- ide the wonderful union—since otherwise all he needed to say was 'introducing two natures, and dividing the marvellous union'.

Κυρίλλου²⁵⁵ ἐκ τῆς πρὸς Σούκενσον ἐπιστολῆς· "Πλὴν τῆς
ἑνώσεως ὁμολογουμένης, οὐκέτι διΐστανται ἀλλήλων τὰ ἑνωθέντα,
ἀλλ' εἷς λοιπὸν Υἱός, μία φύσις αὐτοῦ ὡς σαρκωθέντος."²⁵⁶ Νῦν
δῆλόν ἐστι παντὶ τῷ σοφῶς ἅμα καὶ εὐσεβῶς ἐπισκέπτοντι, ὅτι
μίαν φύσιν Υἱοῦ φησίν, ὡς φύσει Υἱοῦ· οὐ γὰρ ἐστι καὶ χάριτι Υἱὸς
ὁ ἅπαξ τὴν τοῦ φύσει Υἱοῦ φύσιν ἔχων, εἰ καὶ τὴν σαρκὸς φύσιν
προσεκτήσατο μηδέποτε αὐτοῦ ἀποδιαστάσαν, ἵνα καὶ τῆς κατὰ
1876c χάριν υἱοθεσίας δέοιτο, τῆς κατὰ φύσιν οὐκ ἠξιωμένη. Ἀεὶ γὰρ ἐξ
οὗπέρ ἐστι τῇ φύσει υἱωμένη οὐσία, ἡνωμένη ἐστί, καὶ τῇ τῆς
φυσικῆς υἱώσεως ἀξίᾳ συντετιμημένη οὖν δοξάζεταί τε καὶ
συμπροσκυνεῖται.

Μηδὲν δὲ ἀθεράπευτον καταλιπεῖν ὡς οἷόν τε σπουδάζοντες
αὐτοῖς τῶν τῆς πρὸς ἡμᾶς φιλεχθίας²⁵⁷ προφασισμάτων, καὶ τὰς ἐν
παραβάσει τοῦ λόγου εἰωθυίας αὐτοῖς προφέρεσθαι μέμψεις
καθ' ἡμῶν παραγαγόντες, ἐνταυθοῖ που τὸν ἔλεγχον τοῦ κατὰ
τῆς ἐκκλησίας ψεύδους ἀποτερματίσωμεν. Ἐπεὶ γὰρ μήτε
ἀποδεικτικοῖς ἐπιχειρήμασι παραστῆσαι, μήτε γραφικοῖς ἢ
πατρικοῖς μαρτυρήμασι βεβαιῶσαι τὰ οἰκεῖα φρονήματα
δεδύνηνται, ἐν ἐσχατολογίᾳ τῶν αἰτιῶν τῆς ἀφ' ἡμῶν ἐκφοιτήσεως,
1876D [293] φασὶν ἔτι· "Ὡς κἂν τοιάδε²⁵⁸ ὑμεῖς εὐσεβοφανῆ νῦν
δογματίζετε, οὐ συνεκκλησιαζόμεθα ὑμῖν· δέχεσθε γὰρ καὶ σέβετε
τὴν ἐν Χαλκηδόνι σύνοδον, καὶ Λέοντα τὸν πατριάρχην Ῥώμης, οἵ",
1877A καθά φησιν αὐτοῖς ὁ λέγων τινὰ ἑαυτὸν εἶναι διδάσκαλον αὐτῶν, ὁ
ἀπὸ πατριαρχῶν Ἀντιοχείας Σεβῆρος, "πρόφασιν μὲν ἔσχον τῆς ἐπὶ
τὸ αὐτὸ συνελεύσεως τὴν Εὐτυχοῦς καθαίρεσιν, σπούδασμα δὲ ἦσαν
Νεστορίου."

⟨Τ⟩αῦτα γοῦν οἱ λέγοντες, πῶς οὐ τολμηταὶ καὶ αὐθάδεις λίαν;
δόξας γὰρ οὐ τρέμουσι βλασφημοῦντες,²⁵⁹ οἳ λόγον μὲν δώσουσι τῷ
ἑτοίμως ἔχοντι κρῖναι ζῶντας καὶ νεκρούς,²⁶⁰ ὃς καὶ ἀποδώσει
ἑκάστῳ κατὰ τὸ ἔργον αὐτοῦ,²⁶¹ καὶ ἀποκαλύψει τὰς βουλὰς τῶν
καρδιῶν.²⁶² Δείξομεν δὲ καὶ ἡμεῖς σὺν Θεῷ τῇ ἀληθείᾳ πᾶσι τοῖς
ἀκροαταῖς τῶνδε, ὡς καὶ κριταῖς ἀπολογούμενοι, ὅτι χείλη δόλια ἐν
καρδίᾳ²⁶³ αὐτοῖς, καὶ ἐκ καρδίας ἐλάλησαν κακά,²⁶⁴ θυμὸς αὐτοῖς
κατὰ τὴν ὁμοίωσιν τοῦ ὄφεως²⁶⁵ φθονερὸς καὶ μισάνθρωπος, οὐ
θεόζηλος. Οἱ γὰρ τούς τε ἀναθεματίσαντας Νεστόριον, ἤγουν τὴν ἐν
Ἐφέσῳ σύνοδον, ποτνιώμενοι, καὶ τὰ κατὰ Νεστορίου γεγραμμένα
1877B τῷ ὁσιωτάτῳ Κυρίλλῳ καὶ τὰς κατὰ τοῦδε φωνὰς πάσας

---

²⁵⁵ Κυρίλλου] Κυλίλλου sic MS
²⁵⁶ Actually Cyril of Alexandria, Letter 44, ACO i, 1, 4, 36.
²⁵⁷ sic MS = φιλεχθρίας   ²⁵⁸ τοιάδε sic accent. MS
²⁵⁹ 2 Pet. 2: 10   ²⁶⁰ 1 Pet. 4: 5   ²⁶¹ Rom. 2: 6
²⁶² 1 Cor. 4: 5   ²⁶³ Ps. 11: 3 LXX
²⁶⁴ Cf. Ps. 40: 6 and 57: 4 LXX; Luke 6: 45   ²⁶⁵ Ps. 57: 5 LXX

Of Cyril, from the *Letter to Succensus*: 'More than the union that's confessed, the things united no longer stand apart from each other, but from then on there is one Son, there is His one nature as incarnate.' It's clear by now to everyone who examines the matter both wisely and piously that he speaks of the Son's one nature as of a Son by nature, for He who once and for all possesses the nature of a Son by nature isn't a Son by grace, even if He took in addition the nature of flesh that never existed apart from Him in such a way as to stand in need also of sonship by grace because it wasn't worthy of sonship by nature. A substance made into a son 1876c is always united to the nature of that out of which it exists, and being co-honoured with the rank of natural sonship, it's therefore both glorified and co-worshipped with it.

Eager as can be to leave them nothing unaddressed among the allegations of contentiousness made against us, and now that we've turned aside the irrational censures they habitually though irrationally bring against us, we'd like here and now to put a stop to the charge of dishonesty against the church. Since they've been able neither to prove their shared assumptions by scientific arguments, nor to confirm them from scriptural or patristic texts, at the very end of the charges in their publication against us they go on to say: 'Even though you now teach the kind of things that seem to 1876D be orthodox, we don't come together in church with you, for you accept and reverence the council of Chalcedon, and Leo the Patriarch of Rome, people who'—as a self-styled teacher of theirs, Severus, one of the patriarchs of Antioch, tells them—'had as 1877A their pretext for convening the condemnation of Eutyches, but were really an act of zeal for Nestorius.'

How can people who talk like this be anything but *bold* and *wilful* men? They *aren't afraid to revile the glorious ones, who will give account to him who is ready to judge the living and the dead*; who also *will render to each according to his deeds*, and will reveal *the counsels of hearts*. For our part we, with God the truth, are going to demonstrate to all these people's disciples—defending ourselves as if before judges—that the words *deceitful lips in the heart* are for them, and they spoke evil out of their heart; *their soul is in the likeness of the serpent*, envious and full of hatred for the human race, not zealous for God. What possible justification was there for people to be slandered as being zealous for Nestorius who appeal to the anathematizers of Nestorius (the Council of Ephesus, and what the most religious Cyril wrote against Nestorius), who confess every- 1877B

ὁμολογοῦντες, καὶ ὡς μύσός τι αὐτοῦ πανταχόσε μνημονεύοντες,
καὶ πρό γε πάντων τῶν ὑπευθύνων τῇ ἀσεβείᾳ καὶ μετὰ πάντας
τοῦτον ἀναθεματίζοντες, καὶ τοὺς τὰ αὐτοῦ φρονοῦντας, πόθεν
εὐλόγως ὡς Νεστορίῳ σπουδάζοντες διεβλήθησαν;
"Ναί, ἦσάν τινες" φησὶν "ἐν τῇ συνόδῳ, οἳ ἐφωράθησαν
Νεστορίῳ πάλαι προσκείμενοι."

Ἵνα οὖν καὶ κατὰ συνδρομὴν τοῦτο δῶμεν αὐτοῖς—τὸ γὰρ
εὐκαθαίρετον τοῦ λόγου εἰδότες, εἰς μῆκος τὴν ἀπολογίαν ἐκτείνειν
περιττῶς οὐ βουλόμεθα—πῶς πέντε μὲν δικαίων ἕνεκα[266] μόνων
καὶ Σόδομα καὶ Γόμορρα ὅλη ἐσώζετο, ἧς ἡ κραυγὴ τῆς ἀνομίας
1877C καὶ ἕως τῶν ὑψίστων ἀνέβη,[267] ἐν δὲ τούτοις διὰ δεύτερον ἢ τρίτον
τινὰ δεισιδαιμονοῦντα, εἰ καὶ ἄρα ἀγνώστως τέ ἐν αὐτοῖς
ἀσεβοῦντα, πᾶσα ἡ ὁσία πληθὺς καὶ λαὸς ὁ ἅγιος τοῦ τῶν χλ΄
ἱερατεύματος, ὡς γνώμῃ δυσσεβοῦντες, μὴ διαθρῆσαι τὴν ἀλήθειαν
ἐγκατελείφθησαν ὑπὸ τοῦ λέγοντος Θεοῦ· Οὗ εἰσὶ δύο ἢ τρεῖς
συνηγμένοι ἐπὶ τῷ ὀνόματί μου, ἐκεῖ εἰμὶ ἐν μέσῳ αὐτῶν;[268] Καὶ
τοῦτο, οὐκ εἰς αὐτοὺς μόνον συντεινούσης τῆς θείας παροράσεως,
ἀλλὰ καὶ εἰς πᾶσαν Χριστοῦ τὴν καθ᾽ ὅλης τῆς οἰκουμένης ἁγίαν
ἐκκλησίαν τῶν πανδήμων καὶ πανεθνῶν λαῶν ἀφειδέστερον, ὅτι
οὐδὲ προσκαίρως, ἀλλ᾽ ἕως αἰωνίας παραδόσεως ἥκειν ἔμελλε τὰ
τότε ψηφισθέντα φρονήματα, ὡς ὁρῶμεν σὺν Θεῷ μέχρι καὶ νῦν.
1877D Ἆρα οὖν οὐκ εἰς τὸν τῆς θείας προνοίας λόγον ἀσεβήσειε πρῶτος, ὁ
τὸν τῆς πίστεως τῆς οἰκονομίας Χριστοῦ λόγον ἀθετῶν κηρυχθῆναι
τῇ οἰκουμένῃ διὰ τῶν ἁγίων συνόδων, καὶ βεβαιωθῆναι ἐν ταῖς ἑξῆς
γενεαῖς λογιζόμενος; Εἰ δὲ μὴ δὲ ἐκ τοῦ τῆς θείας προνοίας λόγου
μὴ εὐπαραδέκτως ἔχετε πρὸς τὴν ἁγίαν σύνοδον, ἀλ[293ᵛ]λ᾽ ἔτι
1880A ὑποπτεύετε ἐκ τῆς παλαιᾶς προλήψεως τινὰς ἰδικῶς τῶν ἐν αὐτῇ
ὑπούλως ἔχειν καὶ τότε τὴν Νεστορίου κακοδοξίαν, εἰ καὶ τοῖς
λεγομένοις ὑπὸ τοῦ κοινοῦ συναπήγοντο, σκοπήσωμεν καὶ οὕτως,
τίς δικαία κατάκρισις ἐκ τοῦδε τῆς συνόδου. Εἴπατε γάρ, εἰ
ἀδύνατον ἦν τινὰς πάλαι οὐκ εὐφρονοῦντας, ἐν τοῖς ἑξῆς χρόνοις
μεταμαθεῖν τὴν εὐσέβειαν καὶ ὀρθοδοξῆσαι; Αὐτὸ γὰρ δὴ τοῦτο
ὑπ᾽ αὐτῶν πραχθέν, τουτὶ βοᾷ, ἤγουν τὸ κατ᾽ ἐκεῖνο καιροῦ
ἀκραιφνῶς εὐσεβεῖν, εἰ καὶ μὴ πρώην, ἐγγράφως ἀναθεματισάντων
τὰ Νεστορίου φρονήματα, τόδε γάρ, οὐ τῶν ἐνδεχομένων ἐστίν;

---

[266] Gen. 18: 28 LXX   [267] Cf. Gen. 19: 30 LXX   [268] Matt. 18: 20

thing said against this man, commemorate anything of his as a total abomination, and anathematize him, as well as those who agree with him, both before and after all others held responsible for impiety?

'There were unquestionably some people in the council', my friend says, 'who were found to have formerly belonged to Nestorius.'

By way of granting this point to them as a provisional concession—recognizing the weak point of their argument, we have no wish to further extend our defence—how is it that all of Sodom, and all of Gomorrah, were saved *for the sake of only five just men*, though the clamour of their lawlessness rose all the way to heaven, whereas on account of two or three individuals among the [Chalcedonians] (even though those individuals kept their impiety a secret when they were with the participants) the entire blessed assembly and the holy members of the priesthood, all six hundred and thirty of them, have been included under the same sentence (as being ungodly in thought on the grounds of not looking closely into the truth) by the God who says *when two or three are gathered together in my name, there am I in the midst of them*? This is so because, given that the divine tolerance extends not only to them, but also, and even more generously, to all of the holy Church of Christ throughout the world, the Church of all peoples and all nations, He intended the doctrines voted on at Chalcedon to endure, not for a season, but as an everlasting tradition, one which we with God recognize right up to the present. Isn't any man a prime sinner against the concept of divine providence who denies that the meaning of the faith about Christ's Incarnation has been proclaimed to the world through the holy councils, yet considers it to have been confirmed in succeeding generations? If you don't take an acceptable stance towards the holy synod, not even in the light of this understanding of divine providence, but still suspect, on the basis of your long-standing prejudice, that certain of the men at it, acting as individuals and in secret, continued to hold, even then, the false opinion of Nestorius, even though they accommodated themselves to what was said by the majority, then let's also investigate what justice there is in condemning the synod on that score. Tell us, then: was it impossible for people who at one time didn't hold correct opinions to later learn piety instead, and become orthodox? The very action they took proclaims, so to speak, the fact that, when they anathematized Nestorius' ideas in writing, they were utterly pious at that moment, if not before, for

1877C

1877D

1880A

Ὥσπερ γοῦν οὐδὲ ἑτέρους πάλιν τινὰς τῶν ἐν τῇ συνόδῳ, ἀδύνατόν
ἐστι κατ' ἐκεῖνο καιροῦ εὐσεβοῦντας, ὕστερον μεταπεσεῖν εἰς
ἀσέβειαν; Ἢ οὐχὶ καὶ Παῦλος ὁ πρὶν διώκτης ὕστερον
1880B εὐηγγελίζετο τὴν πίστιν ἣν πάλαι ἐπόρθει;²⁶⁹ Ἰούδας δὲ ὁ πρώην
σὺν τοῖς ια' εὐαγγελιζόμενος τὸν Κύριον, ὅτε ἀνὰ δύο²⁷⁰
ἀπεστάλησαν ὑπ' αὐτοῦ, ὕστερον καὶ ἐπεβούλευσεν αὐτῷ; ἄλλως δὲ
εἰ καὶ κατὰ τὸν τῆς συνόδου καιρὸν αὐτὸν κακόφρονες ἦσαν τινὲς
ἐν αὐτοῖς, ὅμως ἐπὶ τοῖς καλῶς πραττομένοις καὶ λεγομένοις
συνετίθεντο, τίς ἡ μέμψις ἐκ τοῦδε καὶ τῇ συνόδῳ; μόνου γὰρ εἶναι
Θεοῦ τὸ καρδίας καὶ νεφροὺς²⁷¹ ἐτάζειν εἴρηται.
"'Αλλ' εἰ ὅλως μέρος ἔσχε ψεκτόν, τὸ ὅλον" φησὶ "λοιπὸν
ἀδόκιμον κρίνεται."
1880C Καὶ πᾶσαν τὴν ἅλω ἄρα διὰ τὸ ἓν ζιζάνιον, καὶ τὸν ὅλον χορὸν
τῶν ἀποστόλων διαβλητέον, διὰ τὴν εἰς τούσδε τοῦ Ἰούδα
συγκαταρίθμησιν. Ἔτι μήν, εἰ ἐκ τοῦ μέρους τὸ ὅλον κρίνειν δεῖ,
ἐπεὶ πολλοὶ καὶ τῶν ἐκ τῆς ἐν Ἐφέσῳ συνόδου ἦσαν ἐν τῇδε τῇ
Χαλκηδόνος συνόδῳ, δῆλον ὅτι ὡς ἐκ τῶνδε μᾶλλον τὸν κατὰ
Νεστορίου σκοπὸν εἶναι καὶ τῇσδε στοχάζεσθαι εὔλογον. Ἢ
ἀγνοεῖτε ὅτι καὶ τῶν ἐν Νικαίᾳ τιη' περὶ τοὺς δέκα καὶ ἑπτά, φόβῳ
τῆς καθαιρέσεως, ὑπέγραψαν κατὰ Ἀρείου, οἳ καὶ ἐπολέμησαν
δεινῶς μετὰ ταῦτα τὸν μέγαν Ἀθανάσιον, καὶ οὐ παρὰ τοῦτο ἡ
σύνοδος ὅλη διαβάλλεται; Εἰ δὲ ἐκ τοῦ μὲν σαφοῦς μέρους οὐκ
εὐδοκεῖτε συνιέναι τὴν τοῦ ὅλου ἀγαθότητα, ἐκ δὲ τοῦ ἀμφιβόλου
διαβάλλειν πειράζετε, ἄρά²⁷² γε ἐκ μέρους διαβληθείσης ὑμῖν τῆσδε
1880D τῆς ἁγίας συνόδου τῆς ὁλότητος πάσης, συνδιαβεβλημένων τῷ ὅλῳ
καὶ τῶν ἐκ τῆς ἐν Ἐφέσῳ εὑρεθέντων ἐν αὐτῇ, οἳ ἦσαν μέρος
ἐκείνης, κἀκείνην ἀνάγκη τὴν ὁλότητα, ἐκ τοῦ ληφθέντος αὐτῆς
μέρους μεμπτοῦ, ὡς σπούδασμα Νεστορίου συνδιαβάλλεσθαι, καὶ
ἐκ τοῦ ὑπολείμματος τῶν δέκα καὶ ἑπτὰ ὡς σπούδασμα Ἀρείου τὴν
ἐν Νικαίᾳ ἀθετεῖσθαι δέον. Ἵνα δὲ μὴ ἀγνοῆτε τῆς ἀθέσμου
1881A λοιδορίας ὑμῶν τὴν προπέτειαν, μνημονεύσατε ὅτι καὶ Συμεὼν ὁ
ἅγιος ὁ ἐν κίονι τὴν ἰδίαν ἡμῖν [294ʳ] στηλώσας ἀρετήν, εἰς ἣν
τῶν ὑπογραψάντων ἐν τῷ ὅρῳ τῇσδε τῆς συνόδου, εἰς ὅν
ἐγκωμιαστικοὺς λόγους καὶ ὕμνους ἐκθειαστικοὺς καὶ ὁ ὑμέτερος
ἔφη πατριάρχης Σεβῆρος αὐτός, καὶ Βαραδάτος δὲ καὶ Ἰάκωβος οἱ

---

²⁶⁹ Gal. 1: 23   ²⁷⁰ Luke 10: 1
²⁷¹ Rev. 2: 23   ²⁷² ἄρά] ἀρά MS

isn't this the action of approved people? Likewise, was it impossible for certain other participants in the council, who were pious at that moment, to later fall into impiety? Didn't Paul, the onetime persecutor, later *preach the faith he* once *tried to destroy?* Didn't Judas, who once proclaimed the Lord along with the eleven when He sent them out *two by two,* later plot against Him? On the contrary, even if, at the very time of the council, there were certain evil-minded people among those present, and they were likewise included among those who acted and spoke rightly, what are the grounds for complaint against the council in that? It's said, after all, that it's for God alone to test *hearts and minds.*

1880B

'But if it had a part that was altogether blameworthy,' my friend says, 'then the whole is condemned as spurious too.'

Well then, you have to find fault with the entire threshing-floor because of a single weed, and with the whole troop of apostles because Judas was numbered among them! If the whole really is to be judged from the part, the reasonable conclusion clearly follows that, since many people from the Council of Ephesus participated in the Council of Chalcedon, the intent of the latter council was all the more anti-Nestorian as a result of their presence! Are you unaware of the fact that, even out of the 318 at Nicaea, seventeen subscribed against Arius for fear they'd be deposed, but later on made terrible war against the great Athanasius, yet the entire council isn't impugned because of it? If you refuse to understand the goodness of the whole from the part of it that's sound, but attempt to impugn the whole on the basis of the dubious part, then consider the implications: since the latter holy council [of Chalcedon] in its entirety is attacked by you on the basis of one part of it, and since the people from the Council of Ephesus who were found at it are included in the attack on the whole—men who were a part of the former council—it follows that the entirety of that former council [of Ephesus] must be attacked along with Chalcedon as an 'act of zeal for Nestorius' on the basis of the selected blameworthy part! The Council of Nicaea, too, must be set aside as an act of zeal for Arius on account of the remnant of seventeen. Just so that you don't fail to realize how rash your illegitimate abuse is, you should remember that even holy Symeon, who displayed his personal virtue to us on a pillar, was one of those who subscribed in the precincts of the Council [of Chalcedon]—Symeon, to whom even your patriarch Severus himself offered eulogies and worshipful hymns—as were

1880C

1880D

1881A

θαυματουργοὶ συνυπέγραψαν. Ἀλλὰ τί ταῦτα, ῥητορικῆς ὄντα πιθανολογίας δεινώματα, τοῖς πρὸς κατάληψιν εὐσεβείας ἐναγωνίως σπεύδουσιν ἐμποδὼν ῥίπτετε τὰ σκάνδαλα, καὶ τοὺς θέλοντας <u>τρέχειν καλῶς, ἐκκόπτετε τῇ ἀληθείᾳ μὴ πείθεσθαι;</u>[273] Ὡς ἂν γοῦν ἐνώπιόν τε Θεοῦ καὶ ἀνθρώπων[274] παραστήσωμεν οὐκ ἐν λόγῳ ὄντα τὸν ὑμέτερον ἀπεκκλησιασμόν, ἰδοὺ πάντα παραδραμόντες ἔλεγχον τῶν προφασισμάτων, προτείνομεν ὑμῖν ὡς,

1881B εἰ τὰ προβασανισθέντα ἡμῖν ὀρθὰ δόγματα συνομολογήσοιτε, "μίαν τὲ φύσιν τοῦ θεοῦ λόγου σεσαρκωμένην" λέγοντες, καὶ δύο φύσεις εἶναι Χριστοῦ ἡνωμένας κατὰ μίαν αὐτοῦ τὴν ὑπόστασιν οὐκ ἀρνούμενοί τε, καὶ τὴν σύνοδον καὶ Λέοντα καὶ ἑαυτούς, <u>ἀλλὰ καὶ ἄγγελον ἐξ οὐρανοῦ,</u>[275] εἰ μὴ οὕτως ἐφρόνουν καὶ ἔλεγον καὶ ἔγραφον, πρὸ ὑμῶν ἀναθεματίζομεν, Σεβῆρόν τε καὶ Διόσκορον καὶ Τιμόθεον καὶ ὑμᾶς, καὶ τὸν οἱονοῦν οὕτως φρονοῦντα, εὐφημοῦμεν καὶ ἀποδεχόμεθα, μηδὲν ἕτερον ἐπιλέγοντες τούτοις, ἀλλὰ τὴν κρίσιν τῶν οὕτως φρονούντων, ἢ ἄλλως μὲν εἰρηκότων, ἑτέρως δὲ νοούντων, τῷ πάντων κριτῇ Θεῷ ἐγκαταλιμπάνοντες. Εἰ δὲ πάντως κρίνειν καὶ ἡμᾶς δεῖ καὶ πληροφορεῖσθαι, τίνες μὲν εὐσεβεῖς εἰσὶ

1881C πατέρες ἡμῶν καὶ <u>ποιμένες</u>[276] καὶ <u>φωστῆρες,</u>[277] τίνες δὲ <u>ἀστέρες πλανῆται,</u>[278] καὶ <u>λῆσται</u>[279]; καὶ <u>λύκοι,</u>[280] εἰς διαίρεσιν καὶ φθορὰν τῆς ἐκκλησίας Χριστοῦ τῷ διαβόλῳ λειτουργήσαντες, εἰκότως, οὒς μὲν εὕρομεν σαφῶς ἐκ τῶν γεγραμμένων τῆς ἀληθείας ὑποφήτας, ὡς <u>διὰ τῆς θύρας</u>[281] εἰσιόντας εἰς τὴν μάνδραν τοῦ Χριστοῦ, ἤγουν δι' αὐτοῦ, ὅς ἐστιν <u>ἡ ἀλήθεια,</u>[282] τούτους σέβομεν, τούτους ἀγαπῶμεν, τούτοις ὑπακούομεν, <u>ἀλλοτρίῳ δὲ οὐχ' ὑπακούομεν, ὅτι οὐκ οἴδαμεν τῶν ἀλλοτρίων τὴν φωνήν,</u>[283] τὰ ἐντὸς πρόβατα τοῦ καλοῦ ποιμένος[284] καὶ ἀρχιποίμενος[285] τοῦ μεγάλου Ἰησοῦ Χριστοῦ.

"Καὶ μὴν" φασὶ "καὶ αὐτοὶ οἱ τῆς συνόδου πατέρες περὶ φωνάς τινὰς ἀλλήλοις διηνέχθησαν, καὶ ἐνέστησαν ὑπὲρ τῆς πρώτης αὐτῶν

1881D ἐκθέσεως τῆς καταργηθείσης θερμῶς. Ἀλλήλως ἂν οὗτοι, καὶ ὑπὲρ Διοσκόρου πρεσβεύοντες τοῦ ὑπευθύνου, πῶς οὖν οὐχ' ὕποπτοι;"

1884A Πλὴν τί τοῦτο ξένον; Καὶ ἐν τῇ γὰρ τῶν τιη΄ πατέρων συνόδῳ τῇ ἐν Νικαίᾳ διηνέχθησάν τινες πρὸς ἀλλήλους, ὡς δηλοῖ Εὐσέβιος ἱστορῶν.

"Ἀλλὰ ναὶ" φησὶν "ἐλέγχει τὴν σύνοδον ἑτεροφρονοῦσαν κατὰ βάθους πρὸς τὰ πολλὰ τῶν εἰρημένων ὑπ' αὐτῆς, καὶ ἄλλα μὲν ὠδίνουσαν, ἄλλα δὲ ἀποτίκτουσαν, καὶ ὁ τοῦ ὅρου αὐτῆς διπλασιασμός, καὶ ἡ ἐπάλληλος ψῆφος, καὶ τῶν ἰδίων ἡ μεταστροφή."

---

[273] Gal. 5: 7   [274] Cf. 2 Cor. 8: 21   [275] Gal. 1: 8
[276] Eph. 4: 11   [277] Phil. 2: 15   [278] Jude 1: 13
[279] John 10: 8   [280] John 10: 12   [281] John 10: 1
[282] John 14: 6   [283] John 10: 5   [284] John 10: 11
[285] 1 Pet. 5: 4

Baradatus and James the wonder-workers.[xii] But why do you set these snares—exaggerated views based on plausible-seeming arguments on the part of people who are pugnaciously eager for an assault on piety—for our feet, and *hinder* those who want *to run well from obeying the truth?* So as to demonstrate, as may be, before God and men that your secession from the Church isn't reasonable, look, we set aside every argument we might make against your allegations, and make you the following offer: If you'll join with us in confessing the tried and true doctrines, saying both 'one incarnate nature of God the Word' and that there are two natures of Christ united in His one hypostasis, and if you also don't repudiate the Council, and Leo, and ourselves, then we, for our part, anathematize even *an angel from heaven* sooner than we do you, if he doesn't think and speak and write likewise; we praise and accept Severus, Dioscorus, Timothy, and you, and anyone at all who shares such views; we add nothing to this, but we leave the judgement on those who think in this way, or who speak in one way but think in another, to God, the judge of all. If we really do have to judge and to assure ourselves fully as to which are our pious fathers, *shepherds*, and fixed *stars*, and which are rather *wandering stars* [that is, planets], *robbers*, and *wolves*, serving the devil for the division and ruin of Christ's Church, then naturally enough the ones we honour, the ones we love, the ones to whom we listen, are those we've clearly found from their writings to be interpreters of the truth, people who enter into Christ's fold *by the door*, i.e. through Him who is *the truth*. We *don't* listen *to a stranger, because we don't know the voice of strangers*, being inwardly sheep of the good shepherd and great chief shepherd, Jesus Christ.

'Certainly even the fathers of the council themselves', they say, 'disagreed with each other about certain phrases, and they enthusiastically replaced their first creed, which was annulled. How could these men not be suspect who, in their mutual disagreement, took precedence over Dioscorus, the one who had that responsibility?'

What's strange about that? Even at the council of the 318 fathers at Nicaea some disagreed with each other, as Eusebius makes clear when he writes the history.

'But certainly', my friend says, 'the remaking of its definition, its successive votes, and its turning away from its own statements prove that the council changed its mind profoundly about the majority of what it had said, that it gave birth to one set of things, though it had been pregnant with another.'

1881B

1881C

1881D

1884A

Ἀλλ' ἔστι μέν, ὦ οὗτοι, ἐκ τῶν κατ' αὐτὴν πεπραγμένων εὔλογον, τήν τε ἐπανάληψιν τοῦ ὅρου καὶ τὴν ἐπιδιόρθωσιν κατανοῆσαι σαφέστατα. Ἵνα δὲ μὴ τοιαύταις δικολογίαις ἀγο[294ᵛ]ραίοις καὶ ἡμεῖς ὑμῖν συνδιασυρώμεθα, καὶ πρὸς τόδε τοῦτό φαμεν· "Πρῶτα μὲν ὡς οὐκ ἐκ πρώτης ἀνθρώποις πᾶσιν, οὐδὲ τοῖς θεοφόροις, ἡ

1884в τελεία γνῶσις εὐθύς, ἀλλ' ἔστι καὶ τοὺς ἁγίους πῆ μὲν ἐκ μέρους τί γινώσκοντας,²⁸⁶ ὕστερον τελεωτέρως τὸ αὐτὸ ἐπιγινώσκειν· ἄλλως δὲ εἰ μὴ τὸ ὅλον πρὸς διαβολὴν μόνον ὁρῶμεν, μᾶλλον ἂν ἐκ τοῦδε προσεχῶς τε καὶ ἐμπερισκέπτως ψηφισαμένη φανεῖται, καὶ οὐδὲν κατὰ συναρπαγὴν ἢ παρόρασιν τῆς χρείας ἐκφωνήσασα."

"Ἀλλὰ καὶ ἑτέρωθεν αὐτήν" φησιν "διαβλητέον. Διοσκόρῳ γὰρ ἀντιπαθῶς ἔχουσα ἐλέγχεται τῷ ἐν Ἀλεξανδρείᾳ ὄντι πάπᾳ ποτέ, ὃς τοῖς Νεστοριανοῖς ἀντέκειτο ἄγαν δόγμασι. Καὶ γὰρ τόνδε οὐκ ἀλόγως ἐξέβαλε τοῦ θρόνου, μόνον ὡς ἐχθρῷ Νεστορίου τούτῳ μηνίσασα, ἀλλὰ τινες αὐτῶν τοιῶνδε συνηγοριῶν καὶ κατηγοριῶν ῥητορικαὶ παραγραφαὶ καὶ διαβολαί, Τερτύλλῳ τῷ ὑπὲρ Ἰουδαίων λέγοντι κατὰ Παύλου πρὸς Φήλικα πρέπουσαι."²⁸⁷

1884с Πρὸς ὑποσύλησιν γὰρ τῶν κουφοτέρων κριτῶν εἰσιν ἐξευρημένα τὰ τοιάδε. Διόσκορον γάρ, ὡς Εὐτυχέα μὲν τὸν κακόφρονα δεξάμενον μετὰ τὴν καθαίρεσιν αὐτοῦ, καὶ ἀναθεματίσαντα τὸν ὅσιον Φλαβιανὸν τὸν δικαίως αὐτὸν καθάραντα, προετρέψατο ἐλθεῖν εἰς ἀνάκρισιν τῶν κατ' αὐτοῦ ἡ σύνοδος, διαφόρως καὶ ἀλληνάλλως ψευδῆ τε προφασιζόμενον ἐπὶ τῇ ἀναμονῇ αὐτοῦ τῇ πρὸς τὴν κλῆσιν φωραθέντα· ὕστερον δὲ καὶ ἀνέδην τέλεον οὐκ εἴξαντα παραγενέσθαι, τηνικαῦτα ἐξέβαλον.

"Πῶς οὖν" φησιν "αὐτὴ ἡ σύνοδος ἔφη Διόσκορον μὴ διὰ δόγμα καθελεῖν, ἀλλ' ὅτι κληθεὶς οὐχ ὑπήκουσε;"

1884D Καὶ γὰρ ὄντως, ὦ οὗτοι, ἐκλήθη μὲν διὰ τὴν τοῦ κακοῦ δόγματος Εὐτυχοῦς ὑποψίαν, μὴ ὑπακούσας δὲ καὶ ἐκδοὺς εἰς βάσανον τὰ καθ' ἑαυτὸν προϋποπέπτωκε καὶ ἑτέρῳ ἐγκλήματι, τῷ τῆς παρακοῆς, ὑπὲρ οὗ καὶ τῆς κατὰ τοὺς κανόνας μερικῆς τέτυχεν

1885A ἀμοιβῆς ἐκβεβλημένος· πλὴν οὐκ ἐν τῷδε τοῦ τῆς κακοδοξίας

---

²⁸⁶ 1 Cor. 13: 9   ²⁸⁷ Acts 24: 1–8

But, my friends, the reasonable thing is to understand the recension of the definition to be very clearly also its correction! For our part, we'd rather not participate in your depreciation of things with this kind of courtroom rhetoric. We do, nonetheless, have this to say by way of response to your charge: 'In the first place, we say that perfect understanding doesn't happen right away for all men, not even for god-bearing men; rather, it's possible even for the saints, when they've somehow *known* something 1884B *in part*, to get to know the same thing more perfectly later on. If we don't view the whole with an eye only to slander, the council appears in this light to have voted with care and circumspection, and to have uttered nothing conducive to fraud or to negligence of the task at hand.'

'But the council is to be faulted on another score as well', my friend says. 'When it behaved adversely towards Dioscorus, it was opposed by him, he being the Pope of Alexandria at the time, and a man much opposed to Nestorian teachings. It wasn't for no reason that it deposed this man from his throne, since it was angry at him solely for being an enemy of Nestorius, but some of the rhetorical mis-statements and accusations of such speeches pro and contra are of the kind that would suit Tertullus, the man who spoke to Felix on behalf of the Jews against Paul.'

Such things are inventions aimed at suborning those not well- 1884C equipped to judge. The council summoned Dioscorus as having received the thoughtless Eutyches after the latter's deposition, and as having anathematized the holy Flavian (who justly deposed Eutyches), and it summoned him to appear for an examination of the allegations against him when he was detected making false excuses in many different ways for his delaying action against the summons. It was later, when he quite freely refused to appear, that they deposed him.

'How is it, then,' my friend says, 'that the same council said it did not condemn Dioscorus on doctrinal grounds, but because he did not comply when he was summoned?'

Well, my friends, Dioscorus really was summoned on suspicion 1884D of harbouring the evil doctrine of Eutyches, but when he wouldn't comply and submit the case against himself to trial, he fell under another accusation, that of disobedience, and it's in connection with the charge of disobedience and the particular penalty prescribed by the canons for it that he happened to be deposed—except he wasn't released from the charge of heresy in 1885A

ἠλευθέρωται. Οὐ γὰρ εἴ τις ἐπὶ ἱεροσυλίᾳ ἐγκαλοῖτο, προτραπεὶς δὲ εἰς τὴν περὶ τοῦδε δίκην καὶ φυγοδικήσας, εἶτα εὐλόγως φυγοδικίαν κατακριθεὶς ὅδε, διὰ τῆς κουφοτέρας κατακρίσεως τῆσδε, περὶ τῆς ἱεροσυλίας τὴν νικῶσαν ἀπενέγκοιτο· τοὐναντίον γὰρ καὶ ἐπιβεβαιοῖ τὴν προτέραν ὑποψίαν τῆς κατ' αὐτοῦ προσαγγελίας, ἡ γενομένη αὐτῷ ἔγκλησις τῆς βασάνου τῆς ὑποθέσεως. Εἰ δὲ λέγοιτε ὅτι οὐ τὸ συνειδὸς αὐτῷ αἴτιον ἦν τῆς φυγοδικίας, ἀλλ' ἡ τῶν δικαστῶν ἀντιπάθεια, ταύτην ἄρα ἐγγράφως καὶ νομίμως καὶ κανονικῶς [295ʳ] δι' εὐλόγου παραιτήσεως ἔδει αὐτὸν συστῆσαι, οὐ μὴν διὰ τῆς τῶν ἐλέγχων ἀποδράσεως· τοῦτο γὰρ ἀπορίᾳ παντελεῖ τῆς περὶ τοῦ ἐγκλήματος ἀπολογίας γίνεται. Τίνας γὰρ ἂν καὶ ἔφη λόγους παραγενόμενος, ὁ βουλόμενος τῶν ὑπεραλγούντων τἀνδρὸς
1885в ἠθοποιείτω.²⁸⁸ Ὅτι μὲν γὰρ ἐδέξατο Εὐτυχέα, φανερόν· ὅτι δὲ οὐ καλῶς ἐδέξατο ἄνδρα μίαν εἶναι μόνην τὴν τοῦ Χριστοῦ φύσιν δοξάζοντα, θείαν τε ἁπλῶς καὶ οὐδὲν ἔχουσαν ἀνθρώπινον, τί ἂν ἀπελογήσατο; Ὑμεῖς οὖν οἱ Διοσκορῖται ἐπινοήσατε.

"Ναί" φησι "μετανοήσαντα γὰρ αὐτὸν ἐπὶ τούτοις ἐδέξατο, καὶ ἀληθῶς ὀρθοδοξοῦντα ὕστερον."

Οἱ γοῦν τοὺς ὁπωσοῦν ὑποπτευθέντας πῶ ποτε Νεστορίῳ συμφρονεῖν τῶν ἐν τῇ συνόδῳ, μὴ μεταστῆναι τῆς δεισιδαιμονίας πειθόμενοι, πῶς νῦν τόνδε οὐχ' ἁπλῶς μόνον ὑποπτευόμενον, ἀλλὰ καὶ ἐγγράφως ὁμολογήσαντα τὴν ἀσέβειαν αὐτοῦ, καὶ
1885с καθαιρεθέντα ἐπὶ τῷδε, ὡς μὴ ἀποστάντα τῆς κακοδοξίας, μεταμαθεῖν τὴν εὐσέβειαν ἐπληροφορήθητε, οὔτε παρουσίᾳ συνόδου, ἢ μαρτύρων τινῶν ἀξιοπίστων, οὔτε ἐν ἐκκλησίᾳ, οὔτε ἐγγράφῳ ὁμολογίᾳ τινὶ τῆς πρώην αὐτὸν ἀποστῆναι κακοδοξίας ὁμολογήσαντα; Ἔτι μὴν εἰ ὄντως ταῦτα ἔχει, καὶ ὡς μετανοήσαντα ἐδέξατο αὐτόν, δῆλον ὅτι ὄντως ἀσεβοῦντα πρώην αὐτὸν ἐφ' οἷς ἔσχατον πρὸς Διόσκορον μετενόησε, καθῆρεν ὁ ὁσιώτατος Φλαβιανός. Πῶς οὖν δεξάμενος τόν δε ὁμολογοῦντα τὴν πάλαι αὐτοῦ κακοδοξίαν, τὸν καθαιρεθέντα δικαίως πρὸ τῆς μετανοίας, Φλαβιανὸν τὸν δικαίως αὐτὸν καθήραντα Εὐτυχῆ, τοῦτό φησι καὶ αὐτὸς πρᾶξαι εἰς αὐτόν; Ἢ οὖν οὐκ ἀληθῶς μετανοήσαντα τοῦτον
1885d ἐδέξατο, ἢ οὐκ ἀδίκως καθελόντα αὐτὸν Φλαβιανόν, ἐκεῖνον αὐτὸς ἀδίκως ἀντικαθεῖλεν.

²⁸⁸ ἠθοποιείτο

this. If someone's charged with sacrilege, but avoids trial even though he's urged [to submit to] trial for it, and then this man's condemned on solid grounds for avoiding trial, he doesn't deflect the first-order judgement for sacrilege on account of this lighter judgement. On the contrary, the accusation that emerged against him of contesting the proposed trial would strengthen the earlier suspicion contained in the information laid against him. If you say it wasn't this realization that caused him to avoid trial, but the antipathy of the judges, what he needed to do was to give written, legal, and canonical proof of this antipathy in the form of a reasoned refusal, not by running away from cross-examination! That completely undermines his defence against the accusation. Let anyone who feels pain for the man note the character of the assertions he made when he was present. That he received Euty- 1885B ches is clear, but what excuse did he offer for incorrectly receiving a man who supposed that there was only one nature of Christ, a nature that was just divine and had nothing human about it? That's what you, the followers of Dioscorus, need to come up with!

'Certainly', my friend says, 'he received [Eutyches] when he repented for these things, and when he later held correct and true opinions.'

How does it happen that you—who are persuaded that, among those at the council, none of those ever suspected in any way of agreeing with Nestorius ever abandoned their superstition—now have become utterly convinced that this man (who isn't just sus- pected of impiety, but even confessed his impiety in writing, and was deposed for it as being someone who didn't abandon his 1885c error) learned piety instead? This though he didn't confess that he abandoned his former error either in the presence of a council or of trustworthy witnesses, or in church, or in any written confes- sion! Furthermore, even if it really is the case that [Dioscorus] received him as being someone who repented, it's clear that the most religious Flavian deposed him when he earlier was impious about things of which he in the end repented to Dioscorus. How is it that Dioscorus, though he received the one who confessed his former error (a man justly deposed before his repentance), says he himself did exactly the same thing to Flavian that Flavian did to Eutyches, that is, justly deposed him? Either he received this man though he didn't truly repent, or he himself unjustly counter- 1885D deposed the very Flavian who not unjustly deposed Eutyches!

"'Αλλὰ ναί" φησι "Νεστοριανὴ πρόληψις ἦν περὶ Φλαβιανοῦ τοῦ Κωνσταντινουπόλεως ἐπισκόπου, ἔνθεν καὶ ὕποπτα τὰ εἰς Εὐτυχῆ γενόμενα ὑπ' αὐτοῦ."

Καὶ τίς ἐντυγχάνων τῇ ἐκθέσει τῆς πίστεως Φλαβιανοῦ, τῷδε συμφήσειεν, ὦ οὗτοι; Φησὶ γάρ· "Κηρύσσομεν τὸν Κύριον ἡμῶν Ἰησοῦν Χριστὸν πρὸ αἰώνων ἐκ Θεοῦ Πατρὸς ἀνάρχως γεννηθέντα
1888A κατὰ τὴν θεότητα, ἐπ' ἐσχάτων δὲ τῶν ἡμερῶν τὸν αὐτὸν δι' ἡμᾶς καὶ διὰ τὴν ἡμετέραν σωτηρίαν ἐκ Μαρίας τεχθέντα κατὰ τὴν ἀνθρωπότητα, Θεὸν τέλειον καὶ ἄνθρωπον τέλειον τὸν αὐτὸν ἐν προσλήψει ψυχῆς καὶ σώματος, ὁμοούσιον τῷ Πατρὶ κατὰ τὴν θεότητα καὶ ὁμοούσιον τῇ μητρὶ τὸν αὐτὸν κατὰ τὴν ἀνθρωπότητα. Καὶ γὰρ ἐκ δύο φύσεων τὸν αὐτὸν Χριστὸν μετὰ τὴν σάρκωσιν τὴν ἐκ τῆς ἁγίας παρθένου καὶ ἐνανθρώπησιν, ἐν μιᾷ ὑποστάσει καὶ ἐν ἑνὶ προσώπῳ ἕνα Χριστόν, ἕνα Υἱόν, ἕνα Κύριον ὁμολογοῦμεν, καὶ μίαν δὲ τοῦ Θεοῦ Λόγου φύσιν σεσαρκωμένην μέντοι καὶ ἐνανθρωπήσασαν λέγειν οὐκ ἀρνούμεθα, [295ᵛ] διὰ τὸ ἐξ ἀμφοῖν ἕνα καὶ τὸν αὐτὸν εἶναι Κύριον ἡμῶν Ἰησοῦν τὸν Χριστόν. Τοὺς δὲ
1888B δύο υἱούς, ἢ δύο ὑποστάσεις, ἢ δύο πρόσωπα καταγγέλλοντας, ἀλλ' οὐχ' ἕνα καὶ τὸν αὐτὸν Κύριον Ἰησοῦν Χριστὸν τὸν Υἱὸν τοῦ Θεοῦ τοῦ ζῶντος κηρύσσοντας ἀναθεματίζομεν, καὶ ἀλλοτρίους τῆς ἐκκλησίας εἶναι κρίνομεν, καὶ πρῶτον πάντων Νεστόριον ἀναθεματίζομεν τὸν δυσσεβῆ, καὶ τοὺς τὰ αὐτοῦ φρονοῦντας ἢ λέγοντας· καὶ ἐκπέσουσιν οἱ τοιοῦτοι τῆς υἱοθεσίας τῆς ἐπηγγελμένης τοῖς ὀρθῶς φρονοῦσιν."[289]

Οὕτω μὲν οὗτος ὁμολογεῖ ὁ ὑπὸ Διοσκόρου, ὡς φησίν, ἅτε Νεστοριανίζων καθαιρεθείς. Εἶτα δὲ ἁπλῶς καὶ τῆς κατὰ Διοσκόρου πάσης μέμψεως σιγηθείσης ἡμῖν, πᾶσα μὲν ἡ τῶν ἱερῶν
1888C καὶ ἁγίων λειτουργῶν σύνοδος ἀντιπαθῶς ἔδοξεν ὑμῖν ἐκβαλεῖν παρόντα καὶ κεκλημένον διαφόρως καὶ προδιαβεβλημένον ἐπὶ προλήψει Εὐτυχοῦς ἕνα τινὰ μόνον αὐτὸν Διόσκορον, Σεβῆρος δὲ ὁ γενόμενος ⟨ἐπίσκοπος⟩ ἐν Ἀντιοχείᾳ, οὔτε ἐν χρόνοις ἢ τόποις αὐτοῦ τὴν ἐν Χαλκηδόνι σύνοδον παροῦσαν, οὔτε προτραπεῖσαν ὑπ' αὐτοῦ, οὔτε δεξαμένην Νεστόριον, ἀλλὰ καὶ ἐκβάλλουσαν αὐτὸν καὶ τὰ αὐτοῦ ἐγγράφως, δεχομένην δὲ τὴν κατ' αὐτοῦ ὀρθοδοξίαν, ἀλλ' οὐχὶ καὶ τὴν ἀντικειμένην αὐτῷ κακοδοξίαν Εὐτυχοῦς, οὐκ ἐκβάλλεσθαι ἁπλῶς καταψηφισάμενος ἀλλὰ καὶ ἀναθέματι κατακρίνειν αὐτοὺς ἅπαντας ἅμα ὑφὲν ὁ εἷς μόνος τολμήσας, πῶς

---

[289] Flavian of Constantinople, *Letter to Theodosius*, *ACO* ii, 1, 1, 35.

'But there certainly was a Nestorian prejudice to Flavian, the Bishop of Constantinople,' my friend says, 'and as a result everything that took place against Eutyches under him is suspect.'

Yet who that happened upon Flavian's exposition of faith would agree with this, my friends? Here's what he says: 'We proclaim our Lord Jesus Christ, eternally begotten of God the Father before all ages vis-à-vis His divinity, but in latter days the same   1888A
born of Mary vis-à-vis his humanity for us and for our salvation; perfect God, and the same perfect man by the acquisition of a soul and a body; consubstantial with the Father in respect of divinity, and the same consubstantial with His mother in respect of His humanity. For we confess the same Christ out of two natures after taking flesh from the holy Virgin and becoming man, one Christ, one Son, one Lord in one hypostasis and in one person, and do not refuse to speak of one nature—incarnate, to be sure, and become man—of the Word of God, on account of our Lord Jesus Christ's being one and the same out of both. But those who proclaim two sons, or two hypostases, or two persons, but not   1888B
one and the same Lord Jesus Christ, the Son of the living God, we anathematize, and judge them to be strangers to the Church. We anathematize first of all the impious Nestorius, along with those who think or speak as he does. Such people will fall away from the adoption as sons announced for those who think aright.'

That's the kind of confession this man makes, the man deposed by Dioscorus, as my friend says, for being a 'Nestorianizer'! So then: while we just kept silent about the whole case against Dioscorus, you took it that the entire council of priests and sacred ministers banished a single individual, Dioscorus himself, who was   1888C
present, who was called in various ways, and who had incurred suspicion of prejudice in favour of Eutyches. Yet when Severus, newly become Bishop of Antioch, didn't just pronounce that the council should be rejected—though it took place at Chalcedon neither in his day nor within his territory, wasn't summoned by him, and didn't receive Nestorius, but rather rejected him and his teachings in writing, and received instead orthodox teaching against him, though it didn't receive Eutyches' error either that was opposed to him—but also dared (one man, alone!) to place all of them at once under anathema by a single pronouncement, how is it that, in your eyes, he didn't seem in these matters to be in the

οὐκ ἔδοξεν ὑμῖν ὅλως ἐμπαθῶς ἔχειν ἢ προπετῶς πρὸς τάδε; Καίτοι
ἀπ᾽ αἰῶνος κἄν τοῖς ἐξωτέροις κἄν τοῖς ἡμετέροις πάντων τῶν
1888D ὁμοειδῶν τὰς τοῦ κοινοῦ κρίσεις, μᾶλλον ἀποδεκτέας ἴσμεν κατά
τινος τῶν ἰδικῶν, ἢ τὰς ἐξ ἰδικοῦ τινὸς κατὰ τοῦ περὶ αὐτὸ κοινοῦ·
καὶ ὑμῖν ἄρα τὸ ὅλον τῆς ἐκκλησιαστικῆς ἱεραρχίας μέρους ἰδίου
ἑνὸς ἀξιοπιστότερον ἔδει νομίζεσθαι, εἰ εὐθείας κρίνετε υἱοὶ τῶν
ἀνθρώπων.²⁹⁰ Τίνα γὰρ καὶ ἄλλον εἴδετε τολμήσαντά ποτε σύνοδον
ἀναθεματίζειν, καὶ οὐ τοὐναντίον πάντας τοὺς αἱρεσιάρχας ὑπὸ
1889A συνόδων ἀναθεματισθέντας; Καὶ γὰρ ὄντως θαυμαστόν, ὅπως οἱ
τοῦ Θεοῦ δοῦλοι τὸν τῆς τάξεως λόγον ἐφύλαξαν ἀεί· οὐ γὰρ
ἔστιν ἀκαταστασίας ὁ Θεός·²⁹¹ Συνόδων γοῦν διαφόρων
δεισιδαιμονησασῶν, κατήργηνται μὲν συνόδοις κυριωτέραις τὰ
ὑπ᾽ αὐτῶν, οὐ μήν τις τῶν θεοφόρων μόνος ἰδικῶς κατακρίνειν,
ἀλλ᾽ οὐδὲ σύνοδος ἀναθεματίσαι σύνοδον ἐτόλμησε. Πόσῳ γε μᾶλλον
ἀναθεματίζειν κοινόν τι θεολάτρου πανηγύρεως, ὁ εἷς ἐνθέσμως
ἀπετόλμησεν;

'Αλλ᾽ ἐν τούτοις πᾶσιν οὐκ ἐκπτύσαντες ὅμως ἀπὸ τῆς ψυχῆς τὸν
ἐγχριφθέντα αὐτοῖς γλοιώδη τῆς ἀλόγου προλήψεως καθ᾽ ἡμῶν
1889B ῥύπον, [296ʳ] τί φασὶ πάλιν· "Ὡς αἱ πλείους τῶν χειροτονιῶν
ὑμῖν διὰ χρυσίου δόσεως καὶ λήψεως εἰσίν, καὶ ἔχουσι τὸ ἐπάρατον
κατὰ τὴν τοῦ μάγου Σίμωνος πρόθεσιν.²⁹² Πῶς οὖν ὑμῖν
συγκοινωνητέον, εἰ μὴ ἄρα κατάρας εἶναι κληρονόμους
περιφρονητέον ἡμῖν;", φασίν.

῏Αρα γοῦν ἐπεὶ τινὲς τῶν ἰατρῶν ἐφωράθησαν μοιχοὶ καὶ
κλέπται, διὰ τόδε τὴν ἰατρείαν λοιδορητέον ἐπὶ τούτοις καὶ
φευκτέον; Πλὴν τάδε ἡμῖν εἰ, ὡς οἱ λεγόμενοι ἀγνοὶ τῷ ἑαυτῶν
ἀνεπιλήπτῳ βίῳ πεποιθότες, προάγουσιν, ὡς Ναυατιανοῖς
ἀποκρινούμεθα λοιπόν, καὶ οὐχ᾽ ὡς μιξοφυσίταις. Εἰ δὲ οὐχὶ,
ἀλλ᾽ ἁπλῶς ὡς φιλοχρύσοις μᾶλλον ἢ φιλοχρίστοις διαμέμφονται,
καὶ τῷ μὲν δόγματι συμφωνεῖν ἡμῖν, τούτῳ δὲ μόνῳ
1889C σκανδαλίζεσθαι συγκοινωνεῖν μεθ᾽ ἡμῶν φασίν, καὶ οὕτως ἄρα
φιλοφρόνως αὐτοὺς ἔδει ἐξομολογουμένοις ἡμῖν τὰς ἁμαρτίας,²⁹³
ἡμῶν ὑπερεύχεσθαι· εὔχεσθαι γὰρ ὑπὲρ ἀλλήλων ἡμᾶς ὅπως
ἰαθῶμεν,²⁹⁴ ἐντετάλμεθα, καὶ οὐ φαρισσαϊκῶς βδελύττεσθαι τοὺς
ὁμοφυεῖς καὶ ὁμοπίστους.²⁹⁵ Πλὴν ἐν Κυρίῳ θαρρούμεν, ὅτι
ἐγκαταλέλοιπεν ἡμῖν Κύριος σπέρμα, καὶ οὐκ ἐγενήθημεν ὡς
Σόδομα, οὐδ᾽ ὡς Γόμορρα ὡμοιώθημεν.²⁹⁶

---

²⁹⁰ Ps. 57: 2 LXX   ²⁹¹ 1 Cor. 14: 33   ²⁹² Acts 8: 20
²⁹³ Mark 1: 5   ²⁹⁴ Jas. 5: 16   ²⁹⁵ Cf. Luke 18: 11
²⁹⁶ Isa. 1: 9

grip of emotion and rashness? Furthermore, it's been a matter of common knowledge time out of mind for the whole human race, foreigners and natives alike, that the judgements of the state against any of its individual members are to be accepted over those of any individual entity against the state on the matter at issue. Even by you, therefore, the whole ecclesiastical hierarchy should have been considered more trustworthy than one individual part of it, if *you judge justly, O sons of men*. What other person have you ever observed daring to anathematize a council, and not the opposite—all the heresiarchs being anathematized by councils? Really, it's amazing how God's servants always preserved respect for order, *for He is not the God of confusion*. If various councils held false beliefs, their actions were nullified by more authoritative councils; none of the theologians dared on his own to pass individual sentence, but neither did council dare to anathematize council. How much more legitimate was it for the one man to venture to anathematize an agreed position of a God-worshipping assembly?

Seeing that, in all these matters, they don't likewise spit out of their souls the sticky filth that's washed over them in the form of their irrational prejudice against us, why do they say by way of contradiction: 'The majority of the votes on your side resulted from the giving and receiving of money, and they fall under the curse pronounced against Simon Magus. How, then, are we supposed to have fellowship with you,' they say, 'unless it is a matter of no concern to us to be inheritors of a curse?'

Does that mean that, just because certain doctors have been caught in adultery and theft, one must therefore revile and avoid the medical treatment they practised? Moreover, if it's as people said to be pure in the confidence of their own blameless life that they are bringing up these points against us, well, we're responding from now on as to Novatianists, not as to nature-mixers! If that's not the case, but they're blaming us simply for being lovers of gold rather than of Christ, and say that, while they agree with us on doctrine, they take offence at coming together with us on this score alone, then the right thing for them to do, in a spirit of friendship towards us *when we confessed our sins*, was to pray for us in a spirit of friendship, for we're commanded to *pray for one another so that we may be healed*, not pharisaically to despise men of the same nature and faith as themselves. Moreover, we trust in the Lord, because *the Lord left descendants for us, and we did not become like Sodom, nor were we made like Gomorrah*.

1888D

1889A

1889B

1889C

Τί δὴ οὖν ἆρα, εἰ δείξομεν πλείστους τῶν ἱεραρχούντων εἰς ἡμᾶς οὐ νοσφιζομένους ἀπὸ σπαρτίου ἕως σφαιρωτῆρος ὑποδήματος,²⁹⁷ ἐπὶ τῷδε λέλυται αὐτῶν ὁ ζῆλος, καὶ κατήργηται τὸ σκάνδαλον καὶ

1889D προσδράμοιεν τῇ ἀληθείᾳ, ἢ οὐδὲ τόδε πάλιν ἱκανὸν ἡμῖν ἔσται εἰς ἀποθεραπείαν αὐτῶν; Ἆρα δ' οὖν εἴποιμεν ἔτι· "Οἱ καθ' ὑμᾶς ἱερεῖς οἱ ἐνδύνοντες εἰς τὰς οἰκίας, καὶ αἰχμαλωτεύοντες γυναικάρια²⁹⁸

1892A αἰσχροῦ κέρδους χάριν,²⁹⁹ οὐ τῆς εἰς τὰς γυναικωνίτιδας καὶ παρὰ πόδας τῆς κλίνης τελουμένης αὐτοῖς ἱερουργίας τοὺς μισθοὺς ἀποβλέποντες, καὶ τοῖς μηνιαίοις καὶ ἐτησίοις ἐράνοις ἐπελπίζουσι;" Δέδοικα λέγειν τὰ πλείω, μήπως καὶ βεβήλοις θριαμβευθῶμεν, οἱ τὴν μόρφωσιν ἔχοντες τῆς εὐσεβείας, τὴν δὲ δύναμιν αὐτῆς ἠρνημένοι·³⁰⁰ πολλὰ γὰρ πταίομεν ἅπαντες.³⁰¹ Καὶ γὰρ μισθὸς τοῦ λουτροῦ τῆς χάριτος, καὶ ἀπὸ τιμῆς ἐκ τῶν λειψάνων τῆς θείας δωρεᾶς εἰ συμπεφώνηται πῇ δι' ὑμῶν, τί ἕτερον ἀκουσόμεθα, ἢ ὅτι τὸ ὄνομά μου δι' ὑμῶν βλασφημεῖται ἐν τοῖς ἔθνεσιν;³⁰² Ἀρκέσει γοῦν ἑκάστῳ ἐκ τοῦ ἰδίου ὀφθαλμοῦ τὴν δοκὸν ἐξαίρειν, καὶ τότε τρανότερον τὸ ἐν τῷ ὀφθαλμῷ κάρφος κατανοεῖν, καθά φησιν ἡμῖν ὁ μόνος ἀναμάρτητος.³⁰³

1892B Τούτων δὲ ἡμῖν σὺν Θεῷ προτεθέντων εἰς κρίσιν καὶ διάσκεψιν πᾶσιν ἀνθρώποις, δυσωποῦμεν ἐνώπιον τοῦ τῆς ἀληθείας Λόγου,³⁰⁴ τοῦ ὄντως κριτοῦ παντὸς ἔργου καὶ λόγου καὶ ἐννοήματος ἡμῶν,³⁰⁵ ἀποθέσθαι ἕκαστον ἐντευξόμενον, κἄν τε τῆς ἡμετέρας, κἄν τε τῆς ἀλλοτρίας ᾖ δόξης, [296ᵛ] τὴν ὡς παρ' οἰκείων καὶ πολεμίων ἀκρόασιν τῶν εἰρημένων, καὶ κρίνειν τὰ ῥηθέντα ὡς παρά τινων πάντη ἀγνώστων αὐτῷ τῶν ἐξ ἑκατέρου μέρους, καὶ ὡς οὔ ποτε θατέρου λόγου προθεματισθέντος κατὰ τὴν διάνοιαν αὐτῷ. Καὶ εἰ³⁰⁶ ὄντως γυμνῷ τῷ κριτηρίῳ ἑαυτῶν χωρὶς παντὸς προσπαθοῦς καὶ ἀντιπαθοῦς ἐπισκοτίσματος ἀληθέστερα κρίνωμεν καὶ εὐλογώτερα

1892C καὶ ἰσχυρότερα καὶ σοφώτερα τὰ παρ' αὐτῶν, οἱ τοῖσδε τοῖς ἐναντίοις ἡμῖν προκείμενοι, ὄντως τολμῶμεν λέγειν, ὡς εἰ καὶ κακῶς ταῦτα ἐκεῖνοι φρονοῖεν οἱ συναπαγόμενοι αὐτοῖς, διὰ τὸ δόξαι τούτοις θεοπρεπέστερον εἶναι δόγμα τὸ κατ' αὐτούς, οὐ κατακριθήσονται ἀσέβειαν ἐν ἡμέρᾳ ὅτε κρινεῖ ὁ Θεὸς τὰ κρυπτὰ³⁰⁷ τῶν καρδιῶν· ἐὰν γάρ φησιν Ἔμπροσθεν αὐτοῦ πείσωμεν τὰς καρδίας ἡμῶν, καὶ ἡ καρδία ἡμῶν μὴ καταγινώσκῃ ἡμῶν, ὁ θεὸς

---

²⁹⁷ Gen. 14: 23
³⁰⁰ 2 Tim. 3: 5
³⁰³ Matt. 7: 3–5
³⁰⁶ εἰ] ἦ a. corr. MS

²⁹⁸ 2 Tim. 3: 6
³⁰¹ Jas. 3: 2
³⁰⁴ Eph. 1: 13
³⁰⁷ Rom. 2: 16

²⁹⁹ Titus 1: 11
³⁰² Isa. 52: 5 LXX
³⁰⁵ Cf. Heb. 4: 12

What then? If we show you that the majority of those who hold ecclesiastical office over us stole *neither a thread nor a sandal-thong*, has their zeal slackened over this business? Has their offence been removed, and are they hastening to the truth? Or will this too not suffice us for achieving their restoration? We therefore have some- 1889D thing more we'd like to say: Aren't priests of your party—*who make their way into households, and captivate weak women for base gain*— keeping a close eye on their wages when the sacrifice is celebrated by them in the women's quarters, and at the foot of the bed, and 1892A aren't they hoping for monthly and yearly contributions? I'm afraid to say more, lest we're being led along by godless people, who *have the form of piety, but deny its power, for we all make many mistakes*! If on your side a fee's ever been agreed upon for the baptism of grace, or as the price for the remains of the divine gift, what are we going to understand from that except that *my name is blasphemed because of you among the nations*? It'll be enough for each person to cast *the beam* out of *his* own *eye*, and then to perceive *the speck in* someone else's *eye*, as He who alone is without sin tells us.

All that having been laid out by us, with God's help, for the 1892B judgement and inspection of all, we have an urgent appeal to make before the *Word of truth*, who's the real judge of our every action, word, and thought: we urge each person—be he of our persuasion, or be he of the contrary persuasion—who comes upon statements to put aside the tendency to hear them according to whether they're from friends or foes, and to judge what's said as though it came from people entirely unknown to him, whatever side they're on, and as though the other interpretation of its meaning had never been presupposed by him. If we really judged by our own unaided judgement, without any kind of clouding of our judgement by prejudices for or against, that their views are truer, more reasonable, stronger, and wiser, then we who're press- 1892C ing these opponents of ours so hard would actually be so bold as to say that, even if the people led astray by them should think wrong things because a doctrine enunciated by our opponents seemed to them to be more worthy of God, they won't be con-demned for heterodoxy *on that day when God judges the secrets* of our hearts. (If, [Saint John] says, *we are to reassure our hearts before Him*, and *our heart is not to condemn us, God is greater than our heart, and knows*

μείζων ἐστὶ τῆς καρδίας ἡμῶν, καὶ γινώσκει πάντα·³⁰⁸ Εἰ δὲ ὁ μὲν
τῆς ἀληθείας Λόγος³⁰⁹ φαιδράζων ἑαυτὸν ἐπιδείκνυσιν ἡμῖν, ἡμεῖς
δὲ τούς τε ὀφθαλμοὺς καμμύομεν καὶ τοῖς ὠσὶ βαρέως ἀκούομεν
αὐτοῦ³¹⁰ ἐθελοκωφοῦντες, καὶ ἀποστρεφόμεθα αὐτόν, ὄντως παντὸς
θρήνου ἀξίους ἑαυτοὺς καταστήσομεν, τὴν αἰσχύνην τῆς μελλούσης
1892D ἀλλοτριώσεως καὶ ἀρνήσεως Χριστοῦ, ἐνώπιον ἀγγέλων³¹¹ καὶ
ἐξουσιῶν παντός τε τοῦ κρινομένου κόσμου, οὐ προϋπιδόμενοι, ὅτε
οὐδὲν ἡμᾶς ὀνήσει, οὔτε ἡ πρὸς τοὺς αἱρεσιάρχας προσπάθεια, οὔτε
ἡ γονικὴ ἢ φιλικὴ ἢ τοπικὴ συνήθεια πρὸς τὴν ἀσέβειαν ἀλύτως
τινὰς καταδεσμεύουσα, οὔτε πορισμὸς χρημάτων, ἢ κέρδη τινὰ
1893A βιωτικὰ δυσαποσπάστους ἡμᾶς ἀπὸ τῆς δεισιδαιμονίας ποιήσαντα,
καὶ τὸν μέγαν πορισμὸν τὴν εὐσέβειαν μετ᾽ αὐταρκείας³¹² παριδεῖν
ὑποπείσαντα. Οὐ γὰρ δὴ φατριαστικοὶ κρότοι, καὶ ἀγῶνες
ἀντιλογικοί, καὶ πρόληψις διδασκαλικῆς ἀξίας, φιλοῦντας λέγεσθαι
ῥαββὶ παρὰ τῶν ἀνθρώπων,³¹³ τοῦ οἰκτροτάτου ἐκείνου
ταλανισμοῦ καὶ τῶν ὀδυνηροτάτων βασάνων, καὶ τῆς εἰς τὸ σκότος
τὸ ἐξώτερον³¹⁴ παραδόσεως ἐξαιροῦνται τούσδε, οἳ τὸ φῶς τῆς
ἀληθείας ἠρνήσαντο, καὶ ηὐδόκησαν ἐν τῷ σκότει τοῦ ψεύδους.
Εὐάρεστον γὰρ Θεῷ τὸ παντὸς προτιθέναι τὴν ἀλήθειαν, καὶ
μάλιστα ἐν τοῖς περὶ Θεοῦ αὐτοῦ τῆς ἀληθείας. Διὰ γοῦν τόδε καὶ
μόνον, Ἀβραὰμ³¹⁵ Χαλδαίων τὴν ἀσέβειαν ἀποπτύσας, μετὰ πατρὸς
καὶ οἴκου καὶ συγγενείας καὶ φίλων καὶ χώρας καὶ λοιπῶν,
1893B προσεχώρησε τῇ εὐσεβείᾳ,³¹⁶ Θεῷ τὲ ἐπὶ τούτῳ πρώτῳ καὶ μόνῳ
ἠγάπηται καὶ πεφύλακται καὶ δεδόξασται [297ʳ] καὶ πεπλήθυνται·
Παῦλος δὲ ὁ ἀπόστολος, ἄτινα ἦν αὐτῷ κέρδη, πάντα σκύβαλα
ἡγήσατο, δι᾽ οὐδὲν ἕτερον, ⟨ἀλλ᾽⟩ ἵνα Χριστὸν κερδανῇ.³¹⁷ καὶ οἱ
λοιποὶ πάντες οἱ ἐξ Ἑλλήνων καὶ Σαμαρειτῶν καὶ Ἰουδαίων πιστοὶ
ἅγιοι ὡσαύτως ἔσχον. Ὁ γὰρ μὴ ἀρνούμενος πατέρα καὶ μητέρα καὶ
ἀδελφοὺς καὶ ἀδελφὰς καὶ τέκνα καὶ ἀγροὺς καὶ οἰκίας, ἔτι δὲ καὶ
τὴν ἑαυτοῦ ψυχὴν ἕνεκεν ἐμοῦ,³¹⁸ οὐκ ἔστι μου ἄξιος³¹⁹ φησὶν ὁ
Κύριος. Καὶ μή τις διαλογιζέσθω λέγων· "Ἀλλ᾽ οὐχ᾽ ἡ κατὰ τὰς
αἱρέσεις διένεξις πρὸς τὴν ὀρθοδοξίαν οὐ τόσον διέστηκεν, ὡς ἡ
Χαλδαίων καὶ Ἑβραίων καὶ Ἑλλήνων ἀσέβεια τῆς ἀληθοῦς
πίστεως, ἵνα ὁμοίως αὐτοῖς ἀλλοτριωθείη ἀπὸ Χριστοῦ, ὁ περὶ
μέρος τί τῆς ὀρθῆς πίστεως μόνον ἀπειθῶν τῷ λόγῳ." Ὁ γὰρ
1893C σμικρόν τι μόριον ὁπωσοῦν εὐσεβείας τοῦ λόγου παρορῶν διὰ
προσπάθειαν ἄλογόν τινος ἑτέρου καὶ συνήθειαν, δῆλός ἐστιν ὡς καὶ
ὅσον εὐσεβεῖν δοκεῖ, οὐδὲ τοῦτο ἐξ αἱρέσεως οἰκείας, ἀλλ᾽ ἀπὸ

---

³⁰⁸ 1 John 3: 19–20   ³⁰⁹ Eph. 1: 13
³¹⁰ Isa. 6: 10 LXX; Matt. 13: 15; Acts 28: 27
³¹¹ Luke 12: 9   ³¹² 1 Tim. 6: 6   ³¹³ Matt. 23: 6–7
³¹⁴ Matt. 8: 12, 22: 13, 25: 30   ³¹⁵ sic spir. MS   ³¹⁶ Gen. 12: 1–5
³¹⁷ Phil. 3: 7–8   ³¹⁸ Matt. 19: 29, 16: 25   ³¹⁹ Matt. 10: 37

everything.) If, on the other hand, the *Word of truth* shows Himself to us with shining brightness, but we *close our eyes, and hear* Him *with heavy ears*, deliberately shutting our ears, and we turn away from Him, we really make ourselves worthy of every lament for not foreseeing the shame of impending estrangement from, and denial by Christ *before angels* and powers of the whole world when the time comes to be judged. On that day nothing will profit you: not passionate attachment to heresiarchs; not the ties of ancestry, family, or place which tie some people indissolubly to heterodoxy; and not the means of gain or certain life-benefits that make it hard to tear us away from superstition, and that gradually persuade us to overlook the *great gain, orthodoxy with contentment*. Certainly factional cheers, and disputatious contests, and a pre-occupation with one's status as a teacher don't free those who *love to be called 'rabbi' by men* from that most pitiable misery, those most painful tortures, and being cast *into outer darkness*, seeing that they're people who denied the light of truth, and delighted in the darkness of the lie. What's well-pleasing to God is to put the truth before everything else, above all in matters that concern the truth about God Himself. It was for this reason, and for this reason alone, that Abraham—despising the impiety of the Chaldeans, and with it his father, home, family, friends, lands, and everything else—put his faith in piety. That's the reason, the first and only reason, why he was loved, protected, magnified, and increased by God. Paul the Apostle considered *whatever was gain* for him *to be dung*, for no other reason than *so that he might gain Christ*. The rest of the faithful saints from among the Greeks, Samaritans, and Jews were the same. He who does not deny *father*, and *mother, brothers* and *sisters, children, fields, homes*, and even *his own soul for my sake, is not worthy of me*, says the Lord. No one's to put up an argument, saying 'The disagreement between heresies and orthodoxy doesn't set them as far apart from each other as the impiety of Chaldeans, Jews, and pagans sets them apart from the true faith, so that the person who won't listen to reason over just some part of the true faith is alienated from Christ to the same degree as they are.' It's clear that the person who in any way whatsoever neglects any little bit of the understanding of piety because of an irrational and habitual preference for something else, in so far as he also appears to be orthodox, has this appearance, not on the basis of personal choice, but as a result of what's been handed down to him from

1892D

1893A

1893B

1893C

συμβεβηκότων γονέων ἢ τόπων, ἢ φίλων παραδόσεως ἔχει, ὡς, εἴπερ καὶ Μανιχαίων ἔτυχεν ἢ Ἑλλήνων ἢ Ἑβραίων υἱὸς εἶναι, ἢ φίλος ἢ σύνοικος, πολλῷ μᾶλλον ἂν ἀπειθεστέρως διέκειτο πρὸς τὴν ἀλήθειαν· εἴπερ γὰρ ὀλίγον ἀφεστὼς οὐ προστρέχει καὶ καθέλκεται τῇ ἀληθείᾳ, πλεῖον διεστηκὼς, μᾶλλον ἂν ἀσπόνδως εἶχε πρὸς αὐτήν.

"'Αλλὰ" φησὶ "κατ' ἐμαυτὸν ἐγὼ νομίζων κρειττόνως φρονεῖν, ἔχομαι τῆς ἐμῆς δόξης ἀμεταθέτως."

1893D   'Αλλὰ καὶ περὶ ὧν φησὶν ὁ ἀπόστολος Ἰουδαίων, ὡς <u>Θεῷ μὴ ἀρεσκόντων, καὶ τὸν Κύριον</u> σταυρωσάντων, καὶ τοὺς ἀποστόλους <u>διωξάντων,</u> καὶ <u>πᾶσιν ἀνθρώποις</u> ἀπειθούντων,[320] ὅμως τοῦτο κἀκείνοις μαρτυρεῖ· φησὶ γάρ πη πάλιν· <u>Μαρτυρῶ γὰρ αὐτοῖς ὅτι ζῆλον Θεοῦ ἔχουσιν, ἀλλ' οὐ κατ' ἐπίγνωσιν.</u>[321] "Αρα οὖν οὐχ' ἁπλῶς ζηλοῦν, ἀλλὰ καὶ ἐν ἐπιγνώσει τοῦ ζηλουμένου δόγματος, δεῖ· καὶ γὰρ καὶ πᾶσα ἄλογος καὶ ἄνομος παράδοσις, καὶ ἐθνῶν καὶ αἱρέσεων, οἴεταί τι καλὸν ποιεῖν, ὥσπερ οὖν καὶ ἀνθρωποθυσίαις οἱ

1896A   Σκύθαι θεοσεβοῦντες. Δέον ἄρα μὴ ἀμελεῖν, ὅση δύναμις, καὶ ἐρευνᾶν τὴν ἀλήθειαν, καὶ <u>πάντα δοκιμάζοντας, τὸ καλὸν</u> φρόνημα <u>κατέχειν.</u>[322] Οἵ γε οὐδὲ ἀργύριον λαμβάνομεν, ἢ ἱμάτιον ὠνούμεθα, εἰ μὴ δοκιμασίαις καὶ πυρώσεσι καὶ παρακόναις καὶ ἐπιδείξεσιν εἰς ἑτέρους πλειόνως αὐτὸ βασανίσομεν, πῶς οὖν εὔλογοι ὦμεν ἀτημελῶς τὴν θείαν δόξαν προσδεχόμενοι; Τὸ γὰρ ἐν τούτοις ἀφρόντιστον, ὡς οὐκ ἀξιόλογόν τι οἰομένους ἡμᾶς τὴν τῆς πίστεως Χριστοῦ χάριν καὶ ἀλήθειαν, διαβάλλει, [297ᵛ] δι' ἧς <u>ἡμῖν τὰ πρὸς ζωὴν πάντα</u> τὰ θεῖα <u>καὶ μέγιστα ἐπαγγέλματα δεδώρηται,</u> ὡς εἴρηται, καὶ ἡ πρὸς τὴν <u>θείαν φύσιν</u> ἁπλῶς <u>κοινωνία.</u>[323] Ὅσον οὖν ἐστὶν ἀγαθὸν ἡ ἀκραιφνεστάτη εὐσέβεια, καὶ ὅσον κακὸν ἡ ἀσέβεια—τῆς γὰρ εἰς πᾶσαν ἁμαρτίαν ἐγκαταλείψεως ὑπὸ Θεοῦ

1896B   αἰτία ἡμῖν αὕτη ἐστὶ μόνη—δηλοῖ ὁ λέγων· <u>Καὶ καθὼς οὐκ ἐδοκίμασαν τὸν Θεὸν ἔχειν ἐν ἐπιγνώσει, παρέδωκεν αὐτοὺς ὁ Θεὸς εἰς ἀδόκιμον νοῦν, ποιεῖν τὰ μὴ καθήκοντα,</u>[324] ἅτινα ἑξῆς κατηρίθμησε. Καὶ τάδε μὲν οὖν μαρτυρεῖ τῇ ἀσεβείᾳ, περὶ δὲ τῆς εὐσεβείας φησὶ πρὸς Τιμόθεον· <u>Γύμναζε σεαυτὸν πρὸς εὐσέβειαν· ἡ γὰρ εὐσέβεια πρὸς πάντα ἐστὶν ὠφέλιμος, ἐπαγγελίαν ἔχουσα ζωῆς, τῆς τε νῦν καὶ τῆς μελλούσης.</u>[325]

---

[320] 1 Thess. 2: 15   [321] Rom. 10: 2   [322] 1 Thess. 5: 21
[323] 2 Pet. 1: 3–4   [324] Rom. 1: 28   [325] 1 Tim. 4: 7–8

the parents, locations, or friends he happened to have—just as, if he happened to be the son, friend, or fellow-countryman of Manichaeans, Greeks, or Jews, he'd be even more disposed to be disobedient towards the truth. If he didn't hasten and feel drawn towards the truth when he'd let it go a bit, then when he'd turned completely away he was surely all the more implacably opposed to it.

'I, on the other hand,' my friend says, 'stick to my opinion without changing, since I am in the habit of thinking more highly of myself.'

The apostle, who says of the Jews that they *displease God*, crucified *the Lord*, *drove out* the apostles, and disobey *all men*, likewise gives the following testimony against them, for he somewhere goes on to say: *I bear witness against them that they have a zeal for God, but not according to full knowledge*. It's necessary, then, not just to be zealous, but to be zealous in full knowledge of the doctrine on behalf of which one is zealous, for every irrational and lawless tradition, both of nations and of heresies, supposes it's doing something good. Such is the case even with the Scythians, who show their piety towards God by human sacrifices! What's needed, however great one's power, is not to be careless, and to seek the truth, and *testing all things, to have the right* mind. We don't accept a silver coin or buy a piece of cloth, unless we fully test it by assays and tests by fire, by paring it, and by proofs in the presence of others. How sensible, then, would we be if we were careless about accepting divine doctrine? The apostle opposes the great thoughtlessness in these matters involved in our thinking that the grace and truth of Christ's faith aren't anything worthy of note—through which all the divine things *that pertain to life* and *the very great promises have been given* to us, as is said, and, quite simply, *participation in the divine nature*. How great a good the purest orthodoxy is, and how great an evil impiety is—for the latter is the sole reason why we're abandoned by God to every sin—is something he makes clear when he says: *And since they did not see fit to acknowledge God, God gave them over to a reprobate mind, to doing what is not right*, which things he went on to enumerate. These things, then, give evidence of impiety, but he talks about piety to Timothy: *Train yourself in piety, for piety is profitable in every way, as it holds the promise of life, life in the present, and life that is to come.*

1893D

1896A

1896B

Ἀλλὰ τί καὶ ἕτερον τούτων τινὲς τῆς πρὸς τὴν ἀλήθειαν
ἀνυποταξίας ποιοῦνται δικαίωμα. Φασὶ γὰρ ὅτι "Πῶς οὐ θεάρεστος
ἡ κατ᾽ αὐτοὺς δόξα, ἔνθα καὶ τῶν ζώντων ἐν σαρκὶ τινὲς αὐτοῖς
1896c   ὁμόδοξοι καὶ τῶν προκοιμηθέντων, ὤφθησαν ἰαμάτων καὶ σημείων
θεόθεν ἔχειν τὸ χάρισμα; Δῆλον γὰρ ὡς ἐξ ἀκοῆς καὶ διδαχῆς ὀρθῆς
πίστεως θεοῦ, αἱ θεῖαι δυνάμεις ἐνεργοῦνται."

Πρὸς ὃ λεκτέον, ὡς οὐκ ἀρκεῖ τόδε πρὸς ἀσφαλῆ πληροφορίαν τῷ
δοκιμωτάτῳ τῶν θείων δογμάτων κριτῇ. Πρῶτον μὲν γὰρ
σπανιώτερον εὕρηται τοῦτο ἐν αὐτοῖς, καὶ οὐκ ἐκ μιᾶς χελιδόνος τὸ
ἔαρ κριτέον· ἄλλως γοῦν καὶ Ἀρειανοί ποτε, καὶ μέχρι νῦν ἐν
Λογγιβάρδοις, καὶ Νεστοριανοὶ παρὰ Πέρσαις ποιοῦσι τοιάδε
θαύματα· ἀλλ᾽ οὐκ εἰς μαρτυρίαν ἁπλῶς τῆς κατ᾽ αὐτοὺς πρὸς ἡμᾶς
αἱρέσεως, ἀλλὰ τῆς τῶν Χριστιανῶν πίστεως, οἵα τις ἐστιν ἥ[326]
1896d   δύναμις πρὸς τοὺς πάντῃ ἀπίστους, ἐπιδεικνυμένου τοῦ πνεύματος.
Ἔτι μήν ἐστιν ὁρᾶν πολλάκις θαυμάτων χαρίσματα ἔν τισιν
ὀρθοδόξοις τὲ καὶ ἑτεροδόξοις ὁμοίως, οὐ δι᾽ εὐσέβειαν μόνον—ἢ
γὰρ ἂν ἦν ἐν τοῖς ἐναντίοις λόγοις καὶ ἀντιφατικοῖς ἡ ἀλήθεια;—
ἀλλὰ διὰ φυσικὴν ἁπλότητα καὶ ἀτυφίαν, μᾶλλόν τὲ νηπιότητα
1897a   ψυχῆς, ἢ δεινότητα, πραΰτητά τε καὶ συμπάθειαν, καὶ ἁπλῶς τῆς
τοιᾶσδε χάριτος ἰδικωτέραν ἐπιτηδειότητα τοῦδέ τινος παρὰ τοὺς
λοιποὺς τῶν ὁμοπίστων αὐτῷ. Εἰ γὰρ ὄντως πᾶσιν ἀεί τε διὰ τὴν
δόξαν μόνον πρόσεστιν ἡ τῶν θαυματουργιῶν δύναμις, ἔδει πάντας
πάντοτε ὁμοίως τοὺς ὁμοδόξους θαυματουργεῖν· καὶ μὴν πολλάκις
τῶν διδασκάλων τῆς πίστεως οὐ θαυματουργούντων, οἱ
μαθητευθέντες ὑπ᾽ αὐτῶν, ἐνεργοῦσι τὰ σημεῖα.

Οὐ γὰρ πάντα ὅσα ἐνεργεῖ τὸ ἓν καὶ τὸ αὐτὸ πνεῦμα,[327] ἑνὶ καὶ τῷ
αὐτῷ χαρίζεται· ᾧ μὲν γὰρ δίδοται λόγος σοφίας, ᾧ δὲ λόγος
1897b   γνώσεως, ἑτέρῳ δὲ χαρίσματα ἰαμάτων, ἑτέρῳ [298ʳ] ἐνεργήματα
δυνάμεων, ἄλλῳ δὲ πίστις κατὰ τὸ αὐτὸ πνεῦμα.[328] Καὶ γὰρ
θαυμαστόν, πῶς ὁ λαλῶν γλώσσαις, οὐ πάντως οὐδὲ τὸ ἐγγύτατον
τῷδε χάρισμα λαβών, καὶ διερμηνεύει·[329] Ἆρα οὖν ἐστι καὶ τινὰς
οὐδὲ λόγον σοφίας ἀκραιφνῆ, οὐδὲ λόγον γνώσεως, οὐδὲ πίστιν[330]
ὑψηλὴν εἰληφότας, θαυμάτων ἔχειν χαρίσματα, καὶ οὐκ εὔλογον ἐκ
θατέρου θάτερον τῶν τοῦ πνεύματος χαρισμάτων κατακρίνεσθαι.

---

[326] ἥ] οἱ a. corr. MS   [327] 1 Cor. 12: 11   [328] 1 Cor. 12: 8–10
[329] 1 Cor. 14: 5   [330] 1 Cor. 12: 8–9

But some people invent a different justification than these for their disobedience to the truth. This is what they say: 'When certain people who hold the same opinion as they do—some of them living in the flesh, and some who have passed on—have been seen to possess the gift of healings and of signs from God, how could the opinion held among them not be pleasing to God? It's clear, after all, that divine powers operate on the basis of hearing and teaching God's correct faith.' 1896C

What's to be said against that argument is the following: to the really reputable judge of divine doctrines, this [working of miracles] is not sufficient grounds for confidence. In the first place, this [phenomenon] is to be found more rarely among our opponents, and 'one swallow doth not a summer make'.[xiii] On the contrary, even Arians (found to this day among the Lombards), and Nestorians (found among the Persians) sometimes work just as great miracles, but that doesn't all on its own have the effect of justifying their choosing against us. Rather, such is the power of Christians' faith over against those entirely outside the faith when 1896D the Spirit's made manifest. Moreover, it is often possible to observe gifts of miracles among orthodox and heterodox persons alike, not on account of orthodoxy alone—for then, truly, there's truth in opposite definitions and contradictions!—but on account of the particular individual's natural simplicity and humility (and even more, innocence of soul), or on account of his gentle and 1897A sympathetic disposition and, to put it simply, his greater personal fitness for so great a gift over the others who share his faith. If the capacity for miracle-working really is present in anyone on account of his opinion alone, then everyone who took the same doctrinal stance must always have worked miracles in the same way. To tell the truth, though, teachers of the faith often aren't miracle-workers; it's those they've taught who perform signs.

One and the same Spirit doesn't give all the miracles He works to one and the same person, *for to one is given a word of wisdom,* but to another *a word of knowledge,* to another *gifts of healing,* to another *the* 1897B *working of miracles,* to another *faith* according to *the same Spirit.* It's remarkable how *the one who speaks in tongues* doesn't receive the most closely related gift to speaking in tongues at all, and *interpret tongues.* It's therefore possible for some people who've received neither a pure *word of wisdom,* nor a *word of knowledge,* nor lofty *faith,* to have gifts of miracles, and there's no sound reason for deciding about

Τὸ δέ γε σαφέστερον εἰπεῖν· εἰ μὲν ἐν τούτοις μόνοις ἦν τὰ
χαρίσματα τῶν θαυμάτων, ἢ εἰ μᾶλλον ἡμῶν ἐν αὐτοῖς ἑωρᾶτο,
εἶχεν ἂν ὄντως αὐτοῖς ἡ δόξα πρόληψιν εὐσεβείας παρὰ τὴν
ἡμετέραν, ὡς τοῦ Κυρίου τὸν λόγον αὐτῶν βεβαιοῦντος μόνων διὰ
1897c τῶν ἐπακολουθούντων σημείων³³¹ κατὰ τὸ γεγραμμένον, ὥσπερ καὶ
τὸ κήρυγμα τῶν ἀποστόλων πάλαι συνιστάνοντος πρὸς ἅπαντα τὰ
ἔθνη, καὶ ὥσπερ τὰ Μωϋσέος καὶ Ἀαρὼν σημεῖα ὑπὲρ τὰ Ἰαννοῦ
καὶ Ἰαμβροῦ πρὸς τοὺς Αἰγυπτίους θριαμβεύοντος.³³² Εἰ δὲ ἐν ἡμῖν
καὶ μείζονα καὶ πλείονα ὁρᾶται τὰ ἐκ τοῦ πνεύματος θαύματα κατὰ
πᾶσαν τὴν οἰκουμένην, πῶς ἐκ θαυματουργιῶν ἀξιοπιστότερον
εἶναι βούλονται τὸ δόγμα; Μὴ δὲ τόδε οὖν ὡς ὀνήσιμον αὐτοῖς
εἰς ἀπολογίαν τινὰ τὴν ὑπὲρ τῆς δεισιδαιμονίας αὐτῶν
προβαλλέτωσαν.

Εἰ γὰρ καὶ Σκευᾶς σὺν τοῖς υἱοῖς αὐτοῦ, Ἰουδαῖος ὤν, ἐν ὀνόματι
Χριστοῦ ἐπορκίζων ἐλαύνει δαίμονας,³³³ καὶ οὐκ ἐν τῷδε ἁπλῶς
1897d τοῖς μαθηταῖς τοῦ Κυρίου συναριθμεῖται, δῆλον, ὡς οὐδὲ οὗτοι ἐκ
τοῦδε πρόφασιν ἔχουσι περὶ τῆς ἁμαρτίας αὐτῶν.³³⁴ Πολλοὶ γάρ
φησιν ἐροῦσί μοι ἐν τῇ ἡμέρᾳ ἐκείνῃ· Κύριε οὐ τῷ σῷ ὀνόματι
προεφητεύσαμεν, καὶ δαιμόνια ἐξεβάλομεν, καὶ δυνάμεις πολλὰς
ἐποιήσαμεν; Καὶ τότε ὁμολογήσω αὐτοῖς, ὅτι οὐδέποτ' ἔγνων
1900a ὑμᾶς.³³⁵ Σαφὲς ἄρα, ὡς οὐκ ἀρκεῖ πρὸς διάκρισιν τῶν ἐγνωσμένων
καὶ ἀπεγνωσμένων Χριστῷ θαύματος ἐμφάνεια, πολλάκις ἢ διὰ τὴν
τοῦ πεισομένου τὴν εὐεργεσίαν πίστιν, ὀρθοτέραν μᾶλλον ἢ τὴν τοῦ
ἐνεργοῦντος, γινομένου τοῦδε, ἢ διὰ τὴν τῶν θεατῶν εἰς τὴν πρὸς
εὐσέβειαν ἁπλουστέραν πληροφορίαν, ἐνίοτε δὲ καὶ κατὰ πρόνοιαν
κοινωφελεστέρας χρείας τῆς κατὰ καιρὸν ἢ τόπον ὑπὸ Θεοῦ καὶ διὰ
τοῦ οἱουδήποτε τῶν παρόντων ἐπιτελουμένου.

Ἐν τοῖς γοῦν καθ' ἡμᾶς ἱστόρηται χρόνοις καὶ τόποις, μῖμος τίς
τῶν θεατρικῶν, καὶ οὗτος ἐπὶ στάσει καὶ φόνῳ ἐγκαλούμενος,
φυγεῖν τὸν δικαστὴν ἐν ταῖς κατὰ τὸ βαρβαρικὸν λεγόμενον λιμιτὸν
ἐρήμοις, καὶ ὑπὸ Σαρακηνῶν ληϊσθεὶς Χριστιανῶν, διὰ τὸ δοκεῖν
αὐτοῖς ἐκ τῆς ἀποτριχώσεως μοναχὸς εἶναι, καὶ ὥσπερ οἱ πρὸς
1900b αὐτοὺς μοναχοὶ παραβάλλοντες, ἱερουργεῖν δύνασθαι τοῦ ζωτικοῦ
ἄρτου τὸ μυστήριον, διὰ νευμάτων εἰσεπράττετο σπουδαίως
ὑπ' αὐτῶν, τῆς θείας θυσίας τὴν λειτουργίαν, μόνος ἀφεθεὶς τῶν
συνδεσμίων αἰχμαλώτων, ἐκτελέσαι. Καὶ ὡς λόγῳ πείθειν αὐτοὺς

---

³³¹ Mark 16: 20　　　³³² 2 Tim. 3: 8　　　³³³ Acts 19: 13–14
³³⁴ John 15: 22　　　³³⁵ Matt. 7: 22–3

one of the Spirit's gifts on the basis of another. Let me make my point more clearly: If gifts of miracles existed solely among these people, or if they were observed to a greater extent among them than among us, then their view really has a prima facie case for its orthodoxy over against ours, since then *the Lord has confirmed* only their *message by the signs that followed*, as it is written, just as He also 1897C once commended the preaching of the apostles to all nations, and just as He made Moses' and Aaron's signs triumph over those of Jannes and Jambres against the Egyptians. If, however, greater and more numerous miracles from the Spirit are to be seen among us throughout the world, how is it that they'd have their doctrine be more trustworthy on the basis of miracles alone? Don't let them propose this line of argument, then, as being of any advantage to them in the way of offering some kind of defence for their superstition!

If Sceva, though a Jew, drove out demons with his sons by adjuring them in the name of Christ, yet isn't counted among the 1897D Lord's disciples for that alone, it's clear that our opponents don't *have an excuse for their sin* on that basis either. *On that day*, He says, *many shall say to me, 'Lord, didn't we prophesy in your name, and cast out demons, and perform many wonders?' And then I shall declare to them, 'I never knew you.'* It's clear, then, that the manifestation of a miracle is not sufficient grounds for distinguishing between those who are 1900A known, and those who are disowned, by Christ; often the miracle happens through the faith (more correct than the miracle-worker's) of the one about to receive the benefit, or through the onlookers' faith, to enhance their simple confidence about religion. Sometimes, too, it happens by means of foreknowledge on God's part of a general need of the moment and the district, and by the agency of whatever person there brought it to pass.

In our own times[xiv] and places the story is told of a certain actor from a theatre company who, being charged with riot and murder, tried to escape from the judge in the deserts near what is called the barbarian border, and was captured by Christian Arabs. Because he seemed to them to be a monk on account of his shaved head, and to be able, like the monks who consort with them, to perform 1900B the mystery of the bread of life, he was earnestly entreated by them with signs to celebrate the liturgy of the divine offering, and was set apart from his fellow prisoners on his own. He found no way to convince them by argument of his own unfitness, and he

ὑπὲρ τῆς ἑαυτοῦ ἀνεπιτηδειότητος οὐκ εὐπόρει, καὶ ἀντιτείνειν τῇ προστάξει αὐτῶν ἐπὶ [298ᵛ] πλεῖον οὐκ εὐτόνει, βωμὸν ἐκ φρυγάνων κατὰ τὴν ἔρημον συστησαμένων καὶ σινδόνα ἐφαπλωσάντων, καὶ προθέντων ἄρτον νεόπτητον, καὶ οἶνον ἐν ξυλοποτηρίῳ κερασάντων, παρεστὼς ἐσφράγισε τὰ δῶρα ἀναβλέψας εἰς τὸν οὐρανόν, καὶ ἐδόξασε τὴν ἁγίαν Τριάδα μόνον, καὶ κλάσας διένειμεν αὐτοῖς. Εἶτα μετὰ τόδε, ὡς ἁγιασθέντα λοιπὸν 1900C ἐν τιμῇ συστέλλουσι τό τε ποτήριον καὶ τὴν σινδόνα, πρὸς τὸ μὴ κοινωθῆναι λοιπὸν τάδε, τοῦ βωμοῦ μόνου περιφρονήσαντες· καὶ ἄφνω πῦρ ἐκ τοῦ οὐρανοῦ πλεῖστον ἐπιπεσόν, αὐτῶν μὲν οὐδενὸς ἥψατο ἢ ἐλύπησέ τινα, τῶν δὲ φρυγάνων τὸν βωμὸν ὅλον κατέφλεξε καὶ ἐξανάλωσεν, ὡς μὴ δὲ τέφραν αὐτῶν καταλιπεῖν. Καὶ τούτῳ ὀφθέντι τῷ τεραστίῳ οἱ βάρβαροι πληροφορηθέντες εἰς τὸν ἱερουργήσαντα, δόμά τι παρ' αὐτῶν αἰτεῖν ὑπὲρ τῆς λειτουργίας ἐξεβίαζον· ὁ δὲ τοὺς συνληϊσθέντας αὐτῷ πάντας καὶ συναφεθῆναι ᾐτήσατο, καὶ τοῦτο ἐλάμβανε, καὶ πάντας ἠλευθέρου τῆς συμφορᾶς τοὺς σὺν αὐτῷ. Ἦν δὲ οὗτος τὴν μὲν δόξαν ἡμέτερος τῷ μόνον ἡμῖν συνεκκλησιάζεσθαι οὐ μὴν εἰδὼς οὐδὲ ὅτι ἔστι τίς σχεδὸν Χριστιανῶν διαφορά. Οἱ δὲ Σαρακηνοὶ ἐκ τῆς τῶν Ἰακωβιτῶν 1900D αἱρέσεως εἰωθότες κοινωνεῖν, οἳ καὶ αὐτοὶ τὴν μίαν φύσιν ἐπὶ τοῦ Κυρίου πρεσβεύουσι, καὶ οὗτοι πρῶτοι τοῖς Σαρακηνοῖς συμπεριάγεσθαι κατὰ τὴν ἔρημον καὶ λειτουργεῖν αὐτοῖς ἐπετήδευσαν ὡς ἐπίπαν· οὔτε μὴν οὐδὲ οὗτοι εἰδότες ἢ διδάσκοντες τῶν ἐν Χριστιανοῖς δογμάτων ἐξέτασιν ἢ σύγκρισιν, ἀλλ' ὥσπερ τοῖς 1901A Νεστορίου Πέρσαι, οὕτως καὶ οἵδε τοῖς Ἰακώβου φρονήμασι προκατειλημμένοι ἐνετυπώθησαν ἀβασανίστως.

was impotent to resist their demand any longer. He made for himself an altar out of sticks in the desert, spread a fine cloth, set out newly baked bread, and mingled wine in a wooden chalice. Offering the gifts, he made the sign of the cross over them as he looked towards heaven, and glorified the Holy Trinity alone. Then he broke [the bread] and distributed it to them. Afterwards, they took away the cup and the cloth with reverence, as being 1900C sanctified, so that they would no longer be put to any profane use. The only thing they overlooked was the altar. Without warning a great fire fell from heaven! It struck none of them, and hurt no one, but it burned up the entire altar of sticks, and destroyed it so completely as to leave behind not even their ashes. The barbarians, given complete confidence in the man who performed the ritual by the marvel they'd seen, insisted that he ask for some gift from them in return for the liturgy. He asked that all those captured with him be released with him; his wish was granted, and he freed all his companions from their unfortunate situation. Now this man was of our persuasion only in that, when he went to church, he gathered with us, though to tell the truth he did so without realizing there was any difference between Christians. The Arabs, however, traditionally shared in the heresy of the 1900D Jacobites, who themselves give pride of place to one nature in the Lord. These Jacobites were the first to make a practice of travelling with the Arabs in the desert and ministering to them in every way. These men neither knew of, nor taught, precision about or comparison between the doctrines held by different Christian groups. Rather, they were converted by the ideas of Jacob [Baradatus], taking the imprint of these ideas without any examination, 1901A much in the way the Persians were converted by the ideas of Nestorius.

Τοῦ πανσόφου μοναχοῦ κύρ Λεοντίου τοῦ Ἱεροσολυμίτου ἀπορίαι πρὸς τοὺς μίαν φύσιν λέγοντας σύνθετον τὸν Κύριον ἡμῶν Ἰησοῦν Χριστὸν

1. [265ʳ] Ἀλλὰ ταῖς αὐτῶν ἀπαντήσαντες ἀπορίαις, ὀλίγα τινὰ νῦν ἐκ πλειόνων καὶ ἡμεῖς αὐτοῖς ἀνταπορήσωμεν, εἴπωμέν τε πρὸς αὐτούς, ὅτι "Εἰ ὁμοούσιος ἡμῖν τὲ καὶ τῷ Πατρὶ ὁ Χριστὸς κατὰ τὴν μίαν αὐτοῦ οὐσίαν, ἣν φατέ, γνωρίζεται, καὶ ἡμεῖς δηλαδὴ ὁμοούσιοι τῷ Πατρί· τὰ γὰρ τῷ αὐτῷ κατὰ τὸ αὐτὸ ὅμοια, καὶ ἀλλήλοις ὅμοια."

2. Φύσιν ἐκ φύσεων γενέσθαι λέγοντες, εἰ μὲν ὁμώνυμον ταῖς πρώην αὐτὴν φασί, δῆλον ὡς οὔτε Θεὸν οὔτε ἄνθρωπον αὐτὴν ἐροῦσιν· εἰ δὲ συνώνυμον, θάτερον ἔσται πάντως—οὐ γὰρ ἀλλήλαις συνώνυμοι ἑκατέρα—· ἢ οὖν Θεός, ἢ ἄνθρωπος ἔσται μόνον καὶ αὐτή. Εἰ γὰρ ἀλλήλαις αἱ δύο μὴ συνώνυμοι, οὐδὲ τὸ τῇ μιᾷ συνώνυμον, καὶ τῇ ἑτέρᾳ συνώνυμον ἔσται· ὥσπερ γὰρ τὸ ἴσου¹ ἄνισον, καὶ τοῦ ἑτέρου τῶν ἴσων ἄνισον, οὕτω καὶ τὸ ἀνίσου ἴσον, ὁμοίως καὶ πρὸς τὸ ἕτερον ἄνισον.

---

¹ ἴσου] ἴσον a. corr. MS

OF THE ALL-WISE MONK, LORD LEONTIUS OF JERUSALEM: APORIAE AGAINST THOSE WHO SAY OUR LORD JESUS CHRIST IS ONE COMPOUND NATURE[i]

1. Seeing that we've confronted these people's aporiae, we'd now like to counter-propose aporiae ourselves on a few points out of many, and say to them: 'If Christ is recognized as being consubstantial both with us and with the Father by this one substance of His that you talk about, then of course we're consubstantial with the Father as well. Things identical with the same thing in the same respect are, after all, identical with each other.'

2. They say that a nature came to be out of natures. If they say it has the same name but not the same definition as the natures that were there before, it's clear they're saying it's neither God nor man. If, on the other hand, they say it has both the same name and the same definition as they do, it'll have to be one or the other of them—for they don't have the same name and definition as each other. It'll therefore be exclusively either God or man. If the two natures don't have the same name and definition as each other, then what has the same name and definition as one of them won't have the same name and definition as the other. Just as something that's unequal to one of a pair of equals is also unequal to the other of them, so also what's equal to one of a pair of unequals is likewise unequal to the other of them.

3. Εἰ ἀεὶ σώζοιτο ἡ ἕνωσις ἐνεργείᾳ οὖσα, εἴτουν ἓν οὖσα ἀεί, τίνα ἑνοῖ; Οὐ γὰρ ὡς ἡ τοῦ χρόνου φύσις μετὰ τὸ γενέσθαι εὐθὺς φθειρομένη, οὕτως καὶ τῆς ἑνώσεως ἡ φύσις· τῶν γὰρ πρός τι οὖσα, ἅμα τῇ φύσει καὶ τῷ χρόνῳ, τοῖς ἑνουμένοις ἐστὶν ἐφ' ὅσον λέγοιντο ἡνωμένα. Ἐν τίσιν οὖν ἑνουμένοις ἐστὶν ἀεί, καθ' ἣν καὶ ἡνωμένα λέγεται ἀπὸ τῆσδε τῆς σχέσεως παρωνύμως. Γενομένης δὲ ἤδη, ὡς οὗτοι φασί, "μιᾶς" ἀληθῶς "φύσεως" ἐκ τῶν δύο φύσεων τῶν ἑνωθεισῶν, χώραν οὐχ' ἕξει λοιπὸν ἡ ἕνωσις. Ἐνοῦται μὴ ἑνουμένης δυάδος, ἣν ἑνώσει αὕτη ἡ ἕνωσις, τοὐλάχιστον ἐν δύο θεωρουμένη πάντως; Τοῖς ἑνουμένοις τὲ γὰρ ἕν, ἢ οὐδὲ ὄν, ἕνωσιν λοιπὸν οὐκ
1772A ἐπιδέχεται· γενόμενον γὰρ ἕν, ἑνώσεως λοιπὸν οὐ δεῖται. Ἢ οὖν ψευδῶς ἓν εἶναι πάντῃ, καθὸ ἥνωται τὰ δύο, εἴρηται αὐτοῖς, ἢ οὐκ ἀληθῶς ἑνοῦσθαι τὰ δύο καθ' ὃ ἤδη γεγόνασιν ἕν, λεχθήσεται. Ὥστε καλῶς φαμέν· "Εἰ δύο φύσεών ἐστιν ἡ ἕνωσις, μίαν εἶναι μᾶλλον τὴν ὑπόστασιν, οὐδὲ γὰρ τὴν φύσιν"· δύο γὰρ κατὰ φύσιν τὰ ἑνούμενα, ὡς ἑνούμενα, ἓν δὲ τὴν ὑπόστασιν, ὡς ἡνωμένα.

4. Πᾶν ἐξ ἀνομοιομερῶν συντεθὲν ὅλον, ἑτερώνυμον ἕξει πρὸς τὸ ἑαυτοῦ εἶδος ἑκάτερον εἶδος φυσικὸν τῶν ἑαυτοῦ μερῶν· οὔτε γὰρ ἁπλῶς σῶμα, οὔτε μόνως ψυχὴ ὁ ἄνθρωπος λέγοιτο, φυσικοῦ εἴδους λόγῳ, οὔτε σῶμα [265ᵛ] καὶ ψυχή· τὸ γὰρ θνητὸν, ἐν
1772B οὐδετέρῳ τῶνδε εἴδει, ἐν δὲ τῷ ἀνθρώπῳ σαφῶς. Εἰ[2] οὖν οὔτε Θεὸς οὔτε ἄνθρωπος, οὔτε Θεὸς καὶ ἄνθρωπος ἅμα, ἀλλ' ἕτερόν τι εἶδος φυσικὸν ὁ Χριστός· καὶ τί τοῦτο, λεγέτωσαν. Εἰ ὁμοειδὲς ἀμφοῖν τοῖς συντεθεῖσι κατὰ πάντα τὸ τοῦ συνθέτου εἶδος, πῶς οὐχὶ καὶ ἰσάριθμον ἔσται αὐτοῖς κατὰ τὸν φυσικὸν λόγον;

---

[2] ἢ

3. If union—a union that exists in actuality—is always pre-served, that is, if it's always one thing, what does it unite? The nature of union isn't like the nature of time, perishing right after it comes into existence: since it belongs to the class of things that exist in relation, along with nature and time, union always exists in things that are united in so far as they may be said to be united. It always exists in specific united things, and it's in respect of union that they're said to be united, and by derivation from this status. Since, however, a 'nature' that's truly 'one' has already come into being out of two united natures, as these people assert, union will no longer be in effect. Is it united when a duality isn't united which this union unites—a union inevitably recognized at least in two? For united things, what's one—otherwise, it doesn't exist—won't accept any further union, for having become one it no longer needs union. They're going to have to say, then, either that 1772A it's a false assertion on their part that there's indeed one thing, given that the two were united, or that the two aren't truly united, given that they've already become one. We're thus right when we say: 'If the union's of two natures, then it's rather the hypostasis that's one, for it's not the nature.' The things united are two by nature as being united, but one by hypostasis as having been united.

4. Every whole compounded out of non-identical parts will have a name for each natural form of its parts that's different from its own form. You wouldn't call man just 'body' or just 'soul' on the basis of natural form, nor would you call him 'body and soul'. The human is in neither of these forms, but rather—clearly enough—in the man. If Christ is, then, neither 'God', nor 'man', 1772B nor 'God and man' together, but some other natural form, it's up to them to tell us just what this form is. If the form of the compound is in all respects of the same form as both of the things compounded, how can it not also be equal to them in number by virtue of what's meant by nature?

5. Εἰ μία φύσις εἴτουν οὐσία μετὰ τὴν ἔνωσιν ὁ Χριστός, μία καὶ ἡ ταύτης ἀρχὴ τοῦ εἶναι· δύο γὰρ ἀρχὰς τῆς αὐτῆς οὐσίας καὶ φύσεως, ἤγουν ἀφ' οὗ πέφυκε καὶ ὑπάρχει, εἶναι ἀδύνατον· αὐτὸ γὰρ τοῦτο τὴν ὕπαρξιν ἡ οὐσία δηλοῦσα, ὅτε γέγονε, τότε καὶ ὑπάρχει. Ἡ οὖν ἀρχὴ τοῦ εἶναι ταύτης τῆς συνθέτου φύσεως, πότε τε καὶ ὅπως; Εἰ μὲν γὰρ πρὸ τῆς ἐνώσεως, οὐ διὰ τὴν ἔνωσιν μία λέγοιτο δηλαδή—ἦν γὰρ καὶ πρὸ τῆς ἐνώσεως μία—οὔτε δὲ ἐνώσεως χρεία ἦν εἰς τὸ μίαν εἶναι αὐτήν. Εἰ δὲ ἀπὸ τῆς προσφάτου ἐνώσεως ἡ ταύτης ἀρχή, πῶς ἀΐδιαν ἔτι καὶ προαιωνίαν καὶ θείαν ὁμολογήσοιμεν τὴν ἐπὶ τῶν Αὐγούστου χρόνων προελθοῦσαν εἰς τὸ εἶναι φύσιν;

1772c

5. If Christ is one nature, that is, substance, after the union, then there's also one beginning of existence for this one nature, for it's impossible for there to be two beginnings of existence for the same substance and nature, that is, two beginnings from which it's taken its being and subsists. This is so because, since 'substance' signifies this very thing, subsistence, when it comes to be, then it subsists. When, and in what way, then, does the beginning of this compound nature's existence take place? If it took place before the union, it would clearly not be called one on account of the union—for it was also one before the union—and there was no need of a union for it to be one. If, however, its beginning dates from the recent union, how are we to confess the nature that came into being in the time of Augustus to be 'eternal', and 'from before all ages', and 'divine'?

1772c

6. Πᾶσα ἕνωσις εἰς φύσιν τινὰ καινοτέραν ἀπαρτιζομένη τέ καὶ
ὁρωμένη, δείκνυσιν αὐτὴν ἔχουσαν τινά, ἃ οὐδεμία τῶν ἐνωθεισῶν
φύσεων καθ' αὑτὴν κέκτηται· καὶ γὰρ οὔτε ψυχῆς φύσις, οὔτε
σώματος καθ' ἑαυτὴν πώποτε πεινᾷ ἢ διψᾷ, ἢ ῥιγᾷ, ἢ καυσοῦται, ἢ
ὑπνοῖ, ἢ ἀποθνήσκει, ἢ γελᾷ, ἢ κλαίει, ἢ ἁπλῶς αἰσθάνεται
αἰσθητῶς αἰσθητοῦ, ὥσπερ οὐδὲ ὁ αὐλὸς ἰδίᾳ, οὐδὲ ὁ αὐλητὴς
1772D καθ' ἑαυτὸν λαλεῖ. Τί οὖν ὁ Κύριος, ὁ μήτε Θεὸς μήτε ἄνθρωπος,
ἰδίᾳ ἔχειν ἐνεδείξατο; "Εἰκὸς οὖν" φασί "ὡς τὸν ἐφ' ὕδατος
σωματικὸν περίπατον καὶ τὰ τοιάδε." Ἀλλὰ τόδε κατανοητέον οὐ
φύσεως ὂν ἰδίωμα συνθέτου· καὶ οἷς γὰρ μὴ κατ' οὐσίαν εἰς φύσιν ἢ
εἰς ὑπόστασιν σύγκειται τῶν ἁγίων ὁ Θεὸς πολλάκις ἐποχεῖσθαι
τῶν ὑδάτων πεποίηκε, σώματι μεταβατικῶς ἐν αὐτοῖς
πορευομένους. Εἰ οὖν οὐδέν ἐστι φυσικὸν ἰδίωμα Χριστοῦ ἰδικῶς,
οὐδὲ φύσις αὐτῷ μία τίς μόνον ἰδική· οὔτε γὰρ κατὰ σύγχυσιν, ὡς
τὰ σίκερα, οὔτε κατὰ μετουσίωσιν, ὡς τὸ ὕδωρ τῶν Αἰγυπτίων αἷμα
γεγονός, οὔτε κατὰ ἀλλοίωσιν, ὡς ὁ χαλκὸς εἰς ἰὸν ἀμείβεται, οὔτε
κατὰ φυσικῆς ἑνώσεως ἀνάγκην, ὡς ψυχὴ εἰς σῶμα ἀνθρώπου
γέγονεν. Ἔτι μὲν τράγου [266ʳ] τὸ μυκαστικὸν ἔχοντος, ἀνθρώπου
1773A δὲ ἰδίως τὸ κηροπλαστικόν, εἴ τις ὁ αὐτὸς κηροπλαστῶν καὶ
μυκάζοι ἀνήρ, μιμηλὸς τῶν ἑτεροφυῶν, οὐ σύνθετον δείκνυσι τὴν
φύσιν αὐτοῦ δηλαδή, ἀλλὰ δύο φύσεων ἰδικὰς ἐνεργείας ἐκ τῆς
αὐτῆς μιᾶς φύσεως αὐτοῦ. Οὕτως γοῦν καὶ τὸ μεταβατικῶς
κινεῖσθαι, ἀνθρωπίνης φύσεως ἦν, τὸ δὲ μὴ καταδύεσθαι τὴν
βαρυτέραν τοῦ σώματος φύσιν ἐποχουμένην τῇ τοῦ ὕδατος
κουφοτέρᾳ φύσει, ἀλλὰ ὑπερείδεσθαι τὴν στερροτέραν τῇ
μανωτέρᾳ, τοῦτο θείας ἐστὶ φύσεως ποιεῖν, ⟨ἡ⟩ ἰδικωτάτως πάσας,
ποιῶσαι καὶ μεταποιῶσαι, καὶ οὐσιῶσαι, καὶ μετουσιῶσαι, καὶ
ἀπουσιῶσαι τὰς φύσεις δύναται, κἂν ἐκ τοῦ αὐτοῦ πρόεισι
προσώπου. Σαφῶς οὖν ἐν τοῖς τοιοῖσδε θεία καὶ ἀνθρωπίνη φύσις
συνενεργοῦσαι ὁρῶνται, οὐ μὴν ἑτέρα φύσις συντεθεῖσα, ἐκ τῶνδε
ἡμῖν καθορᾶται.

6. Every union seen to complete some newer nature shows that nature to possess certain things which neither of the natures united possessed on its own. On its own, neither a soul's nature nor a body's is ever hungry or thirsty, is cold, burns with heat, sleeps, dies, laughs, weeps, or just perceives a sense-object by means of its senses. It's just as in the case of the flute and the flute-player: neither makes music on its own. What then was the 1772D
Lord—who [by their argument] is neither God nor man—shown to possess on His own? 'The reasonable answer', they say, 'is walking on water in a bodily way, and that sort of thing.' One shouldn't consider this to be a property of a compound nature, though, for God has often so arranged it that those of the saints who travel by water are carried bodily on it, though it's agreed there's no compounding by substance into either a nature or an hypostasis in their case! If, then, there's no natural property belonging to Christ in particular, neither is there any one particular nature that belongs only to Him—not by a mixing together, as in the case of fermented liquids, nor by a change of substance, as in the case of the Egyptians' water that became blood, nor by transformation, as in the case of copper that turns into verdigris, nor yet by the necessity of a natural union, as in the case of a man's soul that comes into existence in a body. Though a billy-goat has the ability to bleat, but a man characteristically has the ability to make wax models of things, it's still not the case that, if 1773A
this same model-making man also happens to bleat—being an imitator of things that possess different natures from his—he's plainly showing his nature to be compound! On the contrary, he's revealing operations characteristic of two natures on the basis of that identical one nature of his. Similarly, then, the capacity to be moved from place to place belonged to human nature, but for the heavier nature of the body not to sink, being carried by the lighter nature of water—or rather for the denser nature to be supported by the less dense—that belongs to a divine nature. It has the ability, an ability supremely characteristic of it, to make and remake all natures, to cause them to exist as substances, to cause them to exist as substances again, and to deprive them of substance, even though it springs from the same person. In such cases, then, a divine and a human nature are clearly seen to be operating together; a different nature compounded out of them is definitely not observed.

1773B **7.** Εἰ μηδὲν πλέον ἢ ἔλαττον ταῖς δύο φύσεσιν ἡ σύνθεσις ἡ ἀσύγχυτος πλὴν τῆς πρὸς ἀλλήλας ἑνώσεως δείκνυσιν, ἕνωσις δὲ οὔτε φύσις ἐστίν, οὔτε μὴν ἀλλοίωσις, ἢ λεῖψις, ἢ πρόσθεσις φύσεως, πῶς ἄνευ προσθέσεως, ἢ λείψεως, ἢ ἀλλοιώσεως φύσεως, τὸ κατ᾽ ἀριθμὸν ποσὸν τῶν ἡνωμένων φύσεων, πλέον ἢ ἔλαττον φανήσεται, ἵνα ἢ τρεῖς ἢ μίαν τὰς οὐσίας δύο οὔσας, μεταποιήσῃ; Εἰ δὲ ἄρα καὶ πλεῖόν τι ἑνώσεως ἀσυγχύτου ταῖς φύσεσιν ἐπεισάγειν τολμῶσι ποιητικὸν ἢ παραστατικὸν ἁπλῶς φύσεως, λεγέτωσαν ἡμῖν παρρησίᾳ· "Τί τοῦτο εἶναι διανοοῦνται;"

8. Εἰ ἐκ δύο φύσεων ἡνωμένων ἀσυγχύτως μίαν ποιεῖν ἔστιν, ἐκ δύο φύσεων ἡνωμένων κατὰ σύγχυσιν, τί ἕτερον γίνεται; Ἢ οὖν 1773C δύο εἶναι φύσεις ἐκ τοῦ ⟨τοῦ⟩ ἀσυγχύτου λόγου ἐπὶ Χριστοῦ ἐροῦσιν, ἢ τίς ἡ διαφορὰ τοῦ ἀσυγχύτου πρὸς τὴν σύγχυσιν ἐν τῇ τῶν φύσεων ἑνώσει λέγειν εἰσπραχθήσονται. Εἰ γὰρ καὶ λέγοιεν, ὅτι "Οὐ συγχέομεν"· τί γὰρ πλεῖον ἐρεῖ ὁ λέγων σύγχυσιν; Εἰπάτωσαν γάρ. Καὶ τοῖς Νεστοριανοῖς, δύο ὑποστάσεις λέγουσι καὶ κράζουσιν ἀνέδην, ὅτι "Οὐ διαιροῦμεν", τοῦτο φαμέν· ὅτι τί γὰρ ἄλλο παραστήσει τὸν διορισμόν; Οὐ γάρ ἐστιν ἑτέρως τὰ πάντῃ ἀδιακρίτως συγκείμενα, πλὴν τοῦ λέγειν μιᾶς ὑποστάσεως καὶ φύσεως εἶναι, οὔτε τὰ πάντῃ διακεκριμένα, ἢ τῷ λέγειν δύο φύσεις καὶ ὑποστάσεις εἶναι.

9. Εἰ μία φύσις τοῦ Δεσπότου ἡμῶν Χριστοῦ μετὰ τὴν ἕνωσιν, εἴποιμεν πρὸς αὐτούς· "Ἆρά γε φατέ, ὦ οὗτοι, κρειττωθῆναί πως 1773D ταύτην πᾶσαν μετὰ τὴν ἁγίαν αὐτοῦ ἀνάστασιν, ἢ [266ᵛ] οὐχί· ἢ πᾶσαν μὲν οὐχί, εἶναι δέ τι λέγεται ἐν αὐτῇ ἐν τῇ ἀναστάσει τοῦ Δεσπότου κρειττούμενον, καὶ ἕτερον μὴ κρειττούμενον;" Εἰ μὲν οὖν εἶναί τι τέλειον καὶ φυσικὸν τὸ κρειττούμενον κατὰ φύσιν, καὶ ἕτερον τέλειον φυσικὸν κρειττοῦν κατὰ φύσιν ἐν τῇ ἁγίᾳ αὐτοῦ ἀναστάσει φατέ, αὐτόθεν ἡμῖν ἰδοὺ τὰς δύο φύσεις συνομολογεῖτε· καὶ εὐχαριστία τῷ κοινῷ Πατρὶ ἐπὶ τῇ τῶν ἀδελφῶν ἐν ὑγείᾳ ἀπολήψει.

7. If unconfused composition reveals nothing more nor less for two natures than their union with each other, but a union is neither a nature, nor indeed a change, subtraction, or addition of a nature, how will the numerical quantity of natures united be seen to be higher or lower, so that it changes the existing two natures to three or to one, without an addition, subtraction, or change of nature? If, however, these people have the effrontery to add something greater than an unconfused union to the natures, something simply productive and indicative of nature, the onus is on them to tell us outright just what they think this something greater is. 1773B

8. If it's possible to make one nature out of two natures united in an unconfused way, what different outcome is there if two natures are compounded by confusion? Either they're saying there are two natures in Christ by reason of the word 'unconfused', or they're going to find themselves forced to say just what the difference is between 'unconfused' and 'confusion' in the union of natures. If they say 'We don't confuse [them]!', well, what else is the person who speaks of confusion talking about? Let them tell us. To the Nestorians likewise—who speak of two hypostases, and feel no restraint about crying out 'We don't make a division!'—we say this: what else proves the distinction? It's not possible to talk about things completely and indistinguishably compounded except by saying they're of one hypostasis and nature, nor is it possible to talk about things completely distinguished except by speaking of two natures and hypostases. 1773C

9. If there's one nature of our master Jesus Christ after the union, we'd say this to them: 'Do you then say, my friends, that the whole of this nature has in some way been made better after His holy resurrection, or not? Or do you say that not all of it's been made better, but there's said to be something in it that's made better in the Master's resurrection, and something else that isn't made better?' If, then, you're saying that it's something complete and having the character of a nature that's improved by nature, and that it's something else complete and having the character of a nature that does the improving by nature in His holy resurrection, then notice this: you're instantly joining in our confession of the two natures—and thanks be to our common Father for our brothers' restoration to health! 1773D

10. Οἱ ἐπινοίᾳ μόνον ὁρᾶν φάσκοντες τὸ διττὸν τῶν φύσεων ἐπὶ Χριστοῦ μετὰ τὴν ἕνωσιν, λεγέτωσαν ἡμῖν, τὴν φυσικὴν διαφορὰν τοῦ ἀοράτου καὶ ὁρατοῦ ἐν Χριστῷ, ἐπινοίᾳ ἴσασιν, ἢ οὐχί, ἀλλ᾽ ἑτέρως; Εἰ μὲν οὖν τῇ αὐτῇ ἐπινοίᾳ καὶ τὴν διαφορὰν ἴσασι τὴν φυσικὴν ἐν τῷ αὐτῷ, ὥσπερ ταύτην ὁμολογοῦσι, κἀκείνην ἀναγκασθήσονται· ἢ εἰ πλάσμα ἐστὶν ἐκείνη, καὶ ταύτην οὕτως ἔχειν λέξουσιν. Εἰ δὲ τὴν διαφορὰν οὐκ ἐπινοίᾳ, ἀλλ᾽ αἰσθήσει ὁρᾶν αὐτῇ εἴποιεν, τὸ ἀόρατον αἰσθητῶς ὁρᾶν διαβεβαιούμενοι θαυμασθήσονται. Εἰ δὲ ἐπινοίᾳ μὲν ἄμφω ὁρῶσιν, ἀλλὰ τὴν μὲν διαφοράν, τῇ τῶν ὄντων κριτικῇ καὶ τῶν ὑπὲρ αἴσθησιν καταληπτικῇ, τὴν δὲ δυάδα τῇ τῶν μὴ ὄντων ἀναπλαστικῇ, πρῶτα μὲν τί μὴ καὶ δέκα καὶ εἴκοσι καὶ τριάκοντα φύσεις ἀναπλάττομεν Χριστῷ, ἀλλὰ δύο μόνον; Τίς δὲ καὶ ἐνομοθέτησεν ἡμῖν πλάσματα δογματίζειν ἐπὶ Χριστοῦ τοῦ ἀληθινοῦ Θεοῦ, καὶ φαντασίαις μόναις ἀπαιωρεῖσθαι τὴν πίστιν, εἰδωλολατρεῖν δὲ οὐκ ἔξωθέν πως, ἀλλ᾽ ἐν αὐτῇ ἡμῶν τῇ ψυχῇ, τὰ μὴ ὄντα ἀναπλάττοντας, εἶτα καὶ μυθολογοῦντας αὐτὰ τοῖς λοιποῖς; Ταῦτα γὰρ δοθέντα, πᾶν τὲ τὸ τῆς εὐσεβείας μυστήριον,[3] καὶ τοὺς διδασκάλους πάντας ἅμα μιᾷ προλήψει τῇ τοῦ ψεύδους ἀβεβαιότητι διασύραντα καταστρέφει.

Ἔτι δὲ λεγέτωσαν ἡμῖν ὄντως, εἰ ἀρά γε κατὰ ταύτην αὐτὴν τὴν ἐπίνοιαν, καθ᾽ ἣν δύο φασὶ τὰς φύσεις, ἔξεστι τινὶ τῶν πατέρων ἢ ἀποστόλων εἰπεῖν δέκα τὰς φύσεις Χριστοῦ, ἢ πεντήκοντα, ἢ οὐδενὶ ἀληθῶς; Εἰ μὲν γὰρ ἐξῆν ἀληθῶς εἰπεῖν, τί μὴ ἔφασαν τἀληθές, καίτοι τούτου ζητουμένου πάλαι, πόσαι ἂν εἶεν Χριστοῦ αἱ φύσεις; Εἰ δὲ μὴ ἔστιν ὑπὲρ τὰς δύο ἀληθῶς ἐπινοῆσαι τὰς φύσεις Χριστοῦ, δῆλον ὡς τοῦ πράγματος τὴν ἀλήθειαν ἕως τοῦδε τοῦ ἀριθμοῦ ἔχοντος. Εἰ δὲ πράγματι καὶ ἀληθείᾳ ἐπινενόηται τί,[4] [267ʳ] οὐκ ἀναπλαστικῶς νενόηται, καὶ πεφάνασται ψευδῶς· τούτῳ γὰρ διακριτέον ἁπλῶς τὰς ἐπινοίας, ὅτι ἡ μὲν ἀληθὴς ὑπὸ τῶν ὄντων γεννᾶται ἡμῖν, ἡ δὲ ψευδὴς τὰ μὴ ὄντα γεννᾷ ἐν ἡμῖν. Εἰσὶν οὖν ἀληθῶς δύο τῇ ἐπινοίᾳ αἱ φύσεις Χριστοῦ· καὶ γὰρ καὶ ἡνωμέναι, τῇ

---

[3] 1 Tim. 3: 16
[4] ἐπινενόηται, τί MS

10. Those who say they recognize the duality of natures in Christ after the union only in thought must tell us this: is it in thought that they recognize the natural difference between the invisible and the visible in Christ, or not in thought but in some other way? If they also recognize the natural difference in the same Christ by this same thought, logically they'll have to confess one natural difference in exactly the same way as they confess the other—or if one is a figment of the imagination, they'll say the other is one too. If, on the other hand, they say that it's not in thought that they discern the difference, but by sense-perception itself, they'll find themselves the objects of astonishment for maintaining so strongly that they observe what's invisible by sense-perception! If, again, they discern both in thought, but understand 'difference' by the kind of critical understanding that can comprehend realities beyond the grasp of sense-experience, but 'duality' by the kind of understanding that imagines a form for non-existent things, my first response to that is to ask why we don't then invent ten, twenty, or thirty natures for Christ, but just two? Who decreed that we should teach fictions about Christ the true God, and that the faith should hang upon mere illusions? Who decreed that we should worship as idols, not external realities of any kind, but things we invent in this soul of ours, things that have no existence at all, and then tell stories about them to everyone else? These conclusions, once granted, overturn *the* whole *mystery of orthodoxy* and all of the teachers at once, tearing them apart with the assumption of one false premise!

They really must tell us whether any of the fathers or apostles could have spoken of ten, or fifty natures of Christ by means of this very thought by which they speak of two natures, or could none of them truly have done so? If it truly was possible to speak of them, why didn't they speak the truth, since it was always their goal to discover how many natures of Christ there were? If, though, it's impossible truly to think of more than the two natures of Christ, it's clear that reality supports the truth so far as this number is concerned. If something's understood in reality and truth, it isn't apprehended in a fictitious way and falsely presented to the mind, for one ought to distinguish between thoughts in this simple way: the true thought is produced in us by things that are, but the false thought produces non-realities in us. There are, for thought, truly two natures of Christ. Being united as well, they are

1776A

1776B

1776C

ἐπινοίᾳ ἡμῶν εἰσὶ θεωρηταὶ μόνον· τὸ γὰρ φύσει ἀόρατον, οὐδ' ὅτι
ἥνωταί τινι ὁρατὸν εἰ μὴ τῇ ἐπινοίᾳ. Ἀλλ' ἐπεὶ ἅμα νοεῖν πλείονα
καὶ περὶ πλειόνων νοήματα ὁ νοῦς ἡμῶν οὐ δύναται, ἀναγκαίως καὶ
τὴν ἕνωσιν ἀποδιαστέλλοντες τῶν ἡνωμένων, ἐν τῷ κρίνειν ἕνωσιν
καὶ ἡνωμένα, ὁρῶμεν τὸν διάφορον ἑκάστου λόγον, καὶ τῶν
ἡνωμένων ἕκαστον κατ' ἰδίαν σκοποῦντες, ποῖα καὶ ποῖα ἔχει ἴδια
1776D γνωρίζομεν· Εἰ γὰρ μὴ οὕτως γνῶμεν, οὐδὲ τὴν ἕνωσιν νοοῦμεν·
αὕτη γὰρ διὰ τῆς ἀντιδόσεως τῶν ἰδίων καθορᾶται. Ἅμα δὲ πάντα
τὰ ἡνωμένα, καὶ τὰ ἴδια αὐτῶν, καὶ τὰ τῆς ἑνώσεως ἴδια νοεῖν, οὐκ
ἔστιν οὐδενὶ μιᾷ καὶ ἁπλῇ φαντασίᾳ. Ἀναγκαίως οὖν τὰς μὲν
διαστολὰς τῶν ἡνωμένων κατὰ φαντασίαν ἀναπλάττομεν τῇ
ἐπινοίᾳ, ἀλλὰ καὶ τόδε οὐ διὰ τὸ ψεύσασθαι τῇ ἐπινοίᾳ ἐν ἑαυτοῖς
τὴν διάκρισιν τῶν συγκειμένων—οὐ γὰρ οὗτος ἦν σκοπός—ἀλλὰ
διὰ τὸ τῆς φύσεως ἡμῶν ψευδὲς, ὡς εἰπεῖν· πᾶς γὰρ ἄνθρωπος
ψεύστης,[5] οὐ δυναμένων ὑφ' ἓν τὰ πολλὰ νοεῖν ἡνωμένα, εἰ μὴ διὰ
τοῦδε τοῦ τρόπου ἐπιστῶμεν τῇ τῶν ἡνωμένων ἀληθείᾳ, πόσα τὲ
καὶ ὁποῖα ἰδικῶς ἐστιν ἕκαστον· τούτου δὲ μὴ γνωσθέντος, οὐδ' ὅτι
1777A ὄντως πλείονα ἥνωταί τινα καταληφθήσεται. Ἀγνοεῖται ἄρα καὶ ἡ
ἕνωσις οὐκ οὖσα, καὶ ἐπινοίᾳ ψευδεῖ διάστασις τῶν ἡνωμένων, ἵνα
ἐπινοίᾳ ἀληθεῖ γνωσθῇ ἡ ἕνωσις αὐτῶν, λαμβάνεται· ἐν γὰρ μόνον
ὁρῶσά τι ἡ αἴσθησις, οὔτε εἰ φύσει, οὔτε εἰ ἑνώσει ἐστὶν ἕν, δύναται
διακρίνειν.

11. Ἡ μία φύσις, ἣν φατέ, ἀδελφοί, μετὰ τὴν ἕνωσιν, ἢ ταὐτὴ ἔσται
τῷ ἀριθμῷ μιᾷ τῶν πρὸ τῆς ἑνώσεως φύσεων, ἐξ ὧν λέγετε εἶναι
αὐτὴν δύο φύσεων, ἢ οὐχί. Εἰ μὲν οὖν οὐ ταὐτή, οὐχ' ὁ αὐτὸς Θεὸς ὁ
πρὸ σαρκὸς καὶ ἐν σαρκὶ, ἤγουν ὁ μετὰ τὴν ἕνωσιν καὶ πρὸ τῆς
ἑνώσεως, εἷς τῷ ἀριθμῷ, ἀλλ' ἕτερος ἐν τῷ Λόγῳ, καὶ ἕτερος ἐν
Χριστῷ. Εἰ δὲ ταὐτὴ τῷ ἀριθμῷ τῇ τοῦ Λόγου φύσει ἐστὶν,
ἄσαρκος ἄρα καὶ μετὰ τὴν ἕνωσιν ὁ Λόγος, ἢ σύνθετος σαρκὶ καὶ
1777B πρὸ τῆς ἑνώσεως.

---

[5] Ps. 115: 2 LXX; Rom. 3: 4

perceptible only to our thought, for the invisible by nature doesn't become visible just because it's been united to something, unless it's to thought. Rather, since our mind's incapable of paying attention to multiple apprehensions about multiple things at the same time, we necessarily divide the union from the things united, and discern the different definition of each, when we judge that there are a union and things united. When we examine each of the things united on its own, we recognize what sort of properties each has. If we don't have this kind of understanding, neither do 1776D we apprehend the union, since it's perceived by means of the interchange of properties. It just isn't possible for anyone at exactly the same time to apprehend all of the things united, their properties, and the properties of the union in one, simple perception. Of necessity, then, we represent to our understanding the distinctions between things united by means of an image. Even this doesn't happen because of any mental falsification in ourselves of the distinction between the things compounded—that wasn't the point—but rather because of something false in our nature, so to speak, for *every man is false*, seeing that we're incapable of comprehending the number of united things in one apprehension unless, when it comes to the truth about the things united, we perceive in this way the quantity and quality of each on its own. If this information isn't known, neither will it be understood that several things were in fact united. The union that doesn't exist is 1777A therefore not known, and a separation of things united is accepted by a false act of understanding so that their union may be recognized by a true act of understanding. Sense-perception, when it observes only one object, is incapable of deciding whether it's one by nature, or one by union.

11. The one nature after the union that you talk about, brothers, will either be the same in number as one of the two natures out of which you say it is before the union, or it won't. If it's not the same in number, then neither is the same God who is before flesh and in flesh—that is, after the union and before the union—one in number. Instead, He's one God in the Word, and another in Christ. If, on the other hand, it's the same in number as the nature of the Word, then the Word was without flesh even after the union, or else He was compounded with flesh before the union as well. 1777B

12. Πᾶν τὸ ὄν, κτιστὸν ἢ ἄκτιστόν ἐστι· τὸ γὰρ "τούτων μέσον, οὐδὲ οἱ τοὺς τραγελάφους ἀναπλάττοντες", καθὼς φησὶν ὁ πατήρ, "δώσουσιν".[6] Εἰ οὖν μία φύσις ἐστὶ Χριστοῦ εἴπερ ἄκτιστός ἐστι [267ᵛ] τίς ἡ ἐκ τῆς ἁγίας παρθένου; Εἰ δε κτιστή ἐστι, τίς ἡ ὁμοούσιος τῷ ἀκτίστῳ Πατρί; Ὁμοίως δὲ καὶ εἰ ἀγένητος, καὶ εἰ ἄχρονος αὕτη ἐστί, τίς ἡ γενομένη ἐκ γυναικός,[7] καὶ τοῦτο, ὅτε ἦλθε τὸ πλήρωμα τοῦ χρόνου[8] ἐν ὑστέροις καιροῖς;[9] Εἰ δὲ γενητὴ[10] καὶ ὑπὸ χρόνον, τίς δι' ἧς πάντα γέγονε,[11] καὶ δι' ἧς τοὺς αἰῶνας ὁ πατὴρ ἐποίησε;[12] Καὶ πῶς μήτε ἀρχὴν ζωῆς, μὴ δὲ τέλος ἡμερῶν ἔχων[13] ὁ Χριστὸς, κατά τε τόδε ἀφομοιούμενος τῷ Μελχισεδέκ;[14] Τὸ γὰρ αὐτὸ ἓν κατὰ τὸ αὐτὸ ἐν ταὐτῷ τῶν ἐναντίων τοὺς λόγους οὐκ ἐπιδέξεται, ὡς πολλάκις εἴρηται.

1777c

13. Ὁ μεσίτης θεοῦ καὶ ἀνθρώπων,[15] ἆρά γε μέσος αὐτοῖς εἶναι δοκεῖ ὑμῖν καὶ κατὰ τὸν φυσικὸν λόγον, ἢ μόνον κατὰ γνωμικὴν σχέσιν, καὶ συμβιβαστικὸν σκοπόν; Εἰ μὲν οὖν κατὰ γνώμην μόνον, κατὰ φύσιν ἢ θάτερον τῶν δύο, ἢ ἕτερον τί ἐστι παρὰ τὰ δύο. Εἰ δὲ οὖν, ἀνάγκη καὶ κατὰ φύσιν εἶναι αὐτὸν μέσον· τὸ δὲ μέσον, ἀνάγκη ἢ οὐδετέρου τῶν μεσαζομένων μετέχειν, ἢ ἀπὸ μέρους ἑκατέρου, ἢ ὅλων τῶν ἑκατέρου λόγων. Ὁ βούλεσθε ἡμῖν ἀποκρίνασθε.

14. Ὁ ἀπόστολος μετὰ τὴν ἕνωσιν δηλαδὴ τὴν ἐν Χριστῷ λαβοῦσάν[16] τε καὶ ληφθεῖσαν μορφὴν οἶδεν,[17] ἤγουν φύσιν· αὗται δὲ ὅτι οὔτε μία οὔτε ὁμοίως ἔχουσαι, παντὶ δῆλον.

1777D

---

[6] Gregory of Nazianzus, *Oration* 31, 286
[7] Gal. 4: 4.   [8] Gal. 4: 4.   [9] 1 Tim. 4: 1
[10] γενετὴ MS   [11] John 1: 3   [12] Heb. 1: 2
[13] Heb. 7: 3   [14] Heb. 7: 3
[15] 1 Tim. 2: 5
[16] λαβοῦσάν: β add. MS supra lin.; λαλοῦσάν in textu
[17] Phil. 2: 6–7

12. Everything that exists is either created or uncreated, for 'even those who invent goat-stags aren't going to grant that there's a mean between them', as the father says. If, then, there's one nature of Christ, and if it really is uncreated, what's the nature from the Holy Virgin? If, on the other hand, Christ's one nature is created, what's the nature that's consubstantial with the uncreated Father? Likewise, if this one nature is ungenerated, and if it's independent of time, what's the nature that's *born of a virgin*, and what's this entity which, when *the fullness of time arrived*, existed *in later times*? If there was a temporal hour of birth, too, what nature is it *through* which *all things came to be*, and through which the Father *made the ages*? How is Christ, *who has no beginning for His life nor end of His days*, said in the same text to be *made like* Melchizedek? What's one and the same in relation to something won't admit the predicates of its opposites in the same respect, as is often said.[ii] 1777C

13. Does the *mediator between God and men* really seem to you to be intermediate between them even with reference to what's understood by 'nature', or only with reference to harmony of will and shared purpose? If He's intermediate only in terms of will, He's by nature either one of the two, or something different from the two of them. If, on the other hand, He has to be intermediate between them by nature as well, the mediating reality necessarily participates in neither of the things it mediates between, or in part of each, or in the whole of what we mean by both of them. Tell us which of these things you want to assert!

14. The apostle quite clearly knows, after the union, the *form* (that is, nature) in Christ that did the taking, and the one that was taken.[iii] It's clear to anyone that these forms aren't one, and that they don't exist in the same way. 1777D

15. Εἰ διὰ τὸ τοῦ ἀνθρώπου εἰρημένον τισὶ τῶν πατέρων παράδειγμα τὰς δύο φύσεις οὐχ᾽ οἷόν τε σώζεσθαι ἐν Χριστῷ, λεγέτωσαν ἡμῖν· οἱ ἀποκτείνοντες τὸ σῶμα[18] φύσιν ἀποκτείνουσιν, ἢ οὐχί; καὶ οἱ τὴν ψυχὴν μὴ δυνάμενοι ἀποκτεῖναι,[19] φύσεως οὐ κατισχύουσιν ἑτέρας παρὰ τὸ σῶμα, ἢ οὐ δῆτα; Εἰ οὖν ἄνθρωποι ὄντως ἦσαν οἷς ἐντέταλτο ὑπὸ τοῦ Κυρίου μὴ φοβεῖσθαι[20] ἀπὸ τῶν τοιῶνδε, δῆλον ὡς ἐνουσῶν αὐτοῖς τῶν δύο φύσεων ταῦτα εἴρηται, ἤγουν τῆς τε ἀποκτενομένης καὶ τῆς μὴ ἀποκτενομένης.

16. Εἰ ἔμεινε φύσις τὲ οὖσα καὶ θεότητος ἡ τοῦ Λόγου, καὶ φύσις οὖσα καὶ ἀνθρωπότητος ἡ τῆς σαρκός, πῶς οὐ δύο φύσεις ἄτρεπτοι ἐν τῷ Χριστῷ;

17. Ἔτι ἡ διαφορά, τινῶν διαφορά; τῶν γὰρ ἔν τινι καὶ οὐ τῶν καθ᾽ αὑτὰ νοουμένων ὁ ταύτης λόγος. Διαφορὰν οὖν οἱ λέγοντες, καὶ διαφέροντα εἶναι ἐν Χριστῷ δώσοιτε. Πόσα δὲ ταῦτα, δύο τοὐλάχιστον φήσοιτε. Τίνα δὲ ταῦτα ἐστὶν εἰσπραττόμενοι, θεότητα καὶ ἀνθρωπότητα ὀνομάσοιτε, ὡς οἶμαι. Τί δὲ τάδε τῶν ἐν τοῖς οὖσι[21] γενῶν ἴστε ἀνακριθέντες, εἴπερ μὴ εἴη ποιά, ἢ πόσα, ἢ σχέσεις, ἢ τι τοιόνδε, οὐσίας ὁμολογήσοιτε πάντως. Δύο ἄρα οὐσίας λέγειν ὑμᾶς ἐκ τῆς [268ʳ] διαφορᾶς ἐπὶ Χριστοῦ σαφῶς συνάγεται.

---

[18] Matt. 10: 28   [19] Matt. 10: 28   [20] Matt. 10: 28   [21] οὐσιῶν MS

15. If it's impossible for two natures to be preserved in Christ because of the paradigm of man used by certain of the fathers, let them tell us this: do *those who kill the body* kill a nature, or not? Do those who *cannot kill the soul* lack power over a different nature from the body, or is that clearly not the case? If men really were the ones to whom the Lord gave the command *don't be afraid* of such people, it's clear that these things are said of the two natures that are in men, that is, the one that's killed, and the one that isn't.

16. If there continued to exist a nature of divinity (that of the Word), and a nature of humanity (that of the flesh), how could there not be two unchanged natures in Christ?   1780A

17. Furthermore, difference is difference between certain things. The definition of difference, after all, belongs to things involved in some difference, and not to things understood in and of themselves. Since you're people who speak of a difference, then, you'd grant that there also are things that differ in Christ. As for how many of these there are, you'd have to say there are at least two. If you were driven to say what these differing things are, you would, as I see it, identify divinity and humanity. If you were cross-examined about which of the classes of beings you recognize these as belonging to, and if they're not qualities, or quantities, or states, or something of that kind, you'd have to confess that they are, without question, substances. It follows that you do speak of two substances because of the difference in Christ.

1780B **18.** Ἐρωτῶμεν δὲ ὑμᾶς ἔτι ἀδελφοί· "Λέγετε κατά τι διακρίνεσθαι τοῦ ἰδίου Πατρὸς τὸν Υἱὸν καὶ Λόγον, ἢ οὐχί;" Ἴσμεν οὖν ὅτι λέγετε· καὶ ὅτι τοῦτο εἶναι τὴν ὑπόστασιν ὁμολογεῖτε· μὴ γὰρ εἴη ὑμῖν μὴ δὲ ταῦτα βλασφημεῖν, μὴ δὲ τῶν λειπομένων πρὸς τελείαν εὐσέβειαν ἀμοιρεῖν. Πάλιν οὖν πυθοίμεθα ὑμῶν καὶ τόδε· "Τῆς ἰδίας σαρκὸς λέγετε κατά τι διακρίνεσθαι τὸν Λόγον, ἢ οὐχί;" Εἰ μὲν οὖν κατὰ μηδέν, ἐγγυτέραν ταύτην τῷ Λόγῳ καὶ ἡνωμένην μᾶλλον τοῦ Πατρὸς παρεστήσατε, εἴπερ τοῦ Πατρὸς καθ᾽ ὑπόστασιν, τῆς δὲ σαρκὸς τῆς ἐν αὐτῷ οὐδὲ κατὰ φύσιν, οὐδὲ καθ᾽ ὑπόστασιν διακέκριται ὁ Λόγος. Εἰ δὲ κατά τι καὶ ταύτην τοῦ Λόγου διακρίνετε, διαφορᾶς λόγῳ καὶ οὐ διαιρέσεως, τί τοῦτο, ἀποκρίνασθε. Εἰ μὲν οὖν τῷ αὐτῷ καθὸ καὶ τοῦ Πατρὸς διωρίζετο,

1780C ὑπόστασις δὲ αὐτή, πρῶτον μὲν δύο τὰς ὑποστάσεις Χριστοῦ δεδώκατε, εἶτα δὲ καὶ ἴσην τῷ Πατρὶ κατὰ πάντα τὴν σάρκα παριστάνετε, εἴ γε τοῖς αὐτοῖς καὶ μόνοις ἔκ τε τοῦ Πατρὸς καὶ τῆς οἰκείας σαρκὸς διακρίνεται ὁ Λόγος. Εἰ δὲ καθ᾽ ἕτερόν τι, ἢ φύσιν ἀνάγκη τοῦτο εἶναι, ἢ τί παρὰ τὴν φύσιν καὶ ὑπόστασιν ἐν τῷ Χριστῷ ἔχοιτε εἰδέναι, σημάνατε ἡμῖν. Εἰ δὲ οὐδέν, πάντως κατὰ φύσεως λόγον δίδοτε τὸν διορισμὸν τοῦ Λόγου καὶ τῆς σαρκὸς ἐπὶ Χριστοῦ· τῶν δὲ διοριζομένων καὶ ἀριθμός ἐστιν, ἐπείπερ τῶνδε δύο ὅροι εἰσίν· ὧν δὲ δύο οἱ ὅροι, δῆλον ὅτι καὶ δύο τὰ ὁριστά· εἰ δὲ τῶν φύσεων οἱ ὅροι εἰσί, τὰ ὁριστὰ δῆλον ὅτι αἱ φύσεις ἀποδειχθήσονται· οὐκοῦν ἀριθμηταὶ σαφῶς αἱ φύσεις Χριστοῦ.

1780D Καλῶς οὖν ἡμῖν εἴρηται· ἕνωσις μὲν ὑποστάσεων ἐν μιᾷ φύσει ἐπὶ τῆς ἀγίας καὶ ὑπερουσίου Τριάδος, ἕνωσις δὲ τῶν φύσεων ἐν μιᾷ ὑποστάσει ἐπὶ τῆς ἀγίας καὶ ἀφράστου σαρκώσεως τοῦ Λόγου· τοῦτο γὰρ ἔφη καὶ ὁ λέγων πατήρ· "Ἔμπαλιν ἔχειν τὸν λόγον τοῦ κατὰ Χριστὸν μυστηρίου, ἢ ἐπὶ τῆς ἀγίας Τριάδος."[22]

---

[22] Gregory of Nazianzus, *Letter* 101, 44

18. We'd like to put another question to you, brothers: are you saying that the Son and Word is distinguished in any respect from 1780B His own father, or not? We know that you say He is, and that you confess it's the hypostasis that distinguishes them. God forbid that you should blaspheme against these doctrines, or that you should lose your share in the heritage left to us that leads to perfect orthodoxy! Here's another thing we'd like to learn from you: do you say that the Word is distinguished in any respect from His own flesh, or not? If He isn't distinguished from His flesh in any respect, you're proving that His flesh is closer to the Word, and more united to the Word, than His Father is—if indeed the Word is distinguished from the Father by hypostasis, but from the flesh that's in Him neither by nature nor by hypostasis! If, however, you do in some way distinguish the flesh from the Word by reason of difference, and not of division, give us an answer as to what precisely this consists of. If [the Word] was distinguished [from the flesh] by exactly the same thing—and that thing is a hypostasis— by which He was distinguished from the Father, you've admitted 1780C right off the bat there are two hypostases of Christ. In that case, you've shown the flesh to be equal to the Father in every respect if, that is, the Word is distinguished from the Father and from the flesh proper to Him by the same distinctions, and only those distinctions. If, however, the Word is distinguished from His flesh by something else, either this must be a nature, or you're going to have to indicate to us just what it is you're able to comprehend in Christ beyond a nature and an hypostasis. If you can comprehend nothing of the sort, grant that the distinction between Word and flesh in Christ is entirely a matter of what we understand by 'nature'. There's also a number for the things distinguished, given that there are two definitions for them. It's clear that, when there are two definitions, there are two definable entities. If the definitions are of natures, it's clear that the definable entities in question will be shown to be natures. That's clearly why the natures of Christ are counted. We are, then, right in saying there's a union of hypostases in one nature in the case of the holy and supra- 1780D essential Trinity, but a union of natures in one hypostasis in the case of the holy and ineffable Incarnation of the Word. This is what the father was talking about who said: 'The definition of the mystery in Christ is the opposite of the definition for the Holy Trinity.'

19. Ἐρωτῶμεν ἔτι καὶ τόδε· "Ταύτης τῆς καθ᾽ ὑμᾶς φύσεως Χριστοῦ τοῦ Υἱοῦ τοῦ Θεοῦ τοῦ ζῶντος,²³ κατὰ τὴν τοῦ Πέτρου ἀσφαλῆ ὁμολογίαν, τὸν Θεὸν Λόγον τί φατὲ εἶναι, μέρος ἢ ὅλον;" Εἰ μὲν γὰρ μέρος, καὶ μέρους φύσεως Πατέρα λέγετε τὸν Πατέρα· μερικοῦ δὲ ὄντος τοῦ Λόγου κατὰ τὴν φυσικὴν υἱότητα, καὶ τοῦ Πατρὸς ἔσται κατὰ τὴν φυσικὴν πατρότητα μερικὴ ἡ πατρότης·

1781A ἑκατέρα οὖν τῶν δύο θείων ὑποστάσεων, τοῦ τε Πατρὸς καὶ τοῦ Υἱοῦ, ἀνὰ ἥμισυ λείψει τοῦ κατὰ φύσιν λόγου, καὶ οὐκ ἔσται τελεία φύσις ἔν τινι τῶν προσώπων θεωρουμένη τῆς ἁγίας [268ᵛ] Τριάδος. Εἶτα δὲ καὶ τῷδε ἐπισκεπτέον τῷ ἀτόπῳ, ὅτι ἔσται οὑτωσὶ λέγειν· ὅτι εἰ μετὰ σαρκὸς τελεία γέγονεν ἡ φύσις τοῦ Λόγου, ἐκ τῆς σαρκώσεως τοῦ Υἱοῦ, πρὸς τὸν ἑαυτῶν²⁴ λόγον ὅ τε Υἱὸς καὶ ὁ Πατὴρ προέκοψαν, ἵνα καὶ αὐτὸς τελείου Υἱοῦ τέλειος Πατὴρ εἴη. Εἰ δὲ ταῦτα εὐλαβηθέντες, τὸ ὅλον εἶναι τῆς μιᾶς φύσεως τοῦ Χριστοῦ τὸν ἐν αὐτῷ θεῖον Λόγον φατέ, πρῶτον μὲν ἢ τὸ ὅλον δεδώκατε τοῦ Χριστοῦ, καὶ πρὸ Χριστοῦ εἶναι, ἐπείπερ ἦν ὁ Λόγος καὶ πρὸ τῆς ἑνώσεως αὐτοῦ τῆς πρὸς σάρκα· ἢ τὸν Λόγον οὐ λέγετε ὑπάρξαι πρὸ τῆς σαρκὸς Χριστοῦ. Ἔσται οὖν οὕτως· πρῶτον,

1781B οἰκεῖον τὸ ὅλον, εἴπερ Χριστός, οὗ ἐστι τὸ ὅλον ὁ θεῖος Λόγος ὁ πρὸ αἰώνων, προϋπῆρχε τῆς σαρκὸς ἑαυτοῦ ἤ ἐστι μέρος Χριστοῦ. Εἶτα δὲ πάλιν, πῶς ἕξει καὶ μέρος ἑαυτῆς τόνδε τὸν Λόγον ἡ μία φύσις, ὃν ἔχει ἤδε ὡς ὅλον, οὐκ ἔστιν ἰδεῖν· οὐ γὰρ τὸ αὐτὸ τοῦ αὐτοῦ μέρος τὲ καὶ ὅλον ἔσται πώποτε. Ἔτι μέντοι καὶ ἡ σάρξ, κατὰ ταύτην ὑμῶν τὴν ἀπόκρισιν, ἐκβληθήσεται πάντη Χριστοῦ, τῆς μιᾶς ταύτης ὑμῶν φύσεως ὑπὸ τοῦ Λόγου μόνου συμπληρουμένης ἤδη, ἢ προστεθήσεται καὶ αὐτὴ καὶ οὐκ ἔσται ὑμῖν κατὰ σκοπὸν ἔτι τὸ συναγόμενον· πᾶν γὰρ τὸ μετὰ τὴν οἰκείαν φυσικὴν ὁλότητα τινὶ ἐπιθεωρούμενον, περισσόν τι ποσὸν ἐπεισάξει, εἴπερ ὄντως τούτῳ ἡνωμένον ἐστί· καὶ οὐ μόνον κατὰ λόγον κτίσεως ἴσως ὑπάρχον αὐτῷ ἔξωθεν ἐπινοηθήσεται. Οὐκοῦν εἰ ἄτοπα τάδε ἐστίν, οὐ

1781C δυνατὸν μίαν εἰπεῖν τὴν Χριστοῦ φύσιν, ὡς μέρος ἢ ὡς ὅλον θεωροῦντας τὸν Λόγον ἢ τὴν σάρκα ἐν αὐτῇ· ἢ οὖν ἑτέρα τίς ἐστιν ἡ λεγομένη ὑμῖν μία φύσις, παρὰ τὸν Λόγον πάντη καὶ τὴν σάρκα, καὶ οὔτε Θεὸς οὐδὲ ἄνθρωπός ἐστιν, ἢ οὐ μία πάντως ἀλλὰ δύο ὑπάρχουσιν.

---

²³ Matt. 16: 16   ²⁴ ἑαυτοῦ MS

19. We'd like to pose another question: what do you say God the Word is: a part, or the whole of this (as you put it) nature of *Christ the Son of the living God*, to use the words of Peter's sound confession? If He's a part of it, then you're saying the Father is Father of a part of a nature. Since the Word is then partial vis-à-vis natural sonship, the Father's fatherhood will also be partial vis-à-vis natural fatherhood. That would mean each of the two divine hypostases involved—that of the Father, and that of the Son—will be missing as much as half of its definition by nature, and no complete nature will be observed in either of the persons of the Holy Trinity! 1781A

Consider next that, as a result of this absurdity, it'll be possible to speak as follows: if the Word's nature became complete with flesh, then both the Son and the Father advanced in terms of their own definition as a result of the Son's taking of flesh, so that He too might be complete Father of a complete Son. You may, on the other hand, avoid these conclusions and say that the divine Word in Him is the whole of Christ's one nature. If so, the first implication is either that you've granted that the whole of Christ existed even before Christ, given that the Word existed before His union with flesh, or else that you deny the Word existed before Christ's flesh. Things will then stand as follows: in the first place, the whole does belong to Him, if Christ, the divine Word before the ages, 1781B whose whole it is, pre-existed His own flesh, which is a part of Christ. But then again, it's impossible to understand how the one nature will have this Word as a part of itself which it has as a whole: nothing can ever be both part and whole of the same thing!

Furthermore, according to this answer of yours the flesh too will be entirely divorced from Christ, since this one nature of yours is already completed by the Word alone. Either that, or it'll be added. Then the conclusion won't suit your purpose, for everything observed in an entity beyond its proper natural wholeness entails an increase in quantity if it's really united to that thing, and isn't just thought of as existing equally alongside it, in the fashion of the created order. If these implications are absurd, it's an impossibility for people who consider either the Word or the flesh 1781C as a part or as a whole in Christ's nature to say that it's one. Either, then, this one nature you talk about is some nature entirely other than the Word and the flesh, and is neither God nor man, or else it's not one nature that exists, but two.

20. Ἔτι φαμέν· "Τὰ συνελθόντα ὁ Λόγος ἐστὶ καὶ ἡ σὰρξ ὑφ' ὧν γενομένην τὴν ἐκ δύο ἕνωσιν Χριστοῦ φατέ, ἢ ἕτερόν τι παρὰ τάδε;" Ἀλλὰ ταῦτα εἶναι πάντως ἐρεῖτε· μεμένηκε δὲ καὶ Λόγος ὁ Λόγος, καὶ σὰρξ ἡ σὰρξ μετὰ τὴν ἕνωσιν, εἰ καὶ ἡνωμένη τῷ Λόγῳ, καὶ ἰδίᾳ τοῦ ἰδιοποιουμένου αὐτήν. Πῶς οὖν οὐ δύο καὶ νῦν, ὡς Λόγος καὶ σάρξ, καὶ ὡς ἴδιον καὶ ἰδιοποιούμενον ἔσονται;

1781D **21.** Κύριλλος ὁ πατήρ φησιν ἐν τῷ πρώτῳ τῶν Σχολίων, ὅτι "Τὸ Χριστὸς ὄνομα, οὔτε ὅρου δύναμιν ἔχει, οὔτε μέν τινος οὐσίαν ὅ τί ποτέ ἐστι, [269ʳ] σημαίνειν,²⁵ καθάπερ καὶ τὸ ἄνθρωπος ἢ ἵππος ἢ βοῦς, πράγματος δὲ μᾶλλον ἐνεργουμένου περί τινα ποιεῖται δήλωσιν."²⁶ Εἰ οὖν οὔτε ὁριστικόν, οὔτε σημαντικὸν οὐσίας τοῦτό ἐστι τὸ ὄνομα, δῆλον ὅτι, φυσικῶς οὕτω δὲ προσαγορευτέον τινὶ τὴν καθ' ὑμᾶς μίαν Χριστοῦ φύσιν, ἀλλ' οὐδὲ θεόν—μέρος γὰρ αὐτῆς ὅδε—οὔτε ἄνθρωπον—καὶ τοῦτο γὰρ ὁμοίως ἔχει—τί οὖν τῆς ὁλότητος αὐτῆς ὄνομά ἐστι, εἴπατε· ὥσπερ τῆς ἀνθρωπείας ἕτερόν τι παρὰ ψυχὴν καὶ σῶμα καταφάσκομεν; "Τὸ γὰρ Χριστός, χρίσιν"

1784A φησὶ "σημαίνει περί τινα χριόμενον²⁷." Ὅτι δὲ οὔτε χρίσις ἄνευ οὐσιωμένου χρίσματος, οὔτε χριόμενος ἀνούσιος τίς ἐστιν, οὔτε ἔτι τὸ χρίσμα καὶ τὸ χριόμενον μία ἐστὶν οὐσία, φανερόν. Εἰκότως οὖν καὶ τῶν πραγμάτων καὶ τῶν ὀνομάτων τῶν φυσικῶν διττῶς εὐποροῦντες, δύο φαμὲν τὰς φύσεις Χριστοῦ ἡμεῖς.

---

²⁵ σημαίνειν] ~ν s. lin. MS   ²⁶ Cyril of Alexandria, *Scholia*, 219
²⁷ χριομένου MS

20. We have something else to say: 'Are the Word and the flesh the things by virtue of whose coming together you say Christ's union out of two came to be, or something else apart from them?' You say these are precisely what came together, yet after the union the Word remained Word, and the flesh remained flesh, even though it was united to the Word and was the own flesh of Him who made it His own. How can there not be two things—Word and flesh—now as well, one that was the other's own, and one that made the other its own?

21. The father Cyril says, in the first book of the *Scholia*, that 'the name "Christ" does not have the meaning of a definition, nor can it signify the substance of something (what it is at that moment), as do the words "man", or "horse", or "cow". Rather, it provides an indication of an action done to someone.' If, then, this isn't the kind of name that constitutes a definition or that signifies a substance, it's clear that anyone who wants to give a name in terms of what we mean by 'nature' to your one nature of Christ must do so in this light. Yet he can't call it 'God', for God's a part of it; nor can he call it 'man', for it's the same problem there. What, pray tell, is the name of the whole of it that corresponds to the way we affirm of humanity something more than soul and body? 'The word "Christ"', he says, 'signifies an anointing vis-à-vis someone who's anointed.'[iv] It's evident that there's no anointing where there's no chrism invested with substance, that there's no one who's anointed unless he has substance, and yet that the chrism and the anointed do not constitute one substance. We ourselves are therefore right to speak of Christ's two natures, since we have a twofold stock both of actions and of natural names.

22. Ἔτι δέ φαμεν πρὸς ὑμᾶς· ἐπεὶ τὸ προκείμενον ὑμῖν ἅτε θεῖον, γένους λόγον οὐκ ἐπιδέχεται ὁπωσοῦν—τί γὰρ τοῦδε πρώτου αἰτίου ὄντος, ἀνώτερον ἔσται γένος;—τὸ "ἕν" διττῶς μόνον ἐπὶ Χριστοῦ κατὰ τὰς κυριωτέρας λέγεται φωνάς, εἴ γε καὶ κατὰ ταύτας συγχωρητέον τινὶ λέγειν αὐτὸ ἐνθάδε, καὶ δύο δὲ διττῶς εἶναι τάδε τινὰ λέγονται. Τὸ οὖν ἓν ὄν, ἢ τῷ εἴδει ἢ τῷ ἀριθμῷ ἐστιν ἕν, καὶ τὰ 1784B ὄντα δύο, ἢ τῷ εἴδει ἢ τῷ ἀριθμῷ ἐστι δύο. Τὰ μὲν οὖν ἓν τῷ εἴδει ὄντα, πᾶσαν ἕξει πρὸς ἄλληλα τὴν φυσικὴν ὁμοιότητα· τὰ δὲ δύο ὄντα τῷ εἴδει, πάντως ἔχει τὴν φυσικὴν ἀνομοιότητα· τὰ δὲ τῷ ἀριθμῷ ἓν ὄντα, οὐ κωλύεται ἐν ἑαυτοῖς ἔχειν φυσικὴν ἀνομοιότητα, εἰ καὶ ἀλλήλων χωρὶς μὴ διεστήκασι, καὶ ἐν ἰδίᾳ περιγραφῇ θεωρούμενον ἑκάτερον, ἀριθμοῦνται κατὰ τὸν τοῦ ἀριθμοῦ διωρισμένον λόγον. Οὕτως γὰρ νοοῦντες καὶ ἀριθμοῦντες, ἕνα μὲν πάντα τὸν κοινὸν ἄνθρωπον καὶ ἵππον καὶ ἄγγελον ἀπαραλλάκτως ἔχοντα τῷ εἴδει τῆς αὐτοῦ φύσεως ἐν πᾶσι τοῖς ὑπ' αὐτὸν ἀτόμοις φαμέν, κεχωρισμένως δὲ πολλὰ τοῦδε τὰ ἄτομα τῷ ἀριθμῷ γινώσκομεν—ἀνὰ μέρος γὰρ ἕκαστον αὐτῶν ἀριθμεῖσθαι δυνάμενον ἴσμεν· καὶ πάλιν ἕνα τῷ ἀριθμῷ, τόν τε κόσμον ὅλον 1784C καὶ τὸν τινὰ ἄνθρωπον λέγομεν, φύσεσι μερικαῖς ἢ φυσικοῖς εἴδεσιν οὐχ' ἕνα αὐτὸν ἀριθμοῦντες. Ἐπὶ οὖν τοῦ Δεσπότου ἡμῶν, εἰ μὲν τὴν μονάδα διὰ τὴν τοῦ προσώπου ἑνότητα καὶ τὴν τῶν ἐν αὐτῷ ἀχωρίστων ἐξαρίθμησιν, ὡς ἑνὸς ὄντος τῷ ἀριθμῷ, φατέ, καλῶς λέγετε, καὶ ἡμᾶς δέον σὺν ὑμῖν τοῦτο ἀποδέχεσθαι, ὡμολογημένου τοῦ κατ' αὐτὸ τὸ ἓν πρόσωπον φυσικοῦ διαφόρου. Εἰ δὲ [269ᵛ] κατὰ τὸν τοῦ φυσικοῦ εἴδους λόγον ἀπαριθμῆσαι τὰ ἐν Χριστῷ βουλόμεθα, ἐπεὶ ὡμολόγηται τὰ ἓν τῷ εἴδει ὄντα, κατ' εἶδος ὅμοια δέον εἶναι, ἀναγκαίως ἀνόμοια θεωρήσαντες, οὐκέτι τολμήσομεν τῷ τοῦ εἴδους καταλόγῳ ἓν ταῦτα λέγειν, ἀλλὰ δύο. Οὐκοῦν ἀκολούθως δύο μὲν ταῖς φύσεσιν, ἓν δὲ τῷ ἀριθμῷ τὸν Χριστὸν γινώσκομεν.

22. We have something else to say against you: since what you've proposed, inasmuch as it's divine, doesn't admit of any notion of genus at all—for what genus could transcend this first existent cause?—the word 'one' is used for Christ in only two ways according to the more authoritative statements if, again in the light of these statements, it's to be conceded that anyone may use the word at this point. Such things are also said to be two in two ways. What's one is one either in form or in number. Things that are two likewise are two either in form or in number. Things that are one in form will have complete identity with each other on the level of nature, but things that are two in form have complete dissimilarity on the level of nature. Things that are one in number aren't prevented from having natural dissimilarity in themselves, so long as they haven't also stood apart from each other and, each being considered within its own circumference, been numbered in accordance with the distinction-making understanding of number. Understanding and numbering in this way, we speak of the one whole and universal man (and horse, and angel) which exists unchangeably by the form of its nature in all of the individuals subsumed under it, yet we know its individual iterations to be many in number, for we know each of them can be numbered in turn. Again, we say that the whole cosmos, like the individual man, is one in number, but we aren't counting it as one on the basis of partial natures or natural forms.

1784B

1784C

In the case of our Master, then, if you speak of His single reality on account of the oneness of His person and of the enumeration of undivided things in Him as belonging to one who is one by number, you speak correctly. We have to accept this right along with you, since a natural difference is confessed in respect of the one person itself. If, on the other hand, we want to count up what's in Christ by the logic of natural form, we wouldn't dare to call these one under the category of form, but two, necessarily considering them to be non-identical things, since the consensus is that things one in form must be identical in form. Accordingly, then, we recognize Christ to be two in nature, but one in number.

1784D **23.** Ἔτι ἐρωτητέον αὐτούς· ἐκ δύο φύσεων λέγοντας τὴν μίαν φύσιν, ἣν φασὶ Χριστοῦ· ἆρά γε καὶ ἐκ δύο ὑποστάσεων εἴτουν προσώπων, τὴν μίαν αὐτοῦ ὑπόστασιν λέγουσιν, ἢ οὐχί; Ποῦ οὖν καὶ πῶς ὑφέστηκε θατέρα τῶν φύσεων αὐτοῦ πρὸ τῆς ἑνώσεως, λεγέτωσαν, τίνος τε οὖσα τότε; Οὐ γὰρ Χριστοῦ ἦν, μή πω "χρισθεῖσα θεότητι"²⁸ ἡ ἀνθρωπίνη φύσις. Εἰ δὲ καὶ ἐκ δύο ὑποστάσεων φασὶ τὴν ἕνωσιν, ποῦ ἦν ποτε ἡ τελεία ὑπόστασις ἀνθρωπίνη προϋπάρξασα Χριστοῦ, εἶτα ἐν τῇ μήτρᾳ τῆς ἁγίας παρθένου ἐγκαθειρχθεῖσα; Κατ' ἐκεῖνο γὰρ τὸ ἅγιον χωρίον ἡ ἕνωσις τῶν Χριστοῦ φύσεων ἀπ' ἀρχῆς ἐγένετο, εἰ μὴ ἄρα κατὰ Νεστόριον 1785A τὴν ἕνωσιν τῆς θεότητος μετὰ τὸν τόκον τῆς ἀνθρωπότητος οἴονται γενέσθαι πρὸς αὐτὴν σχετικῶς.

24. Ἔτι ἀνακριτέον αὐτούς· ἐκ δύο φύσεων πράγματι ὑφεστηκυιῶν φασὶ τὸν Χριστόν, ἢ θατέρας αὐτῶν ἤγουν τῆς ἀνθρωπείας, κατ' ἐπίνοιαν προαναπλαττομένης αὐτοῖς πρὸ τῆς ἑνώσεως; Εἰ μὲν γὰρ ἀμφοῖν ὄντως προουσῶν, τίς ἦν, καὶ ποῦ, πάλιν ζητήσωμεν, ἡ ψιλὴ ἀνθρωπίνη φύσις πρὸ Χριστοῦ, εἶτα γέγονεν ἐν Χριστῷ κατὰ τὴν ἁγίαν μήτραν συντεθέντι; Εἰ δὲ θατέραν τῶν φύσεων, ἐξ ὧν φασὶ τὸν Χριστόν, ἐπινοίᾳ προαναπλάττουσι, πρῶτον μέν, ἢ οὐδαμόθεν λαβόντες ἀφορμὴν ἀληθοῦς ἐπινοίας, ψευδὲς ἀνάπλασμα ταύτην παριστῶσιν, ἢ λαβόντες, ἐκ τῆς μετὰ τὴν ἕνωσιν θεωρίας Χριστοῦ, τὴν διάγνωσιν 1785B ὡς δύο φύσεων καὶ τοιῶνδε, ταύτας καὶ προεπινοοῦσιν αὐτοῦ. Πῶς οὖν οὐ δύο ἴσασι μετὰ τὴν ἕνωσιν, οἱ καὶ τὴν προΰπαρξιν αὐτῶν τὴν πρὸ τῆς ἑνώσεως ἐκ τῆς κατὰ τὴν ἕνωσιν διαγνώσεως αὐτῶν ἐπινοήσαντες; Ἔτι ἦν, εἰ μὲν ἐπινοίᾳ θατέραν, καὶ ἀληθείᾳ τὴν ἑτέραν τῶν φύσεων, ἐξ ὧν ὁ Κύριος φασίν, ἀνάγκη καὶ αὐτὸν Χριστὸν τὸ μέν τι μέρος αὐτοῦ ἀληθείᾳ ὑπάρχον ἔχειν, τὸ δὲ ἐπινοίᾳ δοκεῖν μόνον, ὡς εἶναι καὶ τῆς κατὰ τούσδε μιᾶς φύσεως αὐτοῦ, ἀνύπαρκτον τὸ ἥμισυ, καὶ εἰς ἥμισυ φύσεως μόνον καταντῆσαι αὐτῶν τὴν ἐπὶ Χριστοῦ φυσιολογίαν, καὶ μὴ δὲ εἰς μίαν φύσιν τελείαν ὡς λέγουσιν.

---

²⁸ Gregory of Nazianzus, *Oration* 45, 13, 641A.

23. There's another question to be put to these people who say   1784D
that the one nature, the one they say is Christ's nature, is out of
two natures: do they then say that His one hypostasis is out of two
hypostases (that is, persons) as well, or not? [If not,] they must
then explain where and how either of His natures subsisted before
the union, and whose nature it was then, for the human nature
wasn't Christ's, not having yet been 'anointed by divinity'. If, on
the other hand, they do say that the union is out of two hypostases
as well, where did the complete human hypostasis ever exist that
pre-existed Christ—the one that then was shut up in the Holy
Virgin's womb? It was in that holy place that the union of Christ's
natures had its beginning, unless, of course, they consequently
take Nestorius' line that the union of divinity with humanity came   1785A
about by relationship after the latter's birth.

24. One needs to cross-examine them further. Are they saying that Christ is out of two natures that subsisted in reality, or out
of one—the human nature—that's only imagined in thought by
them before the union? If it's a case of both natures actually pre-
existing the union, we need to ask again what the human nature
on its own was before Christ, and where it used to exist, so that
afterwards it came to be in a Christ who was compounded in the
holy womb. If, on the other hand, they imagine the other of the
natures (out of which they say Christ is) only in thought, then in
the first place they're either just taking the starting-point for a true
thought out of thin air, and representing this nature by something
they've falsely imagined, or else accepting the discernment as of
two natures of such and such a kind on the basis of their observation of Christ after the union, and then conceiving of these
natures as pre-existing Him. How can they not recognize two after   1785B
the union when it's on the basis of their discernment of them in
the union that they think of the natures' pre-existence before the
union? Furthermore, if they speak of one of the natures out of
whom the Lord is in thought, and of the other in truth, Christ
Himself must have had one of His parts existing in truth, but the
other only seeming in thought to exist, and so half also of His (in
their view) one nature must have been non-existent. Thus their
inquiry into natural causes with respect to Christ must come down
to only half of a nature, and not to the one complete nature they
talk about!

1785C **25.** Ἔτι ἐπεὶ τῶν φύσεων δηλαδὴ τὴν σύνοδον ἴστε, καὶ σὺν ἡμῖν τὸ ἀσύγχυτον ὁμολογεῖτε τῶν συνελθόντων, πόθεν τοῦτο θεωρεῖτε, ἀπο[270ʳ]κρίνασθε ἡμῖν. Εἰ γὰρ ὅτι ἀνελλιπῆ τὰ θεῖα καὶ τὰ ἀνθρώπεια ἐν τῷ αὐτῷ θεωρεῖτε προσώπῳ, σῷον ἑκάστου τὸν φυσικὸν λόγον διὰ τῆς τῶν ἰδιωμάτων ἀντιδόσεως ἐν τῷ ἑνὶ συγκρίματι γίνωσκετε, δῆλον ἔσται ὅτι ἔκ τινος τελείου τε τοῦδε τὰς ἐνεργείας καὶ τὰ πάθη κατὰ τελείου καὶ οὐ κατ᾽ οὐδενὸς²⁹ λογίζεσθε, ἐπείπερ ἀναγκαῖον καὶ τὰς αἰτίας οὕτως ἔχειν καὶ φυλάττεσθαι διαφόρους καὶ τελείας ὥσπερ τὰ ἴδια τούτων ἰδιώματα καὶ προβλήματα. Ἐπεὶ οὖν διάφορα τέ εἰσι καὶ διττά, θεῖα τέ ὄντα καὶ ἀνθρώπινα, διάφορα ἔσται καὶ δύο καὶ τάδε. Ταῦτα δὲ τὰ αἴτια τῶν ἰδίων, εἴπερ φύσεις εἶναι ὁμολογεῖτε, ἐκ 1785D δύο ἄρα τῶν φύσεων προϊέναι τὰς ἰδιότητας καὶ ὑμεῖς ὁμολογεῖτε.

26. Ἔτι εἰ τὴν φυσικὴν διαφορὰν ὁμολογοῦσιν ἐν Χριστῷ, ἀρά γε τινῶν ὄντων ἤδη εἶναι αὐτὴν διαφοράν, ἢ τινῶν μὴ ὄντων λέγουσιν εἶναι τὴν διαφορὰν ἐν Χριστῷ; Ἐπεὶ οὖν πάντως ὄντων ἐροῦσιν, ἢ δύο τούτων δηλαδὴ ἢ πλειόνων, λεγέτωσαν οὖν ὁπόσων τινῶν βούλονται εἶναι αὐτὴν, καὶ μὴ εὐλαβείσθωσαν.

---

²⁹ καθ᾽ οὐδενος MS

25. Furthermore, since you quite clearly recognize the coming 1785C together of natures, and confess with us the unconfusedness of the things that came together, tell us: where do you draw this observation from? If you know that the natural definition of each is intact in the one compound reality through the exchange of properties, because you observe that the divine and the human are without defect in the same [person], it'll be clear that you're drawing your conclusions about this person's actions and passions on the basis of something realized, and in respect of something realized, not what has no reality. This is so if it's indeed necessary for causes to be, and to be kept, just as different and complete as are their specific characteristics and effects. Since, then, their characteristics and effects are different and twofold, being both divine and human, they too will be different and two in number. If you confess that these causes of characteristics are natures, it follows that you too confess that the properties proceed from the two natures. 1785D

26. Furthermore, if they confess the natural difference in Christ, are they saying that it's a difference between certain things that already exist, or that the difference in Christ is between certain things that don't exist? Since they say it's absolutely a difference between things that do exist—whether there are clearly two of them, or more—they must tell us between how many things they want the difference to be, and not be shy about it.

27. Ἔτι εἰ τὸ λέγειν δύο, χωρίζειν ἐστί, πῶς δύο λέγοντες τὰς ἰδιότητας καὶ αὐτοί, τὴν ἕνωσιν οὐ μερίζουσιν; Ἀλλ' ἴσως εἴποιεν, ὅτι "Τοῦτο χωρίζειν τὴν φύσιν οὐ πέφυκεν· ἰδοὺ γὰρ καὶ ἐν τοῖς καθ' ἕκαστα,³⁰ καὶ ἐν αὐτῇ τῇ ἁγίᾳ Τριάδι, πλείους μὲν τὰς ἰδιότητας, μίαν δὲ τὴν φύσιν ὁρῶμεν." Ταῦτα δὲ οὐχ' οὕτως

1788A φρονοῦντες οἱ πλείους αὐτῶν φασίν, εἰ καὶ πρὸς τὸ παρὸν τάδε ἡμῖν προβάλλονται, ὡς ἐν ἑτέροις ἐδείχθη. Πλὴν εἴποιμεν πρὸς αὐτούς· "Ἐπεὶ οὖν κατὰ ταύτας λέγετε τὸ δύο ὑμεῖς, αἳ πέφυκαν οὐ τὴν φύσιν χωρίζειν, ἀλλὰ τὰς ὑποστάσεις τῶν προσώπων τῆς μιᾶς φύσεως— ταῖς γὰρ ἰδιότησιν αὗται χωρίζονται, καθ' ὑμᾶς τε καὶ καθ' ἡμᾶς— λέγοντες ἄρα κατὰ ταύτας μόνον, ἤγουν τὰς ἰδιότητας, ἐπὶ Χριστοῦ τὴν δυάδα, τὰς ὑποστάσεις τῶν προσώπων, δύο ἴστε τοῦ Χριστοῦ, εἰ καὶ μίαν τὴν φύσιν αὐτοῦ ὁμολογεῖτε· ὅπερ μὴ εἴη ὑμᾶς, ἀδελφοί, καταδέχεσθαι." Εἰ δὲ εἴποιτε μήτε τὴν φύσιν μήτε τὴν ὑπόστασιν τὰς ἰδιότητας χωρίζειν, οὔτε Παῦλος ἄρα Πέτρου, οὔτε τοῦ Πατρὸς ὁ Υἱὸς κατά τι διακρίνεται, τῇ μὲν φύσει ὄντες ταυτοί, ταῖς δὲ ἰδιότησιν ἀδιάκριτοι καὶ ἀδιάγνωστοι.

1788B 28. Εἰ διαφορὰν λέγουσι, καὶ δυάδα πάντως εἰπεῖν τῶν διαφερόντων ἀναγκασθήσονται δηλονότι· τῶν τε γὰρ ἑτεροφυῶν πραγμάτων ἡ ἀπαρίθμησις, τῶν τε συμβεβηκότων τῶν ἐξαλλασσόντων κατά τι, ἢ τό γε ἔσχατον, [270ᵛ] γυμνῶν τῶν τοῦ ἀριθμοῦ μορίων, ἢ ψιλῶν τινῶν ἐπινοημάτων εἰ γένοιτο μέτρησις, ἐκ τῆς διαφορᾶς τῆς κατὰ λόγον, ἢ τάξιν, ἢ χρόνον, ἢ τόπον, ἢ σχέσιν, καὶ αὕτη προβήσεται σαφῶς. Ἢ οὖν μήτε διαφοράν, ἢ καὶ τὸν ἀριθμὸν λεγέτωσαν τῶν διαφερουσῶν φύσεων.

29. Εἰ ἐκ δύο λέγοντες φύσεων τὸν Χριστόν, ὡς ἐκ τῆς κοινῆς θεότητος καὶ ἀνθρωπότητος, δύο τάσδε καὶ μετὰ τὴν ἕνωσιν οὐ γινώσκουσιν, ἆρά γε οὐδὲ ἴσασι μετὰ τὴν οἰκονομίαν τῆς

1788C σαρκώσεως τοῦ Λόγου τὰς κοινὰς δύο φύσεις ἀνθρωπότητος καὶ θεότητος, οὐδὲ διωρισμένως αὐτὰς ἀριθμοῦσιν, οὐδὲ εἶναι ὅλως δύο ἔτι λοιπὸν φασί· τάδε γὰρ πεπαῦσθαι τῆς δυάδος φασὶν οἷς προσγέγονεν ἡ ἕνωσις, εἶναι δὲ ταῦτα τὰς κοινὰς φύσεις ὁμολογοῦσιν.

---

³⁰ καθέκαστα MS

27. Furthermore, if to speak of two is to divide, how is it that, when they themselves speak of two properties, they aren't dividing the union? But perhaps they'll say: 'This doesn't have the effect of dividing the nature, for notice this: even in things taken individually, and in the Holy Trinity itself, we see many properties, but we see one nature.' The majority of them speak of two properties without sharing in this way of thinking, even though they offer us this pretext right up to the present, as was explained elsewhere. 1788A We'd like to add this to the case against them: 'You yourselves use the word "two" for these properties, properties which have the effect, not of dividing the nature, but of dividing the hypostases of the persons of the one nature—for these are divided by their properties on your view just as much as on ours. Therefore, when you speak of the duality in Christ in terms only of these, that is, in terms only of these properties, you're recognizing that the hypostases of Christ's persons are two, even as you confess His one nature—just what you couldn't admit, brothers!' If, on the other hand, you say that properties divide neither nature nor hypostasis, then Paul isn't distinguished from Peter, nor is the Son in any way distinguished from the Father, since they're the same by nature, being undifferentiated and indistinguishable by their properties.

28. If they speak of a difference, they'll be forced, it seems clear, 1788B to speak unreservedly also of a duality of things that differ. The numbering of entities that have different natures, and of things that happen to differ in some respect, whether in the end it's the numbering of fractions or of mere conceptual distinctions, will also evidently be advanced on the basis of differences in definition, order, time, place, or condition, if measurement takes place. Either, then, they mustn't speak of a difference, or they must speak also of the number of differing natures.

29. When they say Christ is out of two natures, as being out of universal divinity and universal humanity, if they don't recognize these as two after the union as well, then they don't know the two universal natures of humanity and divinity after the dispensation of the Incarnation of the Word, nor do they number them separ- 1788C ately, nor do they say that they're fully two any more. They say that those things to which union happened left off their duality, yet they confess these to be universal natures!

30. Εἰ διὰ τὸ ταῖς φύσεσιν ἡνῶσθαι, μίαν οἴδασι φύσιν τὰ συνελθόντα, καὶ διὰ τὸ φύσει διαφέρειν, δύο ταῦτα γινωσκέτωσαν· διά τε γὰρ ἔνωσιν, ἓν πρόσωπον, καὶ διὰ τὴν διαφοράν, δύο αἱ φύσεις. Οὐ γὰρ ὅπερ αὐτῷ ἐστι διὰ τὴν ἔνωσιν, τοῦτο καὶ διὰ τὴν διαφορὰν ὑπολήψονται, ἀλλ' ἐν θατέρῳ τῷ λόγῳ τὸ ἕτερον. Ἐπεὶ οὖν καὶ οὐσιώδης μὲν τοῖς συνελθοῦσιν ἡ διαφορά, ἐπίκτητος δὲ ταῖς οὐσίαις ἡ ἔνωσις, καλῶς τὰς μὲν οὐσίας, τῷ ἰδίῳ αὐτῶν λόγῳ 1788D διακρίναντες, δύο φαμέν, ἤγουν τῇ διαφορᾷ, τὸ δὲ πρόσωπον αὐταῖς ἕν, τῇ ἑνώσει δοξάζομεν.

31. Ἔτι παντὸς συνθέτου τελείου οὐ περιττεύειν οὔτε ἐλλείπειν δεῖ τὸν λόγον, ἀλλ' ἄρτιον εἶναι· δυὰς δὲ πρώτη σύνθεσις, καὶ πρῶτος ἄρτιος ἀριθμός. Πῶς οὖν ἀπρόσφορον ἔσται ἐπὶ τῶν συντεθεισῶν φύσεων καὶ τὸ ἓν τέλειον πληρουσῶν, δυάδα λέγειν, μονάδα δὲ ὑποστάσεως; Οὐ γὰρ συνετέθησαν δύο ἀλλήλαις καὶ ὑποστάσεις, ὡς αἱ φύσεις.

32. Ἔτι πᾶσα μονάς, εἰ πάντη ἐν ταυτῷ λόγῳ λέγεται κατά τινος καθ' ἕν καὶ δυάς, πρὸ τῆς ἐν αὐτῷ κατὰ τὸ αὐτὸ λεγομένης δυάδος, ἔστιν ἥδε. Εἰ δὲ μετὰ τὴν δυάδα λέγοιτο, ἢ οὐκ ἐν ταυτῷ λέγεται λόγῳ, ἢ οὐ μονάς ἐστιν· οὐ γὰρ ἔχει φύσιν ἢ τάξιν ἔν τινι 1789A τῷ αὐτῷ ποτὲ μονὰς μετὰ τὴν δυάδα θεωρεῖσθαι. Πῶς οὖν εἰ τὴν αὐτὴν εἶναί φασι ταῖς ἐξ ὧν ἐστι φύσεσι τὴν μίαν φύσιν, δυὰς πρῶτον γέγονε φύσεων, καὶ τότε μονὰς φύσεως; Μὴ ὑπαρξάσης καὶ[31] γὰρ μονάδος κατά τι, οὐ δυνατὸν τὴν κατὰ τοῦτο αὐτὸ δυάδα φανῆναι, εἴπερ ἐκ μονάδος ἡ δυάς, καὶ οὐκ ἐκ δυάδος ἡ μονάς· Αἱ δὴ[32] οὖν, εἰ προέφθασαν φύσεις δύο εἶναι, οὐδέποτε μία τε, καὶ αἱ αὐταὶ γενήσονται, ἀλλ' ἢ κατ' ἄλλο, ἢ πρὸ αὐτῶν ἔσται ἡ μία.

---

[31] καὶ s. lin. MS　　[32] αἱ δεῖ a. corr. MS

30. If they know the things that come together are one nature on account of their being united in their natures, they must also recognize that these things are two because they differ in their natures. Because of the union there's one person, and because of the difference there are two natures. They aren't going to assume that the very thing that exists in Christ because of the union also exists in Him because of the difference, but rather that something different is implicit in a different definition. Since, then, the difference in things that come together is a difference in the realm of substance, whereas it's the union that's new for the substances, we're right to say there are two substances, distinguishing them by the particular definition of each, that is, by the difference, but to consider that there's one person for them both by virtue of their union. 1788ᴅ

31. Another thing: the sum of every perfect number has to neither exceed, nor fall short, but be even. Two is the first compounding, and the first even number. How, then, could it ever be inappropriate in the case of compounded natures that also make up the one perfect thing to speak of two, but of a unity of hypostasis? (Two hypostases weren't compounded with each other as natures were.)ᵛ

32. Another thing: any unity that's asserted in respect of some separate entity in exactly the same sense as a duality is asserted pre-exists the duality said to be in it in the same respect. If unity is asserted after the duality, either it isn't asserted in the same sense, or else it's not a unity, for no unity ever retains a nature or order to be observed in that same thing after duality. If they say that the 1789ᴀ one nature's the same nature as the [two] natures out of which it is, how did there come to be a duality of natures first, and then a unity of nature? When a unity doesn't exist in something, it's impossible for duality to appear in the very same thing, if duality comes from unity, and not unity from duality. If the existence of two natures came first, these same two natures will never become one. Rather, there'll be one nature in something else, or else it'll pre-exist the two natures.

33. Ἔτι μήν, εἰ καὶ διὰ τὴν ἔνωσιν οὐκέτι δύο τὰς δύο εἰδέναι φασί—τὸν γὰρ χωρισμὸν [271ʳ] αἴτιον τῆς δυάδος εἶναι λέγουσι— πευστέον αὐτῶν, ἀρά γε ἐπὶ τῷ θανάτῳ τοῦ Κυρίου, ἴσασι χωρισμόν τινα τινῶν φύσεων, ἢ οὐχί; Εἰ μὲν οὖν οὐχί, φαντασία τε 1789в ὁ θάνατος, καὶ ψευδὴς ἡ περὶ αὐτοῦ δόξα³³ ἐν τῷ Κυρίῳ—θάνατος γὰρ χωρισμός ἐστι ψυχῆς ἀπὸ σώματος ἀναντιρρήτως—· εἰ δὲ ὄντως χωρισμὸς γέγονε φυσικός, πάντως καὶ κατὰ τούσδε δύο φύσεις τὰ κεχωρισμένα τοῦ³⁴ Χριστοῦ. Ἆρα οὖν εἰ ὁμολογοῦσι τὸν θάνατον τοῦ Κυρίου, καὶ δύο φύσεις αὐτοῦ τινὰς εἶναί ποτε δώσουσι· τοῦτο³⁵ δέ, ἢ τῆς μιᾶς, ἣν φασί, κατακερματισθείσης, ἢ ἑτέρας ἐπιγεννηθείσης³⁶ Χριστῷ φύσεως. Συλλογιστέον δὲ αὐτοὺς ἔτι ἐκ τούτων καὶ ὅτι, ἐπείπερ ἐκ δύο φύσεων τὴν γέννησιν ὁμολογοῦσι Χριστοῦ, ἐκ θεότητός τε καὶ ἀνθρωπότητος ταύτην νοοῦσι· εἰς δύο δὲ φύσεις διαιρεῖσθαι κατὰ τὸν θάνατον δόντες, οὐκ εἰς τοιάσδε, ἀλλ' εἰς ἄψυχον σῶμα καὶ εἰς ἔνθεον ψυχὴν λέξουσι καὶ αὐτοί, 1789c ἀνάγκη πάντως ἑτέρας εἰδέναι τάσδε, τὰς ἐπὶ τῷ χωρισμῷ φανείσας, τῶν πρὸ τῆς ἑνώσεως αὐτοῖς λεγομένων, ἀλλὰ καὶ τὴν μίαν φύσιν κατὰ τούσδε τὴν ἐκ τῶν φύσεων τῆς τε θεότητος καὶ ἀνθρωπότητος οὖσαν, ἑτέραν εἶναι παρὰ τὴν ἐξ ἐνθέου ψυχῆς καὶ ἀψύχου σώματος μίαν φύσιν μετὰ τὴν ἀνάστασιν τοῦ Κυρίου νοουμένην κατ' αὐτούς· ὧν γὰρ διάφορα τὰ ἁπλᾶ μέρη, διάφορα ἔσται καὶ τὰ σύνθετα. Ἔσονται οὖν οἱ δύο φύσεις ἡνωμένας Χριστοῦ μὴ ὁμολογοῦντες σαφῶς, δύο μὲν τὰς πρὸ τῆς κατὰ τὴν σάρκωσιν τοῦ Λόγου, μίαν δὲ τὴν ἐπὶ τῇ ἑνώσει αὐτῶν, καὶ ἑτέρας δύο τὰς ἐπὶ τῷ χωρισμῷ τοῦ θανάτου, καὶ μίαν ἄλλην τὴν ἐπὶ τῇ ἀναστάσει τοῦ Κυρίου καινοτέραν λέγοντες, καὶ ἕξ τε καὶ διαφόρους, καὶ πῆ μὲν ἡνωμένας, πῆ δὲ χωριζομένας φύσεις, καὶ 1789d πάντα σπαραγμὸν Χριστῷ ἐπινοήσαντες, οἱ τῇ ἑνώσει αὐτοῦ συνηγορεῖν προσποιούμενοι.

---

³³ Cf. Heb. 2: 9 and Gal. 6: 14
³⁴ τῶν MS   ³⁵ τοῦτο] ~το supra lin. MS
³⁶ ἐπιγεννηθείσης] ~η¹ - supra lin. MS

33. Furthermore, if they say they no longer know the two to be two on account of the union—for it was division, they say, that caused the duality—the question begs to be asked: do they, or do they not, recognize some division of natures in the Lord's death? If they don't, His death is an illusion, and glorying in the Lord 1789B about it is false, for death is incontrovertibly a division of soul from body. If, on the other hand, a division having to do with nature really took place, the components of Christ that were divided correspond absolutely to these two natures. If, then, they confess the Lord's death, they'll also grant that at that moment there are two specific natures belonging to Him. This was either of the one nature they say was divided into parts, or of another nature produced for Christ afterwards. Another inescapable conclusion for them from all this is that—if indeed they confess Christ's generation out of two natures, and understand this generation to be from divinity and humanity, when they grant that He's divided into two natures in death (but even they say it's into soul-less body and a godly soul, not into natures such as these)— it's absolutely necessary to recognize these natures, which appear 1789C in the division, as different from those spoken of by them before the union, but also that the one nature which is, according to them, out of the natures of divinity and humanity is different from the one nature that, according to them, is understood to be from godly soul and soul-less flesh after the Lord's resurrection. This is so because, when things' separate parts are different, the entities compounded from them will also be different. Those who don't clearly confess Christ's two united natures will find themselves speaking of two natures before the [nature] that exists in the Incarnation of the Word, but of one nature in their union, of another two natures in the division of death, and of another and newer one nature in the resurrection of the Lord, and thus of six different natures [altogether]! They'll find themselves speaking on one side of united natures, and on the other side of divided natures. The inventors of a total dismemberment of Christ, 1789D they'll find themselves pretending to be champions of His union!

34. Πευστέον δὲ αὐτῶν ἔτι καὶ τόδε· "Εἰ τὸν Πατέρα κατ᾽ οὐσίας λόγον διακεκρίσθαι λέγουσι πάσης τῆς ἀνθρωπότητος, εἶτα εἰ καὶ τὸν μίαν φύσιν λεγόμενον αὐτοῖς εἶναι Χριστὸν, κοινωνοῦντα γινώσκουσι τῷ Πατρὶ καὶ ἡνωμένον κατ᾽ οὐσίας λόγον, καθ᾽ ὅνπερ ἡμῶν, ὡς ἔφασαν ἤδη, διακέκριται ὁ Πατήρ." Εἰ γὰρ φάσκοιεν ἡνῶσθαι αὐτὸν τῷ Πατρὶ κατὰ φύσιν, ἡμῶν δηλονότι καὶ αὐτὸς διακέκριται, ἤγουν τῆς ἀνθρωπότητος, οὐκοῦν καὶ τῆς ἰδίας σαρκός, εἰ ἀληθὴς αὕτη σὰρξ καὶ μία τῆς ἀνθρωπότητός ἐστιν.

1792A Ἆρα οὖν ἄσαρκος ὁ Χριστός, διακεκριμένος τῆς σαρκὸς αὐτοῦ, καὶ λέλυται αὐτοῖς ἡ ἕνωσις, καὶ πάντῃ ἡμῖν ἀκοινώνητον τὸ θεῖον ἐν Χριστῷ. Εἰ δὲ τῇ σαρκὶ μὲν ἥνωται ὁ Λόγος κατὰ τὴν [271ᵛ] φύσιν, οὐ κοινωνεῖ δὲ τῷ Πατρὶ τῇ κατὰ φύσιν ἑνώσει, διαιρεῖται ⟨κατὰ⟩ τὴν φύσιν ἐκ τοῦ Πατρός, καὶ ἔσται οὐ Θεός, εἴπερ ὁ Πατήρ ἐστιν ὁ εἷς Θεός, ἢ ὁ Πατὴρ οὐ Θεός, εἰ ὁ Χριστός ἐστιν ὁ εἷς Θεός—πλείους γὰρ διαιρουμένους, οὐ δοξαστέον θεούς—κατὰ θάτερον δὲ τῶν βλασφήμων, τὸ τῆς γεέννης ἂν εἴη κολαστήριον τοῖς αἱρουμένοις τάδε λέγειν ἐπάξιον.

35. Εἰ μὴ καθ᾽ ὃ Χριστός ἐστι κατὰ τοῦτό τις φύσις ἐστί—τοῦτο γὰρ καὶ οἱ πατέρες ἀπείρηκαν—ἢ κατ᾽ οὐδὲν, ἢ καθὸ Θεὸς μόνον, ἢ καθὸ ἄνθρωπος μόνον, ἢ καθὸ τὲ Θεὸς φύσις ἐστί, καὶ καθὸ ἄνθρωπος

1792B πάλιν φύσις ἐστί, ὁ αὐτὸς μὲν εἷς Χριστός, ἀλλ᾽ οὐχ ἡ αὐτὴ φύσις ἐν θεότητι καὶ ἀνθρωπότητι εἶναι νοούμενος. Εἰ δὲ εἴποιεν· "Καθὸ Υἱὸς φύσις ἐστίν, εἷς οὖν Υἱὸς καὶ μία φύσις", ἄρα οὖν φαμὲν καὶ ὁ Πατὴρ φύσις ἐστίν· εἰ οὖν μὴ ταυτὸν Πατὴρ Υἱῷ ἀριθμῷ ἢ λόγῳ, οὐδὲ ταυτὸν τῇ φύσει ὁ Πατὴρ τῷ Υἱῷ, οὔτε ἀριθμῷ οὔτε λόγῳ φυσικῷ, ὡς Ἄρειος βούλεται. Εἰ δὲ πάλιν εἴποιεν, καθ᾽ ὃ πρόσωπον καὶ φύσις ἐστί, τὰ αὐτὰ πάλιν ὑπαντήσεται αὐτοῖς· ἄρα γὰρ ἐπεὶ ἕτερον πρόσωπον τοῦ Πατρὸς καὶ τοῦ ἁγίου Πνεύματος, καὶ ἑτέρα φύσις· ἀλλ᾽ ἐπεὶ καὶ διάφορον πρόσωπον Πέτρου πρὸς Παῦλον, καὶ διάφορος ἡ φύσις, ἅ ἐστι προφανῆ ἄτοπα.

34. This further challenge is in order: 'If they say the Father is distinguished from all humanity on the basis of substance, and if they further say Christ is the one nature they talk about, then they're recognizing that He shares in the reality of—is united to— the Father on the basis of substance, but it's on just that basis, as they've already stated, that the Father's distinguished from us.' If they say He's united to the Father by nature, it's clear He's also divided from us, that is, from humanity, and therefore also from His own flesh, if this is true flesh, and humanity's flesh is one. This means that Christ is without flesh, since He's distinguished from His flesh, that the union's been dissolved by them, and that what's divine in Christ has no fellowship with us whatsoever. If, on the other hand, the Word's been united with flesh by nature, He has no part in union with the Father by nature, He's distinguished by nature from the Father, and He won't be God, if indeed the Father is the one God. Either that, or it's the Father who isn't God, if Christ is the one God—for one mustn't think of many different gods. As for the alternative blasphemy, hell would be the appropriate punishment for those who choose to say such things.

1792A

35. If He isn't a particular nature in exactly the same respect in which He's Christ—for that's something the fathers have forbidden[vi]—the same is understood to be one Christ either in no respect, or in so far as He's God alone, or in so far as He's man alone, or in so far as God's a nature and again in so far as a man's a nature, but He's not understood to be one nature in divinity and humanity! If, on the other hand, they say 'He's a nature in so far as He's Son; therefore there's one Son and one nature', we reply that, by the same token, the Father's a nature too. If, then, the Father's not the same as the Son by number or by definition, the Father isn't the same as the Son by nature, number, or natural definition—just as Arius would have it. If, again, they say there's a nature in so far as there's a person, the same objections are going to be raised against them, for the result is that, since He's a different person from the Father and the Holy Spirit, He's also a different nature from them. But then, since Peter is also a different person from Paul, his nature's different—all of which is manifestly absurd.

1792B

36. Εἰ μία σύνθετος φύσις τοῦ Χριστοῦ, μία δὲ ἁπλῆ φύσις τοῦ Πατρός, πῶς τῷ Πατρὶ ὁ Υἱὸς ὁμοούσιος; οὐ γὰρ ταυτὸν τῷ ἁπλῷ τὸ σύνθετον. Ἢ οὖν οὐ μίαν τοῦ Χριστοῦ, ἢ οὐχ᾽ ὁμοούσιον τῷ Πατρὶ τὴν φύσιν δοξάζουσι. Εἰ δὲ ἐκ μέρους αὐτὴν ὁμοούσιον λέγουσι τῷ Πατρί, ἴστωσαν ὅτι, ὡς προείρηται, οὐκ ἐκ μέρους τις φύσις ἤγουν οὐσία λέγεται τινὶ ὁμοούσιος· οὕτως γὰρ ἂν καὶ ὁ ἄνθρωπος τῷ τε λίθῳ καὶ κυνὶ καὶ ἀγγέλῳ ὁμοούσιος λέγοιτο.

37. Ἡ μία φύσις τοῦ Θεοῦ Λόγου σεσαρκωμένη διαφέρει τῆς μιᾶς τοῦ Θεοῦ Πατρὸς φύσεως τῆς μὴ σεσαρκωμένης, ἢ οὐχί; Ἀνακρινέσθωσαν. Εἰ μὲν οὖν φασὶ διαφέρειν, οὐχ᾽ ὁμοούσιος ἀληθῶς ἔσται τῷ Πατρὶ ὁ Υἱὸς διαφέρων αὐτοῦ κατὰ φύσιν· οὐκ ἐκ μέρους γάρ ἐστιν εἰπεῖν αὐτῶν τὸ ὁμοούσιον· πάντα γὰρ τὰ κυρίως ὁμοούσια, ἐκ τοῦ ὅλου αὐτῶν ὁρῶμεν ἀλλήλοις ὁμοούσια. Εἰ δὲ μὴ διαφέρειν ἐροῦσιν, ἄρα καὶ ἡ τοῦ Θεοῦ Πατρὸς μία φύσις σεσαρκωμένη, ὁμοίως δὲ καὶ τοῦ ἁγίου Πνεύματος.

38. Ἔτι ἐπεὶ ἤ τε ἐξ ὑποστάσεων σύνθετος ὑπόστασις, στρατοῦ τυχὸν ἢ οἴκου, ἤ τε ἐκ φύσεων σύνθετος φύσις, τό τε ἐκ σωμάτων σύνθετον σῶμα, καὶ πᾶν ἁπλῶς τὸ ἔκ τινων συγκείμενον, εἰ καὶ ὁμοίως αὐτοῖς λέγοιτο ὑπόστασις, [272ʳ] ἢ φύσις, ἢ σῶμα, ἀλλ᾽ ἢ χεῖρον ἢ κρεῖττον τῶν ἑαυτοῦ μερῶν ὁρᾶται καὶ λέγεται. Εἰ καὶ ὁ Λόγος φύσις, καὶ ὁ Χριστὸς φύσις συγκρίνεσθαι πρὸς τὸν Λόγον δυναμένη ἐστίν, ἤγουν ὡς ὅλον πρὸς τὸ ἴδιον μέρος, τί ἄρα φησί, χείρων ἢ κρείττων ἐστὶ τοῦ Λόγου ὁ Χριστός;

36. If there's one compound nature of Christ, but one simple nature of the Father, how can the Son be consubstantial with the Father? What's compound isn't the same as what's simple. That means they suppose either that there isn't one nature of Christ, or that it's not consubstantial with the Father. If, on the other hand, 1792C they say that it's partly consubstantial with the Father, they have to realize that, as was said before, no nature, that is, substance, is said to be partly consubstantial with anything, for in that way man could be said to be consubstantial with stones, dogs, and angels!

37. Does the 'one incarnate nature of God the Word' differ from the one non-incarnate nature of God the Father, or not? They have to give us an answer! If they say it does differ from it, the Son won't truly be consubstantial with the Father in that He differs from Him by nature. It isn't possible to speak of their being partly consubstantial, for we observe all properly consubstantial things to be consubstantial with each other in their entirety. If, on the other hand, they say that it doesn't differ from it, then God the 1792D Father's one nature is incarnate too, and so is the Holy Spirit's.

38. Moreover, since the hypostasis that's compounded out of hypostases (the hypostasis of an army, say, or of a house), the nature compounded out of natures, the body compounded out of bodies, and quite simply anything compounded out of any set of things, even if it's called a hypostasis or a nature or a body in the same way as they are, is still observed and said to be either inferior or superior to its own parts. If the Word too is a nature, and Christ is a nature capable of being compared with the Word, that is, as a whole compared with one of its parts, what then does my opponent say? Is Christ inferior or superior to the Word?

39. Ὁ ἀπόστολος φησί· <u>Κατὰ τὴν ἐνέργειαν τοῦ κράτους τῆς</u>
1793A <u>ἰσχύος τοῦ Θεοῦ ἣν ἐνήργησεν ἐν τῷ Χριστῷ ἐγείρας αὐτὸν ἐκ</u>
<u>νεκρῶν.</u>[37] Αὕτη γὰρ ἡ ἐνεργοῦσα ἰσχύς, φύσις ἦν, ἢ οὐχί; Καὶ ἡ
ἐγειρομένη ἐκ νεκρῶν, φύσις ἐστὶν, ἢ οὐχί; Εἰ δὲ ἄμφω μία ἦν φύσις
αὐτὴ ἡ ἐνεργοῦσα καὶ τὸ ἐνεργούμενον τὴν ἀνάστασιν, τίς ἡ
ἐνεργουμένη καὶ τίς ἡ ἐνεργοῦσα καὶ ἐγείρουσα αὐτὴν φύσις; Οὐ
γὰρ ἑαυτὸν λοιπὸν ἀνεστηκέναι Χριστὸς μία ὢν φύσις δειχθήσεται.
Εἴπερ οὖν εὐσεβῶς τὴν ἀνάστασιν αὐτοῦ δοξάζομεν, ἐξ ἑτέρας
αὐτοῦ φύσεως τὴν ἑτέραν ἑαυτοῦ φύσιν ἀνιστᾶν αὐτὴν Χριστὸν
ὁμολογήσομεν, ὥσπερ ἐν ὕπνοις καὶ ψυχὴ σῶμα ἐξεγείρει· τῆς γὰρ
κλίνης αὐτὸ διανίστησι πολλάκις δι' ἐνθυμήσεως. Οὕτω καὶ
γέγραπται· Ἐγὼ ἐκοιμήθην καὶ ὕπνωσα, ἐξηγέρθην ὅτι Κύριος,
δηλονότι ὁ ἐν ἐμοί, φησὶν <u>ἀντελήψατό μου.</u>[38] Καὶ τό· <u>Σκύμνος</u>
<u>λέοντος ἐκ βλαστοῦ Ἰούδα ἐκοιμήθη· τίς ἐξεγείρῃ αὐτόν;</u>[39] οὐχ'
1793B ἕτερος φησίν, ἀλλ' αὐτὸς ἑαυτόν· ἐξουσίαν γὰρ εἶχε καὶ παραθεῖναι
καὶ ἀπολήψεσθαι τὴν ψυχὴν ἑαυτοῦ.[40]

---

[37] Eph. 1: 19–20   [38] Ps. 3: 6   [39] Gen. 49: 9
[40] Cf. John 10: 18

39. The Apostle says: *By the working of the might of God's power which He worked in Christ He raised Him from the dead.* Was this power 1793A that worked a nature, or not? And is what was raised from the dead a nature, or not? If both—the one that worked the resurrection, and the one that was worked upon—were one nature, then what was the nature that was worked upon, and what was the nature that did the work and raised it? A Christ who is one nature will never be shown to have raised Himself! If, then, we think in a pious way about His resurrection, we'll confess that it's out of one of His own natures that Christ raised the other, just as happens in cases of sleep when a soul wakes a body up, for it often rouses it from bed when it feels anxious, as is written: *I went to bed and, while I slept, I was wakened because the Lord*—it's clear He's talking about 'the Lord in me'—*helped me.* There's also the text: *A lion's cub from Judah's stem fell asleep; who would rouse him?* He's saying it's not some- one else, but He Himself who'll rouse Himself, for He had the 1793B power both to lay down and to take up His own soul.

40. Ἵνα δὲ μὴ λεξιδρίοις ὑποδύναντες ἑαυτοὺς συσκιάζωμεν κατ᾽ αὐτούς, γυμνῶς ἐρωτήσωμεν αὐτούς, εἰ τὴν μίαν φύσιν ταύτην τὴν ἐκ δύο φύσεων ἄναρχον γινώσκουσιν ἢ ἀρξαμένην κατὰ χρόνον. Εἰ μὲν γὰρ ἄναρχον, πῶς ἔκ τινων, καὶ ὑστερογενῆ αὐτῶν καὶ σύνθετον; Εἰ δὲ ἦρκται καὶ αἰτίαν ἔσχε καὶ σύγκειται, πῶς Θεός; "Ἀλλ᾽ ἡμεῖς", φασί, "τὴν αὐτὴν ἄναρχον καὶ ἀρξαμένην ὡς οἱ πατέρες λέγομεν." Ἀλλ᾽ οὐ τὴν αὐτὴν ἐν ταυτῷ κατὰ τὸ αὐτό, εἰ καὶ τοῦ αὐτοῦ, οἱ πατέρες φασίν, ὦ οὗτοι· οὐδὲ γὰρ δυνατὸν ἐν ταυτῷ κατὰ τὸ αὐτὸ τῶν ἐναντίων εἶναί τι δεκτικὸν λόγων, ἀλλ᾽ εἰ καὶ λέγεται ὁρατὸς καὶ ἀόρατος ὁ αὐτὸς εἷς ὢν Χριστός, οὐ κατὰ τὸ αὐτό, ὡς οὐδὲ τὸ Θανατωθεὶς μὲν σαρκί· ζωοποιηθεὶς δὲ Πνεύματι,[41] καὶ τὸ Εἰ γὰρ καὶ ἀπέθανεν ἐξ ἀσθενείας, ἀλλὰ ζῇ ἐκ δυνάμεως,[42] καὶ τὰ τοιάδε. Οὐκ ἐν ταυτῷ γάρ ποτε, οὐδὲ τὸ Ἐν ἀρχῇ ἦν ὁ Λόγος, καὶ ὁ Λόγος σὰρξ ἐγένετο, νοητέον· τῷ μὲν γὰρ Λόγῳ μηδὲ καθ᾽ οἱανοῦν ἀρχὴν γεγονέναι μαρτυρῶν, ἀλλ᾽ ἀνάρχως εἶναι, τὴν σάρκα γενέσθαι φησί. Ἀλλ᾽ ἀπειθῶς ἔχοντες δοκοῦσι πιστῶς [272ᵛ] ἀπιστεῖν τῷ Λόγῳ διὰ τῆς ἀλογίας· "Οἶδε γὰρ" φασιν "ὅπως ταῦτα γενήσεται αὐτῷ, κἂν ἡμῖν ἀδύνατα δοκῇ." Ἀλλ᾽ οὐδὲν τοιοῦτον ἄλογον ἢ ἀσύστατον ἔφη περὶ ἑαυτοῦ πώποτε ὁ Λόγος, ὦ ἀδελφοί· τί οὖν δεῖ ἡμᾶς[43] συκοφαντεῖν τὸν Χριστὸν ἵνα τὸ ἴδιον συστήσωμεν κατὰ σκοπὸν ἔχον ἡμῖν ἀγνόημα;

41. Ἔτι ἡ φύσις ἡ θεία πάντη ἁπλῆ. Ἡ οὖν φύσις, ἥν φατὲ μίαν εἶναι τοῦ Χριστοῦ, σύνθετός ἐστιν, ἢ ἁπλῆ; Εἰ μὲν οὖν ἁπλῆ, πῶς σύνθετος ὁ Χριστός; εἰ δὲ σύνθετος ἡ φύσις αὐτοῦ, πῶς θεία; Οὐκοῦν ἀληθῶς μία μὲν σύνθετος ταῖς φύσεσιν ἡ ὑπόστασις, δύο δὲ αἱ φύσεις τοῦ Δεσπότου ἡμῶν Χριστοῦ τοῦ ἀληθινοῦ Θεοῦ.

---

[41] 1 Pet. 3: 18   [42] 2 Cor. 13: 4   [43] ὑμᾶς

40. Lest we should throw ourselves into obscurity, as they see it, by entering into suspect passages, we'd like to ask them openly whether they recognize this one nature—the nature out of two natures—to be without beginning, or to have had a beginning in time? If it's without beginning, how can it be out of anything, and how can it be later in origin than they, and compounded? If it had a beginning, had a cause, and is compounded, how can it be God? 'But we', they say, 'speak of the same [nature] both as being without a beginning and as having had a beginning, as do the fathers.' On the contrary, my friends, the fathers don't speak of the same nature in the same way and in the same respect, even if it belongs to the same thing, for it's impossible for anything to be patient of opposite definitions in the same way and in the same respect. Rather, if the same Christ, being one, is said to be both visible and invisible, it's not in the same respect that He is so. That's true in the texts *put to death in the flesh, but made alive in the* 1793c *Spirit*, and *He was slain in weakness, but He lives in power*, and others of the kind. Nor is one ever to understand *In the beginning was the Word*, and *the Word became flesh*, in the same sense, for [John] says the flesh came into being, while witnessing as to the Word that He didn't come to be by any kind of beginning, but exists without any beginning. Those who understand in a way beyond credulity, however, seem to be faithfully faithless towards the Word on account of their lack of reason: 'He knows', they say, 'how these things will come to pass for Him, even though to us they may seem impossible.' My brothers, the Word never yet said anything so irrational and incoherent as this about Himself! Why then should we misrepresent Christ just so as to establish our own ignorance in the service of some goal of our own?

41. Furthermore, the divine nature's entirely simple. Is Christ's 1793D nature, then, which you say is one, compound or simple? If it's simple, how is Christ compound? If His nature's compound, how's it divine? Truly, therefore, there's one compound hypostasis for the natures, but there are two natures of our master Christ, the true God.

42. Εἰ μίαν φύσιν τοῦ Θεοῦ Λόγου σεσαρκωμένου καὶ οὐ "σεσαρκωμένην" εἴποιτε, πῶς οὐ φανερῶς τὴν πατρικὴν διδασκαλίαν παραχαράξετε; Εἰ δὲ σεσαρκωμένην ὁμολογεῖτε, καὶ οὐ σεσαρκωμένου τοῦ Λόγου μίαν φατέ, διὰ τόδε αὐτὸ δύο φύσεις ἔσται ὁ ἐκ Λόγου καὶ σαρκὸς Χριστός· διότι γὰρ μία φύσις τοῦ Θεοῦ Λόγου[44] ἐντελὴς ἥδε προωμολόγηται καὶ ἄνευ σαρκός, οὐδὲν δείξει καινότερον ἡ ἕνωσις εἰς φύσιν, ἐὰν μία μεμένηκεν. Πυθώμεθα[45] γὰρ ὑμῶν· "Ἆρά γε φύσει σαρκὸς τὴν φύσιν τοῦ Λόγου σεσαρκωμένην ὁμολογεῖτε, ἢ οὐχί"; Εἰ μὲν οὖν οὐχί, ἢ λόγῳ μόνον, ἢ φαντασίᾳ, ἢ τροπῇ τοῦ λόγου, τὴν σάρκωσιν εἰδέναι ὑμᾶς ἀπολείπεται. Εἰ δὲ φύσει σαρκὸς τὴν φύσιν σεσαρκῶσθαι τοῦ Λόγου φατέ, ἄλλην τὴν σαρκοῦσαν καὶ ἄλλην τὴν σαρκουμένην ἐν τῷ ἑνὶ συνθέτῳ προσώπῳ Χριστοῦ γινώσκοντες, πῶς ἀριθμεῖν ἄνευ δυάδος ταύτας δυνήσεσθε;

43. Ἡ μία φύσις τοῦ Θεοῦ Λόγου σεσαρκωμένη, ἢ ταυτόν ἐστι τῇ μιᾷ, καὶ περιττῶς πρόσκειται τὸ "σεσαρκωμένη", εἰς παράστασιν ποσοῦ οὐ συντεῖνον ὅλως, περὶ οὗ νῦν ἡ ζήτησις· ἢ ταῖς δύο φύσεσι ταυτὸν συνάγει, καὶ μάτην ἡμῖν ἀντιφέρονται· ἢ οὔτε μία πάντῃ ἐστίν, οὔτε δύο, καὶ ἀνάγκη μίαν σὺν ἐπιμερισμῷ λέγειν αὐτοὺς ἔσχατα νηπιάζοντας.

44. Ἐκρειττώθη τί τῶν τοῦ Κυρίου, φυσικὴν κρείττωσιν λαβὸν μετὰ τὴν ἁγίαν αὐτοῦ ἀνάστασιν, καθὰ Κύριλλός τε ὁ πατὴρ φησὶ πρὸς Ἀκάκιον καὶ οἱ λοιποὶ πατέρες, ἢ ὁμοίως ἔχουσα πᾶσα αὐτοῦ ἡ φύσις, ἣν φασὶ μίαν, μεμένηκεν; Εἰ μὲν οὖν οὐκ ἐκρειττώθη, ἢ καὶ νῦν παθητή, ἢ οὐδὲ πρὸ τῆς ἀναστάσεως ἦν παθητή, ψευδεῖς τε οἱ λέγοντες τὴν κρείττωσιν τῆς ἀνθρωπότητος αὐτοῦ πάντες οἱ διδάσκαλοι. Εἰ δὲ ἐκρειττώθη τελεία τίς φύσις ἐν αὐτῷ, ἢ ὅλη [273ʳ] ἢ μία αὕτη ἐστὶν ἥν φασι, καὶ ἔσται καὶ ἡ θεότης αὐτοῦ εἰς προκοπὴν ἀπαθείας ἀχθεῖσα, ἢ μέρος αὐτοῦ μόνον. Εἰ δὲ τὸ μέρος αὐτοῦ τὸ προκόψαν τελεία φύσις ἐστί, καὶ τὸ προκοπὴν οὐκ ἐπιδεξάμενον, ἢ μίαν εἶναι τελείαν φύσιν, ἢ μόριον λέγειν ἀναγκασθήσονται, καὶ ἢ βλασφημεῖν ἢ εὐσεβεῖν καὶ ἄκοντες συγκλιθήσονται.[46]

---

[44] post Λόγου spatium MS   [45] πυθόμεθα
[46] συγκλιθήσεται

42. If you speak of 'one nature of the Word of God incarnate', and not of 'one incarnate nature of God the Word', won't you plainly be falsifying the fathers' teaching? If you confess one incarnate nature, and don't speak of one nature of the incarnate   1796A
Word, the Christ who is out of Word and flesh will be two natures for that very reason. Because this one nature of the Word of God was already confessed to be complete even without flesh, the union in a nature will reveal nothing new if it's remained one. We'd like to find something out from you: Do you confess that the Word's nature has been made incarnate by a nature of flesh, or not? If not, you're left to perceive the Incarnation by reflection alone, or by imagination, or by a change in vocabulary. If, on the other hand, you say the nature of the Word was made incarnate by a nature of flesh, then, since you know in the one compound person of Christ one nature that makes incarnate, and another that is made incarnate, how are you going to be able to count these natures without duality?

43. The one incarnate nature of God the Word is either the same thing as the one, and in that case the word 'incarnate' is   1796B
added superfluously, since it bears not at all on the signification of quantity, which is what the present inquiry is about; or it introduces the same thing as the two natures, and our opponents are fighting against us for no reason; or it's not entirely either one or two, and they're forced to speak of one nature with a division, behaving like children in the face of ultimate things.

44. Was anything belonging to the Lord made better by receiving a natural improvement after His holy resurrection—as the father Cyril says to Acacius, and as the rest of the fathers say—or did His whole nature, which they say is one, stay the same?[vii] If it wasn't improved, either it's still subject to passion, or it wasn't subject to passion before the resurrection either, and all the teachers who speak of His humanity's improvement are liars. If,   1796C
on the other hand, some complete nature in Him was improved, this nature they talk of is whole or one, and His divinity will take the lead in progress towards freedom from passion, or else just a part of Him will. If, however, the part of Him that made progress is a complete nature, they'll be forced to say that the part that doesn't admit of progress is either one complete nature too, or a portion of one—and they'll be inclined, even against their will, either to blaspheme or to be pious.

45. Εἰ ὁμοίως τῷ ἀνθρώπῳ μίαν τὴν φύσιν ἐπὶ τοῦ Δεσπότου φασίν, ὁμοίως τῷ ἀνθρώπῳ καὶ τὸ ἐκ δύο φύσεων ἐπὶ τοῦ αὐτοῦ εἶναι λέγουσιν. Ἀλλ' ὁ ἄνθρωπος οὐκ ἐκ προϋπαρχούσης ψυχῆς τε καὶ σώματος δέδοται· ἐπινοίᾳ γὰρ μόνῃ τοῦ οἰκείου ὅλου

1796D προτιθέντες τὰ ἴδια μέρη,⁴⁷ τὸ ἐκ δύο ἐπὶ τοῦδε φαμέν, ἐπὶ δὲ τοῦ Κυρίου οὐκ ἐπινοίᾳ προϋπάρχειν τὸν Λόγον τῆς ἰδίας συνθέσεως φαμὲν ὁμοίως τῷ ἀνθρώπῳ. Εἰ δὲ οὐχ ὁμοίως τὸ ἐκ δύο ἐπὶ τοῦ Κυρίου καὶ ἀνθρώπου ψιλοῦ, οὐδὲ τῇ μιᾷ τοῦ ἀνθρώπου φύσει ὁμοίως ἐνοῦμεν τὸν Κύριον· τὰ γὰρ ἐξ ἀνομοίων τε καὶ ἀνομοίως συγκείμενα, ἀνόμοια γραμμικαῖς ἀνάγκαις. Οὐκ ἄρα οἰκεῖον αὐτοῖς πάντῃ τὸ παράδειγμα, εἰ καὶ ὄντως μία ἐλέγετο καὶ μόνως ἀεὶ μία ἐδείκνυτο ἡ τοῦ ἀνθρώπου φύσις.

46. Εἰ ἡ φύσει παθητὴ σάρξ τοῦ Λόγου οὐκ ὤφθη ἀπαθὴς διὰ τὴν πρὸς αὐτὸν ἕνωσιν, πόσῳ γε μᾶλλον ὁ φύσει ἀπαθὴς Λόγος, αὐτὸς οὐ γέγονε παθητός, διὰ τὴν πρὸς τὸ παθητὸν ἕνωσιν. Τί οὖν

1797A πυνθάνεσθε ἡμῶν ὡς ἀμφιβαλλομένου ὄντος ποία φύσις προσήλωτο, εἰ μὴ θεοπάθειαν φυσικὴν καὶ οὐ τὴν κατ' οἰκείωσιν λέγετε;

47. Εἰ ἔστιν ὁ Λόγος φύσει ἀπαθής, κατὰ δὲ τὸ εἰωθὸς λέγεσθαι αὐτοῖς ἔπαθεν αὐτὸς ὡς οἶδε, οἶδεν ἑαυτὸν οὐκ ἀπαθῆ πάντῃ, εἰ μὴ ἀγνοεῖ ἑαυτὸν παθητὸν ὄντα.

48. Εἰ ὥσπερ τὴν ψυχὴν καὶ τὸ σῶμα μέρη ὅλου τοῦ ἀνθρώπου ὡς φυσικοῦ εἴδους φαμέν, οὕτω καὶ τὸν Λόγον καὶ τὴν σάρκα μέρη Χριστοῦ, οὐχ ὡς συνθέτου τινὸς μόνον, ἀλλ' ὡς φυσικοῦ εἴδους λέγομεν, εἰπὲ "Τί τὸ⁴⁸ ὅλον τοῦτο εἶδος;"

---

⁴⁷ In marg. ση(μείωσαι)   ⁴⁸ τὸ] iteravit MS

45. If they say that, in the case of the Master, His nature's one in the same way as man's is, they're by the same token saying that His being out of two natures is the same as man's is. Man isn't admitted to be out of a pre-existing soul and body, for we speak of 'out of two' in his case by positing in thought alone the individual 1796D parts of the common whole. In the Lord's case, however, we don't speak of the Word's pre-existing in thought His own compounding, as we do in a man's case. If the expression 'out of two' doesn't obtain in the same way in the Lord's case as in the case of a mere man, however, neither do we unite the Lord in the same way as we do the one nature of man, for things that are put together out of dissimilar things and in dissimilar ways are, by the rules of geometry, dissimilar. The paradigm doesn't, therefore, apply across the board to both of these, even though man's nature really was said to be one, and was always shown to be only one.

46. If the Word's flesh, by nature subject to passion, wasn't seen to be impassible as a result of union with Him, so much the more has the Word, by nature impassible, Himself not become passible as a result of His union with the passible. Why, then, do you ask 1797A us, as though it were a matter of doubt, what kind of nature was nailed [to the Cross]?—unless you're speaking of a natural divine suffering, and not the suffering that's by appropriation?

47. If the Word is by nature impassible, but—as they're in the habit of saying—He suffered in a manner known to Himself, He knows Himself to be not entirely impassible, unless He's ignorant of the fact that He's subject to passion.

48. If we call the Word and the flesh parts of Christ, just as we call soul and body parts of the whole man as of a natural form, that is, not just as belonging to a particular compounded entity, but as belonging to a natural form, then tell us: what is this whole form?

49. *Τῷ ἑνὶ πάθει τῆς μιᾶς σαρκός, πῶς τὸ μὲν τοῦ ἀνθρώπου*
1797B *πάσχει, τὸ δὲ συμπάσχει τῇ αὐτοῦ σαρκί, καὶ οὐκ ἐν⁴⁹ ἑαυτῷ; Καὶ ὁ*
συμπάσχων γὰρ ἐν ἑαυτῷ πάσχει. Πῶς καὶ οὐκ ἐν τῷ πάσχοντι, εἰ
καὶ ⟨μὴ⟩ δι᾽ ἑαυτοῦ, ὥσπερ καὶ ὁ πάσχων ἐν ἑαυτῷ πάσχει, καὶ οὐκ
ἐν τῷ συμπάσχοντι;

50. *Τοῦ Κυρίου ἡμῶν Ἰησοῦ Χριστοῦ δύο αἱ φύσεις, εἷς δὲ ὁ*
θάνατος. Οὗτος οὖν εἰ μὲν κατὰ φύσιν αὐτῷ μόνον ἐστί, τῆς θνητῆς
αὐτοῦ φύσεως μόνης, εἰ δὲ καὶ παρὰ φύσιν, καὶ τῆς ἀθανάτου. Πῶς
οὖν εἴποιτε κατὰ φύσιν ἢ παρὰ φύσιν [273ᵛ] *παθεῖν τὸν Λόγον*
εὐδοκεῖν;

51. *Εἰ πάντως ἰσαρίθμους εἶναι δέον τὰς ὑποστάσεις ταῖς φύσεσιν,*
ὡς φασίν, ἐπεὶ μίαν φαμὲν τῆς ἁγίας Τριάδος τὴν φύσιν, μίαν
λεγέτωσαν καὶ τὴν ὑπόστασιν· ἢ ἐπεὶ τρεῖς φαμὲν τὰς ὑποστάσεις,
τρεῖς λεγέτωσαν καὶ τὰς φύσεις· πολλῷ γὰρ μᾶλλον οὐκ ἔστιν
1797C *ὑπόστασις ἀνούσιος, ἤπερ οὐσία ἀνυπόστατος.*

52. *Εἰ ἡ ἕνωσις καὶ τὰ ἡνωμένα τῶν πρός τι ἔστι πᾶσιν*
ὡμολογημένως, πῶς μετὰ τὴν ἕνωσιν οὐκ εἶναι δύο τάδε, ἃ καὶ
ἡνωμένα εἶναι ὀνομάζουσιν ἀληθῶς, οἴονται οἶδε; Τῆς γὰρ ἑνώσεως
μὴ παυθείσης, ἀνάγκη καὶ τὰ ἡνωμένα συνεισάγεσθαι. Ἔτι μὴν εἰ
μὴ πρὸ τῆς ἑνώσεως δύο ἦν τάδε αὐτὰ τὰ κατὰ Χριστὸν ἡνωμένα
κυρίως—οὐ γὰρ δή, ὡς Νεστόριος βούλεται, καὶ προϋπῆρξε τὸ
ἀνθρώπινον τοῦ Κυρίου, εἶτα ἑνοῦται—μήτε μετὰ τὴν ἕνωσιν
ὁρᾶται δύο—οὐ γάρ ἐστι λῆξις τῆσδε τῆς ἀπεράντου ἑνώσεως—ἢ
οὐδέποτε, ἢ ἐν τῇ ἑνώσει ἐστὶ δύο τὰ ἡνωμένα ἐν Χριστῷ
ἀσυγχύτως.

---

⁴⁹ οὐκ ἐν] οὐχ ἐν

49. How is it that, for the one suffering of the one flesh, one of man's [components] suffers, but the other co-suffers with its flesh and not in itself? Even the one who co-suffers suffers in himself. How can it be that he doesn't also suffer in the one that suffers, even though he doesn't suffer on his own account, as does the one who suffers in himself and not in the co-suffering one? 1797ʙ

50. Our Lord Jesus Christ's natures are two, but His death is one. If, then, this death exists for Him only by nature, it belongs to His mortal nature alone, but if it exists in a way beyond nature, then it belongs to His immortal nature as well. In what way do you say the Word agrees to suffer: by nature, or in a way beyond nature?

51. If it's necessary, as they say, for there to be exactly the same number of hypostases as there are natures, then they have to say there's one hypostasis of the Holy Trinity, since we say the Trinity's nature is one, or that there are three natures, since we say there are three hypostases—for it's far more the case that there's no hypostasis without a substance, than that there's no substance without an hypostasis.ᵛⁱⁱⁱ 1797ᴄ

52. If 'union' and 'things united' belong—as everyone agrees—to the class of things in relation, how can these people suppose that these things, which they correctly specify as also being united, aren't two after the union? Since the union hasn't been brought to an end, it must be that the things united are still held together. Furthermore, if these same things actually united in Christ weren't two before the union (for certainly the Lord's human reality wasn't also in existence before, and then became united, as Nestorius would have it, neither are two entities observed after the union, for there's no end to this endless union), either they never were two, or the things unconfusedly united in Christ are two in the union.

1797D **53.** Ἐκ δύο φύσεων, ἢ κοινῶν ἢ ἰδικῶν, φασὶ τὸν Κύριον ἡμῶν Ἰησοῦν Χριστόν. Εἰ μὲν οὖν κοινῶν, καὶ πᾶσα ἡ ἁγία Τριὰς ἐσαρκώθη καὶ ἐσταυρώθη, καὶ πᾶσα ἡ ἀνθρωπότης ἐν αὐτῷ. Εἰ δὲ ἐξ ἰδικῶν, ἢ δυνάμει, ἢ ἐνεργείᾳ εἶναι προεπινοουμένων αὐτοῖς πρὸ Χριστοῦ. Εἰ μὲν οὖν δυνάμει μόνον, ἢ μετὰ τὴν ἕνωσιν εὐθὺς γέγοναν αὐτῷ καὶ ἐνεργείᾳ δύο φύσεις, ἢ οὔπω μέν, ἔσονται δὲ ποτέ, ἢ οὐδέποτε γίνονται ἐνεργείᾳ, καὶ νοοῖντ᾽ ἂν οὑτωσὶ ἀεί τε ἀτελεῖς καὶ μάτην ἔχουσαι τοῦτο δυνάμει, εἰς ὃ οὔποτε ἥξουσιν ἐνεργείᾳ. Εἰ δὲ ἐνεργείᾳ οὔσας καὶ πρὸ τῆς κατὰ τὴν οἰκονομίαν ἑνώσεως ἴσασι τάσδε ἰδικάς τε καὶ διεστώσας καὶ ὑφεστώσας τὰς δύο, ἐν τίνι πρὸς Νεστόριον διαφωνοῦσι, λεγέτωσαν

1800A **54.** Εἰ τὸ ὅλον τοῦ συνθέτου Χριστοῦ Θεὸν καὶ ἄνθρωπον. ὁμολογεῖς, ἰδοὺ τὴν ὁλότητα τῇ τῶν ἀποτελεστικῶν αὐτῆς μερῶν ἐπωνυμίᾳ προσαγορεύεις. Πῶς οὖν τὴν δυάδα τῶν φύσεων ἡνωμένην οὐ λέγεις εἶναι Χριστόν, αἵ εἰσι Θεὸς καὶ ἄνθρωπος, καὶ μέρη τῆς ὅλης ὑποστάσεως Χριστοῦ;

55. Εἰ μὴ δύο φύσεις Θεοῦ καὶ ἀνθρώπου ἀλλὰ μία τίς ἰδίως Χριστοῦ ἐστὶ φύσις, ἆρά γε ὄντως καθ᾽ ὑμᾶς, Χριστοτόκος ἡ ἁγία παρθένος, καὶ οὐ Θεοτόκος λέγοιτο, φύσιν [274] ἑτέραν παρὰ τὴν ἁπλῶς θείαν καὶ ἀνθρωπείαν τεκοῦσα.

53. They say our Lord Jesus Christ is out of two natures, either universal or particular. If He's out of universal natures, then the whole of the Holy Trinity was incarnated and crucified too, and the whole of humanity is in Him. If, on the other hand, He's out of particular natures, He's out of particular natures conceived by them as pre-existing Christ either in potentiality or in actuality. If they're conceived as pre-existing Him only in potentiality, either there suddenly came to be two natures for Him in actuality as well after the union or, though they don't yet exist, they will exist sometime; or they never come to exist in actuality, and they might be considered, perhaps, as being thus for ever incomplete, and as vainly having in potentiality what they'll never achieve in actuality. If, on the other hand, they know these particular two natures as also being actually distinct and subsistent before the union that came to be in the Incarnation, they're going to have to tell us in what way they differ from Nestorius!

54. If you confess that the whole of the compound Christ is God and man, notice that you're calling the whole by the name of its constituent parts. How, then, can you not say that Christ is the duality of united natures, which are God and man, and parts of Christ's whole hypostasis?

55. If there aren't two natures of God and man, but rather one particular nature that's specifically Christ's, it follows that, in your view, the Holy Virgin really would be said to be 'Christ-bearer', and not 'God-bearer', since she's the bearer of a different nature from the divine and human natures in themselves.

56. Ἔτι ἐρωτητέον αὐτοὺς λέγοντας τὴν διαφορὰν καὶ οὐκ ἀριθμοῦντας τὰ διαφέροντα, ὡς "Διακεκριμένα τῷ λόγῳ φαμέν, καὶ οὐχ ὡς διωρισμένα ταῖς ὑποστάσεσιν"· Ἆρα φασὶ τὸν διορισμὸν πρὸ τῆς διαφορᾶς εἶναι φύσει, ἢ σὺν τῇ διαφορᾷ, ἢ μετὰ τὴν διαφοράν; Εἰ μὲν οὖν πρὸ τῆς διαφορᾶς εἴποιεν, ἔσται καὶ ἐν τοῖς πάντῃ ἀδιαφόροις ὁ διορισμός, ὡς διωρίσθαι καὶ στιγμήν, καὶ μονάδα, καὶ νοῦν, καὶ αὐτὴν καθ᾽ αὑτὴν τὴν ἀδιάφορον θείαν φύσιν· καὶ ⟨εἰ⟩ ἡ μία οὖν αὐτοῖς φύσις, καθὸ μία, διώρισται, καθὸ δὲ διώρισται, καὶ ἀριθμῷ ὑπέπεσεν, οὐ μόνου τε Χριστοῦ ἀριθμόν, ἀλλὰ καὶ τοῦ ἐν αὐτῷ νοῦ ἰδίᾳ καὶ τῆς ἐν αὐτῷ θεότητος διδόασιν ἀριθμόν. Εἰ δὲ σὺν τῇ διαφορᾷ ἢ μετὰ τὴν διαφορὰν τὸν διορισμὸν ἀναγκαίως ὁρῶσι τῶν διαφερόντων, πῶς διαφορὰν λέγοντες, τὸν κατὰ τὸν λόγον τῶν διαφερόντων διορισμὸν οὐ φασί, καὶ ὁμολογουμένως, καὶ τῆς καθ᾽ ὑπόστασιν αὐτῶν ἐνώσεως φυλαττομένης, τὰ διαφέροντα τῷ λόγῳ καὶ διαφόροις ὁριστικοῖς λόγοις οἷόν τισιν ὅροις διοριζόμενα[50] ⟨οὐκ⟩ ἀπαριθμοῦσιν;

57. Ὁ ἀριθμὸς ἢ προϋπάρχει, ἢ συνυπάρχει, ἢ μεθυπάρχει τῆς διαφορᾶς πάντως. Τὴν οὖν διαφορὰν τῶν ἡνωμένων φύσεων τοῦ Κυρίου οἱ ὁμολογοῦντες, τὸν ἀριθμὸν τὸν κατ᾽ αὐτήν, ἤγουν τὰ διαφέροντα πράγματα, εἰ μὲν πρὸ αὐτῆς ἴσασι, λεγέτωσαν ποῦ ἰδόντες αὐτὰ ἢ πότε ἀδιάφορα ἠρίθμησαν, ἵνα ἐκ δύο μὲν ἀδιαφόρων[51] μία δὲ φύσις εἴη αὐτοῖς νῦν ἡ ἀδιάφορος, ὅτε διίστατο, ἔχουσα τὸ ὅμοιον, ὅτε δὲ ἡνώθη τάδε, λαβοῦσα τὸ διάφορον. Εἰ δὲ σὺν τῇ διαφορᾷ ἢ μετὰ ταύτην ὁ ἀριθμός ἐστιν, ἀναγκαίως διαφορὰν δόντες, ἢ σὺν αὐτῇ ἢ ἐπ᾽ αὐτῇ καὶ τὸν ἀριθμὸν τῶν διαφερόντων εἰσπραχθήσονται.

---

[50] intellege οὐκ   [51] ἀδιαφόρων] ἀ~ supra lin. MS διαφόρων a. corr.

56. There's a further question to be asked of those who speak of difference and yet don't number the things that differ, saying 'We're talking about things distinguished by reason, and not as separated by their hypostases.' Are they saying the distinction exists before the difference in nature, or along with the difference, or after the difference? If they're saying it exists before the difference, then there'll be a distinction even between things between which there's no difference, as if a point, a monad, a mind, and the divine nature itself—which is undifferentiated in respect of itself—were to have distinctions made in them! If this one nature of theirs has a distinction made in it in so far as it's one, but is subject to being numbered, too, in so far as a distinction is made, they're granting not only Christ's ability to be numbered as well, but also the ability to be numbered separately of both the mind that's in Him and the divinity! If, on the other hand, it's along with difference, or after it, that they necessarily discern the distinction between differing things, how is it that, when they speak of a difference, they don't speak of the distinction according to what's understood by things that differ, and in accordance with what's generally agreed? How is it that they don't also count up the things that differ by definition, and are distinguished by their different specific definitions, such as particular species, though their hypostases are preserved?

57. It's always the case that number exists either before, or at the same time as, or after difference. It follows that, if those who confess the difference between the Lord's united natures recognize the number that corresponds to that difference—that is, if they recognize the differing realities—before the difference, they'll have to tell us where or when it was that they recognized and numbered them as undifferentiated so that there might now be, for them, the one undifferentiated nature out of two undifferentiated natures! Once it was divided when it had identity, but then it was united vis-à-vis these [undifferentiated realities?] when it took on difference! But if number exists at the same time as, or after difference, they'll have an answer wrung from them—when they can't avoid granting that there is a difference—as to whether the number of the things that differ also exists along with it, or after it.

1800B

1800C

58. Εἰ μίαν ἐκ δύο, οὐχὶ δὲ καὶ δύο φύσεις τοῦ Κυρίου ἡμῶν Ἰησοῦ Χριστοῦ εἶναι φασί, λεγέτωσαν, τῆς θείας ὑπὲρ τὸν τοῦ κοινοῦ καὶ 1800D ἰδικοῦ λόγον οὔσης φύσεως ὁμολογουμένως, τὴν ἑτέραν τῶν δύο ἐξ ὧν ὁ Σωτήρ, ἤγουν τὴν ἀνθρωπείαν, ὁποίαν φασί, κοινὴν ἢ ἰδικήν; Εἰ μὲν οὖν ἰδικήν τινα ἰδιάζουσάν τε χωρὶς τοῦ Λόγου ποτὲ ταύτην οἴονται, δῆλον ὡς Νεστοριανῶς ἀσεβοῦσιν. Εἰ δὲ κοινὴν τήνδε λέγουσιν, ἢ τὴν ἐπινοίᾳ ἢ τὴν πράγματι, ὅλου δὲ τοῦ εἴδους οὐσίαν φασίν. Εἰ μὲν οὖν τὴν ἐπινοίᾳ λέγουσι μίαν εἶναι, τῶν ἐξ ὧν ὁ Σωτὴρ σύνθετός ἐστι κατὰ μίαν φύσιν ὑφεστώς, σαφὲς ὡς τὸ ἥμισυ τοῦ κατ᾽ αὐτὸν φυσικοῦ λόγου ἐπινοίᾳ ἔσται ἔχων καὶ οὐ πράγματι, ἤγουν τὸ ἀνθρώπειον μέρος τῆς συνθέσεως αὐτοῦ· εἰ δὲ κατὰ τοῦτο καὶ ἐκ τῆς παρθένου σαρκοῦται, καὶ ἀνθρώποις ὡράθη, καὶ 1801A ἐσταυρώθη, καὶ τὰ λοιπά, πάντως καὶ ταῦτα ἐπινοίᾳ καὶ οὐ πράγματι ἀληθῶς γεγένηται. Εἰ δὲ πράγματι μέν, κοινὴν δὲ τὴν κατ᾽ αὐτὸν φύσιν τῆς ἀνθρωπότητος [274ʳ] φασίν, ἐπεὶ ἐν τῇ κοινῇ, τῇ πράγματι εἶναι λεγομένῃ, Ἰούδας τὲ καὶ Πιλάτος ἐστίν, ἄρα καὶ οὗτοι οὐδὲν ἧττον τοῦ Δεσπότου ἐσταυρώθησαν καὶ ἐκ νεκρῶν ἀνέστησαν, αὐτός τε οὐδὲν ἧττον προέδωκέ τε καὶ ἐσταύρωσεν αὐτούς τε καὶ ἑαυτόν· οὕτω δὲ καὶ συγγεννηθῆναι αὐτῷ Ἄννας τε καὶ Καϊάφας ἐκ τῆς ἁγίας παρθένου νοοῖντο ἄν· ἀλλὰ μὴν καὶ ὁ προπάτωρ αὐτῆς Δαβίδ, καὶ αὐτὴ ἡ ἄχραντος μία τις οὖσα τῆς κοινῆς φύσεως, ὑφ᾽ ἑαυτῆς γεννηθῆναι σὺν τῷ Θεῷ Λόγῳ τὴν κοινὴν φύσιν τῆς ἀνθρωπότητος γεννώσης λογισθείη· ὧν τί ἀτοπώτερον

58. If they say there's one nature out of two, but don't also say there are two natures of our Lord Jesus Christ, they must explain something to us: Since the divine nature is, as all agree, beyond 1800D the categories of universal and particular, what kind of nature do they say the other of the two natures out of which the Saviour comes, that is, the human nature, is? Is it universal, or is it particular? If ever they imagine it's some particular human nature on its own and without the Word, it's obvious they're talking in the impious way of Nestorians. If, on the other hand, they say it's a universal nature, whether in thought or in actuality, they're talking about the substance of the entire form. If they say it's in thought that there exists one nature of the two out of which the Saviour is compounded, subsisting in one nature, it's clear He'll exist by possessing half of the natural definition relative to Him—the human part of His composition—in thought, not in act. If it's in these terms, too, that He took on flesh from the Virgin, was seen by men, was crucified, and so on, then these things too have come 1801A to pass entirely in thought, and not truly in act. If, however, the human nature exists in actuality, but it's the universal nature of humanity they're speaking of in Him, it's Judas and Pilate too— since it exists in the universal said to exist in actuality—and therefore these men were crucified no less than the Master, and rose from the dead, and He no less than they betrayed and crucified them, and Himself too. By the same token, Annas and Caiaphas will be considered to have come into existence at the same time as He did from the Holy Virgin, but so would her forefather David. She, the undefiled, being one participant in the universal nature, will be considered to have given birth to herself along with God the Word, since she gives birth to the universal nature of humanity. What could you find more absurd or blasphemous than that?

ἐξεύροι τις, ἢ βλασφημότερον; Εἰ δὲ λέγοιεν· "Ὑμεῖς οὖν ἐκ δύο καὶ
180IB ἐν δύο φύσεσι τὸν Δεσπότην δοξάζοντες, ὁποίων τούτων φατέ;",
ἀφθόνως αὐτοῖς ἐροῦμεν, ὡς "Ἐκ δύο μέν, τῆς τε θείας καὶ τῆς
κοινῆς ἀνθρωπείας, ἄμφω προϋπαρχουσῶν τῆς ἑνώσεως Χριστοῦ
φαμέν, ἐν δύο δέ, τῆς τε ὑπὲρ τὸν κοινὸν λόγον καὶ ἰδικὸν οὔσης
κοινῆς θεότητος καὶ τῆς ἰδικῆς μόνου αὐτοῦ ἀνθρωπότητος." Τὴν
μὲν γὰρ ἐκ δύο φύσεων φωνὴν συνιστᾶν δυνατόν, καὶ ἐκ τῆς κατὰ
ἀφαίρεσιν λαμβανομένης φύσεως ἐκ τοῦ κοινοῦ τῶν ἀνθρώπων πρὸς
τῇ ἐνυπάρκτῳ θεότητι ἐπινοίᾳ οὖσαν—ἐπινοίᾳ γὰρ καὶ θεωροῦμεν
πρὸ Χριστοῦ τὰ Χριστοῦ—τὰ δὲ ἐν αὐτῷ ὑφεστώτως ὄντα
ὁμολογεῖν οὐκ ἔστι πρὸ αὐτοῦ, ἀλλ' ἐν αὐτῷ, ὥστε τὴν ὑφεστῶσαν
αὐτοῦ ἀνθρωπότητα, οἱ δύο φύσεις εἰδότες ἡνωμένας ἐν Χριστῷ
180IC φασιν μᾶλλον, ἤπερ οἱ ἐκ δύο φύσεων λέγοντες αὐτόν.

59. Ἔτι ἡ μία φύσις τοῦ Θεοῦ Λόγου ἡ νῦν σεσαρκωμένη, ἦν ποτὲ
οὐ σεσαρκωμένη, ἢ οὐχί; Εἰ δὲ τοῦτο ἀναμφίβολον καὶ αὐτοῖς,
ἀκουστέον παρ' αὐτῶν, εἰ Θεοῦ τε Λόγου ἦν, καὶ φύσις ἦν, καὶ μία
ἦν καὶ πρὸ τοῦ σαρκωθῆναι, σαρκωθεῖσα τί ἐπεκτήσατο, ἢ τί
ἀπεβάλετο; Εἰ μὲν οὐδὲν ἀπεβάλετο—οὐ γὰρ κατὰ τροπὴν εἴρηται
καὶ μετουσίωσιν τὸ σεσαρκωμένη, ὥσπερ φαμὲν ἐπὶ τοῦ
κρυστάλλου μία φύσις ὕδατος λελιθωμένη—δῆλον ὡς ἐπεκτήσατο
σάρκα ἤγουν ἀνθρωπότητα· αὕτη δὲ τί ἐστι, ποιότης ἢ φύσις τις; Εἰ
δὲ πάντως φύσις, αὕτη ἡ κτηθεῖσα φύσις, πρὸς τῇ κτησαμένῃ αὐτὴν
μιᾷ τοῦ Θεοῦ Λόγου φύσει, πόσαι ἂν εἶεν, εἰπάτωσαν ἡμῖν
εὐγνωμόνως.

If they say, 'You yourselves, who suppose the Master's out of two natures, and in two natures: what sort of natures do you call 1801B them?', we give them the following wholehearted answer: 'We say He's out of two natures, the divine nature and the universal human nature, both of which pre-existed Christ's union, but we also say that He's in two natures—the shared divinity that's beyond the logic of universal and particular, and the particular humanity that's His alone.' It's possible to maintain simultaneously the expression 'out of two natures', since it exists in thought on the basis of the nature grasped through abstraction from the universality of men, as compared with the actually existing divinity—for we do contemplate the realities of Christ before Christ in thought. It's not possible, though, to confess the realities that actually subsisted in Christ before Christ, but in Him, so that those who recognize two natures united in Christ affirm His actually subsisting humanity more than those who say He's out of two 1801C natures.

59. Again, was the one nature of the Word of God, now the incarnate nature, ever not incarnate, or was that never the case? If this is an unambiguous issue for them, one needs to hear from them: if it belonged to God the Word, and was a nature, and was one even before the taking on of flesh, what did it take on when it became flesh, or what did it lose? If it didn't take anything on—for the word 'incarnate' isn't used in the sense of change and transformation, as when we say of ice that water's one nature 'turned to stone'—it's clear that it took on flesh, that is, humanity. But what is this humanity, a quality, or some nature? If this nature that's taken on is unquestionably a nature in addition to the one nature of the Word of God that took it on, they're going to have to tell us candidly just how many natures there are!

180ID **60.** Ἔτι ἐκ δύο φύσεων τὴν μίαν φύσιν, τοῦ Θεοῦ Λόγου, τὴν σεσαρκωμένην, ἴσασιν, ἢ Χριστοῦ μόνον; Εἰ μὲν οὖν Χριστοῦ μόνον, κακούργως, περὶ Χριστοῦ ἀνακρινόμενοι παρ' ἡμῶν, οὐ διὰ τοῦ αὐτοῦ ὀνόματος, ἀλλὰ διὰ τοῦ Θεοῦ Λόγου τὴν περὶ τῶν φύσεων ἀπολογίαν ποιοῦνται. Εἰ δὲ καὶ τοῦ Λόγου τὴν μίαν φύσιν ἐκ δύο λέγειν τολμῶσιν, ἔσται καὶ αὐτὴ δηλαδὴ ἐκ θεότητός τε καὶ ἀνθρωπότητος καθ' αὑτὴν νοουμένη, [275ʳ] καὶ σαρκουμένη δὲ πάλιν, ἑτέραν φύσιν σαρκὸς ἐπικτησαμένη, τριπλῆ τε ἀντὶ διπλῆς ἐκ δύο σαρκῶν καὶ μιᾶς θεότητος συγκεκροτημένη.

60. Another thing: do they recognize the one incarnate nature
out of two natures as belonging to God the Word, or to Christ   1801D
alone? If it belongs to Christ alone, it's mischievous of them,
when we interrogate them about Christ, to make their defence of
the natures, not in terms of Christ's name, but in terms of the
Word of God's name. If, however, they have the nerve to say that
the Word's one nature also is out of two, then it too will clearly be
understood to be out of divinity and humanity in its own right,
and to become incarnate a second time, taking on an additional
nature of flesh, and welded together as a threefold nature
(replacing a twofold one) out of two fleshes and one divinity!

61. Ἔτι ἐπεὶ ἐκ δύο φύσεων ἕν τι γενέσθαι φασί, πευστέον αὐτῶν· τὸ ἓν τοῦτο, τίνι λόγῳ ἓν φασίν; Ἢ γὰρ τῷ ὀνόματι, ἢ τῷ γένει, ἢ τῷ εἴδει, ἢ τῷ ἀριθμῷ ἓν εἶναί τι λέγουσι· παρὰ γὰρ τάδε, ἑτέρως ἓν τι λέγειν οὐκ ἔστιν. Εἰ οὖν τῷ ὀνόματι ἕν τι γέγονε, μόνον ὁμωνυμίᾳ ἡνώθησαν τὰ δύο, ἑτεροφυῆ δὲ καὶ ἀσύνθετα ἀλλήλοις ἔτι ἐστίν, ἄνθρωπός τε μόνον, ἢ Θεὸς μόνον, ἢ ἕτερόν τι, ὃ μήτε Θεοῦ μήτε ἀνθρώπου ἐστὶν ὄνομα, ἑκατέρῳ ἐπικληθήσεται. Εἰ δὲ τῷ γένει ἐστὶν ἓν τὸ γενόμενον, ὑφ᾽ ὃ τελεῖ Θεὸς καὶ ἄνθρωπος ὁμογενῆ ἄρα τάδε· τί δὲ ἄρα τὸ κοινόν τε αὐτοῖς καθολικώτερόν τε Θεοῦ γένος ζητητέον, πῶς τε ἀπὸ προσφάτου ἑνώσεως τόδε ἀρχαιότατον γένος αὐτοῖς ἐπενοήθη. Εἰ δὲ τῷ εἴδει ἓν αὐτὸ φασίν, δύο πάντως, ἢ καὶ πλείονά ἐστι τὰ ὑπ᾽ αὐτὸ ἄτομα, ἤγουν ὑποστάσεις, καὶ ἐν δύο προσώποις νοεῖται ἢ ἐν πλείοσι Χριστός· ἐν δὲ εἶδος θεότητός τε καὶ ἀνθρωπότητος εἶναι ὅπως λογιστέον ἀδιανόητον. Εἰ δὲ τούτων οὐδὲν εὔλογον, ἐξ ἀνάγκης ἓν τῷ ἀριθμῷ εἶναι τὸ ἐκ δύο φύσεων γενόμενον ὑπολείπεται· τὸ δὲ ἀριθμῷ ἓν λεγόμενον, τὸ τῇ ὑποστάσει ἓν ὂν φαμέν, καὶ οὐ τὸ τῇ φύσει ἕν· διότι ὥσπερ ἀριθμὸς ἕκαστος συνθέσει ἀριθμῶν ἢ μονάδων τὸ ἕν τι εἶναι ἔχει, οὕτως καὶ αἱ ὑποστάσεις συνθέσει φύσεων καὶ ἰδιωμάτων συμπαραλήψει ὑφίστανται, ἢ τοὐλάχιστον συμπλοκῇ φύσεως μιᾶς καὶ ἰδιώματος· τὸ γὰρ φύσει ἓν εἶναι, ἀσυνθέτου πάντῃ μονάδος ἴδιόν ἐστιν.

62. Εἰ διὰ τὸ μὴ εἰρηκέναι τοὺς πατέρας δύο φύσεις αὐτολεξεὶ ἐπὶ Χριστοῦ ὑποστέλλεσθαί φασι τὴν καινοφωνίαν, ἢ δειξάτωσαν τινὰ μίαν φύσιν ἁπλῶς λέγοντα, ἢ καὶ αὐτοὶ τὴν τοιάνδε φωνὴν μὴ προπετευέσθωσαν, ὅπου γε ἡμεῖς καὶ φύσεις, ἀλλὰ καὶ δύο λέγοντας ἀκούομεν τοὺς ἐκκρίτους τῶν διδασκάλων.

61. Since they say that one thing came to be out of two natures, there's more to be found out from them. This one thing, now: in what sense are they saying it's one? They say that something's one either in name, or in genus, or in form, or in number; apart from these, it's impossible to say anything's one. If it's in name that there's come to be one thing, the two have been united only in that they have the same name, though they go on being of different natures and uncombined with each other, and it'll be called by either name, just 'man', or just 'God', or some other name that's the name neither for God nor man. If, on the other hand, what's come into existence is one by genus, by which God and men are completed, then these two things are of the same genus. But then one has to try to find out what common genus they share—a genus greater in scope than God!—and how the idea of this most ancient of unions came to them on the basis of a recent union. If, again, they say it's one in form, then the individual entities (i.e. hypostases) under that form number two at least, if not more, and Christ is thought to be in two or more persons. How one's to calculate that there's one form of divinity and humanity boggles the mind! If, though, none of this makes any sense, what came into existence out of two natures necessarily ends up being one in number. What's called one by number, however, is what we speak of as being one by hypostasis, and not what's one by nature. This is so because, just as each number is able to be the one thing by a compounding of numbers or units, so also hypostases subsist by a compounding of natures and a combining of properties, or at the very least by a combination of one nature and one property. To be one thing by nature belongs uniquely to a single entity that's entirely uncompounded.

62. If they speak of the introduction of new terms because the fathers haven't spoken of two natures in Christ in so many words, either they must point out some father who speaks unequivocally of one nature, or else they themselves are going to have to refrain from rashly using that kind of expression whenever we too, for our part, hear the most eminent of the teachers speaking of natures, but *two* natures.

1804A

1804B

1804C

63. Ἡ τοῦ Θεοῦ Λόγου φύσις μία ὡς σεσαρκωμένου ἐστὶν, ἢ καὶ ὡς ἀσάρκου; Εἰ μὲν οὖν ὡς σεσαρκωμένου, πρὸ τῆς σαρκώσεως, οὐ μία ἦν, ἀλλ' ἥμιση μιᾶς, ἤ τι τοιόνδε μόριον· ἔτι μὴν οὐδὲ ὁ Πατὴρ ἢ τὸ ἅγιον Πνεῦμα μιᾶς ἔσται φύσεως τελείας. Εἰ δὲ καὶ πρὸ τῆς σαρκώσεως μία ἦν, ἢ οὐδὲν προσέθηκε φυσικὸν ἡ σὰρξ τῇ ὑποστάσει τοῦ Λόγου, καὶ ψευδὴς ἡ καθ' ὑπόστασιν ἕνωσις φύσεων δοξαζομένη, ἢ προσθεῖσα, μίαν φύσιν ἢ μόριον φύσεως ἐπισυνῆψε τῇ προτέρᾳ φύσει μιᾷ τοῦ Λόγου.

63. Is God the Word's nature one in its incarnated state, or is it also one when it's without flesh? If it's one in its incarnated state, it wasn't one before the Incarnation, but half of one, or some such fraction. Furthermore, neither the Father nor the Holy Spirit will then have one complete nature. If, on the other hand, it was one even before the Incarnation, either the flesh added nothing at the level of nature to the Word's hypostasis, and the union of natures by hypostasis is considered false, or else, if it did add something, it joined one nature or part of a nature to the pre-existing one nature of the Word.[ix]

NOTES

i. The MS heading for the whole of *Against the Monophysites*, found immediately before the *Aporiae*: Τοῦ πανσόφου μοναχοῦ κύρ Λεοντίου τοῦ Ἱεροσολυμίτου ἀπορίαι πρὸς τοὺς μίαν φύσιν λέγοντας σύνθετον τὸν Κύριον ἡμῶν Ἰησοῦν Χριστὸν· καὶ μαρτυρίαι τῶν ἁγίων, καὶ ἀνάλυσις τοῦ δόγματος αὐτῶν. Alternative translations to 'analysis' include 'freeing', if Leontius means that he is freeing the fathers' teaching from misunderstandings, and 'destruction', if Leontius intends by the 'they' of 'their teaching' the anti-Chalcedonians, though the obvious referent for 'their' is 'the saints'. On the whole, it seems best to assume that the referent is 'the saints', and that the word carries the positive sense of 'analysis'. That describes pretty well what Leontius does.

ii. Severus is cited to this effect at 1841D.

iii. A common way to speak of John, the writer of the fourth gospel.

iv. A reference to a common principle of patristic biblical exegesis: if a statement is manifestly untrue or unworthy on the literal level, it is to be interpreted in some other manner, e.g. allegorically.

v. Or 'rub'.

vi. An ironic reference, surely, to Severus' *The Friend of Truth*, in which Severus championed a Cyril (the 'friend of truth' of the title) who was to be understood only in terms of a strict—Leontius implies heretical—reading of this formula.

vii. The translation of Wickham, *Cyril*, 89–91.

viii. These are produced at 1841A–1849C.

ix. Not among the passages preserved in the Latin original: *Explanatio symboli*, in B. Botte (ed. and tr.), *De Sacramentis*, *SC* 25^2 (Paris: Editions du Cest, 1994), 46–58.

x. i.e. saying opposite things. In 1 Cor. 12: 13 it is said to be impossible for one to say both 'Jesus is cursed' and 'Jesus is Lord'.

xi. The scribe neither provides nor leaves room for the title so clearly missing here.

xii. On Symeon Stylites, Baradatus, and James of Cyrrhestica see R. M. Price's translation of Theodoret of Cyrrhus, *A History of the Monks of Syria*, *Cistercian Studies* 88 (Kalamazoo: Cistercian Publication, 1985), esp. 148 n. 1.

xiii. The aphorism is first found in Aristotle.

XIV. The following account is certainly a scribal addition from a later time. See Introduction, section XI.

APORIAE

I. In the MS this description is followed immediately by a description of *Testimonies of the Saints*: καὶ μαρτυρίαι τῶν ἁγίων, καὶ ἀνάλυσις τοῦ δόγματος αὐτῶν.

II. Found in Aristotle, *Categories* 5b and 6a; widely repeated in later works on logic.

III. A reference to Phil. 2:6–7: 'the form of God' and 'the form of a servant'.

IV. Cf. Cyril of Alexandria, *That Christ is One*, 342.

V. A logical sleight of hand. The argument here depends on the fact that Leontius and his opponents agree that hypostases were not compounded in Christ, as is stated in the closing sentence. Both agree that natures were compounded in Him, though his opponents think He was compounded 'out of' two natures, while Leontius prefers to say He was compounded 'in' two natures. It depends, too, on a commonplace of Byzantine number theory: the sum of a perfect number's factors equals itself (e.g. $1 + 2 + 3 = 6$ and $1 \times 2 \times 3 = 6$), 'filling up' that number. Beginning with those assumptions, Leontius plays games with a whole set of double meanings: the expression for 'complete compound' can also mean 'perfect number' in the mathematical sense; the word for 'complete' in the quantitative sense can also mean 'perfect' in the qualitative sense; the word for 'first' can mean either 'first in a sequence' or 'pre-eminent'; the word for 'excessive' can also mean 'odd' in the mathematical sense; the word for 'exact' or 'appropriate' can also mean 'even' in the mathematical sense. The argument unfolds in the following way. The first sentence asserts the commonplace of number theory with which any reader would have to agree: 'the sum of [the factors of] every [mathematically] perfect number has neither to exceed, nor fall short, but be even [fill it up].' Substituting alternative meanings for the same words, though, Leontius would have the reader agreeing that 'the sum of [the components of] every [qualitatively] perfect compound has to be [mathematically] even.' The next sentence works in much the same way. Any reader would agree that 'two is the first compounding, and the first [mathematically] even number.' Leontius, by substituting alternative meanings for words, would have the reader agreeing that 'two is ... the pre-eminent even number.' That would also mean agreement with the proposition that '[t]wo is ... the pre-eminent *appropriate* number', to use yet another meaning for the word. The 'logical' implication of the reader's assumed agreement to these propositions is that the incarnate Word ('the one [qualitatively] perfect thing', and therefore the perfect compound) could have only an even number of components; since two is the 'pre-eminent compounding' *and* the 'pre-eminent appropriate number', the incarnate Word could be compounded only of two components. In the

penultimate sentence Leontius has one last romp with the double meanings of words: 'How . . . could it ever be [mathematically] odd . . . to speak of [the mathematically even] two . . .?' A debt of gratitude is owed to Joel Kalvesmaki for his invaluable help in making sense of this aporia.

VI. See the citation from Cyril in Aporia 21.

VII. The allusion may be to Cyril of Alexandria, *Letter* 41, *ACO* i, 1, 4, p. 46: 'for when he rose from the dead, he put off corruption and with it all that is from it.' Translated from *FC* lxxvi[1], 178.

VIII. The source in Cyril for the Severian assertion is cited and discussed in *Testimonies* at 1824D–1825B.

IX. At this point there are eight blank lines in the text before *Testimonies*.

APPENDIX: THE ARGUMENT OF
TESTIMONIES OF THE SAINTS SUMMARIZED

Note: The text falls into two main sections, each addressing a fundamental charge made by the anti-Chalcedonians used as a justification for
remaining in schism. The first charge is the charge of novelty: the
fathers use 'one incarnate nature', but 'the expression you use . . . is a
strange one we don't find being used explicitly by the fathers anywhere,
i.e. "two natures, albeit undivided, of Christ".'[1] The very long conversation that addresses this issue takes up slightly more than three-quarters
of the text.[2] The second charge is 'the charge of falsehood against the
Church', the falsehood involved being the fact that, 'though you now
teach the kind of things that seem to be orthodox . . . you accept and
reverence . . . Chalcedon, and Leo . . . who had as their pretext for
convening the condemnation of Eutyches, but were really an act of zeal
for Nestorius.'[3] The section addressing this charge completes the text.
The narrative about a local miracle at the end is a scribal addition.[4]

Within these two main sections, the conversation meanders through
the issues, with Leontius supplying the anti-Chalcedonians' responses
along the way, probably imagining some and citing others. The
conversation's progress is as follows:

SECTION I THE NOVELTY OF 'TWO NATURES'

A (Anti-Chalcedonians): The fathers say 'one incarnate nature', but you
    say 'two united natures of Christ'. (1804D–1805A)

L (Leontius): 1. The fathers do in fact speak of two natures, as even
    Severus recognizes. (1805A)
      2. We accept both expressions as meaning the same thing: 'one
incarnate nature of God the Word' = 'two natures united in one
hypostasis'. (1805A–B)
      3. Different ways of expressing things are both common and
necessary. The meaning is what is important, not the particular
words. (1805B–1808B)

A: 'One incarnate nature' captured christological truth exactly. Why
    add another expression? (1808B–C)

---

[1] 1804D   [2] 1804D–1876C   [3] 1876D   [4] 1876C–1900A

L: 1. Each has its use. Just as 'one incarnate nature' was introduced as a way of expressing both the duality and the unity of Christ that could exclude Nestorianism's misuse of 'two natures', so 'two natures united in one hypostasis' was brought in to express that duality and unity in a way that could exclude Eutychianism's misuse of 'one nature'. Again, the point is what they mean underneath the form of words: you need to reject people who impute an incorrect meaning to either expression, and accept those who impute a correct meaning. (1808c–1812c)

2. Do not confuse two meanings of 'nature'. (1812d)

3. Cyril himself intended by 'one incarnate nature' exactly what correct-thinking people intend by 'two natures united in one hypostasis'. He was not inconsistent. (1813a–c)

4. For Cyril to say there is one incarnate nature of Christ does not necessarily mean that there is only one nature in the sense of substance. If so, both humanity and divinity would be replaced by some other nature. Cyril, however, was using 'nature' in the sense of 'hypostasis', and in a hypostatic union the natures united persist, but exist in a single entity. (1813c–1816d)

5. Now you cannot any longer use confusion about the meaning of 'nature' as an excuse for not rejoining us. (1816d–1817b)

L: A first, brief florilegium shows that the fathers speak of natures in Christ that persist after the union. (1817c–1820b)

A second, long florilegium shows that the fathers speak of a union by hypostasis of two natures, whatever terms they use to refer to the union and the duality. (1820b–1841a)

A third florilegium shows that even anti-Chalcedonians like Severus cannot help recognizing this kind of union and duality. (1841a–1849c)

A: You pick only the patristic texts that suit your purposes, and ignore those that support our position. (1849c)

L: The select fathers never disagree with themselves or with each other. Whereas you claim to find them saying the opposite of what we found them to say, that is only because you are looking at the form of words they use, rather than the underlying meaning, which is actually the same. Bring forward your evidence, then, and we shall show that we are right about this. Remember, though, that terms were often used imprecisely by the fathers. Do not be confused by this. (1849c–1852b)

A: The expression 'two natures' that you use is a Nestorian expression, but Cyril spoke of 'one nature'. (1852d)

L: 1. The fact that Nestorius used the expression does not prove it is, of itself, erroneous. (1852d–1853a)

2. When it comes to texts of Cyril that speak of one nature, however, it can be shown from what he says in the context that what he means by 'nature' is 'person' or 'hypostasis'. When Cyril says Christ is 'out of two natures' after the union, and says he does not divide the natures after the union, he makes it clear from the context that he means that he does not divide the one Son whose natures they are, and that there are two natures there to be discerned by 'the eyes of the soul'. (1853A–1860A)

3. Cyril's paradigm for union, the union of body and soul in man that produces one, means the production of one person and hypostasis, not of one nature in the sense of substance. (1860A–1861C)

4. Either Cyril means 'one person' and 'one hypostasis' when he says 'one nature', or he is is—unimagineably—inconsistent. (1861C–1864A)

5. Texts claimed to be from Athanasius, Julius of Rome, and Gregory Thaumaturgus that use 'one nature' can be shown by historical investigation to be forgeries produced by Apollinarians, though Cyril cited them in good faith and as bearing an orthodox meaning. (1864A–1876C)

SECTION II THE FALSEHOOD OF THE CHALCEDONIAN CHURCH (1876C–1900A)

A: Chalcedon pretended it met to condemn Eutyches, but really it wanted to preserve a disguised Nestorianism. (1876C–D)

L: Chalcedon actually confirmed everything Cyril and the Council of Ephesus said and did against Nestorius, and anathematized him and all who agreed with him. (1877A–B)

A: Some participants in Chalcedon had been Nestorian sympathizers. (1877B)

L: Two or three closet Nestorians could not taint the whole council, which was established by divine providence to enunciate lasting doctrine. (1877B–1880B)

A: Their error made the whole culpable. (1880B)

L: If so, then those at Chalcedon who had been at Ephesus were culpable, and Ephesus was by the same token tainted by their culpability. Why not leave the few deceivers to the judgment of God, and agree with us on the underlying single meaning of both christological expressions? (1880B–1881C)

A: Chalcedon replaced its first creed by a second, showing the instability of their belief. (1881C–D)

L: All councils involved disagreement, even Nicaea. (1881D–1884A)

A: The remaking of its creed demonstrated a profound change of opinion from what it first believed. (1884A)

L: Chalcedon remade its creed because it realized what it had first said needed to be corrected. The change shows how assiduous it was about the truth. (1884A–B)

A: Chalcedon really deposed Dioscorus because he attacked Nestorianism, but misrepresented the reason for condemning him as being his refusal to appear when summoned. (1884B)

L: He was summoned for receiving Eutyches and anathematizing Flavian, but then he made false excuses for not appearing, and eventually was deposed for refusing to appear. (1884C)

A: Why did Chalcedon condemn him for refusing to appear rather than on doctrinal grounds? (1884C)

L: Dioscorus was suspected of holding the Eutychian heresy, and that was the real reason why he was summoned, but he was condemned when he refused to appear. The doctrinal charge was not withdrawn or misrepresented; it simply never came to trial. Note that Dioscorus did, damningly, receive Eutyches. (1884D–1885B)

A: Dioscorus received Eutyches only when he renounced his error. (1885B)

L: If that is true, then Eutyches admitted he had been in error, in which case Dioscorus ought not to have condemned Flavian for deposing him. (1885B–D)

A: Flavian was tainted by Nestorian sympathies, though, which taints everything he did against Eutyches. (1885D)

L: Flavian's own statements show that was not the case. You have assumed that our silence about Dioscorus' suspected Eutychianism meant Chalcedon deposed him unjustly. In fact, Chalcedon's decisions represented the careful deliberations of a great assembly. Compare that with Severus' arrogant unilateral condemnation of that same great assembly! Individuals do not anathematize councils! It is the other way around. (1885D–1889A)

A: Most votes at Chalcedon were the result of bribery. (1889B)

L: The council could have enunciated true doctrine all the same. You should be forgiving of the sinners involved, especially given the acceptance of money for performing sacraments by some of your clergy. Anyway, our clergy are almost all blameless. (1889B–1892A)

We urge everyone to treat theological statements objectively, as if they came from complete strangers, rather than from 'friends' or 'enemies'. Judge where the truth is being clearly spoken, remembering that we shall be judged by Christ at His coming. Loyalty to one's

teacher [Severus!] and factional solidarity will mean nothing then.   (1892B–1893C)

A: I have too much self-respect to change my opinion.   (1893C)

L: That is to be zealous without paying attention to what you are being zealous for.   (1893D–1896B)

A: The truth of what our people say is confirmed by God's gift of miracle-working power to them.   (1896B–C)

L: There is no necessary or observed connection between being able to work miracles and being able to enunciate sound doctrine. Anyway, our people perform just as many miracles as they do, indeed more. Moreover, there may be many reasons why God gives the gift of miracle-working which have nothing to do with one's doctrinal position.   (1896C–1900A)

SELECT BIBLIOGRAPHY

ABRAMOWSKI, L., 'Ein nestorianischer Traktat bei Leontius von Jerusalem', *III* *Symposium Syriacum 1980*, OCA 221 (Rome: Pont. Institutum Studiorum Orientalium, 1983), 43–55.

ALLEN, P., 'The Definition and Enforcement of Orthodoxy', in A. Cameron, B. Ward-Perkins, and M. Whitby (eds.), *The Cambridge Ancient History*, xiv (Cambridge: Cambridge University Press, 2000), 824–5.

BASDEKIS, ATHANASIOS, *Die Christologie des Leontius von Jerusalem: seine Logoslehre* (Diss. Münster, 1974).

BREYDY, M., 'Les Attestations patristiques parallèles et leurs nuances chez les ps-Léonce et Jean Maron', in R. Stempel (ed.), *Nubia et Oriens Christianus: Festschrift für C. Detlef G. Müller zum 60. Geburtstag* (Cologne: Dinter, 1987), 3–16.

—— *Exposé de la foi et autres opuscules*, *CSCO*, Scriptores Syri, ccx (Louvain: E. Peeters, 1988), 497–8.

BROCK, S., 'The Conversations with the Syrian Orthodox under Justinian (532)', *OCP* 47 (1981), 87–121.

FRACEA, I., Ὁ Λεόντιος Βιζάντιος. Βίος καὶ Συγγράμματα (Κριτική Θεώρικη) (Athens, 1984), 217–46.

GRAY, P. T. R., *The Defense of Chalcedon in the East (451–553)*, SHCT 20 (Leiden: E. J. Brill, 1979), 122–41.

—— 'An Anonymous Severian Monophysite of the Mid-Sixth Century', *Patristic and Byzantine Review*, 1 (1982), 117–26.

—— 'Neo-Chalcedonianism and the Tradition: From Patristic to Byzantine Theology', *BF* 8 (1982), 61–70.

—— 'The Soteriological Case for a "Synthetic" Union in Christ', *Papers of the Ninth International Conference on Patristics Studies, Oxford 1983*, StudPat 18, 1 (Kalamazoo, Mich.: Cistercian Publications, 1985), 151–4.

—— 'Forgery as an Instrument of Progress: Reconstructing the Theological Tradition in the Sixth Century', *BZ* 81 (1988), 284–9.

—— '"The Select Fathers": Canonizing the Patristic Past', *Papers presented to the Tenth International Conference on Patristic Studies held in Oxford 1987*, *StudPat* 23 (Leuven: Peeters Press, 1989), 21–36.

—— 'Neuchalkedonismus', *TRE* xxiv, 1/2 (Berlin and New York: Walter de Gruyter, 1994), 289–96.

—— 'Through the Tunnel with Leontius of Jerusalem: The Sixth Century Transformation of Theology', in P. Allen and E. Jeffreys

(eds.), *The Sixth Century: End or Beginning?*, *BA* 10 (Brisbane: Australian Association for Byzantine Studies, 1996), 187–96.

—— 'Covering the Nakedness of Noah: Reconstruction and Denial in the Age of Justinian', in L. Garland (ed.), *Conformity and Non-Conformity in Byzantium = BF* 24 (1997), 193–206.

—— 'The Sabaite Monasteries and the Christological Controversies (478–533)', in J. Patrich (ed.), *The Sabaite Heritage in the Orthodox Church from the Fifth Century to the Present*, *OLA* 98 (Leuven: Uitgeverij Peeters en Departement Oosterse Studies, 2001), 241–3.

GRILLMEIER, A., 'Der Neu-Chalkedonismus: um die Berechtigung eines neuen Kapitals in der Dogmengeschichte', *HistJb* 77 (1958), pp. 151–66 = *Mit ihm und in ihm: Christologische Forschungen und Perspektiven* (Freiburg: Herder, 1975), 376–85.

—— 'Ὁ κυριακὸς ἄνθρωπος: eine Studie zu einer christologischen Bezeichnung der Väterzeit', *Trad* 33 (1977), 47–51.

GRILLMEIER, A. (with T. Hainthaler), *From the Council of Chalcedon (451) to Gregory the Great (590–604) = Christ in Christian Tradition*, II², tr. P. Allen and J. Cawte (London and Oxford: Mowbray, 1995), 271–312.

GRUMEL, V., 'Léonce de Byzance', *DTC* 9 (Paris: Letouzey et Ané, 1926), 400–26.

HELMER, S., *Der Neuchalkedonismus: Geschichte, Berechtigung und Bedeutung eines dogmengeschichtlichen Begriffs* (Diss. Bonn, 1962), 202–15.

JUNGLAS, J. P., *Leontius von Byzanz: Studien zu seinen Schriften, Quellen und Anschauungen*, *FCLDG* 7³ (Paderborn, 1908).

KRAUSMÜLLER, D., 'Leontius of Jerusalem, a Theologian of the Seventh Century', *JTS* NS 522 (2001), 637–57.

LOOFS, F., *Leontius von Byzanz und die gleichnamigen Schriftsteller der griechischen Kirche*, *TU* 3 (Leipzig: Hinrichs, 1887), 175–97.

LUDWIG, E. M., 'Neo-Chalcedonism and the Council of 553' (Diss. Berkeley, 1983), 117–28.

MACDONALD, J., 'Leontius of Jerusalem's *Against the Monophysites* as a Possible Source for Justinian's *Letter to the Alexandrian Monks*', *Byzantion*, 67 (1997), 373–82.

MEYENDORFF, J., *Christ in Eastern Christian Thought* (Crestwood, NY: St Vladimir's Seminary Press, 1975), 73–82.

MOELLER, C., 'Le Chalcédonisme et le néo-chalcédonisme en Orient de 451 à la fin du VIᵉ siècle', in A. Grillmeier and H. Bacht (eds.), *Das Konzil von Chalkedon: Geschichte und Gegenwart*, i (Würzburg: Echter-Verlag, 1951), 686–7.

—— 'Textes "monophysite" de Léonce de Jerusalem', *EphThLov* 27 (1951), 467–82.

PERRONE, L., *La Chiesa di Palestina e le controversie cristologiche: dal concilio di Efeso (431) al secondo concilio di Costantinopoli (553)*, Testi e ricerche di Scienze religiose 18 (Brescia: Paideia Editrice, 1980), 274–85.

—— 'Leonzio de Gerusalemme', in A. di Berardino (ed.), *Dal Concilio de Calcedonia (451) a Giovanni Damasceno (750): I Padri Orientali* = *Patrologia* 5 (Genoa, 2000), 312–14.

REES, S., 'The Literary Activity of Leontius of Byzantium', *JTS* 19 (1968), 229–42.

RICHARD, M., 'Le Néo-chalcédonisme', *Opera Minora*, i (Turnhout: Brepols, 1977), no. 56, 156–61.

—— 'Les Florilèges diphysites du Ve et du VIe siècle', *Opera Minora*, ii (Turnhout: Brepols, 1976), no. 3, 740–42.

—— 'Léonce de Jérusalem et Léonce de Byzance', *Opera Minora*, iii (Turnhout: Brepols, 1977), no. 59, 35–8.

RÜGAMER, M., *Leontius von Byzanz: ein Polemiker aus dem Zeitalter Justinians* (Diss. Würzburg, 1894), 33–43.

STIERNON, D., 'Léonce de Byzance', *DSp* 9 (Paris: Beauchesne, 1976), 651–60, esp. 655.

WATT, J. H. I., 'The Authenticity of the Writings Ascribed to Leontius of Byzantium: A New Approach by Means of Statistics', *Papers presented to the Fourth International Conference on Patristic Studies held at Christ Church, Oxford, 1963*, StudPat 7 = *TU* 92 (Berlin: Akademie-Verlag, 1966), 321–36.

WESCHE, K. P., *The Defense of Chalcedon in the 6th Century: The Doctrine of 'Hypostasis' and Deification in the Christology of Leontius of Jerusalem* (Thesis, Fordham, 1986).

—— 'The Christology of Leontius of Jerusalem: Monophysite or Chalcedonian?', *SVTQ* 31 (1987), 65–95.

Note: Those wishing to gain a broader perspective on Leontius and his period might wish to read more widely in the section by P. Allen listed above; in the relevant sections of H. Chadwick, *The Church in Ancient Society: From Galilee to Gregory the Great* (Oxford: Oxford University Press, 2001); and idem, *East and West: The Making of a Rift in the Church. From Apostolic Times until the Council of Florence* (Oxford: Oxford University Press, 2003). For an introductory survey of the christological controversies culminating in Leontius' time, see P. T. R. Gray, 'The Legacy of Chalcedon: Christological Problems and their Significance', in M. Maas (ed.), *The Cambridge Companion to the Age of Justinian* (Cambridge: Cambridge University Press, 2005), 215–38.

INDEX OF BIBLICAL CITATIONS

INDEX OF PATRISTIC CITATIONS

INDEX OF NAMES

INDEX OF SUBJECTS